SERIOUS MENTAL
ILLNESS AND THE FAMILY

WILEY SERIES IN COUPLES AND FAMILY
DYNAMICS AND TREATMENT
Florence W. Kaslow, Editor

Treating the Changing Family: Handling Normative and Unusual Events
edited by Michele Harway

In-Laws: A Guide to Extended-Family Therapy
by Gloria Call Horsley

Handbook of Relational Diagnosis and Dysfunctional Family Patterns
edited by Florence W. Kaslow

Child-Centered Family Therapy
by Lucille L. Andreozzi

Strange Attractors: Chaos, Complexity, and the Art of Family Therapy
by Michael Bütz, William G. McCown, and Linda L. Chamberlain

Infertility: Psychological Issues and Counseling Strategies
by Sandra R. Leiblum

The Self in the Family: A Classification of Personality, Criminality, and
Psychopathology
by Luciano L'Abate and Margaret Baggett

Painful Partings: Divorce and Its Aftermath
by Lita Linzer Schwartz and Florence W. Kaslow

Ethical and Legal Issues in Professional Practice with Families
edited by Diane T. Marsh and Richard D. Magee

Serious Mental Illness and the Family: The Practitioner's Guide
by Diane T. Marsh

SERIOUS MENTAL ILLNESS AND THE FAMILY

THE PRACTITIONER'S GUIDE

Diane T. Marsh

John Wiley & Sons, Inc.

New York • Chichester • Weinheim • Brisbane • Singapore • Toronto

This book is printed on acid-free paper. ⊚

Copyright © 1998 by John Wiley & Sons, Inc. All rights reserved.

Published simultaneously in Canada.

No part of this publication may be reproduced, stored in a retrieval system or transmitted in any form or by any means, electronic, mechanical, photocopying, recording, scanning or otherwise, except as permitted under Sections 107 or 108 of the 1976 United States Copyright Act, without either the prior written permission of the Publisher, or authorization through payment of the appropriate per-copy fee to the Copyright Clearance Center, 222 Rosewood Drive, Danvers, MA 01923, (978) 750-8400, fax (978) 750-4744. Requests to the Publisher for permission should be addressed to the Permissions Department, John Wiley & Sons, Inc., 605 Third Avenue, New York, NY 10158-0012, (212) 850-6011, fax (212) 850-6008, E-Mail: PERMREQ@WILEY.COM.

This publication is designed to provide accurate and authoritative information in regard to the subject matter covered. It is sold with the understanding that the publisher is not engaged in rendering professional services. If legal, accounting, medical, psychological or any other expert assistance is required, the services of a competent professional person should be sought.

Library of Congress Cataloging-in-Publication Data:

Marsh, Diane T.
    Serious mental illness and the family : the practitioner's guide /
Diane T. Marsh.
        p.   cm. — (Wiley series in couples and family dynamics and
treatment)
    Includes bibliographical references and index.
    ISBN 0-471-18180-3 (cloth : alk. paper)
    1. Mentally ill—Family relationships.   2. Adjustment (Psychology)
I. Title.   II. Series.
RC455.4.F3M365   1998
616.89—dc21   98-9521

Printed in the United States of America.

10   9   8   7   6   5   4   3   2   1

Series Preface

Our ability to form strong interpersonal bonds with romantic partners, children, parents, siblings, and other relations is one of the key qualities that defines our humanity. These relationships shape who we are and what we become—they can be a source of great gratification, or tremendous pain. Yet, only in the mid-20th century did behavioral and social scientists really begin focusing on couples and family dynamics, and only in the past several decades have the theory and findings that emerged from those students been used to develop effective therapeutic interventions for troubled couples and families.

We have made great progress in understanding the structure, function, and interactional patterns of couples and families—and have made tremendous strides in treatment. However, as we stand poised on the beginning of a new millennium, it seems quite clear that both intimate partnerships and family relationships are in a period of tremendous flux. Economic factors are changing work patterns, parenting responsibilities, and relational dynamics. Modern medicine has helped lengthen the life span, giving rise to the need for transgenerational caretaking. Cohabitation, divorce, and remarriage are quite commonplace, and these social changes make it necessary for us to rethink and broaden our definition of what constitutes a family.

Thus, it is no longer enough simply to embrace the concept of the family as a system. In order to understand and effectively treat the evolving family, our theoretical formulations and clinical interventions must be informed by an understanding of ethnicity, culture, religion, gender, sexual preference, family life cycle, socioeconomic status, education, physical and mental health, values, and belief systems.

The purpose of the *Wiley Series in Couples and Family Dynamics and Treatment* is to provide a forum for cutting-edge relational and family theory, practice, and research. Its scope is intended to be broad, diverse, and international, but all books published in this series share a common mission: to reflect on the past, offer state-of-the-art information on the present, and speculate on, as well as attempt to shape, the future of the field.

FLORENCE W. KASLOW
Florida Couples and Family Institute

v

Acknowledgments

S*erious Mental Illness and the Family* is about professional practice with families of people who have serious mental illness. I am enormously thankful for my own professional family of colleagues who share my commitment to this challenging and important area. Because the book is written for an interdisciplinary audience, I asked outstanding representatives of each of five mental health disciplines to review the manuscript and offer suggestions. Heartfelt appreciation is expressed to social worker Kia Bentley, psychiatric nurse Vicky Conn, psychologist June Husted, family therapist Edie Mannion, and psychiatrist and psychoanalyst Marty Willick. They have read the entire manuscript, shared their wisdom, and greatly improved the quality of the book.

Other members of my professional family have also contributed to the book, including Chris Amenson, Ann Begler, Joyce Burland, Bob Coursey, Thomasine Cubine, Lisa Dixon, Claire Griffin-Francell, Fred Frese, Marsali Hansen, Agnes Hatfield, Rich Hunter, Dale Johnson, Janice Katz, Karen Kinsella, Sam Knapp, Laura LaBarbera, Harriet Lefley, Sheila Le Gacy, Ann List, Bill McFarland, Mary Moller, LeRoy Spaniol, and Mona Wasow. I am grateful to all of you.

In addition, the book has profited significantly from the contributions of many individuals I have come to know through NAMI, the national mental health advocacy organization. Special thanks to Diane Ammons, Kathy Bayes and her spouse support group, Rex Dickens, Judy Flanigan, Linda Lattner, Penny Frese, Marilyn Meisel, Rita Packard, and Vivian Spiese. These family members have generously shared their experiences and expertise for the benefit of my readers. As advocates, we are joined in our quest for a more humane and responsive system of mental health care, believing it is better to light a candle than to curse the darkness.

For more than 25 years, I have been associated with the University of Pittsburgh at Greensburg, which has allowed me to do work that I love. It is wonderful to have colleagues who share some of my enthusiasms. With affection and appreciation, I note Lillian Beeson, Rich Blevins, Mark McColloch, Frank McGlynn, Don Reilly, Guy Rossetti, Norm Scanlon, Cathy Schmidt, Margie Vinkler, and Judy Vollmer.

For the opportunity to work again with Kelly Franklin, my editor at John Wiley & Sons, I am very grateful. I have benefited considerably from her unfailing support and perceptive advice.

My acknowledgments began with my professional family of colleagues. I end with my personal family, which has nurtured and sustained me during the writing of this book and throughout my life. All have enriched my life in countless ways: my husband, Rabe; our sons, Chris, Dan, and Steve; and my siblings and their spouses, Meredith and Dave Kuhn, Jerry and Jane Thimme, and Fred and Sue Thimme.

To all who wondered what I was actually doing on my sabbatical, while I lived on a sailboat moored on the Chesapeake Bay, I hope I can now persuade you that I was indeed working on my book (at least occasionally).

DIANE T. MARSH

Contents

PART ONE

Background

CHAPTER 1

Working with Families

Over the course of the winter term, Paul Cassidy, a freshman honors stu-
dent at St. Joseph's College, began behaving strangely. At first, his friends
ascribed his increasingly erratic moods and lack of focus to academic
pressures. After his grooming deteriorated and he began conversing with
himself in public, the resident assistant in his dorm became concerned
enough to bring Paul to the local hospital. During his evaluation by the
emergency room physician, Paul reported hearing voices, claimed un-
named people were plotting against him, and appeared frightened and
confused. In light of Paul's psychotic symptoms, the physician decided to
admit him to the psychiatric unit, where Dr. Bill Patterson is a new staff
psychologist assigned to work with families. Dr. Patterson is scheduled
to meet with Paul's family, which consists of his parents and two
younger siblings: 13-year-old Elaine and 16-year-old Jim. Although Bill
has many years of experience as a private practitioner, he has had little
contact with patients who have serious mental illness, and even less con-
tact with their families. What special challenges and opportunities do
the Cassidy family, and other families coping with mental illness, present
for Dr. Patterson?

Like mental health practitioners across a wide range of disciplines
and provider settings, Bill Patterson is facing a kaleidoscopic marketplace. In the wake of managed care, he and other clinicians are
redefining their scope of professional practice to encompass new opportunities and roles. One area of increasing interest is serious mental illness, which includes schizophrenia, bipolar disorder, major depression,
and other severe and persistent disorders.

More than 5 million adults in the United States have serious mental illness. An additional 3 million children and adolescents have a serious
emotional disturbance that undermines their present functioning and

3

imperils their future.[1] All of these individuals have family members who share in the many losses that accompany the illness. Because mental illness can have a cataclysmic impact on families as well as individuals, effective practice with these patients requires a family-focused approach that incorporates a variety of professional roles, intervention strategies, and outcome variables.

There is a strong rationale for involving families in the treatment process. First, as with patients who have chronic medical problems, families can play a constructive role in their relative's treatment, rehabilitation, and recovery. They can provide essential information to professionals about their relative and their family, and they often serve in essential roles as primary caregivers, informal case managers, and advocates. Moreover, because family attitudes and behaviors can influence the course of mental illness, a capable and informed family is a considerable asset to patients and to professionals.

Second, families have important needs of their own. Serious mental illness is a catastrophic stressor that can leave families traumatized and debilitated. Based on an expanding body of literature in the area, practitioners now have a solid foundation for professional practice with these families, including an understanding of family experiences and needs and the availability of an array of effective family interventions.

At the core of the family experience of mental illness is a powerful subjective and objective burden.[2] *Subjective burden* refers to the personal suffering endured by family members in response to their relative's illness, as attested by one mother: "The problems with my daughter were like a black hole inside of me into which everything else had been drawn."[3] Young family members are also profoundly affected by mental illness. Responding to one of my surveys, an adult offspring lamented "my loss of a healthy mother, a normal childhood, and a stable home."[4]

Objective burden refers to the daily problems and challenges associated with the illness, including the need to deal with the symptoms of mental illness, caregiving responsibilities, family disruption and stress, limitations of the service delivery system, and social stigma. As one family member complained, "Caring families get socked with most of the responsibility and blame, but little legal or therapeutic support."[5] Another wrote of feeling like a "perpetual outsider" in a stigmatizing society.

This book has been written to assist practitioners in addressing the needs of these highly stressed families. The material should be useful across the full range of mental health disciplines, including psychology, psychiatry, social work, nursing, marriage and family therapy, counseling, and psychosocial rehabilitation. It should also be helpful to other professionals, such as family physicians, who have considerable contact with these families. Building on their existing competencies, clinicians will acquire new knowledge and skills that can assist families in facilitating the treatment and recovery of their relative and in meeting their own needs. My objective is to provide a practical guide that can be translated into clinical practice. Throughout, I draw on my work with families as a practitioner, researcher, and advocate.

This chapter offers a sketch of the changing landscape in professional practice with families, and an overview of the historical context. New modes and models of professional practice are then highlighted, as are the current opportunities for practitioners. Suggestions are offered for engaging and assessing families and for conducting an initial session. The chapter ends with Bill Patterson's first meeting with the Cassidy family.

A Changing Landscape

Particularly within the past decade, there have been significant developments in professional practice with families. These include:

- Increasing evidence for the role of biological factors in serious mental illness
- Deinstitutionalization and downsizing, which have resulted in a service delivery system that is as much family-based as community-based
- Documentation of the devastating impact of mental illness on families
- Acknowledgment of the legitimate rights and needs of family caregivers
- Greater recognition of family contributions and expertise regarding their relative's treatment and recovery
- Managed care, which sometimes emphasizes the *cost* of services, at the expense of their *quality*
- National initiatives that mandate the involvement of people with mental illness, and their families, in the design, delivery, and evaluation of mental health services
- Emergence of a national consumer advocacy movement, which has moved families into more assertive, informed, and involved roles

The Historical Context

The family-professional partnerships that characterize current clinical practice stand in distinct contrast to the unsatisfactory relationships of the past.[6] The history of relationships between families and mental health professionals is inextricably tied to the evolution of theory, research, and practice concerned with serious mental illness. This evolution can be understood in terms of three eras, each of which had an attendant mode of family-professional relationships.

Prior to World War II, during the institutional era, patients with mental illness were sequestered in state mental hospitals and isolated from their families and communities. Years of living in remote institutions rendered these patients marginal to their families, who generally had little contact with their hospitalized relatives or with professionals.[7] Thus, during the institutional era, the characteristic mode of family-professional relationships was distant.

The legitimacy of such institutions was increasingly questioned during the postwar period, and a number of powerful forces culminated in the next era, which was characterized by deinstitutionalization. On February 5, 1963, President John F. Kennedy declared, in a message to Congress, that there was to be a "bold new approach" to the treatment of people with serious mental illness. Lasting until approximately the mid-1980s, this second era was defined by two goals: (a) to transfer the residents of state hospitals to community-based programs, and (b) to avoid the need for residential care through early treatment. The population of state mental hospitals declined from a peak of 560,000 residents in 1955 to fewer than 90,000 by the mid-1990s.[8]

As is widely recognized now, however, the initial promise of deinstitutionalization was not fully realized. Shortcomings included the failure to allocate sufficient resources for community-based care, the absence of a full range of essential services, and the fragmentation of existing services. Many people with mental illness did not receive appropriate treatment—or any treatment at all—and others participated in what was actually a process of transinstitutionalization that placed them in other institutions, such as nursing homes. Compounding these deficiencies were pervasively negative attitudes and low priorities associated with serious mental illness.[9]

Many of these problems—most notably, inadequate funding for the full range of community-based services, and relative neglect of people with the most severe and persistent symptoms—continue in the present. As many people with mental illness reside in our jails and prisons as in all of our hospitals, and at least one-third of the homeless are estimated to have a mental illness.[10] These failures have a significant impact not only on people with mental illness but also on their family members and on society at large.

During the era of deinstitutionalization, contact increased between professionals and families; the latter frequently served as the first and last resort for their relatives, often with little guidance and support.[11] Unfortunately, contact with professionals had the potential to magnify problems of families. Based on earlier theories that assumed mental illness resulted from a dysfunctional or pathogenic family environment, families often found themselves held accountable for the illness of their relatives and were catapulted, sometimes without their consent, into family therapy that met few of their own needs.[12] Describing this earlier era, Samuel Keith[13] has written that families were "four times punished: blamed for causing the illness, forced to watch the deterioration of their loved one, excluded from treatment plans, and required to pay for such treatment."

Earlier theories had many adverse consequences for families and for family-professional relationships. They included: intensifying the feelings of guilt and responsibility experienced by families; alienating families from the mental health system; creating a climate of blame that eroded family relationships; and undermining the ability of families to support the treatment and recovery of their ill relatives. In this context, clinicians became the patients' protectors and, in many cases, the families antagonists.[14] Thus, during the early years of deinstitutionalization, professional modes of practice were rarely collaborative. Far more often, they were intrusive, adversarial, and insensitive to the needs of families.

As a society, we have now embarked on a third era, which is distinguished by increasing community integration and participation of people with mental illness. The hallmark of this era is the availability of a comprehensive system of care that can meet the essential needs of these individuals, that respects their rights and dignity, that affirms their potential for recovery, and that maximizes opportunities for them to lead meaningful and productive lives in their communities. As this vision is gradually transformed into reality, families share in their relative's improved quality of life.

Moreover, the current era of community support has witnessed a constructive shift in family-professional relationships. The ascendant mode is collaborative, and it builds on the strengths and contributions of both groups. Many practitioners now think in terms of a *working alliance* that is designed to meet the needs of all members of the family and to complement the therapeutic alliance formed with their relative for purposes of treatment.[15] Both alliances are essential ingredients of effective professional practice.

Senior family members who have had many years of experience with the changing system may have encountered all of these modes: ignored during their early encounters, later blamed and chastised, and finally invited into full partnership with professionals. One of the older mothers I interviewed had experienced both the terminal illness of her daughter and the schizophrenia of her son. A health care professional herself, she remarked on the contrasting roles of professionals who supported her during her daughter's leukemia but seemed to blame her for her son's schizophrenia. Another mother who had had many years of experience with the system noted the growth of collaboration. She observed that "professionals are listening instead of blaming."[16]

A Systemic Perspective

The family experience of mental illness is tied not only to this historical context, but also to the sociocultural matrix in which the experience is embedded. Thus, an ecological perspective is essential for understanding and working with families.[17] Indeed, the family experience of mental illness cannot be understood apart from the larger society, which shapes that experience in many ways. Society defines mental illness and provides diagnostic labels; establishes social priorities and policies; determines the locus and nature of mental health services; and creates the climate in which families adapt to mental illness.

The family is simply one niche in the larger ecosystem. From an ecological perspective, the family system operates at an intermediate level in a general hierarchy that includes individual family members at a lower level and the sociocultural context at a higher level. Individuals are nested within the family system, and the family is nested within the social system. The value of an ecological perspective in family practice is increasingly recognized in the areas of disability, chronic health problems, and serious mental illness.[18] At the same time, professionals need to be sensitive to individual family members, whose experiences and needs are colored by their particular roles within the family and by their own characteristics. Later in the book, these roles are examined in some detail, focusing on the parents, spouses, siblings, and offspring whose relatives have mental illness.

Practitioners also need to respond to the diversity among families. As we are regularly informed by a barrage of statistics, the American family has been undergoing dramatic change. The traditional nuclear family (breadwinning father, homemaker mother, and children), although clearly more viable than earlier projections of imminent demise implied, is no longer the modal family system. Alternate family structures have become more prevalent, including: ethnic minority, two-career, single-parent, teenage, cohabiting, blended, and gay and lesbian families. With the decline of narrow sex role prescriptions, gender roles and relationships have also been changing, and males and females are more likely to share financial and caregiving responsibilities.

All of these changes influence the family experience of mental illness. For example, the discrimination experienced by ethnic minority families is intensified by the stigma that accompanies a diagnosis of mental illness. Similarly, the problems of single-parent families are likely to be magnified by the stress associated with mental illness. In addition to structural and cultural differences, families vary in their ability to cope with mental illness.[19] Some families appear to be unusually competent— able to cope effectively with the most challenging circumstances. Most families remain at or near the middle of a continuum of competence, exhibiting both strengths and limitations. And some families have difficulty fulfilling their basic functions, perhaps because they are struggling with poverty, violence inside or outside the home, addictions, or debilitating health problems.

Against this backdrop of family diversity, there is nevertheless general agreement that the characteristics of effective families include:[20]

- Open and direct communication
- Mutual tolerance and respect
- Caring, commitment, and affection
- Age-appropriate roles and responsibilities
- Problem-solving and coping ability
- A flexible and adaptive response to stress
- Encouragement of individual growth and development
- A sense of family satisfaction and cohesion

While respecting the diversity among families and evaluating each family on its own terms, practitioners can assist families in building on their existing strengths, surviving their crises, meeting their challenges, and enhancing the quality of their lives. The serious mental illness needs to be placed in the larger family life space, as part of an intricate familial tapestry woven of common bonds, memories, celebrations, and losses.

New Models and Modes of Professional Practice

Many traditional models of help-giving behavior have emphasized pathology and dysfunction, fostered learned helplessness, increased dependency, and undermined self-esteem.[21] A competence paradigm provides a constructive alternative that underscores the positive qualities of families, which have received little acknowledgment in the past.[22]

A COMPETENCE PARADIGM

In contrast to a pathology paradigm, a competence paradigm offers a developmental and educational model that focuses on family coping and adaptation; emphasizes the family's strengths, resources, and expertise; defines family-professional relationships as collaborative; promotes a sense of familial mastery; and encourages feelings of hopefulness. A competence paradigm offers many advantages for practitioners.[23] The paradigm fosters the formation of alliances between families and professionals; focuses on the development of relevant competencies; encourages more precise theory and research concerned with families; and provides a blueprint for more effective services.

A COLLABORATIVE MODE OF WORKING WITH FAMILIES

Reflecting the collaborative spirit of the competence paradigm, the emergent mode of professional practice is a three-way partnership among people with mental illness, their family members, and professionals. Our concern is with the family-professional part of this partnership,[24] which is designed to:

- Build on the strengths and expertise of both parties
- Respect the needs, desires, concerns, and priorities of families
- Enable families to play an active role in decisions that affect them
- Establish mutual goals for their relative's treatment and rehabilitation

In the current era, families often serve as the cornerstone of their relative's support system, and they fulfill valuable roles as primary caregivers and informal case managers. Under these circumstances, a collaborative mode offers obvious benefits: mutual engagement in a process of much importance to all parties; joint satisfaction with decisions that reflect their perspectives; shared challenges and resources; and enhanced treatment and rehabilitation.

In spite of its advantages, the translation of a collaborative mode into practice faces many hurdles.[25] Among the barriers to collaboration are the attitudes, perceptions, and perspectives of families and professionals. Both groups may have had unsatisfactory interactions in the past, which can imprint their relationships in the present. Their initial encounter often occurs in the midst of a crisis, when families may appear confused and distraught, and when overburdened professionals may seem insensitive to family distress.[26] In addition, the two groups differ in terms of training, experience, priorities, responsibilities, and commitments. These differences are likely to influence their views of mental illness and its treatment, the importance of family concerns and needs, and the nature of family-professional relationships.

Another barrier to collaboration is the persistence of earlier models of family dysfunction or pathogenesis.[27] Although these models are not supported by a satisfactory empirical database, they continue to influence clinical practice, often with disastrous consequences for families.[28] One mother, informed of her son's poor prognosis and the presumed causal role of his early relationship with her, said she felt "as if I were being told my son was dying and I was responsible for his death. It was absolutely devastating."[29] In response to one of our surveys, a sibling responded, "I am angry at the doctors for blaming my parents, which hurt them as much as the tragedy of losing a daughter to mental illness."[30]

In addition, systemic policies may limit contact with families to crisis intervention, history taking, and telephone contact, and practitioners may be encouraged to increase the proportion of time spent in direct service to patients. As a result, professionals may have little opportunity or reinforcement for providing services to families. Family-professional alliances may also be threatened by concern about confidentiality, which is sometimes viewed as a rigid barrier to collaboration (see Chapter 2).

Commenting on an early draft of this chapter, one practitioner remarked on another barrier that has accompanied the emergence of the family advocacy movement: "I note a continuing core of families who denigrate the expertise of professionals and portray themselves as the *only* experts—no collaborative spirit at all." She added that although families are experts on their own experiences and needs, providers have expertise regarding treatment, rehabilitation, and family interventions.

There are several ways to minimize these barriers and to facilitate collaboration. At the level of the mental health system, collaborative principles and practices should be incorporated.[31] For example, the system needs to be restructured to acknowledge the rights and contributions of families, to ensure better communication between families and professionals, to provide family-focused services, to involve families in decisions that affect them, and to offer continuing education designed to update providers on our rapidly expanding knowledge of mental illness.

As providers of services to families, individual practitioners can do much to foster collaboration, which depends on the same qualities that are essential to a therapeutic alliance: empathy and understanding, tolerance and respect, an absence of labeling and blame, and acknowledgment of family strengths and contributions. Effective communication is also essential, and families should have an avenue to express their concerns and share their observations. Opportunities for questions and feedback should be provided, so that both parties have the chance for clarification.

Opportunities for Practitioners

New models and modes offer many opportunities for professionals to assist families in supporting their relative's treatment and recovery and in meeting their own needs. These broad objectives require a flexible approach to family practice, as well as a variety of family interventions.[32] As discussed later in more detail, researchers have consistently found that families have three central needs: (a) *information* about mental illness and the service delivery system; (b) *skills* to cope with the illness and its consequences for their family; and (c) *support* for themselves. Not surprisingly, families consistently rate most highly the services that address these needs.[33]

Practitioners bring many existing competencies to professional practice with these families. For example, most clinicians will have little difficulty responding to families with understanding and support, providing general education about mental illness and its treatment, and assisting families in enhancing their communication, problem-solving, assertiveness, and stress management skills. They can also make appropriate referrals to community resources, such as the local affiliate of NAMI (formerly the National Alliance for the Mentally Ill), a national mental health advocacy organization with more than 1,000 state and local affiliates throughout the country.[34] NAMI offers a wide range of services, including educational programs and support groups for families.

Other competencies may need to be strengthened or developed. Practitioners need current knowledge about serious mental illness, about the family experience of mental illness, and about effective family interventions. They also need familiarity with the ethical and legal issues that are likely to arise in professional practice with families, and with the strategies that can facilitate resolution of conflicts. These topics are discussed in later chapters.

Many constructive roles are open to professionals who work with families. Within a service plan designed to meet the needs of individual families, practitioners can serve as family consultants who offer direct services to families for a wide range of illness-related concerns; as providers of educational programs, coping skills workshops, and support groups; or as therapists who offer individual, couple, family, or group therapy. These are natural roles for clinicians, who can build on existing skills to offer a range of family-focused services.

Engaging Families

Practitioners may welcome the opportunity to work with families that include a member with mental illness. But opportunities will not materialize unless families can be engaged in the process.[35] Engagement involves several steps. First, professionals need to *establish rapport* with families. Rapport is enhanced when practitioners have an understanding of the family experience of mental illness, a respectful and humane attitude toward families, and a commitment to family empowerment.

Second, it is essential to *communicate effectively* with families. Particularly during their initial contacts with professionals, families will respond best to listening that is active, nonjudgmental, responsive, and empathic; and to expression that is clear, complete, direct, and supportive. Families also benefit from written materials that provide information about mental illness, the service delivery system, and community resources.

Third, practitioners should *acknowledge the strengths, resources, and expertise of families.* Most families are struggling to do their best under extremely difficult circumstances. Their efforts need to be reinforced and their input encouraged. Clinicians can promote a sense of mastery and control as families acquire the knowledge and skills necessary for coping with mental illness.

Fourth, professionals can *normalize the family experience of mental illness.* Especially at the time of the initial diagnosis, families often feel stigmatized and isolated. It is helpful for professionals to make a referral to a family support group and to share research concerned with family experiences, concerns, and needs. In response to one of my workshops, a family member told me she could see for the first time that she was having a normal reaction to an abnormal family situation.

Fifth, it is vital to *address the expressed needs of families themselves.* Depending on their responsibilities, clinicians may also have other duties, such as obtaining a patient history from families or gaining their support for the treatment plan. At the same time, families have legitimate needs of their own that merit attention. They need a channel of communication to ask questions, express their concerns, and share their observations.

Sixth, practitioners need to *adapt their style to a particular family.* For families that appear confused and overwhelmed in the midst of a crisis, an active and structured approach may be best. Other families may need an opportunity to express their grief or frustration. Listen to their stories and encourage them to share their feelings. Still other families may have specific concerns or questions that merit immediate attention.

Seventh, it is important to *emphasize the value of family involvement* in treatment and rehabilitation. There is substantial research support for the importance of family interventions that educate families about mental illness and assist them in acquiring relevant skills. Families should be acknowledged as full partners in the treatment enterprise, and encouraged to participate in programs that can maximize their contributions. At the same time, families need to be free to define their level of involvement, which is likely to vary over the course of their lives.

Finally, practitioners should *initiate a family service plan* designed to address their present and long-term needs. Few families have much understanding of mental illness or its meaning for their household. Offering immediate assistance, clinicians can share practical suggestions for daily coping and provide written information about mental illness and community resources. They can also encourage families to begin thinking about long-term goals and to maintain a sense of hopefulness.

Assessing Families

Practitioners need to approach family assessment with sensitivity and care.[36] Families are particularly vulnerable at the time of their relative's initial diagnosis, and are likely to have intense feelings of guilt and accountability. As a result, they may regard requests for information as blaming or chastising their family; even the most neutral questions may seem laden with meaning. Illustrating this risk are the perceptions of two family members whom I encountered.

Describing his experiences at the hospital where his son had just been admitted, one father told me that the professionals who interviewed him and his wife seemed to be trying to find out how they had caused their son's illness. Already drained by their efforts to get help for their son, the parents were devastated by their encounter with professionals who appeared to hold them responsible. The father, a retired steelworker, told me they cried all the way home and commented that it was one of the worst days of their lives.

I recently spoke with a woman who described similar feelings at the time of her sister's initial hospitalization at a prestigious university medical center. A teenager at the time, she and her parents had arrived for their appointment hoping to learn how they could help their beloved relative. Instead, they found themselves unexpectedly ushered onto a stage, where their family was questioned in front of an audience of professionals and trainees. Remarking with tears that the experience was the most traumatic of her life, this sibling said she had felt like a butterfly under a microscope.

In light of these risks, practitioners need to engage families before beginning a family assessment and to explain the role of the assessment in meeting their needs. Components of an initial family assessment include:

- Current issues facing the family, such as concern about the risk of harm to their relative or to others
- Level of knowledge of mental illness, including any misconceptions the family might have
- Skills for coping with family stress in general and with mental illness in particular
- Strengths, resources, and potential contributions to their relative's treatment plan
- The impact of mental illness on their family as a unit, and on individual family members
- Other past or present problems that may affect the family's ability to cope with the illness
- The level of support available to the family
- The family's immediate and long-term needs and goals

Results of this assessment will allow practitioners to respond to any urgent family concerns and to begin formulating a family service plan. Future sessions can explore these issues in more detail. Professionals should be flexible and responsive to the needs of individual families. Some families need an opportunity to ventilate; others may be more ready to focus on long-term planning. Either during the family assessment or in a separate session, families will be asked to provide information about their relative's history, current symptoms, and level of functioning.

The Initial Session

Ideally, the first family session should occur as close as possible to the time of the relative's diagnosis. In reality, however, as Kayla Bernheim points out, the initial session may occur at different points in their experience with mental illness.[37] A given family may be actively seeking information at point A, acquiring specific skills at point B, grieving their loss at point C, and dealing with non-illness-related concerns at point D. There is no single format or agenda for all families, or even for all members within a given family.

Bernheim has offered a helpful description of the initial session. As she observes, goals of this session will vary somewhat, depending on family circumstances, the patient's situation, and professional constraints, such as the time available for consultation with a given family. Nevertheless, there are some general considerations. For instance, practitioners should encourage families to talk about their experiences and feelings. For most families, the opportunity to focus on their experience of illness is more beneficial than collecting a formal "objective" history.

It is also useful to explore their previous experiences with mental health providers. Families that have felt neglected, chastised, or pathologized will be understandably wary. In contrast, earlier positive experiences may foster the development of a working alliance. Especially in the initial session, the focus should be on areas of strength and competence rather than deficits or mistakes. Once the working alliance has been established, practitioners can assist the family to make appropriate changes and deal with any inadequacies.

In spite of the diversity among families, practitioners are likely to be dealing with several general subjects during the initial session. Particularly if a crisis or period of hospitalization has preceded the session, these may include:

- The patient's current status and recent history
- The family's reaction to these circumstances
- Questions and concerns
- The need for information, skills, and assistance
- The relative's program and treatment plan
- Realistic expectations for the patient and the family
- The family's wish for involvement in the patient's treatment
- Potential conflict with the patient's desire for autonomy and privacy
- The relationship with the patient's treatment team
- Anxiety about the future

Working with individual families, professionals can assess the relative importance of each of these issues, adapt the content and pacing of the session to their needs, and begin to develop an individualized service plan. The end product is a plan that specifies: the nature of family involvement with the patient and the mental health system; the services that will be provided to the family; and the schedule for reviewing the plan. For some families, the service plan may consist of nothing more than an occasional call. Others may benefit from reading material, case conferences, family support meetings, educational or psychoeducational programs, or coping skills workshops. Still others may request ongoing consultation or psychotherapy for themselves.

Plan of the Book

This book is designed to assist practitioners in developing the competencies necessary for working with families, and in applying their new knowledge and skills to professional practice. The focus of the book is on families that include an adult member with serious mental illness. Because much common ground exists between the child and adult territories, however, the material is also likely to be helpful for clinicians who work with children, adolescents, and their families. For example, many severe and persistent mental disorders, including schizophrenia, bipolar disorder, major depression, and obsessive-compulsive disorder, can be diagnosed during childhood and adolescence.

Moreover, many children and adolescents with these disorders continue to need services as adults. Without transitional planning that links them with appropriate mental health services, these young adults may fall through the cracks, perhaps joining the ranks of those who reside on our streets or in our jails. At any age, severe mental disorders are likely to be profoundly disabling for individuals, and devastating for their families. Thus, a life span perspective is essential for understanding these disorders and their impact on individuals and families.

Throughout, the terms *family* and *family member* are used to refer to close relatives of people with mental illness. A number of terms are used to describe the latter group; often, they are referred to as *clients* in outpatient settings and as *patients* in inpatient settings. Particularly when they are active as mental health advocates, these individuals often use other terms to refer to themselves, such as *consumers* or *survivors.* I have generally used the term *patient* to facilitate communication, but usually prefer to speak of *people* with mental illness. They are, after all, human beings who should not be defined by their illness or by their role as recipients of mental health services.

The book is organized in four parts: One. Background, Two. Family Experiences and Needs, Three. Family Interventions, and Four. Working with Individual Family Members. Completing Part One, Chapter 2 specifies the competencies essential for effective practice, the ethical

and legal issues that are likely to arise, and diagnosis and reimbursement in family practice.

Part Two focuses on family experiences, needs, and concerns. Chapter 3 discusses the family experience of mental illness. Chapter 4 charts
life span perspectives, integrating the life courses of individual family
members, the family system, and the mental illness. The process of family coping and adaptation is addressed in Chapter 5, with emphasis on
the strategies and resources that can assist families in dealing with a
catastrophic stressor. In Chapter 6, clinicians will learn how to assist
family members in developing a Family Action Plan, to meet the needs
of their family as a unit, and a Personal Action Plan, to address their individual concerns.

Part Three covers a range of family interventions that can be modified to
meet the requirements of individual families, practitioners, and treatment
settings. Chapter 7 describes family consultation, which offers a useful role
for assisting families to handle illness-related concerns and to make an informed choice about their use of available services. In Chapters 8 and 9,
four family intervention strategies are described: family support and advocacy groups, family education, family psychoeducation, and psychotherapy. Chapter 10 details some problems that can arise in working with
families and offers suggestions for their resolution.

Part Four focuses largely on family subsystems, including the parents,
spouses, siblings, and offspring of people with mental illness. In Chapters 11 through 14, practitioners will gain understanding of these roles;
their associated experiences, needs, and concerns; and targeted intervention strategies. Chapter 15 describes several family-focused programs,
both generic and specialized. Aside from the final chapter, each chapter
begins with a professional vignette that captures some of the issues to be
addressed. At the end of the chapter, the issues are reconsidered in light
of the material presented, using clinical dialogue, practice-oriented suggestions, or other applications.

From Theory to Practice

Let's return to the opening vignette and see how Dr. Bill Patterson might
begin with the Cassidy family:

PRACTITIONER: *Hello. I'm Dr. Patterson, a psychologist at the medical
center where Paul has been admitted. At the center, our policy is to
work closely with the families of our patients, and we appreciate your
willingness to collaborate with our treatment team. We believe that a*

well-informed family is essential to treatment. In addition, we need your input; no one knows your family better than you do. I will do my best to answer your questions, to assist you in meeting your needs, and to work with you on long-term planning. I am very pleased to have the opportunity to meet with all four of you. Mr. and Mrs. Cassidy, let me begin with you. This must be extremely difficult for both of you.

MOTHER: *It is devastating. We knew Paul was having some problems, but thought he was struggling to adjust to living away from home. Although we live in the area, we felt it would be best for Paul to live on campus. Now we worry that we made a mistake. As his problems got worse, we wondered if he was on drugs. With each week, we felt more helpless. And it was hard for Elaine and Jim, not knowing what was happening. We're a close family and have been torn apart by this.*

PRACTITIONER: *Your feelings of devastation and helplessness are understandable under these circumstances, as is your concern about Elaine and Jim. When a teenager develops mental illness, it has an impact on all members of the family.*

FATHER: *I understand Paul has been diagnosed as having schizophrenia, but I know very little about that illness—apart from the horror stories I've seen on television. Actually, what I have heard about the disorder hasn't helped me understand it any better. Lots of young people have difficulty at his age. Maybe he's just trying to avoid his academic responsibilities. How much do you really know at this point?*

PRACTITIONER: *Sounds like you're confused. Let me see if I can help. To begin with, Paul has been hospitalized for only 3 days, so there's much we don't know. As we gain a better understanding, we'll do our best to keep you informed. And it's true that many young people have problems at this age, which sometimes makes it difficult to obtain an accurate diagnosis. In Paul's case, as you know, he has reported hearing voices, which are called hallucinations, along with false beliefs, which are called delusions. These symptoms are often experienced by people who have schizophrenia. Here is some written material on schizophrenia, which may answer some of your questions. In addition, we have some services designed to help families learn about schizophrenia and other forms of serious mental illness. We offer a 1-day workshop that includes information about mental illness and about the services and resources available for Paul and for your family. After the workshop, you'll have an opportunity to meet with other families and with our professional staff. We also offer a support group for parents and spouses, as well as some services for siblings. And I'll do my best to answer your questions when we meet.*

FATHER: *I'll look over the material. And the workshop sounds like a good idea. At least it's a start.*

MOTHER: *I suppose so. At this point, I feel terribly upset and confused.*

PRACTITIONER: *Your feelings of distress and confusion are understandable. Many parents have told me they feel a child's severe mental illness is the most difficult problem they have faced.*

MOTHER: *You know, I almost feel as if I've lost my son, even though I realize I haven't. I'm sure it's hard for Elaine and Jim to see me crying so much. I'm not usually like this.*

PRACTITIONER: *Feelings of grief and loss are often experienced by parents. There are real losses associated with mental illness. When we meet next time, I can share some personal accounts of parents with you. I think you'll see that your reactions are shared by many mothers. Then we can talk more about your feelings. I understand your concern about your other children. This is heartbreaking for all of you. Elaine and Jim, let me hear from you. How are you feeling about Paul's hospitalization?*

SISTER: *I'm not sure how I feel right now. It's as if Paul has become a stranger, someone I hardly recognize. It's been hard for me to concentrate at school. I start to cry every time I think about it.*

PRACTITIONER: *It sounds like you're also feeling confused and upset.*

BROTHER: *Me, too. And I don't know what to tell my friends. They make fun of "wackos" and "loonies," and I worry about their reaction. And my girlfriend won't understand, either. To be honest, I'm a little afraid of Paul. He acts so weird now. Aren't people with mental illness dangerous?*

PRACTITIONER: *It's normal for teenagers to worry about what their friends think, even when things are going smoothly. When you're upset and confused about something like mental illness, it's hard to know what to say to others. And your question is a good one. Actually, most people with mental illness are no more dangerous than the general population, although their symptoms can be frightening to family members. Both of you are raising issues that are shared by other teenagers. We have a sibling group for the brothers and sisters of our hospitalized patients. I'm sure you have many questions and concerns, and it's usually helpful to talk to someone who's been through a similar experience and can offer suggestions. I'll meet with both of you briefly today after we have ended our joint meeting. Do any of you have additional questions at this point?*

MOTHER: *I can't think of anything right now, but I'm sure I'll have questions later. What if you're not available when I call?*

PRACTITIONER: *The hospital answers 24 hours a day, with professional staff on call. Here is some written information about the services we offer* for families, as well as my telephone number. Hospital hours and policies are also listed. At the workshop, you'll receive material on mental illness and community resources. I don't want to overload you during our first meeting. Mr. and Mrs. Cassidy, I want to schedule another appointment with you so that I can learn more about Paul and your family. Again, I appreciate your involvement in our program and will do all I can to help you during this difficult period. I look forward to seeing you again. Now, let me meet with Elaine and Jim for a few minutes, so I can see what we can do for them.

CHAPTER 2

Foundations of Professional Practice

Susan Murphy is a social worker in private practice who provides services to clients of several managed care organizations. During the past year, she has been receiving increasing referrals of patients with serious mental illness and often has contact with their families. One of her patients is 34-year-old David Endicott, who has been treated for bipolar disorder for more than a decade and continues to reside with his parents. He participates in a day treatment program and is hoping to begin classes at a local community college. Susan was surprised to hear from David's parents, who have asked to meet with her to discuss his progress, as well as their concerns as primary caregivers. David gets along fairly well with his parents and has no objection to the meeting, although he does not wish to attend. Nor does he want Susan to speak freely about his therapy sessions. She wonders about the best way to approach her meeting with the Endicotts and also about the legal and ethical issues involved, such as confidentiality. Neither her training nor her previous experience has prepared her for such a meeting. What new competencies does she need to develop? How might she proceed?

Although experienced practitioners like Susan Murphy have much to offer families of people with mental illness, effective practice also requires certain specialized knowledge and skills. In addition to professional competencies, clinicians need to be familiar with the ethical and legal issues likely to arise in professional practice with these families, such as confidentiality, and with the strategies for their resolution. Another professional concern is diagnosis and reimbursement in family practice. These topics are the focus of this chapter.

Professional Competencies

All mental health professionals are mandated by their ethical codes to maintain minimal standards of competence, to recognize the boundaries of their competence, and to provide only those services for which they are qualified.[1] There have been several attempts to specify the competencies needed for professional practice with families that include a member with mental illness. Working at the Human Interaction Research Institute in Northridge, California, Shirley Glynn, Robert Liberman, and Thomas Backer in collaboration with NAMI have developed a guide for mental health workers that specifies the competencies needed for involving families in mental health services.[2] Defining a competency as an organized set of specific knowledge, skills, and attitudes, they have identified seven family involvement competencies:

- Developing a collaboration with the family
- Providing basic information on serious psychiatric disorders
- Enhancing stress management skills of families
- Helping families utilize the mental health treatment system
- Helping the family meet its own needs
- Helping the family deal with special characteristics of their relative
- Managing professional issues successfully

As members of the Adult Panel of the Center for Mental Health Services (CMHS) Managed Care Initiative (1998), my colleague Victoria Conn and I have also formulated a set of core competencies for working with families, including the requisite values, attitudes, knowledge, skills, and ethics. This book incorporates the results of our work on the panel, including the values reflected in the competence-based models and collaborative modes already discussed; facilitative attitudes such as tolerance, respect, and compassion; current knowledge of serious mental illness and family concerns; skills that can enhance stress management, communication, assertiveness, symptom management, problem solving, consensus building, and conflict resolution; and the ethical issues discussed in this chapter.

All of the relevant competencies will be covered in this book, beginning with an overview of information about serious mental illness that is needed by practitioners and by families themselves.

Serious Mental Illness

Traditionally, serious mental illness has been defined in terms of diagnosis, duration, and disability.[3] The term refers to mental disorders that carry specific diagnoses, such as schizophrenia, bipolar disorder, and major depression; that are relatively persistent (e.g., lasting at least a year); and that result in comparatively severe impairment in major areas of functioning, such as vocational capacity or social relationships. Mental disorders of all types cost the United States an estimated $148 million in 1990, a figure that includes direct treatment costs of $67 billion—10% of the total annual direct cost of health care. This figure also includes the social costs of disorders that reduce life expectancy, lessen productivity, and increase demands on both the social service and criminal justice systems.[4] For people with mental illness and for their families, of course, the human costs are incalculable.

In 1996, the Center for Mental Health Services (CMHS) published the most recent data regarding serious mental illness, indicating a 12-month prevalence (number of total cases within a year) in the United States that is estimated to be 5.4% (10.0 million adults).[5] The CMHS document reports that almost half of individuals with serious mental illness report receiving some type of treatment during the year, although only 29% are seen by a mental health specialist.

This lack of satisfactory—or indeed, any—treatment has devastating consequences for these individuals, their families, and society. Effective interventions *are available* for the treatment of serious mental illness. A special issue of *Schizophrenia Bulletin* includes a series of articles summarizing results of treatment outcomes research for schizophrenia.[6] Using a range of outcome criteria, including symptom control, rate of relapse, and enhanced quality of life, researchers summarize evidence for the effectiveness of psychopharmacological and psychosocial interventions.

Effective interventions are also available for bipolar disorder, major depression, and other severe and persistent disorders.[7] Treatment outcomes for serious mental illness compare favorably with those of general medical problems.[8] Following short-term treatment, for instance, the percentage of patients improved (reduction of symptoms) was 60% for schizophrenia, 80% for bipolar disorder, and 65% for major depression. Similarly, 1-year relapse rates differed significantly between those in active treatment and in placebo groups for schizophrenia (25% vs. 80%), bipolar disorder (34% vs. 81%), and major depression (18% vs. 65%).

Thus, in contrast to the message of hopelessness that was so often conveyed to patients and their families in the past, current practitioners are able to offer genuine assistance and hope. Recovery from serious mental illness, once thought impossible, is being documented in long-term studies that suggest a life process open to multiple influences and characterized by many outcomes, a majority of them positive.[9] In the case of schizophrenia, for example, one report indicated that one-half to two-thirds of more than 1,300 people who were studied for longer than 20 years had achieved recovery or significant improvement.[10]

Based on his review of long-term outcome studies, E. Fuller Torrey summarizes the 30-year course of schizophrenia as follows: 25% are completely recovered; 35% are much improved and relatively independent; 15% are improved but requiring an extensive support network; 10% are hospitalized and unimproved; and 15% are dead, most often from suicide.[11] As discussed in Chapter 3, each of these outcomes has implications for people with these disorders, for their family members, and for professionals.

Ultimately, mental illness is a human experience, which provides the essential context for professional practice. Much can be learned about the subjective experience of mental illness from the personal accounts of those who have endured it. For example, there are powerful depictions of schizophrenia by Lori Schiller, of bipolar disorder by Kay Redfield Jamison, and of major depression by William Styron. A recent book, *Psychological and Social Aspects of Psychiatric Disability*, includes many eloquent personal accounts.[12]

Writing anonymously, a physician described his experience with bipolar disorder.[13] He writes of his long struggle to accept the illness as well as himself, of the suicidal feelings that resulted in hospitalization ("I thought my life had ended, and that I had been sent to Hell"), and of the disastrous consequences for his marriage. Now recovering with medication and therapy, he remarks:

All in all, I am grateful to still be alive. Dealing with bipolar illness on a day-to-day basis is probably the greatest challenge I will ever face. In a way, I am grateful for the fullness of emotions this illness has afforded me. But I remain bitter to this day for what this illness has taken from me—my personality, my memories, my future—for it has altered me in ways that I am only beginning to understand.

EDUCATING FAMILIES

Practitioners who work with families of such patients need to remain abreast of current developments so they can provide basic information in a way that is accurate, understandable, and useful.[14] Psychologist Christopher Amenson, director of Pacific Clinics Institute in Pasadena, CA, has developed an exemplary program of family education (see the description of his multimodal program in Chapter 7).[15] His approach to family education in schizophrenia is detailed in *Schizophrenia: A Family Education Curriculum* and a companion manual, *Schizophrenia: Family Education Methods*, that is used for professional training.

As Amenson points out, much of our current understanding of biological factors in serious mental illness has resulted from major technological developments that have been available only for the past 15 years, including brain imaging techniques such as positron emission tomography (PET) and nuclear magnetic resonance imaging (MRI). Likewise, recent years have witnessed the development of an array of new medications and psychosocial interventions. In the area of schizophrenia, for example, professionals should be familiar with the following:

- Characteristics of schizophrenia, including prevalence and correlates, diagnostic criteria, symptoms, onset, and course
- Biological factors, including evidence for genetic predisposition and other biological risk factors
- Research findings regarding brain abnormalities, as well as their relationship to symptoms and functioning
- The role of psychosocial variables, including potential exacerbators, such as psychosocial stress, and potential protectors, such as social support
- General principles of intervention, including the importance of early treatment
- Traditional and newer antipsychotics, their effects on brain functions and symptoms, side effects and their management, and the relationship between dose and relapse
- Effective psychosocial interventions, such as social skills training, family interventions, and rehabilitation
- Prognostic and outcome variables, including illness, treatment, personal, family, and social variables
- The recovery process

Sharing this information with families, practitioners need to use an educational approach that maximizes their knowledge and skills and that assists them in applying their new competencies. The concept of vulnerability-stress provides a useful structure for family education. The concept assumes that a vulnerability (a biological predisposition) interacts with a range of biological and psychosocial stressors that can trigger the onset of the disorder and affect its course.[16]

As Paul Fink has discussed, this broad biopsychosocial perspective provides a framework for examining relationships among the mind, brain, body, and world at large; and for incorporating important scientific, technological, and humanistic developments.[17] Vulnerability-stress also provides a useful framework for integrating the biological, personal, and familial aspects of serious mental illness, for understanding the reciprocal interactions among these different levels, and for developing effective interventions.[18]

Applying this framework to family education in schizophrenia, families need to be informed that schizophrenia is a brain disorder marked by alterations in brain activity, chemistry, and structure. One common finding in schizophrenia research is ventricular enlargement, which may indicate that the brain has atrophied or shrunk due to damage or death of some brain cells. Slides or photographs illustrating this and other brain abnormalities are an effective teaching device. Practitioners can also explain the role of neurotransmitters as chemical messengers, observing that abnormalities in these messengers may relate to the disorganization of thought processes that is symptomatic of schizophrenia.

Likewise, other brain abnormalities can be discussed, including deficits in frontal and temporal lobes, the basal ganglia, and the limbic system. Following Amenson's example, professionals can explain the normal functions of these structures, examine the deficits associated with schizophrenia, and tie these deficits to symptoms and functional limitations. For example, new brain imaging techniques demonstrate lower levels of frontal lobe activity in some people with schizophrenia, which may have an adverse impact on abstract thinking, problem solving, cognitive flexibility, planning ability, and social awareness.

These techniques also demonstrate abnormalities in temporal lobe function, which may affect perception, reality orientation, and memory. In turn, these impairments may be linked to symptoms such as hallucinations, delusions, and difficulty learning from experience. Deficits in the basal ganglia may impair the brain's ability to inhibit unwanted sensory input, to filter out irrelevant sensory input, to regulate arousal, and to maintain concentration. Similarly, deficits in the limbic system may have an adverse impact on working memory and on the ability to understand emotional events, to connect current perceptions to past experience, and to learn from experience.

Although there is significant individual variability, these neurobiological deficits and their associated symptoms typically result in increased vulnerability to stress and in persistent limitations in cognitive and social functioning.[19] As families become familiar with current biological research findings, their debilitating feelings of guilt and responsibility are likely to diminish. Families are also likely to gain insight into the role of medication, which can control the symptoms of schizophrenia, and of psychosocial interventions designed to improve stress management skills, cognitive functioning, and social competence.

Practitioners can explain that these research findings have important implications for families.[20] Because their relatives may have deficiencies in attention and information processing, families need to develop good communication skills. Similarly, because schizophrenia is often marked by unusual vulnerability to stress and to acrimonious and intrusive inter-personal interactions, families need to learn how to anticipate and defuse difficult situations, reduce overstimulation, and avoid hostile criticism and excessive emotional involvement. Families also need to develop ap-propriate expectations and refrain from making performance demands that cannot be met.

As David Miklowitz and Michael Goldstein discuss in *Bipolar Disorder: A Family-Focused Treatment Approach,* the vulnerability-stress framework can also be applied fruitfully to family education in mood disorders.[21] Accordingly, families of these patients can benefit from interventions that educate them about biological factors in bipolar disorder and major depression, associated symptoms and functional limitations, and helpful family skills and adaptations.[22] For example, it is useful for families to offer assistance in obtaining treatment and services, maintain a low-stress environment, avoid hostile and intrusive interactions, enhance their communication and problem-solving skills, and develop appropri-ate expectations for their relative.

In *Overcoming Depression,* Demitri Papolos and Janice Papolos offer a comprehensive review of bipolar disorder and depression that can provide a foundation for family education.[23] As they observe, mood disorders are the "common cold" of serious mental illness; more than 20 million Ameri-cans will suffer an episode of depression or mania during their lifetimes. Topics covered in the book include:

- Characteristics of these disorders, including the personal experience, prevalence and correlates, diagnostic criteria, symptoms, onset, and course
- Biological factors, including molecular and genetic aspects, the limbic-diencephalic system, neurotransmitters, and hormone secretion
- Psychosocial factors, including the role of stress and loss
- Circadian rhythms, including the sleep-wake cycle, sleep architec-ture, pacemakers, and light and time cues
- The kindling-sensitization hypothesis, which assumes that once a particular stressor has triggered an affective episode in a genetically

predisposed individual, there is increased susceptibility to future episodes, which can be triggered by less significant stressors

- Current approaches to treatment, including somatic therapies (medication and electroconvulsive shock treatment), patient and family education, psychotherapy, and special aspects of the disorders (e.g., seasonal affective disorders)
- Living with the illness, including obtaining good treatment, family concerns and coping strategies, charting mood disorders, dealing with hospitalization, and insurance coverage
- The recovery process

Ethical Issues

In a recent book I edited with Richard Magee, *Ethical and Legal Issues in Professional Practice with Families,* I presented an overview of ethical issues in family practice, as well as an examination of the issues most applicable to clinical practice in the area of serious mental illness. Summarizing that material here, I apply the model of ethical decision making developed by Karen Kitchener and consider selected ethical issues that may arise at each of three hierarchically tiered levels.[24] These levels include *ethical rules,* such as those specified in professional codes of ethics and in other sets of rules or laws; *ethical principles,* which are enduring beliefs and specific modes of conduct that protect the interests and welfare of all involved; and *ethical theories,* which offer a metalevel of analysis that can be used to resolve conflicts between ethical rules or principles.

Ethical Rules

Ethical rules that merit particular consideration in family practice include competence, relationships, informed consent, and confidentiality.

Competence

When working with families of people who have mental illness, in addition to general clinical competence, practitioners need to be knowledgeable about serious mental illness and relevant family issues.

Relationships

With respect to relationships, professionals need to clarify their own role in working with families. They also should clarify at the outset which family members are clients, the relationship the practitioner will have with each, and policies regarding communication with family members who are not clients. For example, when clinicians are offering services to patients with mental illness, they may have collateral contacts with families that focus on history taking, crisis intervention, and telephone contact.

Families may also participate in family-focused interventions, including family consultation, family support groups, family education, family psychoeducation, and psychotherapy. As discussed later, professional roles differ significantly across these family interventions. Some interventions are primarily designed to assist families to cope with mental illness; others involve traditional clinical services, including individual, couple, family, and group therapy. This distinction is important because many families do not see themselves as needing or wanting therapy, yet may welcome professional assistance in dealing with illness-related concerns.

Informed Consent

Informed consent is important in family practice. Given the range of family interventions available to practitioners, they need to ensure that family members have information about available services, their potential risks and benefits, the risks of forgoing services, and possible alternatives. Research support for various services might also be shared with families. For example, there is strong evidence that a low-stress family environment can reduce the risk of patient relapse. Families that have difficulty providing such an environment might be encouraged to participate in a psychoeducational program designed to help them reduce their level of ambient stress (see Chapter 8).

Confidentiality

There are important distinctions among confidentiality, which is a professional ethical standard that offers protection against unauthorized disclosures; privileged communication, which is a legal right that offers protection under certain circumstances from having confidences revealed during legal proceedings without permission; and privacy, which is a constitutional right to protection against invasion of privacy.

Although practitioners may have occasion to deal with all of these concerns, the present focus is on the ethical standard of confidentiality. This standard requires professionals to discuss relevant limitations on confidentiality at the beginning of therapy and thereafter as new circumstances warrant. Potential limitations include the presence of other people in couple, family, and group therapy, as well as applicable laws, institutional rules, and professional or scientific relationships.

In addition, practitioners need to discuss any foreseeable uses of information generated through their services and take reasonable precautions to maintain confidentiality and minimize intrusions on privacy. Written and oral reports should include only pertinent information, and information should be shared only for appropriate purposes and with relevant individuals. Clinicians should also maintain appropriate confidentiality in record keeping. When there are multiple clients, such as family members, records may be kept individually or comingled. In either case, at the outset family members need to be informed about record-keeping practices and about procedures necessary to release records and to disclose confidential information.

In the absence of client consent, disclosures of confidential information should be made only as mandated by law or where permitted by law for a valid purpose, such as to provide needed professional services, to obtain appropriate professional consultations, to protect the client or others from harm, or to obtain payment for services. Practitioners may also disclose confidential information with the appropriate consent of the client unless prohibited by law. Even when there is informed consent, clinicians need to discuss the boundaries of confidentiality with patients before sharing information with families.

When consulting with colleagues, professionals should protect the confidentiality of the relationship unless they have obtained the prior consent of the client or the disclosure cannot be avoided, and they should share information only to the extent necessary to achieve the purposes of the consultation. When there are multiple clients, each legally competent party needs to provide consent for disclosure of confidential information, as in the case of participants in marital therapy who decide to divorce.

ETHICAL PRINCIPLES

Ethical dilemmas sometimes arise that have no obvious resolution at the level of ethical rules. In a given case, for instance, a clinician might believe that the welfare of a patient, a young man with bipolar disorder, is best served by working closely with his family with whom the patient resides. However, there has been much family conflict during this difficult period, and the patient refuses to allow the therapist to speak with his parents, threatening to terminate therapy. At the same time, the parents are understandably concerned about their adult son and are asserting their right to be involved in treatment, for which they are paying.

Another dilemma might arise for a practitioner who believes that family therapy is the most appropriate intervention for a particular family and also that participation of all family members is necessary for effective treatment. Perhaps the family does not wish to become involved in family therapy or only certain members are willing to participate. What is the most ethical course of action under each of these circumstances? A shift to the second level of ethical principles may be helpful, including consideration of autonomy (freedom), beneficence (welfare of others), and nonmaleficence (do no harm).

Autonomy

The principle of autonomy would appear to ensure that families have a right to choose their degree of participation in therapy, to decline to participate at all, to set or alter goals, and to withdraw without undue pressure.[25] However, this right may conflict with other ethical concerns, such as the welfare of a patient with mental illness. Indeed, some agencies and individual practitioners require families to participate in family therapy as a condition for obtaining services for their relative, based on the assumption that family involvement is essential for effective treatment.

When the needs and desires of families are not taken into consideration, such mandated family therapy increases the potential for negative treatment effects.[26] In family practice, it is generally best to use a flexible approach that addresses both ethical issues (informed choice and welfare of the patient); that respects the rights and preferences of all parties; and that assists families in choosing the nature of their involvement in their relative's treatment. Assuming an initial role as family consultant, practitioners can describe the available services and assist families in selecting those that best meet their needs. Any service is more likely to be accepted and beneficial when families have made an informed choice based on their specific requirements and preferences.

During one of my interviews, a mother told me that she and her husband were required to attend family therapy twice a week in order to visit their daughter in the hospital. In the midst of winter, these parents borrowed a car for the 2-hour round trip for therapy sessions they did not wish to attend. What she needed instead, this mother declared, was information about her daughter's mental illness and suggestions to help her family cope. Her verdict on the mandated family therapy: "It was an extreme waste of my time."[27]

Beneficence

Beneficence requires professionals to contribute actively to the good of others. Given the diversity among families, the goal of professional practice is to achieve an optimal match between the needs, desires, and resources of particular families and the available services. Practitioners should conduct a cost-benefit analysis of various alternatives and discuss this analysis with families. Consistent with the principle of least intervention, they should recommend the form of intervention that offers the maximum benefits with fewest risks and reasonable costs.[28] Research support for the effectiveness of various family interventions is also an important consideration, as is family perception of their value.[29]

Nonmaleficence

Nonmaleficence, the directive to do no harm, is defined broadly to include a range of adverse consequences, including negative treatment effects. The potential for negative effects appears to be relatively high among families that include a member with mental illness.[30] For example, negative effects may result when practitioners inappropriately assume that families are dysfunctional or pathogenic.[31] One sibling talked about his adolescence, remarking that his brother's hospitalization was the most devastating episode of his life. He added, "I was in family therapy sessions that put the blame on the family. It was awful."[32] Additional risks attend general prescriptions of family therapy that do not take into account the needs, desires, and resources of individual family members. As one woman remarked, "Family therapy is fine, but I think you should have a choice. We all have rights and needs and feelings, just like our mentally ill family member."[33]

ETHICAL THEORIES

When there are conflicts between ethical rules or principles, practitioners can shift to a third level—ethical theories. This level of analysis requires an examination of all possible consequences of decisions and defines the scope of ethical practice to include all relevant parties, including family members who are not clients. For instance, the ethical theory of utilitarianism mandates that all possible benefits be weighed against all possible costs for all affected individuals.[34] Utilitarian theory pertains to families of patients with mental illness, especially if they are serving as primary caregivers. The ethical course of action is that which results in the least amount of avoidable harm, based on an assessment of the potential impact of alternative decisions on the family system and on all individual members.

Legal Issues

In our book on ethical and legal issues in professional practice with families, the legal overview was written by Ann Lee Begler, an attorney who practices in Pittsburgh. With her generous permission, material in this section is adapted from her chapter, which encompasses a range of legal considerations relevant to family practice.[35]

It is essential for practitioners to have a sound base of knowledge about the ways in which the law intersects with clinical practice and to understand the differences between the legal and mental health systems. In theory, the legal system has been designed to ensure the determination of truth and the accomplishment of justice. In contrast, mental health professionals are primarily concerned with assisting clients to lead healthier and more satisfying lives. Given the inherent subjectivity of the therapeutic process, finding truth and reaching justice are typically not clinical objectives. Thus, when encountering the legal system, therapists need to remember that legal interests, goals, and processes are different from those to which they are accustomed.

Professionals also need to be aware of the possible negative legal consequences of treatment recommendations; when they occur, clinicians are vulnerable to later complaints of malpractice. Begler discusses a range of legal issues of general importance to family practitioners, including sexual contact with clients, other boundary violations, supervision, failure to report, risk management, and professional testimony as a court witness. The following topics have particular relevance to serious mental illness: legal problems in the lives of clients; negligence and professional malpractice; diagnosis, competence, and referrals; confidentiality and privilege; suicide; and harm to others. Each of these topics is discussed briefly.

LEGAL PROBLEMS IN THE LIVES OF FAMILIES

Legal problems facing families are likely to have an impact on the therapeutic process. Such problems might include divorce and custody determination, infertility and adoption, appropriate education for children with disabilities, hospitalization of children with serious emotional disturbance, Social Security for elderly family members, or employment problems such as job discrimination or work-related injuries.

In addition to these general legal problems, over the course of a lifetime, families that include a member with mental illness may need legal consultation regarding a range of illness-related problems. For instance, families often need information regarding their relative's eligibility for Social Security Disability Insurance (SSDI), Supplementary Security Income (SSI), and public assistance, as well as associated health care benefits. Some families may also need knowledge about procedures for filing advance directives that allow patients to specify preferred treatment decisions if they are not capable of making an informed choice or about state regulations governing involuntary commitment.

As their relative ages, families may need legal consultation for estate planning that ensures continuity of caregiving without jeopardizing their relative's eligibility for benefits; for establishing health care proxy (concerned with treatment decisions) and durable power of attorney (concerned with legal and financial matters); and for appointing a guardian (with authority over personal and financial decisions) or conservator (with authority over property and money issues).[36] Knowledgeable clinicians can support families who are dealing with these difficult issues and can make timely and appropriate referrals.

NEGLIGENCE AND PROFESSIONAL MALPRACTICE

Negligence and professional malpractice are of central concern to family practitioners. Lawsuits might be filed by clients who are unhappy with their treatment, by their family members (e.g., in the case of the client's suicide), or by others outside the family (e.g., when negligent care has resulted in harm to others). Although malpractice claims against mental health practitioners generally are far fewer than those against other types of health care providers, recent years have seen an increase in the frequency of claims.[37]

Malpractice suits against mental health professionals are most often concerned with negligence, which is defined in terms of breach of duty and a resultant injury.[38] With a few exceptions (e.g., when there is a duty to protect an identifiable third party), the ultimate issue is whether the professional acted reasonably; that is, whether a standard of care was violated. There are many potential areas of negligence and malpractice in clinical practice, including the remaining topics in this section.

DIAGNOSIS, COMPETENCE, AND REFERRALS

Consistent with the general requirements of clinical practice, practitioners who provide services to patients with serious mental illness need to assign a diagnosis and to formulate and implement an appropriate treatment plan. Clinicians who offer services to these patients need to be familiar with recent models of serious mental illness; relevant diagnostic categories and their associated symptoms; current approaches to assessment, treatment, and rehabilitation; and results of long-term studies that encourage a sense of hopefulness regarding prognosis. Shortcomings in any of these areas can have life-threatening consequences for patients with mental illness, a devastating impact on their families, and malpractice implications for practitioners.

The referral process also carries a risk of liability. The original practitioner must handle the referral and transfer of the client in a competent manner and must refer to a competent individual. Because liability may be incurred by the referring clinician if the client is injured by the incompetence of the professional receiving the referral, clinicians need a network of colleagues who have expertise in the areas of serious mental illness and family concerns and who are receptive to referrals. Therapists may also be liable if, after having begun to offer treatment, they neglect to see the client, fail to make a reasonable referral, or fail to act appropriately in carrying out the actual transfer of the client. In such cases, the practitioner may be deemed to have abandoned the client and is vulnerable to claims of malpractice.

CONFIDENTIALITY AND PRIVILEGE

Confidentiality is a legal as well as an ethical duty. If this duty is breached and if there is a resulting injury to the client, practitioners can be liable for malpractice. Lawsuits can be brought under a general theory of negligence involving breach of contract, based on the assumption that confidentiality was explicitly expressed or implicit in the relationship or as a suit for an intentional invasion of privacy. Thus, professionals should act in accord with the requirements of their ethical codes and with sensitivity to the legal implications of these requirements.

In the absence of client consent, the duty to protect confidentiality applies when professionals receive a written request for client records, when they are asked by an attorney or other party to discuss the case, and even when they receive a subpoena seeking records or testimony in court. When a release is given, it must be given freely and voluntarily; it must be fully informed; it should always be in writing; ramifications of the release should be discussed with the client; and those discussions should be well documented in the client record.

If the client has not signed a release, upon receipt of a subpoena, the practitioner should immediately notify the client and may have an obligation to challenge the subpoena. If the client cannot be located and a court appearance is required, professionals must assert the duty of confidentiality and, to the extent that privilege is applicable, raise it on behalf of the client. Therapists who receive a subpoena should generally consult legal counsel.

Apart from these legal considerations, a breach of confidentiality also has significant clinical implications: Trauma to the client can be significant.

Many participants in therapy have difficulty managing current relationships, and some bring a history of childhood experiences that have undermined their capacity for trust and intimacy. Often, the therapeutic relationship offers a corrective emotional and interpersonal experience that allows clients to build healthier and more satisfying relationships in the present. Indeed, for many clients, the crux of therapeutic work focuses on the re-establishment of trust and the enhancement of relationships. When the bond of trust is broken through a breach of confidentiality, the resulting harm can be severe for the client and the legal liability extensive for the professional.

SUICIDE

Practitioners must act reasonably in assessing the risk of suicide and can be liable in the event of harm if they failed to follow acceptable standards in diagnosing and treating a suicidal patient. Although they are not required to prevent all suicide, reasonable steps must be taken to do so.[39] Assessing the potential for harm is among the most difficult tasks facing clinicians. Moreover, the duty to assess and act, within reason, is juxtaposed with the professional's duty to maintain confidences and respect the client's right to privacy, and with the client's rights to be free from restraint and from the risks associated with certain treatments, such as medication and electroconvulsive therapies.

The challenge of assessing suicidal risk is compounded by the need for practitioners to differentiate between acute and chronic suicidal states, to decide where clients stand on this continuum, and to determine the appropriate level of intervention. Therapists can take and document a number of steps to protect themselves when dealing with the risk of suicide.[40] These include: (a) discussing with the client the chronic risk and the possibilities for managing that risk, (b) examining specific approaches that might be warranted, (c) informing and involving the family, and (d) considering a second opinion. If, during this process, the clinician decides against continuation of treatment, then termination or transfer of treatment must be conscientiously and carefully managed. Again, the treating professional's breach of duty in managing termination is always a potentially viable lawsuit waiting to happen.

The risk of suicide is of considerable importance for practitioners who work with patients who have serious mental illness. The current *Diagnostic and Statistical Manual of Mental Disorders (DSM-IV)* places the rate of suicide between 10% and 15% for the diagnoses of schizophrenia, bipolar disorder, and major depression.[41] Should client suicide occur, a determination of dereliction of duty is based on the court's finding that the practitioner

failed to possess the degree of skill possessed by others similarly qualified, to exercise reasonable care, and to use his or her best judgment. Fortunately, courts recognize that custodial care decisions are complex and
do not demand protection at any cost.[42]

HARM TO OTHERS

Professionals have a duty to take reasonable steps to protect others from
harm that can be perpetrated by dangerous clients. This duty to protect
first emerged in the landmark case of *Tarasoff v. Board of Regents of the University of California*.[43] Although parameters of the duty to protect differ
from state to state, most jurisdictions do have some law, whether by statute
or decisional case law, that imposes some aspect of this duty upon mental
health practitioners. The duty to protect may involve one or more of several
possible options, including seeking a hospitalization; getting the patient on
medication; involving the family in treatment; or warning the intended victim, the police, or a person likely to warn the intended victim.

Early cases in this area focused on protection of an identifiable victim from acts of physical violence by a client. In the context of family
practice, there is a frequent need for risk assessment. The prevalence of
domestic violence is now well established and most victims of homicide
are killed by someone they know. The high incidence of violence within
families has prompted most states to enact laws that offer protection for
victims through restraining orders and household evictions. More recently, the duty to protect has been considered in connection with other
risks, including the transmission of life-threatening illness such as the
HIV virus.[44]

As with other situations that carry risks of malpractice, the duty to
protect requires careful risk assessment, which has always been a formidable task.[45] Nevertheless, professionals are obliged to undertake such an
assessment when appropriate, exercising professional judgment in determining the degree of risk. The duty to protect has clinical as well as legal
ramifications. For instance, even when clients are advised in advance that
such threats may require the therapist to breach confidentiality, such a
breach may ultimately mark the end of the therapist-client relationship,
with its potential for longer term benefits.

The potential for harm to others is an area of much concern in the area
of serious mental illness. Most people with mental illness are not more
dangerous than the general population, although they are often portrayed as such by the mass media. For example, three-fourths of prime-
time television portrayals of serious mental illness depict dangerous
behavior, a great overestimate of the actual incidence.[46] Nevertheless, as

E. Fuller Torrey discusses at length, some people with mental illness have the potential for violence, especially if they fail to take medication or if they have a history of violence or a concurrent problem with drug or alcohol abuse. Moreover, family members are often the target of this violence.[47] Therefore, families need to be able to recognize the warning signs of potentially violent behavior, to respond in a manner that defuses the situation, and to protect themselves and obtain professional assistance if necessary.

Dealing with Confidentiality

Practitioners often view confidentiality as a rigid barrier to working with families.[48] Yet such a stance is rarely in the best interest of patients, family members, or therapists. Thus, clinicians need to understand potential conflicts regarding confidentiality and the ways in which these conflicts can be resolved. The ethical codes of professionals protect the right of patients to a confidential therapeutic relationship. At the same time, family members also have rights, particularly if they are serving as primary caregivers.

Several strategies are available for resolving the conflict between the patient's right to confidentiality and the needs of families.[49] Initially, it is important to distinguish between nonconfidential and confidential information. Much nonconfidential information regarding serious mental illness is available to the general public and can be shared with families, including information about diagnostic categories, etiology, symptoms, treatment, medication, and prognosis. Such information is essential for family members, who can benefit from written materials and educational programs.

When confidentiality does pertain, practitioners can use a release of information form designed specifically for families.[50] If the release form is presented at the right time (when the patient is able to provide informed consent) and in the right manner (as something that is likely to enhance treatment), most patients are willing to authorize the release of relevant information to their families. In the Pittsburgh area, for example, where there are standard confidentiality procedures in the public mental health system, 90% of patients approached in this manner choose to sign the release form.

Practitioners can also function as mediators, negotiating the boundaries of confidentiality to meet the needs of particular patients and families. Clinicians can discuss with patients the importance of keeping their families informed and can work with both parties in deciding what specific information will be shared. In group practice or institutional settings, separate staff members can be designated as family advocates, who can provide relevant information to families and consult with the therapist to enhance treatment planning and coordination. With the consent of the patient, in many settings families can be actively involved in treatment, perhaps as members of the treatment team. As active participants, family members can offer suggestions and observations; they can also play a meaningful role in decisions that affect them.

Confidentiality does not prohibit practitioners from listening to family members, although it may be clinically unwise in certain cases. Even when therapists feel it is best not to have contact with families (perhaps to protect a fragile therapeutic relationship), they should ensure that families have an avenue to express their concerns and to share their observations about the risk of imminent harm, indications of substance abuse, evidence of treatment or medication nonadherence, or other serious matters. I recently heard from a mother who had tried unsuccessfully to communicate her concern about her daughter's potential for a suicide attempt, which might have been avoided with better communication.

There are a number of additional considerations concerning confidentiality. Patients can always reveal information to their families. They can also assign that role to their therapists by signing a release form. Thus, patients should be encouraged as early as possible to make an informed choice about the information that will be shared with family members and the ways in which information will be shared. Moreover, consent requires competence; a decision should be deferred if the patient is experiencing severe psychotic symptoms. Other ethical principles may conflict with (and take precedence over) confidentiality, such as the risk of imminent harm to the patient or to others. Under such circumstances, practitioners may be ethically and legally required to contact family members. The next case illustrates the problems that can result when potential conflicts regarding confidentiality are ignored:

Following a weekend visit, a mother called a taxi to return her son to his community residence. When she contacted the agency to check on his arrival, she was told that staff were not permitted to give out any information about the residents.

A policy that encouraged residents to contact their families upon arrival might have prevented this situation, which was understandably frustrating for this parent. Moreover, decisions regarding the disclosure of information should be made not by staff but by patients, who should be given a timely opportunity to make an informed choice about these matters.

Diagnosis and Reimbursement in Family Practice

Family practitioners are well aware of the problems that attend diagnosis and reimbursement in couple and family therapy. Professional and managed care organizations continue to assume an individual model of practice that generalizes only partly to multiperson therapies. Moreover, although professional practice with couples and families often focuses on distressed relationships, present diagnostic systems do not include relational disorders, a term used to describe problems in relationships.

As Florence Kaslow has discussed, family practitioners consequently face the dilemma of providing a diagnosis that accurately reflects their systems approach to interpersonal problems without neglecting individual clients and without committing insurance fraud.[51] Consider, for instance, a husband and wife whose individual problems do not meet the criteria for a *DSM-IV* diagnosis but who have sought therapy to deal with significant marital conflict. In cases such as this, the widespread practice of giving individual diagnoses in multiperson therapy misrepresents the focus and method of treatment and raises both ethical and legal concerns.

These and other issues are explored in a groundbreaking book edited by Kaslow, *Handbook of Relational Diagnosis and Dysfunctional Family Patterns.*[52] The book offers a valuable perspective for family practitioners in general, as well as those specifically concerned with serious mental illness.

GENERAL CONSIDERATIONS

Terence Patterson and Don-David Lusterman offer an incisive analysis of the "relational reimbursement dilemma," noting that practitioners of couple, family, and parent-child therapy frequently have a need to provide formal diagnosis for reimbursement, quality assurance, and other purposes. They describe three alternatives for dealing with this issue in multiperson therapy, none really satisfactory.[53]

First, practitioners can use *DSM-IV* V codes, which are, by definition, not disorders themselves but are the focus of treatment. Relational problems specified as V codes include: Relational Problem Related to a Mental Disorder or General Medical Condition, Parent-Child Relational Problem, Partner Relational Problem, Sibling Relational Problem, and Relational Problem Not Otherwise Specified (NOS). Unfortunately, insurers often question the necessity of treating a condition that is not a mental disorder and generally view such codes as ineligible for reimbursement.

Second, clinicians can assign the family member a *DSM-IV* individual diagnosis of adjustment disorder, which is defined as the development of clinically significant emotional or behavioral symptoms in response to an identifiable psychosocial stressor or stressors. When the diagnostic criteria are met, as they often are in couple and family therapy, this alternative may be appropriate. However, this alternative requires a psychiatric diagnosis of an individual in the couple or family system, which may misrepresent the nature of the problem and of the therapy. Moreover, insurers sometimes question the need for treatment of stressful reactions to normal life events.

For purposes of reimbursement, many practitioners of multiperson therapy select the third alternative, which is to assign both a psychiatric diagnosis to an individual and a relational code to describe the family pattern. This method is acceptable to some insurers and poses no ethical dilemma if the individual diagnosis is accurate. However, such an approach may lead to an overemphasis on individual concerns and an underemphasis on relational problems. In addition, there may be adverse consequences for the diagnosed individual with respect to employment, future insurance coverage, custody hearings, or other important matters. Not surprisingly, Patterson and Lusterman argue the case for relational assessment, treatment, and reimbursement.

SERIOUS MENTAL ILLNESS

Given this context, how should practitioners approach diagnosis and reimbursement in their work with families that include a member with serious mental illness? In many settings, the focus is on the patient with mental illness, who receives an Axis I diagnosis of schizophrenia, bipolar disorder, major depression, or other severe and persistent disorder. The family sessions are viewed as an integral part of the patient's treatment, and services for families are largely designed to assist them in fostering their relative's recovery. This patient-focused approach is both clinically and empirically sound. For example, there is strong support for the value of certain family interventions in reducing the risk of patient relapse (see Chapter 8).[54] Giving the patient a *DSM-IV* diagnosis reduces problems with reimbursement.

On the other hand, families may seek services for themselves, quite apart from the services received by their relative. Under these circumstances, both diagnosis and reimbursement are problematic. Let us consider two scenarios:

In the first case, family members appear to be appropriate candidates for traditional clinical services, such as individual, couple, or family therapy. Possibly there were pre-existing problems in individual or family functioning that were exacerbated by the stress associated with mental illness; or perhaps the family developed persistent maladaptive patterns in response to the illness.

When clinical services are provided to families such as these, the problems in diagnosis and reimbursement are similar to those discussed by Patterson and Lusterman, as are the alternative solutions. Namely, practitioners can assign a DSM-IV V code to describe the relational problem, a DSM-IV individual diagnosis of adjustment disorder to a family member, or both an individual psychiatric diagnosis and a relational code. As noted, none of these alternatives is satisfactory.

The second scenario raises a different set of issues. In this case, the family is functioning well, although experiencing considerable distress in response to their relative's mental illness. They have joined NAMI, the mental health advocacy organization, and participated in its family education and support program. At present, they neither need nor desire psychotherapy but do have specific illness-related concerns. Thus, they are appropriate candidates for family consultation (see Chapter 7).[55] Unfortunately, often this intervention is not reimbursable.

In the absence of dysfunction, neither an individual nor a relational diagnosis is indicated. In fact, a relational diagnosis may be harmful to family members who are feeling needlessly guilty for causing a biologically-based disorder.[56] Moreover, there are problems with the applicable *DSM-IV* V code, Relational Problem Related to a Mental Disorder or General Medical Condition, which requires "a pattern of impaired interaction that is associated with a mental disorder . . . in a family member."[57] Such a pattern is not present in the family under consideration. In the absence of a *DSM-IV* diagnosis, the cost of services is likely to be shouldered by families. This cost may prevent some families from receiving needed services, with the loss of potential benefits for them and for their relative with mental illness:

One family I have known for over a decade has received three kinds of services. During their daughter's initial hospitalization, they received family services (largely undesired family therapy) as part of a standard patient-focused program. Their daughter appropriately received the diagnosis, and family services were reimbursed under her insurance coverage. The mother, although functioning well in other respects, sought individual therapy to assist her in working through her intense feelings of grief and loss. The mother's diagnosis was adjustment disorder with depressed mood, which was covered under her own policy.

A number of years later, the parents, who were serving as primary caregivers for their daughter, had some immediate and long-term illness-related concerns. They met several times with a practitioner who worked with them on resolving their present concerns and planning for their family's future. As all parties agreed during the initial session, a diagnosis was not appropriate under these circumstances, and the parents paid for the sessions themselves. Thus, this middle-class family had access to services that met their changing needs. Another family, with fewer resources, might not have been so fortunate.

From Theory to Practice

Let's return to Susan Murphy, the social worker in private practice who finds herself unprepared to work with the families of patients like David Endicott, who has bipolar disorder. The easy solution would be for her to refer to another therapist who is competent in this area of practice. However, easy solutions are not always available or desirable. For instance, in some rural or inner city areas, "services referred are services denied." Likewise, there are advantages to working with both patients and families, which provides an opportunity for practitioners to gain a fuller understanding of the family context and to meet the needs of all members.

Assuming Susan wishes to develop the requisite competencies for professional practice with these families, how might she proceed? A general rule is that competency is best obtained by submitting oneself to external feedback, such as through a proctorship. Several additional strategies are available:

1. Susan can attend continuing education programs concerned with serious mental illness and family concerns. State and national professional organizations increasingly offer programs that cover such topics.
2. She can familiarize herself with the extensive literature concerned with serious mental illness and its corresponding family experience, as well as with local services and resources. Both will assist her in meeting the needs of families.
3. She can contact her local NAMI affiliate and offer to provide consultation and programs to the group. By participating in meetings, practitioners will become acquainted with the group; equally important, group members will feel comfortable contacting the clinician when needed. Professionals can also benefit from attending state and national NAMI conventions, which offer a wide range of presentations concerned with mental illness and innovative treatment, with family experiences and needs, and with effective coping strategies.
4. Susan might obtain supervision from a practitioner who has expertise concerned with serious mental illness and the family experience

of mental illness. Professional organizations can usually provide a referral to knowledgeable colleagues.

5. She can begin networking with other professionals who share her interest in serious mental illness and family issues. Many opportunities are available at interdisciplinary conferences and through collaborative activities on local, state, and national levels.

6. She can contact her professional organization to locate special initiatives concerned with serious mental illness. I am a member of the American Psychological Association Task Force on Serious Mental Illness and Serious Emotional Disturbance. As a group and as individuals, we often hear from psychologists who want to learn more about our work or to contribute their expertise.

7. Susan needs to develop sound practice habits and risk management strategies.[58] Consistent with best standards of practice, she should be knowledgeable about her professional code of ethics and about applicable federal and state law; should consult with colleagues as appropriate; should establish positive and collaborative relationships with her clients and their families; should communicate effectively to relevant parties; should anticipate problems and develop strategies for their resolution; should document treatment carefully; and should remain abreast of current theory and research to ensure that her treatment is appropriate and effective.

Assuming that Susan has developed the requisite competencies for professional practice with the families of her clients, how might she approach her meeting with David's parents? Susan is aware of the need to engage the family and begin a family assessment. In addition, she plans to address several professional issues, including the nature of her relationship with the Endicotts, confidentiality, recording keeping, and insurance reimbursement.

PRACTITIONER: *Good afternoon, Mr. and Mrs. Endicott. I'm pleased to meet you and hope I can be helpful. I know David has appreciated your support over the years.*

FATHER: *We've wanted for a long time to talk with the professionals who have worked with David, assuming they would want our input and would help us cope with this difficult situation. But we were never contacted by anyone after his hospitalization over a decade ago. Now that he's been seeing you for several months, we decided to call you.*

PRACTITIONER: *I'm glad you did. I can understand your frustration with a mental health system that often seems to ignore families, even when* they are serving as primary caregivers, as you are for David. Actually, there are some matters we need to discuss before we continue. I've spoken with David about your visit today. As you probably know, I have an ethical and legal obligation to maintain the confidentiality of my therapeutic relationship with him. It would be very difficult to help people like David if they weren't able to trust us with their disclosures. On the other hand, I realize you both have legitimate interests as well. He is, after all, your son, and he continues to live with you. And I agree that your involvement is important. You need to be able to share your observations, to ask questions, and to have a say in decisions that affect you.

MOTHER: You know, you're the only professional we've met who seems to recognize the importance of parents. We do understand the value of a confidential therapeutic relationship and have no interest in David's therapy sessions. But we do want to know how he's doing and what the future holds. We also want to know how we can be helpful to him. I sometimes wonder if we should encourage him to move out or to get a job, but we don't want to see him on the streets or in the hospital again.

PRACTITIONER: I understand your concern. Later, we'll talk about these possibilities. David and I have discussed this meeting and decided what can be shared with you. He has signed a release form allowing me to talk with you, which protects all of us. There may be questions I can't answer, but I'll do my best to meet your needs. There is another issue I want to discuss with you. I spoke with the managed care organization that covers David's treatment and told them it would be helpful for David if I met with you. They agreed to cover four sessions, so we'll have a chance to discuss your concerns. Unless you want to pay for additional sessions yourselves, we need to plan our sessions carefully. Of course, if it turns out that you need more time, we can discuss some possibilities. And we can always ask the insurance company to pay for an occasional session in the future.

FATHER: We really have no major problems ourselves apart from David. My company went through some downsizing last year, and I was forced to retire early. Although we both work part time and I have a small pension, our budget is tight. We can't afford to pay for additional sessions ourselves. So let's plan on four sessions, at least for a start.

PRACTITIONER: Okay, that's fine with me. Since your major concerns are related to David's mental illness, I'll work with you as a family consultant rather than a therapist. We can make a list of your concerns today and plan our sessions accordingly. I'll be keeping your file separate from David's, and you should know that I also have a confidential relationship *with you. Should you wish to release your records for any reason, both of you would need to sign a release. We'll need to decide what I'll share with David, just as he decided what I could share with you. Here is some written information about my office policies and procedures. When you have read it over, let me know if you have any questions. Now, let's talk about your concerns. How can I help you?*

FATHER: *First of all, we would like to know more about David's mental illness and how to cope with his symptoms. At the onset of David's illness, a few professionals talked briefly to us about manic depression. How does that differ from bipolar disorder, a term we've also heard?*

PRACTITIONER: *The terms refer to the same disorder, which is sometimes confusing. Manic depression is still used frequently, but the official name is now bipolar disorder. The disorder is characterized by extreme mood swings. During the manic phase, individuals may have an elevated or irritable mood—kind of like a revved up motor. In addition, they may need less sleep, be more talkative than usual, or spend too much money. During the depressive phase, people may feel despondent and lose interest in their activities. Additional symptoms may include changes in appetite or sleep, decreased energy, feelings of worthlessness or guilt, difficulty concentrating, and sometimes thoughts of death or suicide. Here is some written information about bipolar disorder.*

MOTHER: *David has had all of those symptoms, though he seems to be much better now that he's taking lithium. I recently read a book by Kay Jamison called* An Unquiet Mind: A Memoir of Moods and Madness.[59] *A friend who knows about David recommended it. I thought it was a wonderful book. It helped me understand more about David and appreciate his struggle with this terrible illness. Are there other books about bipolar disorder?*

PRACTITIONER: *Yes, let me write down some titles for you. You should be able to get them at the library. You might also want to contact your local affiliate of NAMI, an organization that provides free services to families who are dealing with mental illness. They offer educational programs and support groups for families, as well as a library. Here is their number. You can ask about their programs and see if any interest you. It usually helps to speak with other parents who can offer practical advice on handling day-to-day problems. The families I have worked with often find the group very helpful. It's nice to know you're not alone! Now, what else concerns you?*

FATHER: *We worry about the future. We're getting older and have some health problems. Who will take care of David when we're gone? And how can we plan our finances to take care of him? We don't have much money, but we plan to leave it all to David, who is our only child.*

PRACTITIONER: *That's a complicated problem for parents who have a son or daughter with mental illness. At the next session I'll give you some information on long-term planning, along with the names of a few attorneys who have expertise in that area. You'll want to make sure your financial plans don't threaten David's benefits, including his Social Security payments and health care coverage. You may wish to establish a trust fund and appoint a trustee to administer the trust in the future. It's also important to learn about the community residential arrangements available for David. The family organization I mentioned may have some suggestions. They can tell you about the Planned Lifetime Assistance Network (PLAN), which is available for families like yours. At some point, it might make sense for us to have a joint session with David to discuss your long-term plans. It's usually best if the entire family works together on this.*

MOTHER: *That sounds like a good idea. Another thing that has always bothered me is David's depression. He'd never hurt someone else, but sometimes he seems so down and talks about wanting to die. Is there a risk that he might commit suicide? How should we handle that?*

PRACTITIONER: *That is often a realistic concern for close relatives of people who have a serious mood disorder, such as bipolar disorder or major depression. Tell me more about your uneasiness. Does David seem suicidal at present?*

FATHER: *No, he seems to be doing fine right now. But from time to time, he talks about not wanting to live. He looks at his former friends, who all have families and jobs. His life seems so empty. I think that would depress almost anyone.*

PRACTITIONER: *I agree with you. There are often significant losses that accompany mental illness, both for the patient and for the family. Some feelings of depression are normal for all of you. We can talk about suicide during the next session, so you know how to recognize any serious signs and what steps to take. Although it's painful to talk about, it's important to be prepared. I'm glad you shared this concern with me. Do you have any other pressing issues?*

MOTHER: *No, nothing that's urgent. I feel better already. It seems we're finally getting the help we need. When you live with someone as ill as David, your own problems don't seem to matter. But we really need help with this and appreciate your willingness to meet with us. Sometimes I get very depressed myself. The sense of what might have been is overwhelming. You know, we've been so focused on David's needs all these years. It's almost as if I didn't feel my own pain mattered. I know David grieves for his lost hopes and dreams—for a real job, for a wife and children. But those are losses for us, too.*

PRACTITIONER: *Yes, they are enormous losses for parents. And your feelings do matter; we can talk more about them next time we meet. Your feelings deserve our attention along with your other concerns. It's often helpful for parents to have an opportunity to talk about their own experiences. Do you have any additional concerns, Mr. Endicott?*

FATHER: *No, not right now. I'm sure I'll have more questions later. But we finally seem to be making some progress.*

PRACTITIONER: *Why don't we plan to meet once a week for the next 3 weeks. How about next week at the same time? As we've discussed, we can talk about bipolar disorder and I can try to answer your questions. In addition, we can talk about your experiences and feelings, and I can share the experiences of other parents if you like. We'll also talk about how you can be most helpful to David, about future financial planning, about community resources, and about suicidal risk factors. Think about other issues you might want to discuss and let me know when we meet next time.*

FATHER: *We look forward to seeing you again. And thanks for telling us about the family group. That sounds like a good idea.*

PART TWO

Family Experiences
and Needs

CHAPTER 3

The Family Experience of Mental Illness

In his work at a community mental health center, family therapist Robert Guardez has been asked to expand services for families of patients who are hospitalized with serious mental illness. At his initial meeting with families of current patients, two family members remained to speak with him afterwards. The first was Fred Pisano, the husband of a woman with major depression. He said he was struggling to hold down his job as a maintenance supervisor and to meet the needs of his three teenagers, adding that he didn't see how his family could continue much longer to deal with his wife's illness, which has involved several suicide attempts and hospitalizations. The second family member was Deborah Newman, a middle-aged African American woman who was caring for an adult son with schizoaffective disorder. Both family members said they had received little assistance from staff during their relatives' prior hospitalizations. Mr. Pisano remarked in frustration, "You professionals have no idea how mental illness tears families apart." And Ms. Newman added, "The staff here doesn't have a clue about what families need!" Robert has mental illness in his family as well, so he is not surprised by their complaints. He invites them to present a program for staff, sharing their experiences and offering suggestions. What can professionals learn from these family members?

Robert Guardez has taken a useful first step in assisting the staff to understand the experiences and needs of families. Although there is extensive literature in the area, it is rarely included in professional training programs. Furthermore, especially in inpatient settings, meetings between families and professionals are largely focused on the patient, often under crisis conditions. In outpatient settings, practitioners may have little or no contact with families. Under these circumstances, families rarely take the initiative to ask questions or express their concerns. In fact, they may have been informed that confidentiality prevents professionals from communicating with them. Thus, an inservice presentation by family members offers a rich resource for staff.

Based on an expanding literature written by professionals and by family members themselves, this chapter explores the family experience of mental illness.[1] Topics include family burden, family risks, family resilience, multiple perspectives, family diversity, and family needs. An understanding of these topics is essential for practitioners working with families, who often feel neglected and misunderstood. I recently received a letter from a mother whose adult son has schizophrenia. She had requested one of my articles and was responding to thank me, remarking that she was so glad to see that professionals were beginning to understand the need to support families of those "afflicted with these heinous illnesses." She added, "The tortures of families need to be brought to the awareness of all humankind, so that we families can learn the necessary coping skills."

Family Burden

Serious mental illness is typically a catastrophic stressor for families that is woven into the familial fabric in an enduring way. In the words of one family member, "This terrible illness colors everything—a family cannot escape."[2] Researchers have repeatedly documented the devastating impact of mental illness on families in terms of family or caregiver burden, which is the overall level of distress experienced as a result of the illness. As noted earlier, researchers have distinguished between subjective and objective burden, defined respectively as the personal suffering experienced by family members in response to their relative's illness and as the practical problems and hardships associated with the illness.[3]

Although there are many situational, social, and iatrogenic sources of family burden, the distinction between subjective and objective burden remains a useful way of conceptualizing the family experience of mental illness. From a family process perspective, even the most well-functioning family will be unsettled by the mental illness of a member and by the internal and external aftershocks that accost the family system. Some families are able to absorb these aftershocks and go on with their lives, albeit transfigured; others struggle to fulfill their basic functions under daunting conditions; and still others do not survive as a unit.

The robust research finding of family burden has in many respects defined the family experience of mental illness, increasing the risk that other important dimensions of this experience will be ignored, such as the potential for family resilience. Resilience is the ability to rebound from adversity and prevail over difficult life circumstances. As with any catastrophic stressor, mental illness may serve as a catalyst for constructive individual or family change. As one family member told me, "When a family experiences something like this, it makes for very compassionate people—people of substance. My brother has created a bond among us all that we will not allow to be broken."[4] Such an exclusive emphasis on family burden also ignores the contributions of people with mental illness to their families and to society.[5]

Professionals are now developing an expanded view of the family experience of mental illness, one that incorporates family resilience as well as family burden, that acknowledges the diversity within and among families, and that maintains a life span perspective on family adaptation to mental illness. Nevertheless, any discussion of the topic must begin with subjective and objective family burden, which serves as the context for understanding other dimensions of the family experience.

SUBJECTIVE BURDEN

In response to the mental illness of a beloved relative, family members often experience intense feelings of grief and loss, as well as a range of other powerful emotions, including shock, disbelief, anger, despair, guilt, anxiety, and shame. Describing the impact of mental illness on her family, one mother wrote, "In the dark soul of the night, I grieve for all of us: for the anguish of the past and the present and for the uncertainty of the future. Most of all, I grieve for my son and for his lost hopes and dreams."[6]

Several components of the subjective burden are discussed, including grief, symbolic loss, chronic sorrow, the emotional roller coaster, and empathic pain.

Grief

At the heart of the family experience of mental illness is a powerful grieving process.[7] Family members may mourn for the relative they knew and loved before the onset of the illness, for the anguish of their family, and for their personal losses. Years after the onset of her son's mental illness, one mother told me she continued to grieve for the irrevocable losses that followed in the wake of the illness. There was a noticeable shift, she said, from their collective sense of a happy and effective family to a very different image: one of a family that had survived—and even prevailed—but that had lost its luster and joy.

Symbolic Loss

In addition to grief, family members experience many symbolic losses that pertain to hopes, dreams, and expectations, and to individual and family myths and identity. A working class father told me of his earlier pride in his son, the first to attend college and the personification of the family's dream of unlimited possibilities. In the wake of his son's mental illness, this father remarked on his own "shattered dreams."

Chronic Sorrow

Although family members often undergo a grieving process in response to their relative's illness, rarely do they proceed through a series of stages that culminate in a state of serene acceptance. Far more often, they experience continuing feelings of grief and loss that wax and wane in response to the course of their relative's illness or to events in their own lives. Their heartache is woven into the familial fabric on a continuing basis, with the potential for periodic emotional firestorms. In my research, I asked mothers whose children (of all ages) were receiving mental health services whether they had experienced chronic sorrow; three-fourths of the mothers responded affirmatively, occasionally distinguishing between mental illness and biological death. In the words of one family member, "It's like someone close died, but there's no closure. It's never over."[8]

In fact, as Curtis Flory and Rose Marie Friedrich have detailed, families may also be dealing with the biological death of their relative: Mortality rates of people with mental illness for both natural and unnatural causes of death are more than twice those of the general population.[9] A recent study found that individuals with serious mental illness died 19 years prematurely; their average age of death was 52.4 years (versus 72.8 years for nonpatients). The largest single contributor to premature death is suicide, with a rate 10 to 15 times higher than expected. More than two-fifths (42%) of patients in their study had attempted suicide; most of those had made multiple attempts. Other causes of death include poor health habits, such as heavy smoking, obesity, and alcohol abuse; diseases, such as heart disease and diabetes, which too often remain undiagnosed and untreated in this population; and accidental deaths, also much higher among these individuals.

When people with mental illness die prematurely, their families are left with sorrow that persists for a lifetime; with a tangle of intense emotions, irrevocable losses, and unanswerable questions; and with unending frustration over the failures of a system that contributes to these deaths. Following her son's suicide, one mother wrote that "the victims of suicide are also those who are left behind to wonder what they might have done differently and who ache from thoughts of the torment their loved one suffered."[10] Whatever their expertise, practitioners may have little to offer such families beyond a protected forum for resolving their grief and finding the courage to go on. As Judith Viorst has written, "So perhaps the only choice we have is to choose what to do with our dead: To die when they die. To live crippled. Or to forge, out of pain and memory, new adaptations."[11]

Emotional Roller Coaster

Families sometimes feel as if they are riding an emotional roller coaster, their ride punctuated by the alternating periods of remission and relapse that typically distinguish the course of mental illness. These cycles create substantial turmoil for family members, who often experience intense distress when renewed hope is shattered by yet another relapse. One mother told me the relapse of her daughter felt "like a small death," as if she were more vulnerable for having dared to hope again.[12]

Empathic Pain

Over time—and often with great difficulty—most family members largely resolve their emotional burden. Even as they re-invest their energy in other aspects of their lives, however, they may continue to experience empathic pain for the continuing losses of their relative and their family. Witnessing their relative's anguish over an impoverished life and his or her struggle against the forces of psychosis, family members may share in this suffering. Speaking for legions of parents, one mother spoke of her devastation at seeing her daughter "so crushed and destroyed and broken."[13]

OBJECTIVE BURDEN

Powerful subjective burden is accompanied by an equally debilitating objective burden, which consists of the practical problems that accompany the mental illness. Responding to one of my surveys, an adult offspring wrote of the consequences of his father's mental illness for his own childhood and adolescence: "My father's paranoid schizophrenia meant we moved frequently, because he felt the conspiracy was closing in on him. . . . I couldn't have friendships with peers because my father felt they might 'poison' my mind against him."[14] Elements of the objective burden include the symptoms of mental illness, caregiving responsibilities, family disruption and stress, limitations of the service delivery system, and social stigma.

Symptomatic Behavior

The symptoms of mental illness often evoke significant frustration among family members. Depending on their relative's diagnosis, family members may have to deal with:

- Positive (psychotic) symptoms, such as hallucinations, delusions, disorganized thought and speech, and bizarre behavior
- Negative symptoms, which are characterized by a decline in normal thoughts, experiences, and feelings (e.g., lack of motivation or of pleasure)
- Disturbances of mood, including severely depressed mood, unusually elevated mood, or extreme mood swings
- Potentially harmful or self-destructive behavior
- Socially inappropriate or disruptive behavior
- Poor daily living habits

People with mental illness are the undeniable victims of symptoms such as these, which may undermine the quality and productivity of their lives. Still, family members are also victimized by symptomatic behaviors, either directly when they are the target of their relative's behavior or indirectly when they are helpless observers. Other potential symptoms of mental illness may also pose problems in family relationships, such as an extreme sensitivity to perceived criticism or a limited capacity for empathy or reciprocity. As Kenneth Terkelsen has observed, "If the patient no longer cares about them, some essential aspect of what it means to be a family has been lost"; "an invisible, an unspeakable emotional deadness exists in the family."[15]

Furthermore, the specter of harm is a reality for families whose relatives confront a death rate from suicide and other causes of death that is significantly higher than the rate of the general population.[16] In addition, although the great majority of people with mental illness are no more dangerous than the general population, some may indeed be more violent, including those who fail to receive treatment or have a concurrent substance abuse problem.[17] When violence does occur, it is often directed at family members, particularly mothers who reside with the patient.[18] The challenge is to acknowledge and reduce the real risks for these family members while countering the stereotypical overemphasis on violence in the media.

Caregiving

Family members, assuming roles for which they are unprepared and untrained, gradually learn to cope with the requirements of daily life with someone who has mental illness; to obtain services from the mental health, welfare, and medical systems; and perhaps to negotiate with the legal and criminal justice systems.[19] Psychologist June Husted has written eloquently of her experiences with the criminal justice system as the mother of a son with serious mental illness, stating that at least 40% of families report that their relatives have been arrested at least once.[20] The consequences are often disastrous for these individuals, who are often treated as criminals rather than patients:

Despite federal laws to provide them their needed medical treatment, these patients are too often ignored and suffer in jail with their delusions; are given substandard care and kept for weeks before transfer to a hospital unit—despite the gravity of their condition; or die in suicide attempts.

Family Disruption and Stress

Although most caregiving families do survive the catastrophic stressor of mental illness, none do so without experiencing family disruption and stress. In the words of one family member, "Mental illness is a ravaging, devastating disease."[21] Problems may include household disarray, financial difficulties, employment problems, strained marital and family relationships, impaired physical and mental health, and diminished social life. All families experience some of these problems, at least occasionally. Some may experience many of them on a long-term basis, with little opportunity for respite. Under such circumstances, exhaustion and burnout are virtually inevitable.

Indeed, these circumstances would be disruptive and stressful for any family. Practitioners may hear of their struggles with their relative's homelessness, incarceration, isolation and abuse, life-threatening accidents and injuries, untreated medical problems, and premature death. For example, describing results of their research with 220 NAMI families in 23 states, Flory and Friedrich report that approximately 20% of patients had experienced homelessness; many had been victims of violence.[22] One parent described the steady deterioration of her son's quality of life as he sank from managing his own art gallery to living alone in a tent in the woods and surviving on handouts.

Another parent related that her homeless daughter had been beaten and injected with intravenous drugs while someone attempted to steal her money; had developed hepatitis and received burns on her abdomen;

and had been hit by a car. In the absence of treatment, her daughter deteriorated to the point where she could not speak. Still another parent reported that her son, having been refused admittance to a crisis unit, was hit when he ran in front of a car, remaining in a coma for 5 weeks. Bones in both legs were fractured; he was left with severe ambulatory problems and brain damage.

The Service Delivery System

To support their recovery process, people with mental illness often require a wide range of mental health, physical health, social, rehabilitative, vocational, and residential services. Unfortunately, these services are not always available; nor are they always satisfactory when available. Researchers have documented many shortcomings of the service delivery system, including the absence of treatment for large numbers of people with serious mental illness, the relative neglect of people with the most severe and persistent problems, inadequate funding for the full range of community-based services, and fragmentation of existing services.[23] These problems may intensify with managed care, which sometimes emphasizes the cost of services at the expense of their quality.

For people with mental illness, the consequences of these shortcomings are considerable: Many of their lives are marked by poverty, isolation, and abuse. These problems also affect the lives of their families, who pay the price for the absence of treatment in the criminal justice system and for people with mental illness who have joined the ranks of the homeless. As one adult sibling declared, "I see my brother in every disheveled and disoriented homeless person."[24]

An additional problem is the lack of services for families themselves, who often decry the insensitivity of the service delivery system. In numerous studies, family members have reported unsatisfactory handling of crises and emergencies, insufficient communication and availability on the part of professionals, an absence of programs and services for families, and minimal involvement of families in treatment planning. As discussed earlier, families may also be adversely affected by earlier unsupported theories that held families accountable for the mental illness. Thus, during a period of intense distress, families may find that the system not only fails to address their expressed needs; it also magnifies their anguish.

Stigma

From the perspective of both patients and families, the most oppressive component of family burden is stigma. Corrosive stigmatization in the larger society results in the marginalization and ostracism of people with mental illness; discrimination in insurance, housing, and employment; an adverse impact on all aspects of their functioning; and decreased likelihood that they will receive treatment. As professionals, we need to counter the negative attitudes and expectations that are often internalized by patients.

There have been many constructive developments, including the enactment in 1990 of the Americans with Disabilities Act. Nevertheless, stigmatization remains a pervasive problem for patients, for families, and even for professionals who work in this area.[25] A National Institute of Mental Health document describes stigma as the most debilitating handicap surrounding mental illness.[26] For example, researchers have found that mental illness is viewed as one of the two worst things that can happen to an individual (the other is leprosy); that exconvicts stand higher on the ladder of acceptance than former mental patients; and that mental illness is at the bottom of a list of 21 categories of disability that were ranked according to degree of offensiveness.

In his incisive book, *Media Madness: Public Images of Mental Illness*, Otto Wahl has documented the pervasiveness of stigmatization in the mass media, including film, television, print, and other media. In fact, mental illness is the most common disability portrayed in the media. For example, one of 10 films involves mental illness; one television character per night is portrayed as having a mental illness; half of the daytime soap operas have featured a character with mental illness; and mental illness is featured in a large number of magazines, newspapers, plays, and lyrics. As Wahl demonstrates, these portrayals are often insensitive, inaccurate, and unfavorable—and sometimes stigmatizing and pernicious.

Based on his own research and that of others, Wahl denounces the overemphasis on violence in the media, reporting that although 72% of characters with mental illness commit violent acts on prime-time television, the actual incidence is 12% or less. In addition, he provides many examples of disparaging stereotypes in lurid headlines (e.g., "Village Beast May Go Free"); in insensitive ads (e.g., a "schizophrenic lawn mower" that has three "sides" to its personality: mulcher, rear bagger, and side discharger); and in dehumanized film portrayals (e.g., a psychiatrist who describes his former patient as having "nothing within him . . . that was even remotely human").

For family members, adverse effects of stigma may include lowered self-esteem and damaged family relationships, risk of self-stigmatization, and feelings of isolation and shame.[27] Reflecting these risks, one family member remarked that the stigma had "translated into an internalized feeling that something is wrong with me."[28]

FAMILY CIRCUMSTANCES AND FAMILY BURDEN

For caring and involved families, burden is an inescapable part of the experience of serious mental illness. But what of families who no longer have contact with their relatives? Some of these families may be protected from the objective burden; others may suffer in their relative's absence, as when a primary wage earner has mental illness. And what of their subjective burden? Some families have no (or diminished) contact with their relative through circumstances beyond their control, such as homelessness or incarceration. Surely, there is no decrease in personal suffering among these family members.[29]

Other families may choose to terminate their contacts with their relative, usually because of severe conflict and repeated crises. In the absence of relevant research, there is no way to determine the emotional cost of mental illness for such families. Nevertheless, in my contacts with some of these families, I have sensed a profound ambivalence, marked both by a belief that the termination was necessary to protect other family members and by intense feelings of loss.

In addition to the universal dimensions of family burden already discussed, each diagnosis presents its own challenges. Much of the literature has focused on the family experience of schizophrenia. As David Moltz has discussed, however, bipolar disorder has specific characteristics that define its impact on affected individuals and their families.[30] First, bipolar disorder is *episodic,* with a frequent return to the previous level of functioning between episodes. People with bipolar disorder tend to work, to marry, and to have children in spite of their illness. As a result, the patient is often a spouse and parent in the family rather than an adult son or daughter, as is more often the case in schizophrenia.

Second, bipolar disorder is *affective,* which likewise has important consequences for families. As Moltz discusses, affect is "contagious"— interacting with someone who is depressed is an extremely depressing experience. In one study, during a depressive episode, 40% of family members were found to be sufficiently depressed to merit professional attention themselves; this distress was absent between episodes. Likewise, during a manic episode, although the euphoria and elation may be infectious at first, family members are also subject to the irritability and anger that characterize mania.

Third, bipolar disorder is *ambiguous* because affective symptoms can easily be confused with normal moods. As a result, families may be uncertain about the difference between moods and symptoms, perhaps developing inappropriate attitudes about responsibility and self-control. Although patients can often exert some control over early or mild episodes, manic episodes are in fact characterized by impairment of judgment and depressive episodes by paralysis of will. This ambiguity may also cause families to pathologize ordinary manifestations of mood or to experience considerable anxiety regarding potentially positive aspects of mania, such as creativity, which may be the first sign of an affective episode. Additional confusion may result from the dramatic shifts in personality that accompany manic and depressive episodes, leaving family members wondering what is "real" and what is a manifestation of the illness.

As Moltz discusses, the episodic, affective, and ambiguous characteristics of bipolar disorder have long-term consequences for families. In particular, these features converge in the family's fear of relapse, which may become a focus—even a preoccupation—of patient and family alike. Long-term consequences of this preoccupation may include hypervigilance, which is marked by a pervasive pattern of alarm; constraints on the range of acceptable behavior in the family, such as mistrust of emotional intensity; and a taboo on discussion, which limits opportunities to resolve painful feelings, correct misunderstandings, and learn how to manage future episodes. Ultimately, these long-term consequences may inhibit the growth and development of family members.

Prognosis, Recovery, and Families

Results of long-term outcome studies and personal accounts of recovery offer a hopeful outlook on serious mental illness that was often absent in the past. This new sense of hopefulness should not deter us as individual practitioners or as a society from confronting the devastation wrought by these disorders. As noted earlier, long-term outcome studies reported by Torrey project the 30-year course for schizophrenia as follows: 25% are completely recovered; 35% are much improved and relatively independent; 15% are improved but requiring an extensive support network; 10% are hospitalized and unimproved; and 15% are dead, most often from suicide. Let us examine these figures from the perspective of people with mental illness and their families.

Approximately 60% of people with schizophrenia are expected to eventually recover completely or to improve significantly. These are long-term outcomes, however, that fail to reflect the enormous hardships often encountered along the way. For example, Frederick Frese and Kay Jamison have led enormously productive lives in spite of their mental illness. Frese was first hospitalized over 25 years ago with a diagnosis of schizophrenia and has gone on to a distinguished career as a psychologist and mental health advocate. Also a psychologist, Jamison is a professor at Johns Hopkins University and an expert on manic depression, the disorder she has lived with for more than 3 decades.

Certainly, the recovery and accomplishments of these psychologists can serve as an inspiration for others who share their diagnoses. Still, during the early years of the illness, each experienced numerous breakdowns and hospitalizations. In a powerful personal account, Frese has written of his certainty that his "enemies" would kill him during his initial hospitalization; of his terror that "I was descending into a total insanity from which I might never return"; of the "considerable anguish" he experienced from the side effects of his medications; of humiliating psychiatric interviews in front of an audience of "spectators"; and of long periods in bed because "life while I was awake was too painful for me to face."[31]

Similarly, Jamison has written a personal account of her experience with bipolar disorder, the "quicksilver" illness defined by its mercurial moods and its "peculiar kind of pain, elation, loneliness, and terror."[32] She shares her early resistance to relinquishing the exhilarating highs of the illness—"the intensity, glory, and absolute assuredness of my mind's flight"—for a life that seemed restrictive, less productive, and "maddeningly less intoxicating." Yet these manic highs left her "irritable, angry, frightened, uncontrollable, and enmeshed totally in the blackest caves of the mind"; moreover, "the depressions that inevitably followed nearly cost me my life." As the accounts of these psychologists demonstrate, their remarkable recoveries required an extraordinary level of courage and perseverance.

Another 15% of patients are improved but require an extensive support network, which often includes their families. About 40% of people with serious mental illness live at home at any given time; the percentage may be even higher among ethnic minority families.[33] These families fulfill many roles as primary caregivers, informal case managers, crisis intervention specialists, mediators with the welfare and legal systems, and advocates for their relative. Family members, especially mothers, pay a high price for these roles, which are likely to magnify their subjective and objective burden and to interfere with their personal plans. Their family life is often chaotic; and their problems defy easy solution. Professionals who fail to understand this reality may dismiss these families as dysfunctional and offer little concrete assistance.

A psychologist who often works with families shared some of her experiences:

One case involves aging parents who reside with a middle-aged daughter who does not groom or bathe herself. The daughter does not want to leave home; the ailing father does not want to force her to move out; and the mother is stressed out. Their daughter's psychiatrist refuses to talk with them. Another case involves parents of an adult son with mental illness who occasionally abuses cocaine, which triggers psychotic symptoms along with poor judgment. In his drug-induced wanderings, *he has been beaten and mugged. His parents paid $6000 to get their son into a dual diagnosis program, which terminated him for having a beer. My colleague told me she hears the pain and concern of these and other parents and sees their ongoing support of their adult children; and this knowledgeable and experienced clinician often wonders how she can help.*

Around 10% of people with mental illness remain hospitalized and unimproved. In an era that celebrates recovery, the lives of these individuals often seem bleak and meaningless. Most families remain in contact with their relatives, sharing this sense of desolation. Encountering the institutions that remain a last resort for those with the most unremitting conditions, family members may suffer the dismay of this woman:

Thinking about visiting my sister in the state institution still brings back feelings of horror. It was distressingly like the hospital in One Flew Over the Cuckoo's Nest. *My sister had been taken there the night before, hauled off by the police. The place was huge, shabby, crowded, frightening—not a place to get well in.*[34]

Three decades after their initial diagnosis of serious mental illness, 15% of these individuals are no longer alive. Their premature deaths leave families shadowed by intense feelings of loss and society deprived of their contributions and gifts. As I was completing this book, the front page headlines of my local paper screamed: "Journey into Madness: Dead Man's Family Blames System for Failing Mentally Ill Son."[35] Chased into the woods by a team of state troopers who put seven bullets into his body, this former premed student had spent the final weeks of his life living outdoors, taunted by voices that commanded him to harm others. Just 5 days before his death, his parents had tried unsuccessfully to get treatment for their son. Told that their son did not pose a threat to himself or to others, his desperate father asked the hearing officer if they had to wait until someone was harmed. Within a week, he had his answer.

Family Risks

This often relentless subjective and objective burden poses many risks for families, including denial or disbelief, family limitations, maladaptive coping strategies, and family disintegration.

DENIAL OR DISBELIEF

Family therapists sometimes use the phrase *the elephant in the living room* to refer to significant problems that cannot be discussed openly. Family members may walk around the "elephant" and ignore its presence, which may prevent painful feelings and conflicts from surfacing. But this denial or disbelief also keeps traumatized family members from dealing with an overarching problem in their lives.

Families may treat the mental illness as forbidden—or even nonexistent—territory for many reasons. They may be poorly informed about the illness, thinking the symptoms are due to a difficult stage or life problem. At the onset of the illness, they may be confused about the diagnosis (often with good reason), the most appropriate treatment, and the expected outcome. In response to this confusion—and their own anguish—family members may refuse to acknowledge the mental illness or may minimize its seriousness. With knowledge and time, most families do come to terms with mental illness, although individual members may vary in their coping strategies, pacing, and ultimate degree of acceptance.

Sometimes family members internalize the stigma that pervades the larger society and retreat behind a facade of normalcy, fearful that the "family secret" of mental illness will be revealed. This suppression keeps families from coping effectively. Reflecting on his family history, an adult offspring concluded that acceptance of his mother's illness might have allowed his family to survive as a unit; instead, "the denial hamstrung us, caused us to fly apart."[36] Another lamented that her mother devoted much of her life to trying to make her father appear "normal" to the outside world.

FAMILY LIMITATIONS

In spite of their diversity, all families fulfill some basic functions, including:

- Ensuring survival of their members
- Providing for safety and security
- Meeting economic and physical needs, including food, clothing, and shelter
- Supplying daily caregiving
- Facilitating socialization, including basic knowledge, skills, values, and behaviors
- Fostering self-definition, including personal and family identity
- Fulfilling emotional needs, including love, affection, companionship, and support
- Satisfying recreational and leisure needs

- Addressing educational and vocational needs
- Coping with crisis
- Advocating for members
- Promoting individual and family development

Given the disruptive force of mental illness, some shortcomings in family functioning are to be expected.[37]

Although most families are able to fulfill their essential survival functions in spite of the mental illness, there are some exceptions, including families who are living in poverty, whose main wage earner develops the illness, who are living with the threat of violence, or who face multiple problems. The remaining family functions are likely to be negatively affected by mental illness, which can act as a sinkhole that consumes family energy and undermines its caregiving, socialization, and definitional functions. Particularly in the beginning, family members—individually and collectively—may have few reserves to meet the emotional needs of others or to engage in recreational and leisure activities. When these functions cannot be fulfilled, the family's quality of life may be eroded.

The ability of families to perform their educational and vocational function may also deteriorate. Parents may be less available to teach social and academic skills to young family members. Teenagers may get little support in formulating appropriate career goals or in translating these goals into reality. Likewise, because of the stigma that encircles mental illness, families may find themselves cut off from important sources of support outside the family. As the mental illness continues to siphon their energy, families may have difficulty coping with other crises, advocating for individual members, and encouraging their development.

Especially during emergencies, all families experience some difficulty fulfilling their basic functions. Some families never really recover. In portraying the impact of her mother's mental illness on her own life, an adult offspring wrote that her mother's illness had a profound effect, shattering her own safety, security, and trust: "I was very scared and very confused."[38] Still, families vary in their response to mental illness and in their overall competence, and many regain their balance. Describing her family, one woman wrote, "As terrible as it has been, I have gained a great sense of love and admiration for my family. We support one another through discussion, problem solving, and humor."[39] Likewise, a sibling remarked that her brother's mental illness had only been a part of her family life, adding, "My parents were there for me, too, and I felt loved and valued."[40]

MALADAPTIVE COPING STRATEGIES

During the course of their lives, families cope with many expected and unexpected events. There is considerable variability in coping effectiveness among families and even within families across situations and through time. Nevertheless, as discussed later, there are certain hallmarks of functional family coping, including the absence of physical violence and substance abuse. One adult sibling reflected on her adolescence, which was marked by the serious mental illness of both her sister and her father. The family's illness-related problems were compounded by the behavior of her well parent: "Mother was exhausted and had started drinking. I grew up suddenly, helping to run the household."[41]

DISINTEGRATION

Serious mental illness can assault individuals and families with a vengeance, leaving behind a wake of damaged lives and ruptured relationships. This onslaught may result in partial or complete disintegration of the family, which can occur in several ways. The relative with mental illness may be lost to institutional care, to suicide, or to homelessness. Likewise, well family members may abandon the family in their effort to ensure their own preservation; or children may be placed in foster care when their needs can no longer be met by their beleaguered family.

Young family members who have experienced the mental illness of one parent and the withdrawal of the other are likely to experience the intense feelings of abandonment. One adult offspring recounted her family history, describing her mother's initial hospitalization when she herself was 7 or 8. Her father later abandoned the family, leaving five young children alone to cope with their mother's mental illness. Feeling frightened and helpless, the children "would just run and hide."[42]

Family Resilience

This chapter began with a discussion of family burden, which is the most salient aspect of the family experience of serious mental illness. As with any catastrophic stressor, however, the illness offers families an opportunity to change in constructive ways, which is an important consideration for practitioners. In recent research, for instance, we found evidence for family resilience.[43] When asked about any strengths that had developed as a result of the mental illness in their family, our survey participants told us about their family bonds and commitments, their expanded knowledge and skills, their advocacy activities, and their role in their relative's recovery.

In addition, participants affirmed their potential for personal resilience, noting that they had become better, stronger, and more compassionate people. Here are the words of one mother:

I have become much more tolerant of imperfection in myself and others. . . . I have learned to appreciate the strengths of other people who appear to be different or are handicapped in some way. Our daughter's younger siblings accept her and make special efforts to help her feel a part of the family. I can face adversity with courage. My husband and I are closer and more honest with each other as a result of our shared grief and stress. . . . We are proud that our family has remained intact and strong.[44]

These family members also commented on the resilience of their relative with mental illness. Describing her adult son, one mother wrote, "It is gratifying to witness our son's courage as he deals with his illness."[45]

Practitioners need to weigh these research findings in balance with the compelling evidence for family burden. In fact, in responding to open-ended questions specifically designed to elicit positive responses, almost two-fifths of participants offered negative comments, such as the following: "I was and am devastated by her illness and discouraged by the system."[46] Even when responding more positively, their answers were often infused with a sense of loss: "I thought that my son's tragedy would completely ruin our lives because it broke our hearts. But we've learned—finally, painfully—not to let this tragedy totally dominate our lives."[47] Although these family members could acknowledge their resilience, they were well aware of the terrible price paid. As one family member declared, "Any increased sensitivity to others or any other side effects would be traded in an eyeblink for a healthy relative."[48]

Nevertheless, resilience is also part of the family experience. In our study of family resilience, three-fourths of our participants reported they had undergone a process of adaptation as they acquired the competencies needed for successful coping. Commenting on the strengths of his family, one adult offspring reminds us, "Just because there is mental illness in a family doesn't mean the family has to stop growing as a unit or that the person cannot lead a constructive life."[49]

Multiple Perspectives

The impact of mental illness on family members depends partly on its timing in their life span and on their roles and responsibilities within the family. As a result, individual members of the family have unique experiences, needs, and concerns in their role as parent, spouse, sibling, or offspring, as Mona Wasow has discussed in her insightful book, *The Skipping Stone: Ripple Effects of Mental Illness on the Family*.[50] In turn, each of their experiences affects other members of the family. In some cases, extended family members play a central role, including grandparents, aunts, uncles, cousins, and even close friends who function as informal members of the extended family.

These members, too, may be profoundly affected by the mental illness in their extended family, sharing in the subjective and objective burden shouldered by the rest of the family. They may also offer life-enhancing love and support. One woman told us that her mother's aunt and uncle— "in essence our grandparents"—were an enormous help to her beleaguered family. "For my entire childhood," she wrote, "they lived right down the street from us and were a shelter when needed."[51]

Relatives are the most important source of informal caregiving for people with serious mental illness. Allan Horwitz and his associates have described the hierarchy of obligations that determines which kin provide caregiving for dependent adults.[52] Spouses, parents, and adult offspring are viewed as having central caregiving responsibilities. Siblings have fewer mandated caregiving responsibilities, although sibling relationships may become increasingly important in later life. There are many reasons for providing caregiving to close relatives who have disabilities such as mental illness, including a sense of duty to close kin, bonds of affection among family members, a value of reciprocity, and personal and family satisfactions and rewards.

Family caregiving responsibilities and burden are also related to gender and marital status. Not surprisingly, researchers have found that caregiving for relatives with mental illness is largely a female responsibility, one that intensifies the family burden.[53] In one study, mothers manifested significantly higher levels of anxiety, depression, fear, and emotional drain than fathers.[54] A similar pattern might be expected among young female spouses, siblings, and offspring who assume caregiving roles, which are accorded little value in modern societies and which may conflict with their personal agendas.[55] The problems of female caregivers are magnified when they shoulder the burden alone. For example, one study found that single parents were more likely to be a support for the patient, to experience high levels of stress, and to lack appropriate information and resources.[56]

In many respects, families are like mobiles that can be set in motion by movement in one part, which in turn can affect the entire construction. Changes in individual family members affect the system in much the same way. Moreover, the family mobile changes through time, reflecting the metamorphosis of individuals, the fluctuations in family roles and relationships, and gusts that blow from inside and outside the family. But always these individuals are joined to others in the family mobile—by a complex web of shared history, sorrows, and triumphs.

Over a lifetime, individual family members will dance to their own tempo and cadence: alternately giving and receiving support, seeking and avoiding closeness, pursuing personal and family goals, and perhaps assuming or avoiding caregiving responsibilities. Mental illness is likely to bring a special intensity to these normal cycles of family cohesion and disengagement, heightening the inevitable conflicts in family relationships. But with time—and often with much hardship—families have the potential to recreate their family mobile in a way that nurtures individuals as well as the larger unit.

From the vantage point of midlife, the following family member recounts one family's development:

I started to understand how difficult it must have been for my family and how they did the best they could. I was able to forgive them and forgive myself for all the anger I had for them. My mother and I can now discuss what has happened and empathize with each other.[57]

These multiple and changing perspectives have important implications for practitioners. Not only do they need an understanding of the impact of mental illness on the family system and on individual members; they also need familiarity with the developmental context. In later chapters, both of these perspectives are addressed.

Family Diversity

Numerous variables influence the impact of mental illness on individuals and families, including their particular strengths and limitations, their roles and responsibilities, and other prior or current problems. Increasingly, practitioners are also focusing on the role of culture and ethnicity in mental illness. Some excellent resources are now available for therapists who wish to learn more about cultural diversity and its implications for practice. For instance, *Ethnicity and Family Therapy,* edited by Monica McGoldrick and her associates, encompasses 42 different ethnic groups and offers a rich picture of cultural diversity and its role in professional practice.[58]

In the past, professionals were often encouraged to maintain a stance of "cultural blindness," based on an assumption that effective professional practice required only an absence of bias. In contrast, the current philosophy urges therapists to acknowledge and respect different cultures and to provide culturally sensitive services for patients and families. In fact, *DSM-IV* now includes an outline for cultural formulation, which directs practitioners to write a narrative summary for the following: cultural identity of the individual, cultural explanations of the individual's illness, cultural factors related to psychosocial environment and levels of functioning, cultural elements of the relationship between the individual and the clinician, and overall cultural assessment for diagnosis and care.

Ethnic minorities, including African Americans, Hispanics, Asian Americans, and Native Americans, already comprise an important segment (26.4% in 1995) of the population in the United States. The term ethnic minorities will be a misnomer in the future, however, because these groups are expected to constitute a majority soon after 2050.[59] Unfortunately, many minority families find mainstream mental health services alien to their cultural values and traditions. As a result, they may choose not to seek services, may terminate services prematurely, or may find treatment unhelpful.[60]

My contacts with families have repeatedly highlighted the importance of cultural variables. A young African American sibling told me her family felt a sense of alienation when dealing with the mental health system, noting they had not met a single African American physician or therapist. From a more personal perspective, one man remarked that the Japanese "restraint on expression of strong feelings and shame about mental illness" had prevented his family from communicating openly.[61]

ETHNICITY AND MENTAL ILLNESS

Researchers have frequently documented the importance of cultural and ethnic variables in serious mental illness. For example, Deborah Plummer reports that African American patients are overrepresented in public psychiatric institutions and more likely than caucasian patients to be committed involuntarily; that low socioeconomic status and minority status jointly influence the quality and degree of services African Americans receive; and that individuals who are poor and African American often receive temporary services over which their community has no control (and that are eliminated when funds are no longer available).[62]

Laurene Finley has also reviewed research concerned with ethnicity and serious mental illness, reporting that in comparison with nonwhites, whites tend to remain in treatment longer, to obtain more service hours, and to receive residential and social rehabilitation services.[63] She observes that although people with serious mental illness are characterized by socioeconomic, ethnic, and cultural heterogeneity, this diversity is poorly reflected in the literature. Moreover, there are significant gaps in research, theory, knowledge, and innovative methods for dealing with diverse patients and families.

In addition, researchers have documented the central roles of culture, ethnicity, and social status in shaping the family experience of caregiving. As Lefley has pointed out, ethnicity interacts with and may be confounded with socioeconomic status; thus, these differences may reflect the realities of poverty and social deprivation rather than cultural practice.[64] Nevertheless, ethnic group differences have important implications for professional practice. Compared with European Americans, for example, Hispanics and African Americans maintain closer family ties, are more likely to expect unmarried family members to remain at home, and more often provide home caregiving for their relative. There is also evidence that the three groups vary in social characteristics, in their perception of caregiving burden and social support, in their experience with the mental health system, and in their conception of the illness.[65]

Finley has examined several cultural variables related to family issues in serious mental illness, such as family structure. Discussing the African American community, she observes that there is a rich fabric of kinship relationships that may include many nonblood relatives, such as close friends, neighbors, and partners. The church family is also a source of considerable strength for these families. This informal support network may partly account for the finding that African American families report less burden than whites.[66]

Other ethnic minority groups also have unique family structures, such as the close ties of Puerto Rican families with relatives in Puerto Rico and the central role of the extended family in all aspects of Italian American family life. For all of these groups, this extended network serves as a great resource and protector against difficulties. Often, separation from the family is not desired, expected, or easily accepted. In contrast, among professionals who espouse the traditional Western values of separation, individuation, and self-determination, these close family ties may be viewed as enmeshed or interfering families.

The cultural context is also likely to have a significant impact on family appraisal of mental illness and its management, as Finely discusses. For instance, ethnic minority families may perceive symptoms of mental illness as spiritual problems, emphasizing the role of religion and the supernatural. Similarly, these groups may seek out culturally compatible healers either in place of or in addition to Western methods and approaches. Such folk healers speak the same language, live in the community, are sanctioned by community members, and may use cultural remedies both familiar and compatible with the extended family's religious and spiritual beliefs. Ethnic and cultural variables may also influence the patient's symptom content, expression, and intensity; the verbal and nonverbal behavior of patients and families; and their perception of appropriate goals and strategies.

Finley describes several barriers to the participation of ethnic minority families in mainstream support groups.[67] For example, ethnic minority families may distrust mainstream institutions or prefer to meet their support needs inside their family system. In addition, these families may find the organizational structure and leadership styles incompatible with their preferred cultural style, the content of these groups unresponsive to their needs, the approach insensitive to issues of diversity, and the social activities inconsistent with their own preferences. Other potential problems include the lack of aggressive and innovative outreach to ethnic families, the discomfort experienced in a group that includes few ethnic family members, and the presence of competing demands, such as child care, transportation, or multiple jobs.

Acknowledging these barriers, practitioners have developed programs designed specifically for ethnic minority families.[68] All families can benefit from improved services for their relative, from education about mental illness and symptom management strategies, and from support groups.[69] Nevertheless, there is a need for multiple models of family psychoeducation that are sensitive to social and cultural diversity.[70] Methods that may be helpful with ethnic minority families include family network approaches, home-based intervention, long-term linkages with churches and local community groups, and sustained outreach and personal contacts with family members.[71]

SUGGESTIONS FOR PRACTITIONERS

Practitioners can use a number of strategies to enhance their effectiveness in working with ethnic minority families.[72] These include:

- Maintaining an ecological systems perspective that incorporates the levels of the individual, the family, the local community, the culture, and the global community
- Developing respect and appreciation for cultural diversity
- Acknowledging the strengths and resources of ethnic minority families, as well as their expertise regarding their own lives, needs, and goals
- Recognizing the heterogeneity within ethnic minority groups and viewing their characteristics as differences rather than deficiencies

- Identifying the cultural variables that can influence the patient and family experience of mental illness, including socialization practices, a history of oppression, racism and discrimination, poverty, religious practices, and values and attitudes

- Understanding personal cultural influences and examining personal cultural biases, prejudices, and stereotypes

- Learning about the cultures of patients and families and working with their family structure and informal support network

- Becoming comfortable speaking with patients and families about cultural and ethnic minority issues

Family Needs

In spite of their diversity, families that include a member with serious mental illness share a number of essential needs, including their need for a truly comprehensive and humane system of care that can support their relative in leading a meaningful and productive life in the community. Indeed, if such a system were available, it would transform the lives of these families. Families also have separate needs of their own.[73]

First, families need *information* about serious mental illness and its treatment, available services and resources, and caregiving and management issues. As one family member asserted, "Knowledge has kept me from the depths of hopelessness."[74]

Second, families need *skills* to cope with the illness and its consequences for their family. Pertinent skills include communication, problem-solving, conflict management, assertiveness, symptom management, and stress management skills.

Third, families need *support* for themselves. In the words of one family member, "The isolation was profound."[75] Sources of support include their informal support network, which includes the nuclear family, the extended family, friends and acquaintances, neighbors, and coworkers; their formal support network, which includes professionals and service providers, social and religious institutions, and the government; and advocacy groups, such as NAMI.

In light of the diversity among families, a given family may have other needs related to family dynamics, functions, or relationships. Thus, an individualized family service plan should always be developed in consultation with the family. Nevertheless, there is much common ground among families that are coping with mental illness.

From Theory to Practice

A cornerstone of professional practice with these families is an understanding of their experiences, needs, and concerns. Like Robert Guardez, practitioners can invite families to tell their stories, to share their observations, and to offer suggestions. Publications written by family members are also a valuable resource. Their powerful personal accounts convey the texture of the family experience of mental illness in a way that no research findings can equal. In addition, both professionals and families can serve in consultative roles, with benefits for family advocacy groups and for provider organizations.

Translating their new insights into effective practice, practitioners can assist families in:

- Understanding and normalizing the family experience of mental illness

- Focusing on the strengths and competencies of their family and their relative

- Learning about mental illness, the mental health system, and community resources

- Developing skills in stress management, communication, and problem solving

- Strengthening their informal and formal support network

- Resolving their feelings of grief and loss

- Coping with the symptoms of mental illness and its repercussions for their family

- Identifying and responding to the signs of impending relapse

- Creating a supportive family environment

- Developing realistic expectations for all members of the family

- Playing a meaningful role in their relative's treatment, rehabilitation, and recovery

- Maintaining a balance that meets the needs of all members of the family

In later chapters, a range of intervention strategies are examined that can facilitate the accomplishment of these objectives and address the concerns of particular families.

Let's return to family therapist Robert Guardez, who is scheduled to meet with the mother of a newly admitted patient, 17-year-old Karen Bernstein, whose first psychotic episode resulted in her hospitalization. Robert is scheduled to meet with Karen's mother, Susan, who is an attorney and single parent. In setting up the appointment, Susan explained that she wondered if there were any hope for her daughter, a high school senior who had been an excellent student and championship tennis player until recently. Anticipating their meeting, Robert wondered what the mental illness might mean for the lives of such a promising young woman and for her accomplished mother—and for their expectations, hopes, and dreams:

> PRACTITIONER: *It must be terribly difficult for you to be here under these circumstances.*
> MOTHER: *Karen and I have been through some trying times together, especially after my divorce from her father. But I never imagined I would be faced with something like this. Karen was such a good child, such a gifted teenager. I can't even begin to contemplate her future—or mine. After hearing her diagnosis was schizophrenia, I went to the library. Everything I read seemed to indicate that this is an incurable and progressive disorder.*
> PRACTITIONER: *Schizophrenia does pose special challenges for individuals and for their families. But this is Karen's first episode, and we really can't predict her future. In long-term studies, we find that some individuals never have a recurrence, others are much improved, and still others have continuing problems.*
> MOTHER: *But what about treatment? Does anything work? The books I read seemed to offer little hope.*
> PRACTITIONER: *You probably found earlier books, which did indeed portray schizophrenia as a chronic and progressive disorder for which there were few effective treatments. Unfortunately, some professionals still hold those views and convey their pessimism to patients and their families. But there are genuine grounds for hope now, with many effective treatments and reasonable hope for recovery. For example, new medications are now available that are generally more effective than those available earlier. Let me give you some articles that contain current information about serious mental illness and its treatment. Next time we meet, I can answer your questions and offer further suggestions for reading if you like.*
> MOTHER: *I feel overwhelmed right now. Karen and I were in the midst of planning for college. She was offered a full scholarship. Does she have to give up her plans?*

PRACTITIONER: *Your sense of being overwhelmed is understandable. Karen has just been a patient for a few days, so we need to get a better sense of her problems and needs. But many people with serious mental illness do attend college. Sometimes they need to modify their program, taking courses part time for a while. And it may take a while to determine which treatment is most effective. We have several months before college starts. Karen will continue as an outpatient after she is released, so we have time to work with both of you. In the meantime, I also want to address your needs. We offer an educational program for families; here is some information. There is also a local chapter of NAMI; here is their number. They offer a support group as well as excellent educational programs. It is usually helpful to speak with family members who have shared your experiences and can offer practical suggestions.*

MOTHER: *I appreciate your help and will give the family organization a call. But is there any assistance for Karen if she is able to begin classes in the fall?*

PRACTITIONER: *Yes, there are some resources available. Most universities have services for students with psychiatric disabilities. In fact, with the passage of the Americans with Disabilities Act in 1990, universities are required to provide "reasonable accommodations" to meet the needs of these students. As it turns out, the university she plans to attend has a program of supported education for students with psychiatric disabilities. The program includes individualized counseling, assistance with scheduling and other academic matters, and opportunities to meet with other students who have similar disabilities. But we all need time to gain a better understanding of Karen's needs and to make future plans. I will do all I can to assist you. Let's set up another appointment. Here is my card. Please don't hesitate to call if you have questions.*

CHAPTER 4

Life Span Perspectives

During his years as a psychologist in private practice, Steve Branson has occasionally worked with families that included a member with mental illness. Often providing services on an as-needed basis, he has noticed that the needs of these families change over the course of their lives. Steve recently received a call from Joan and Ed Paterson, a couple he has seen periodically since their son Mark was diagnosed with schizophrenia more than 30 years ago. At the onset, their son's illness threatened to destroy the entire family. Joan was overcome with grief, Ed could not accept the illness, Mark refused to remain in treatment, and their daughter Pam wanted to leave home as soon as possible to escape the turmoil. After many difficult years, the family has come to terms with the illness, working together to support Mark, who is doing well in treatment, living in a supervised apartment near their home, and working part time at a consumer-run drop-in center. When scheduling the appointment, Joan said that as aging parents in declining health, she and Ed want to ensure that Mark's needs will be met when they are no longer around. Joan asked if Pam, who now has a family of her own, could join them to talk about the future, because she wants to play a more active role in her brother's life. Mark is also willing to attend the session. In anticipation of his first appointment with the entire family, Steve contemplates the changing needs of families like the Patersons and wonders if there is a general pattern to their lives.

As practitioners, we are well aware of the developmental context of individual lives and of the family system. This context is profoundly affected by a catastrophic stressor such as serious mental illness, which can leave a residue of unfinished business in its wake. From the perspective of individual family members, their personal legacy reflects the specific developmental tasks that were interrupted as a result of the mental illness. For example, the illness might undermine the acquisition of basic trust during infancy; the development of peer relationships and academic skills during childhood; and the establishment of a secure sense of identity during adolescence. A child who is confronted from birth with the mental illness of a primary caregiver may be vulnerable to all of these risks. Likewise, a young adult sibling may have difficulty with separation and intimacy, and middle-aged parents may have little energy for their midlife issues.

This developmental context is an important consideration for practitioners, who need an understanding of the individual life cycle, the family life cycle, and the mental illness life cycle, as well as interactions among these cycles. This chapter examines all of these topics.

A Developmental Framework

John Rolland has provided a model for examining the impact of chronic physical illness on the development of family members and of the family as a unit.[1] His model is also useful in understanding the impact of serious mental illness on family members. He poses the essential developmental question as follows: "It is vital to ask what life plans the family or individual members had to cancel, postpone, or alter as a result of the diagnosis. It is useful to know whose plans are most and least affected."

Rolland's model incorporates three developmental strands: the individual life cycle, the family life cycle, and the illness life cycle. His model is a dynamic one that examines the impact of chronic illness through time. This ongoing process is affected by changes in individual family members, in the family system, and in the illness itself. This chapter considers each of these life cycles from the perspective of his model, discusses its application to families that include a member with mental illness, and examines the implications for professional practice.

The Individual Life Cycle

There is a vast body of literature concerned with the nature of individual development and with the universal processes and sequences underlying the individual life cycle. Human development is often discussed in terms of the tasks or issues confronting individuals at particular phases, which provide an useful framework for anticipating and understanding the impact of life events on personal lives. The tasks that are associated with successive phases of development throughout the life span include the following:

Infancy

    Survival

    Attachment

    Basic trust

Preschool period

    Socialization

    Cognitive development

    Social development

    Emotional development

    Behavioral development

    Identification

    Gender identity

    Self-concept

Middle childhood

    Academic adjustment

    Peer relations

Adolescence

    Identity

    Sexuality

    Career plans

    Autonomy and separation

Young adulthood

    Intimacy

    Marriage/Partnership

    Parenthood

    Vocational commitment

Middle adulthood

    Renegotiating earlier commitments

    Launching of children

Late adulthood

    Retirement

    Financial security

    Loss of intimate relationships

    Personal illness and mortality

    Life review

    Grandparenthood

Initially, each of the developmental phases will be examined, as well as its associated tasks. Before proceeding, however, it is important to note the limitations of phase-based conceptions of development. For example, although there is a degree of patterning and predictability in individual development, there is also an inherent circularity and uncertainty. Individuals deal with issues of trust, autonomy, identity, intimacy, generativity, and mortality throughout their lives. The successive tasks of development are not so much problems to be solved as issues that merit periodic reconsideration. In response to changing circumstances, we reformulate our identity, renegotiate our intimate relationships, and reallocate our energy. In addition, universal models of development do not apply to all individuals or families, particularly during an era of significant change in family structure and function.

    Indeed, the "expected" phases of adulthood are often shuffled in response to increases in female employment; in divorce, remarriage, and cohabitation; in pregnancies outside of marriage and in later life; and in life expectancy. The developmental phases and tasks of childhood and adolescence remain more predictable. Even so, in contrast to earlier generations, more recent cohorts often experience a prolonged adolescence that may postpone, circumvent, or reverse the tasks of young, middle, and late adulthood.

In *New Passages*, author Gail Sheehy captures these generational patterns, distinguishing among the World War II Generation (born between 1914 and 1929); the Silent Generation (1930–45); the Vietnam Generation (1946–55); the Me Generation (1956–65); and the Endangered Generation (1966–80), the first to grow up with the increase in divorce, AIDS, violence, and downward mobility. Differentiating between first adulthood (lasting until approximately age 45) and second adulthood (45 to 65), Sheehy describes a "middlescence" that is comparable to adolescence and that precedes the passage into midlife and establishes the foundation for successful aging.[2]

In spite of these limitations, developmental models that focus on successive phases and tasks provide a valuable framework for examining growth and change in the individual life cycle and for understanding the impact of mental illness on family members.

INFANCY

During the first 2 years, infants enter a world in which they are poorly equipped to navigate on their own. It will be many years before these young human beings have the resources to survive without assistance. Because of their prolonged dependency, they are precariously reliant on the adequacy of their human and physical environment. The central tasks of infancy include:

- Biological and psychological survival in an inconsistent and sometimes inhospitable world
- Attachment, as infants bond with their earliest caregivers and build a foundation for future relationships
- The establishment of basic trust, which requires a relatively secure and nurturing environment

THE PRESCHOOL PERIOD

During the preschool period, young children acquire many of the competencies that will allow them to function effectively in the world outside their family. The tasks of this period fall into the following areas:

- Socialization, as children acquire the knowledge, skills, and dispositions that will enable them to participate in their society
- Cognitive development, including accomplishments in the areas of language, memory, attention, and perception
- Social development, including the capacity for reciprocal and satisfying relationships with others
- Emotional development, including the ability to experience a full range of feelings and to express them appropriately
- Behavioral development, including the acquisition of age-appropriate habits and patterns
- Identification, including the internalization of a culturally appropriate value system
- Gender identity, including a sense of being male or female and of the meaning of gender in one's culture
- Self-concept, including a belief that one is a valuable and competent person

Middle Childhood

Shifting from the family to the larger social context in middle childhood, children learn new academic and interpersonal skills. Their developmental tasks center on:

- Academic adjustment, as children acquire the basic building blocks that allow them to succeed in our society
- Peer relations, as they establish a social network outside their family

Adolescence

Adolescents who are preparing for an independent and productive adulthood confront a new set of issues. Some of the most important include:

- Forging a sense of personal identity that can serve as an internal compass in a world in flux
- Coming to terms with emerging sexuality in a world of changing sex roles, values, standards, and behaviors
- Charting a tentative career path that can guide educational and vocational plans and goals

- Achieving separation and preparing to leave a secure home base for an uncertain future

YOUNG ADULTHOOD

During young adulthood, we typically complete our separation from our family of origin. Following resolution of the personal, interpersonal, and vocational issues of adolescence, we are ready to make more sustained commitments to other people and to our career. Important tasks of this early phase of adulthood involve:

- Intimacy, as we form close relationships with others
- Marriage or partnership, as we formalize our long-term commitment to another person
- Parenthood, as we contribute to the continuity of our family and of our species
- Vocational commitment, as we establish and build our career

MIDDLE ADULTHOOD

Middle adulthood is often a transitional period, characterized both by increased stress and by an opportunity for constructive change and renewal. During midlife, individuals often reconsider and modify their earlier commitments in light of changing circumstances. The central tasks of middle adulthood usually include:

- Re-evaluation of earlier personal, interpersonal, and vocational commitments
- Launching of children, with a return to a narrower family structure

LATE ADULTHOOD

Late adulthood brings a new set of challenges and opportunities for most individuals. During this period, we generally adapt to more restricted vocational, financial, and social circumstances; confront the imminence of our own mortality; and strive to attain a sense of meaning and coherence in our lives. This phase of development also brings the opportunity for a period of successful aging marked by growth, vitality, and creativity. Important tasks during late adulthood may involve:

- Grandparenthood, which offers continuity with past and future generations

- Retirement, as we relinquish the structure, challenges, and satisfactions of our career
- Financial security during a period of potentially depleted resources
- Loss of intimate relationships, as our companions face illness and death
- Personal illness and mortality, as we deal with similar issues ourselves
- Life review, as we search for a sense of order and meaning in our lives

The Family Life Cycle

Because individual development takes place largely within the family, however defined, the family life cycle is also an important developmental strand. This life cycle can also be viewed in terms of successive phases and tasks. Betty Carter and Monica McGoldrick have described six phases in the family life cycle:

- Launching of the single young adult from the family of origin
- Joining of families through marriage
- Becoming parents and adjusting to young children
- Transformation of the family system in adolescence
- Launching children and moving on
- Changes in later life

As they discuss, disruptions of the family life cycle can occur in response to a number of stressful events.[3] Some of these include family patterns, myths, secrets, expectations, and attitudes that are transmitted from generation to generation. Other stressful events include predictable developmental (normative) events, such as the changes associated with parenthood, and unpredictable (nonnormative) events, such as untimely death or chronic illness.

For both individuals and families, it is assumed that transition points, such as adolescence and midlife, are associated with increased stress, which may interact with other stressful life events, such as mental illness. Transition points have an inherent quality of upheaval and disruption that may be heightened by—and exacerbate—the disarray that accompanies mental illness. Thus, we might expect adolescent or middle-aged family members to be particularly vulnerable to the adverse consequences of a relative's mental illness. At the same time, transitional periods offer an opportunity to reevaluate and modify existing patterns in the face of changing circumstances.

On the other hand, if mental illness coincides with a period of consolidation, there may be conflict between the family's need to protect the existing life structure and the demands of the illness for flexibility and adaptation. Over time, families may encounter both of these poles, with an escalating level of stress. As one mother remarked, her family seemed to be living on a fault in the midst of an earthquake.

The Mental Illness Life Cycle

In Rolland's model, the life cycles of individuals and families form two developmental strands that determine the life plans and tasks that may be affected by the serious mental illness of a member. The mental illness also has a life cycle, reflecting changes in the illness through time. Rolland specifies four dimensions of illness, each of which is assumed to have an impact on the family: onset, course, outcome, and incapacitation.

ONSET

The first dimension, onset of illness, represents a continuum that ranges from acute to chronic. Illnesses with a sudden onset confront the family with pressing demands for adaptation, whereas gradual onset allows for an extended period of family adjustment. For most forms of serious mental illness, the onset may be either sudden or gradual, as may subsequent episodes. Sudden onset is likely to cause intense distress for family members as they attempt to cope with an unanticipated and disruptive event, whereas gradual onset may pose problems for families who fail to recognize the emergence of the illness. Whatever their particular circumstances, at least periodically families are likely to face crisis conditions, urgent demands for adjustment, and increases in family stress and disruption.

COURSE

The second dimension, course of illness, may be progressive, constant, or relapsing/episodic. A progressive illness is continually symptomatic and advances in severity. Periods of relief may be minimal, and there are inherent risks of exhaustion for primary caregivers. In a constant-course illness, the initial event results in some deficit or functional limitation that remains relatively stable and that again poses the risk of exhaustion.

In a relapsing or episodic illness, periods of remission alternate with periods of flare-up or exacerbation, a pattern that may freeze families in a state of vigilance.

Although the course of serious mental illness is variable, schizophrenia is often characterized by alternating periods of relapse and remission, as well as persistent functional limitations. Bipolar disorder and major depression tend to be episodic, with a return to prior level of functioning between episodes, thus requiring families to shift roles and authority. These frequent transitions and accommodations are even more stressful when episodes alternate between mania and depression or when there is rapid cycling between episodes.

Responding to the unpredictable course of mental illness, family members may struggle—sometimes simultaneously—with recurrent crises, with frequent transitions and accommodations, and with uncertainty and exhaustion. Although families can often return to periods of relatively normal functioning, the specter of a recurrence may leave them feeling compelled to maintain a crisis structure. They are also likely to experience considerable distress in response to the discrepancy between the normality that characterizes periods of remission and the disintegration that accompanies decompensation.

The variable and uncertain course of serious mental illness has a major impact on families. One woman who has lived with her mother's schizophrenia for over 30 years talked about her early years: "She was a perfectly loving mother, but you never knew what to expect when you walked in the door after school. You never knew what was going to meet you, if it was the loving mother or the crazy person."[4] Another woman recalled her mother's recurrent episodes of major depression and the "pain of welcoming her back only to lose her again to the illness."[5]

OUTCOME

With respect to Rolland's third dimension, outcome, serious mental illness is again characterized by significant variability, with the potential for full recovery, partial recovery, or no recovery. Particularly at the time of the initial diagnosis, it is impossible to predict the outcome for a given patient. As a result, all members of the family may remain in a kind of prognostic limbo, hoping for recovery but fearing recurrence. The following family member conveys the difficulties of dealing with an uncertain prognosis and charts one family's positive outcome:

My brother's involuntary commitment and subsequent hospitalization were very stressful for my family. Don't give up hope. Given his original prognosis, his recovery has been just short of miraculous. Although this could change, the future looks very bright. He still receives medication, lives quietly on his own, and holds a full-time job again.[6]

INCAPACITATION

The final dimension is incapacitation, which includes both actual impairment and social stigma. The net effect of incapacitation is a function of the nature and extent of impairment, the prior role of the relative with mental illness, and the family's structure, flexibility, and resources. In the case of serious mental illness, the nature and degree of impairment are variable across diagnostic categories, within specific diagnoses, and for a given individual through time.

Schizophrenia is associated with a range of negative and positive symptoms and of functional limitations. For instance, family members may need to cope with such negative symptoms as apathy, lack of motivation, and poor grooming and hygiene; and with such positive symptoms as hallucinations, delusions, disorganized speech, and bizarre behavior. Functional limitations may occur in many domains, including cognitive, emotional, behavioral, interpersonal, and occupational capacities.

Functional impairment is generally less with bipolar disorder and major depression, and most people with mood disorders recover, remain well for long periods of time, and lead reasonably normal lives. Nevertheless, episodes of mania and depression can be extremely incapacitating, requiring families to cope with severely depressed mood, unusually elevated mood, or extreme mood swings.

The patient's role in the family is likely to vary across diagnostic categories. People with mood disorders tend to work, to marry, and to have children in spite of their illness. Thus, the patient is often a spouse and parent in the family. As a consequence, a severe manic or depressive illness may leave the family without the contributions of a primary wage earner or full-time parent. In the case of schizophrenia, the patient is more likely to be an adult son or daughter, which has implications for parental caregivers.[7]

In addition to the risk of actual impairment that accompanies serious mental illness, there is incapacitation resulting from stigma, which is often experienced as a greater burden than the mental illness itself.

The Evolving Family

The life cycles of the individual, the family, and the mental illness provide an important framework both for understanding the impact of mental illness on families and for designing appropriate services. When the mental illness erupts in a family, it may undermine the accomplishment of their developmental tasks in the present, and alter their hopes, plans, and expectations for the future. Family adaptation to mental illness is a prolonged and complex process that is characterized by diversity and fluidity within and among family members, and by dramatic forward strides and equally dramatic reversals.[8] Thus, the mental illness can have a profoundly disruptive impact on individual and family development. Asked what she missed most as a result of the mental illness in her family, one primary caregiver answered, "My life."

Placing the family experience of mental illness in this developmental context, the implications of the three life cycles are considered from the perspective of professional practice.

IMPACT ON CHILDHOOD AND ADOLESCENCE

It is generally assumed that young siblings and children are more vulnerable than older family members to the disruptive force of mental illness. Infants and young children have not yet developed the resources and strategies for dealing with traumatic events. Moreover, young family members are precariously dependent upon the external environment for meeting their needs during a period of prolonged dependency.

As a result, a young child is likely to be deeply affected by the mental illness of a caregiver whose own energy is consumed by the mental illness, whose reality contact may be impaired, and whose false beliefs and distorted perceptions may be presented as real. A young sibling may be similarly affected, both directly by the mental illness of a brother or sister and indirectly by the depletion of parental resources. In both of these cases, achievement of the developmental tasks of early childhood may be undermined, including the attainment of basic trust and of self-esteem. Illustrating this risk, one man developed a blueprint for avoiding pain in the future: "I swore I would never trust anyone for the rest of my life. . . . I learned to develop a complete wall mentally to protect myself."[9]

During middle childhood, as children shift from the family to the larger social world, the school environment and peer relationships become increasingly important. Young family members may experience difficulty in school as a result of their preoccupation with problems at home and may feel alienated from the "normal" world of their peers. One family member recalled sitting in class and being unable to concentrate, "all of my energy directed toward what was happening at home and what was going to become of our family."[10]

Adolescents are also likely to be profoundly influenced by the mental illness in their family. They may worry about developing mental illness themselves as they deal with identity issues, may find that their losses and vulnerability affect their emerging sexuality, may be influenced by their family circumstances as they formulate educational and career plans, and may have difficulty separating from a family that has come to depend on them. A woman who grew up with a brother who had schizophrenia talked about her adolescent struggle: "I was trying to find my place in the world, and my brother disrupted this world."[11]

Impact on Adulthood

All of the developmental tasks of adulthood may be affected. Young adults are likely to confront the hazards of intimacy as they deal with the mental illness of someone they love, to reconsider marriage in light of their troubled family history, to weigh the genetic risks of mental illness as they consider having children, and to find their career choices influenced by their earlier encounter with mental illness. One man wrote about the legacy of growing up with a brother and sister who both suffered from schizophrenia:

As an adult, I've found intimacy and sexual relationships extremely difficult. I find it difficult to talk to people about my family and feel like a perpetual outsider. I'm still ashamed and self-critical. I tend to deal with emotionally-threatening situations by withdrawing. I'm afraid of having children.[12]

During middle adulthood, the developmental agenda may continue to be disrupted by the mental illness. For instance, parents whose energy is depleted by caregiving responsibilities may need to defer—or cancel—their midlife tasks, including their opportunity to close the gap between former hopes and current achievements. As I have written elsewhere:

The main task of family life, which is the launching of children into the adult world, may never be completed. Adult-to-adult relationships with grown children may never be realized. . . . Parents may long for an "empty nest" that never arrives, and for the freedom and independence that are expected to characterize middle and late adulthood.[13]

Discussing the restrictions imposed by her daughter's mental illness, one mother complained, "You're just not free. You are never, never free. The biggest problem is the prison that it puts us in."[14]

During late adulthood, family members may serve as caregivers, case managers, or guardians for their relatives. In the absence of adequate community resources, this caregiving burden poses particular problems for aging parents. Caregiving burden may actually intensify with parental age, as increasing numbers of adults with mental illness, some in their 40s and 50s, reside with their aging parents, themselves at risk for the geriatric illnesses and other hardships of old age.[15] Many variables influence the experiences of elderly parents, including the contributions and level of functioning of their adult son or daughter. Nonetheless, these parents may be left with substantial responsibilities during a period of diminishing personal resources.

With these added responsibilities, aging parents may have little energy for their own life review or for the uncluttered joys of retirement and grandchildren. Alternatively, they may find themselves pressed into a parental role for the children of their adult son or daughter—an unanticipated and perhaps joyful role but hardly an uncluttered one! In addition, late adulthood is a period of loss and impending loss of intimate relationships; these losses may be heightened by those that accompany the mental illness of a beloved relative. Although a central task of late adulthood involves personal mortality, this issue is barely on the agenda for many aging parents, who confront a far more pressing matter: How can they ensure continuity of caregiving for their adult child? Anticipating her son's bleak future after her death, one elderly mother exclaimed, "I hope to God I live for another 20 to 25 years."[16]

INTERSECTIONS AMONG CYCLES

Whatever their personal choices and family configurations, the life course of family members is imprinted by the mental illness. Moreover, as Rolland discusses, other developmental themes intersect with the life cycles of the individual, the family, and the mental illness, including the distinctions between centripetal and centrifugal phases and between normative and nonnormative illnesses. Centripetal and centrifugal phases are viewed as alternating periods of family cohesion and disengagement. During centripetal periods, such as early child rearing, families move toward their center, tightening external boundaries and emphasizing the primacy of family relationships. Throughout centrifugal periods, such as adolescence, families move away from their center, with emphasis on the identity and autonomy of individual family members.

Like other chronic illnesses, serious mental illness exerts a centripetal pull on the family system, which can potentiate an existing cohesive mode, with adverse consequences for all members of the family. For example, a serious emotional disturbance in a child or adolescent may maintain a centripetal family mode over a long period of time, ultimately freezing the family into a permanent state of fusion and fixation on the illness.

Such a freeze may undermine the autonomy of individual family members, foreclose opportunities outside the family, and undermine other family relationships, including the marital relationship. Well siblings are also affected by this narrow familial focus. As one sibling lamented, "I lost out on my childhood. Most of my memories include a sickly older sister who got all of the attention by having repeated crises."[17]

Another important developmental motif is normative and nonnormative illnesses, which are defined in terms of their timing in the life cycle. Chronic illness in late adulthood is an expected and therefore normative event for families, however difficult the circumstances. In contrast, serious mental illness, typically diagnosed in late adolescence or early adulthood, is a nonnormative event that is out-of-phase with normal developmental expectations. Young adults are expected to separate from their families and to move on in their lives, an expectation that is at often in conflict with the limitations imposed by the illness. As an out-of-phase and nonnormative event, serious mental illness may disrupt the family's sense of continuity and rhythm in the life cycle.[18]

From Theory to Practice

In working with families, practitioners encounter an enormously complex and evolving family life space. When serious mental illness intrudes, the life space becomes infinitely more complex. Some issues that merit attention include:

- The current life cycle phase and tasks of the family, as well as its history and unfinished business
- The current life cycle phases and tasks of each individual family member, as well as their histories and unfinished business
- The current life cycle phase of the mental illness, as well as its history and meaning for the patient
- Family patterns, myths, secrets, expectations, and attitudes that are transmitted from generation to generation
- Other prior or concurrent stressors confronting the family
- The role of individual and family transition points, such as adolescence and midlife

Let's return to the Paterson family and chart their life span issues, beginning with the onset of Mark's mental illness and following the family for the subsequent 3 decades. Table 4.1 summarizes information about the

TABLE 4.1
LIFE SPAN ISSUES IN SERIOUS MENTAL ILLNESS

Family Member	Status: Residential Marital Employment	Family Interactions	Central Issues	Services
Onset and First Year				
Joan				
Mother	Home	Tense	Grief	Educational program
Age 45	Married		Family turmoil	Support group
	Part time			
Ed				
Father	Home	Distant	Denial	Educational program
Age 47	Married			
	Full time			
Mark				
Patient	Home	Angry	Symptoms	Inpatient services
Age 18	Single		Multiple losses	Outpatient services
	Part time			Partial hospitalization
Pam				
Sister	Home	Ambivalent	Grief	None
Age 16	Single		Guilt	
	Part time		Shame	
First Decade				
Joan, 45–55	Home	Conflicted	Family problems	Marital therapy
	Separated briefly		Mark's illness	
	Full time			
Ed, 47–57	Home	Estranged	Family problems	Marital therapy
	Separated briefly		Mark's illness	
	Full time			
Mark, 18–28	Homeless	Angry	Survival	Irregular
	Single			
	None			
Pam, 16–26	Apartment	Ambivalent	Separation	Individual therapy
	Engaged		Intimacy	
	Full time			
Second Decade				
Joan, 55–65	Home	Improved	Midlife concerns	Family consultation
	Married		Mark's illness	
	Full time			
Ed, 57–67	Home	Improved	Midlife concerns	Family consultation
	Married		Mark's illness	
	Full time			

(continued)

TABLE 4.1 Continued

Family Member	Status: Residential Marital Employment	Family Interactions	Central Issues	Services
Mark, 28–38	Group home Single Part time	Distant	Recovery	Outpatient services Rehabilitation program Consumer group
Pam, 26–36	Own home Married Part time	Ambivalent	Marriage Motherhood	None
Third Decade				
Joan, 65–75	Home Married Retired	Comfortable	Late-life concerns Mark's future	Family consultation
Ed, 67–77	Home Married Retired	Comfortable	Late-life concerns Mark's future	Family consultation
Mark, 38–48	Apartment Female partner Full time	Comfortable	Recovery	Outpatient services Consumer group
Pam, 36–46	Own home Married Full Time	Comfortable	Multiple roles	Support group

residential, marital, and employment status of these family members; the quality of their family interactions; their central issues; and the services they received.

ONSET AND FIRST YEAR

At the onset of his mental illness, 18-year-old Mark is single, living at home, and trying to work part time at a hardware store. Beset with hallucinations and delusions, he is confused and angry. Hospitalized during a psychotic episode, he denies he has a mental illness and resists the recommended treatment plan. Despite pressure from his family, Mark attends sessions only intermittently and spends most of his time in his room.

Joan, Mark's 45-year-old mother, works part time as a substitute teacher. Mark's illness has left her consumed with feelings of grief and responsibility, overwhelmed with the family turmoil, and beset with symptoms of anxiety. Her husband, Ed, is a 47-year-old civil engineer. He is unable to discuss Mark's illness without getting angry, has difficulty accepting his son's diagnosis, and spends increasingly less time at home. Both parents attended an educational program during Mark's hospitalization; Joan also participates in an ongoing support group.

Pam is 16 at the time of her brother's hospitalization. She is a junior in high school and works part time after school. Like her mother, Pam is subject to intense feelings of grief and guilt, wondering if her frequent arguments with Mark have somehow contributed to his problems. At the same time, she is ashamed of his bizarre behavior and refuses to bring friends home. She also worries about the reactions of her friends and dates and about the genetic risks for her future children. No services are offered to Pam, nor does she request assistance; everyone else's problems seem so much more important.

FIRST DECADE

Throughout the first decade after his diagnosis, Mark struggles to come to terms with his diagnosis, his symptoms, his treatment, and his life. He is often gone for days or weeks at a time, sometimes living in a local park, where he has been beaten and abused. Belligerent when home, Mark resists both medication and outpatient services. Feeling helpless and hopeless most of the time, he thinks about suicide during his darkest periods, unable to imagine a better future.

Other members of the family have been devastated by Mark's illness and by the family's inability to deal with it. Now working full time as a high school teacher, Joan oscillates between feelings of grief on one hand and anger on the other, because so much of the burden has fallen on her shoulders. She argues frequently with Ed and Pam, and with Mark when he is home. Ed feels estranged from Joan, angry with Mark, and worried about Pam, who seems so forlorn. Following a brief separation triggered by their continuing distress, Joan initiates a course of marital therapy, which Ed attends only reluctantly. Both parents feel their marriage has come to be defined solely by Mark's illness and by their family problems.

Pam graduates from high school and leaves for college, hoping she can shut the door on her family problems. Yet she continues to feel responsible for her troubled family and often returns home on weekends. An excellent student, she graduates from college with an accounting degree and moves into an apartment when she begins a new job. In spite of her accomplishments, Pam feels guilty for having been spared mental illness herself, embarrassed by her family circumstances, and responsible for her family. Engaged during the year following graduation, Pam has some problems in her relationship with her fiance and wonders how her difficulties relate to her family history. Wanting to resolve her issues before getting married, Pam begins individual therapy. She spends much of her first session talking about her family and crying uncontrollably, feeling as if a dam has broken.

SECOND DECADE

Mark has largely accepted his illness and the need for continuing treatment. Although resenting the side effects of his medication, he wants to avoid another relapse and hospitalization. Mark has benefitted from outpatient treatment and rehabilitation, and now works part time at a local consumer-run drop-in center. He is also learning about recovery and developing the skills and strategies needed to manage his illness. After many difficult years at home, he prefers to spend his spare time at the center.

Having resolved their marital problems, Joan and Ed are able to discuss Mark's illness, to manage family concerns together, and to experience the satisfactions of their careers and their marriage. They continue to worry about Mark's illness and to schedule family consultation sessions with Steve Branson on an as-needed basis. Both describe their family relationships as improved, and they derive great pleasure from their grandchildren.

Now married and the mother of two young children, Pam's primary consideration is her responsibilities as wife, mother, and part-time accountant. Yet she remains concerned about her parents, about Mark, and about the future. Pam feels she should do more for her parents and brother, but can't seem to find additional time in her already overburdened life.

THIRD DECADE

Mark continues to do well in treatment. It has been many years since his last hospitalization, and he enjoys his work at the drop-in center. He organizes programs for the center, facilitates a support group for other consumers, and enjoys playing guitar in his rock group. He lives in a supervised apartment and spends much of his free time with a female companion he met at the center. Mark's primary source of income is government benefits, although his work at the drop-in center offers some compensation. Reasonably happy with his life, he sometimes thinks about having a regular full-time job and a family of his own. At age 48, he doubts he will fulfill those dreams; still, he hasn't relinquished them entirely.

Joan and Ed are approaching retirement with mixed feelings. They welcome the leisure time and opportunity to travel but will miss the contacts with coworkers and the satisfactions of their careers. Anticipating the future, they worry about their finances and their health. They despair about Mark's future, which he is unwilling to discuss. They have set up an appointment with Steve Branson to review and finalize their long-term plans.

To their surprise, Mark is willing to accompany them, as is Pam, who told her parents she wants to be involved in the planning process.

Pam strives to juggle the responsibilities of wife, mother, and now full-time employee. She and her two daughters see their grandparents regularly. The girls are sometimes uneasy about their Uncle Mark, however, and Pam wonders what to tell them about mental illness. She has joined a support group for adult siblings and offspring, which she finds very helpful. During her first meeting, she was amazed that her experiences and concerns were shared by so many other family members. Educating herself about mental illness and community resources, Pam is preparing to play a larger role in her brother's life. In light of her parents' increasing age and health problems, she is concerned about her future caregiving responsibilities. Anticipating the family session with Steve Branson, Pam plans to ask him about the needs of her children. Pam continues to worry about balancing her commitments to her husband and children, to her parents and brother, and to herself. Her support group members assure her that this is normal!

CHAPTER 5

The Family Adaptation Process

Elizabeth Lewis works as a psychiatric nurse in a state-operated hospital that is planning to expand services for families of patients. The hospital administrator has asked her to serve as a family advocate who can meet with family members and assist them in coping with their relative's mental illness. Elizabeth is scheduled to meet with the family of Patrick Horner, a newly admitted patient who was involuntarily committed following an episode in which he got drunk and flailed a large knife while threatening the neighbors who called the police. That incident was the culmination of months of escalating problems for Patrick, who had been increasingly confused, paranoid, and belligerent, and for his parents, Barbara and Charles, who had been desperately trying to obtain professional assistance. Patrick's mental illness and the traumatic commitment process have left the family shaken and angry with Patrick as well as the mental health system. Only reluctantly did Mrs. Horner agree to schedule an appointment, indicating that she and her husband wanted no further contact with Patrick and adding tearfully that they were on the brink of "losing it" themselves. Anticipating their meeting, Elizabeth feels compassion for the Horners, wondering how any family could cope with circumstances such as these.

With time, most families do learn to cope with serious mental illness. They learn about the illness and the service delivery system, acquire the skills needed for effective coping, and develop new sources of social support. There is much that practitioners can do to facilitate this process of family adaptation, the topic of the present chapter.

Many catastrophic events can traumatize families. Some of these are natural disasters, such as floods, earthquakes, and tornadoes. Others are unnatural disasters, such as poverty, discrimination, and war. Other more personal disasters include domestic violence, sexual abuse, and loss of a family member through death or divorce. Although serious mental illness shares many characteristics with these and other catastrophic stressors, mental illness is unique in some important respects. Unlike other time-limited disasters, the illness one is woven into the lives of individuals and families on a continuing basis; unlike environmental disasters, mental illness is profoundly personal; and unlike other personal disasters with accountable perpetrators, mental illness involves someone else who is also victimized and traumatized. Furthermore, unlike most other traumatic events, there is little social validation and support, and mental illness brings with it a corrosive stigmatization that often isolates and alienates family members.

To understand the impact of mental illness on families, professionals need to be aware both of the general characteristics of catastrophic stressors and of the unique attributes of mental illness. Serious mental illness meets the criteria for catastrophic stressors specified by Charles Figley.[1] Mental illness is generally an unanticipated event, with little time to prepare, slight previous experience, few sources of guidance, and a high emotional impact. Moreover, family members may spend a lifetime dealing with intermittent crises, family disruption, and feelings of loss and helplessness. Many family members worry about the risk of harm to their relative or to others. As noted, for instance, the death rate from suicide and other causes of death is significantly higher than the rate of the general population.

There is now a voluminous literature concerned with family adaptation to stressful events and with the variables that can affect that process. Building on that literature, this chapter examines the stressor of serious mental illness and assists practitioners in facilitating family adaptation.

Family Adaptation

Family adaptation provides a useful framework for understanding the family experience of mental illness and for designing effective interventions. As has long been recognized, an adaptation framework offers many advantages for professional practice.[2] Such an approach is:

- Balanced, because it emphasizes both healthy and pathological aspects of family functioning
- Validating, because it recognizes the courage and tenacity that families exhibit in coping with the mental illness of their relative
- Hopeful, because it acknowledges the potential for effective coping as well as for family resilience

- Humanizing, because it fosters an atmosphere of empathy and support rather than blame
- Healing, since professional services can be based on real needs rather than on theoretical assumptions about families

Family adaptation involves acceptance of the mental illness and its meaning for the family, accommodation to the altered family circumstances, acquisition of pertinent knowledge and skills, and resolution of the emotional burden. One of the earliest models for conceptualizing family adaptation to stressful events is the ABCX model, now expanded to the Double ABCX model to reflect adaptation through time.[3] Applied to the family experience of mental illness, the model includes four components:[4]

A: *Family life events*, including the serious mental illness and other prior or concurrent stressors that may have depleted family energy

B: *Family resources*, which include the personal, family, and social variables that can facilitate family coping and adaptation

C: *Family appraisal*, which is the collective set of beliefs about the stressor that may or may not make it traumatizing for a particular family

X: *Family adaptation*, as measured by the family's coping effectiveness, sense of well-being and satisfaction, and level of distress

The family life event of serious mental illness and its life span correlates have already been explored. It is important to note that the overall level of family stress reflects other concurrent stressors, such as unemployment or chronic medical problems, as well as prior stressors that may have depleted the family's ability to cope with present circumstances. Focusing now on the other components of the ABCX model, this section examines family appraisal, resources, coping strategies, and recovery. Each of these topics has important implications for professional practice.

Appraisal

A life event becomes stressful for families only after it has been perceived as threatening. Thus, the family's beliefs about mental illness influence its impact on families and on individual members.[5] Families may view the illness as temporary or permanent, their relative's prospects for recovery as hopeless or hopeful, and their own burden as challenging or crushing. Similarly, they may see themselves as helpless victims or active agents, as effective or ineffective problem solvers, and as a strong or weak family system.

Thus, it is not simply the reality of mental illness that determines the family's process of adaptation. It is also their perception of the illness, its meaning for them, and their ability to cope with it. Many variables can influence the family appraisal of mental illness, including their involvement in primary caregiving; their models of causation, symptoms, and outcomes; and their particular circumstances and attributes.[6] Of central importance are the family paradigm, the family's sense of meaning and coherence, and their model of serious mental illness.

David Reiss has investigated the role of the family paradigm in mediating the response of families to stressful events.[7] The family paradigm consists of the underlying assumptions about reality that are shared by family members and that guide their construction of reality. For instance, families may differ in their sense of mastery, in their commitment to family solidarity, and in their openness to current experience and new coping strategies. In the face of severe stress, families may need to reformulate their family paradigm, which may be inconsistent with their altered circumstances. Families who lack the flexibility to modify their paradigm may be at risk for family disintegration.

A cornerstone of the appraisal process is the ability of families to restore a sense of meaning and coherence to their lives. Successful adaptation to threatening events often involves a search for meaning in the experience and an effort to regain mastery and restore self-esteem.[8] Professionals have also underscored the importance of changing one's life scheme to restore a sense of order and purpose in life following a stressful event and re-establishing a view of the world as a comprehensible, manageable, and meaningful place. Researchers have found that a family sense of meaning and coherence is associated with successful adaptation to a stressful family event.[9]

In *Composing a Life,* Mary Catherine Bateson writes of the human search for meaning, remarking that we give meaning to the present through a continual process of reinterpreting the past and reimagining the future.[10] In her view, we are all storytellers. One woman related her own effort to find meaning in her family circumstances: "I wonder sometimes what our family would have been like without the presence of this illness. I am proud that through the heartaches there was a profound sense of love and commitment to each other that could not be dispelled. That is the legacy I'm going to carry on."[11]

The family's model of serious mental illness also imprints their appraisal of mental illness.[12] An interpersonal theory of etiology, such as one that assumes family pathogenesis or dysfunction, may significantly increase the feelings of guilt experienced by family members. Alternatively, a narrow biological model may reduce their guilt and offer hope of more effective treatment, as new medications and other intervention strategies become available. However, neither of these models incorporates the broad biopsychosocial perspective discussed earlier; nor does either suggest a constructive role for families. In contrast, the vulnerability-stress model incorporates current biological and psychosocial research findings, as well as their implications for families.

Appraisal also affects many other dimensions of the family experience, including their attitudes and caregiving patterns.[13] One family member described his model of mental illness, as well as its implications:

Remember that mental illness is mainly caused by brain dysfunction. Don't feel responsible for it. Protect yourself from becoming an enabler, overly devoted caretaker, or escape artist. Treat the ill person as an ill person. Care for him or her while maintaining a balanced life for yourself.[14]

Family Resources

Family resources include the personal, family, and social variables that can offer assistance under conditions of severe stress. A wide range of variables can serve as protectors or exacerbators during the adaptation process.

PERSONAL VARIABLES

There is general agreement that coping effectiveness is enhanced by such personal qualities as wellness (overall physical and mental health), self-esteem (positive feelings about oneself), and self-efficacy (expectations of personal mastery). Similarly, adaptation can be affected by personal beliefs, such as those concerned with religion or locus of control, and commitments, such as those to other family members.[15]

For individual family members, other important variables include:

- Their age, birth order, and chronological proximity to their relative, which may affect their vulnerability and family responsibilities
- Their gender, which may influence their caregiving responsibilities and tendency to identify with a same-sex relative
- Their role, since mental illness has different consequences for parents, spouses, siblings, and offspring
- Their own personality, physical health, and mental health
- Their living arrangements, which are likely to determine their degree of involvement in their relative's life
- The meaning of mental illness for their own life

- The defense mechanisms they employ to cope with this traumatic event

Many of these variables have already been discussed; each can have a major impact. For instance, one woman talked about her change of residence, noting "It is much more difficult for me to be available to 'rescue' my sister when she calls."[16] Likewise, the personal meaning of the mental illness is of central importance, as family members struggle to make sense of this unanticipated family event and to place it in perspective. One family member shares her personal view:

The illness isn't you, and you are not responsible for it in your relative. You can be loving and helpful without taking the illness on as your responsibility. Sometimes the best thing you can do is to pull back a bit. Try to separate your relative from the illness and remember the really wonderful things about your relative as a person.[17]

For clinicians who work with family members in psychotherapy, their defense mechanisms may require considerable therapeutic attention. When confronted with a catastrophic stressor, individuals universally employ defenses to shield themselves from its full impact. George Vaillant has described defense mechanisms as "psychological white corpuscles, scavenging and mastering potential sources of pain and incapacity."[18] All defense mechanisms alter perception to some extent. As a result, although such mechanisms serve an important protective function, they are not adaptive in terms of coping with reality, since they do not increase knowledge or enhance problem solving.

Defense mechanisms vary in their degree of pathology and adaptiveness. At the pathological end of the continuum are denial and distortion of external reality. Such defenses are invariably maladaptive for those who use them, since they preclude effective coping. In contrast, mature defenses, such as sublimation (diversion of energy into more constructive avenues), allow us to cope in flexible and gratifying ways. With respect to mental illness, continuing denial of the mental illness is an example of a pathological defense mechanism. In contrast, involvement in advocacy activities represents a more adaptive response.

FAMILY VARIABLES

Family variables that affect their experience of mental illness include:

- Life cycle issues, such as the developmental tasks confronting individuals and families

- Other stressful events confronting the family, such as poverty, substance abuse, or domestic violence
- Family characteristics, including their composition, social class, ethnic group, and religious affiliation
- Overall level of family effectiveness
- The nature and quality of relationships among family members
- The meaning of mental illness for the family

Again, many of these variables have already been discussed; others may assume particular importance for a given family. For instance, the utilitarian resources of the family, such as parental level of education and yearly income, can make a substantial difference in their ability to locate and access appropriate services. Members of NAMI have relatively high levels of education and income, which has undoubtedly enhanced its effectiveness as an advocacy organization.[19] Many family members outside of the organization do not share these educational and financial advantages or the sense of empowerment resulting from membership in such a group.

Given the devastating impact of serious mental illness on the family system, the nature and quality of the marital relationship is an important variable, as the following mother attests:

My husband and I never learned to make joint decisions. So we divided up the decisions like his and her towels. He decided everything about money, and I about the children. But when our daughter became ill, we were in a bind, because I couldn't handle it alone.[20]

Coping effectiveness is also likely to be influenced by separation or divorce, the level of marital satisfaction, the degree to which caregiving and other responsibilities are shared, and the extent of consensus regarding the mental illness and its treatment. For children who have a parent with mental illness, the well parent can make a substantial difference in alleviating or intensifying the family stress and disruption. Here is one woman's account:

My manic mother, with my father's complicity, would go on enormous spending sprees—buy literally housefuls of furniture in one day, buy lavish gifts. Not surprisingly, they were always in debt; our furniture would get repossessed. They would pawn presents they gave us—a feast/famine pattern. I liked all the presents, but felt betrayed when they were taken back. Adults were not to be trusted.[21]

The family's adaptation process is affected by their overall level of functioning, including the characteristics of effective families and potential for family resilience already noted. For example, the concepts of family coherence and family hardiness predict the ability of families to manage normative family stressors and to recover from nonnormative family crises.[22] Defined as a fundamental coping strategy employed in the management of family problems, family coherence is operationalized as the family's emphasis on acceptance, loyalty, pride, faith, trust, respect, caring, and shared values in the management of tension and strain. Family hardiness is defined as the family's internal strengths and durability; it is characterized by an internal sense of control of life events and hardships, a sense of meaningfulness in life, involvement in activities, and a commitment to learn and explore new and challenging experiences.

In contrast, families that are dealing with multiple problems may demonstrate relatively low levels of family coherence and family hardiness, a pattern that can potentiate family burden and undermine coping effectiveness. Aside from the mental illness, such problems might include separation or divorce, chronic medical problems or disabilities, substance abuse, child maltreatment or domestic violence, unemployment or job-related problems, or poverty. One family member wrote of suffering "the dual taboos of mental illness and divorce" when her parents divorced as a result of her father's illness. Another recalled the relentless fear for her own safety that propelled her from her home:

I left home at 13. I would just run away. When my schizophrenic brother would strike out, I was afraid for my safety. I tried numerous times to get into foster care or group homes. I finally got out by getting pregnant and married. They couldn't send me back then. After I left, my brother sexually abused my younger sister.[23]

Social Variables

From an ecological perspective, many social variables affect family adaptation. In turn, these variables interact with the personal and family factors already mentioned. Important social variables include:

- Services available for the patient, such as mental health, physical health, social, rehabilitative, vocational, and residential services
- Professional services available for the family, such an educational or psychoeducational program, a support group, or psychotherapy
- Other family resources, such as a local family advocacy group or religious organization
- Sociocultural characteristics, such as social values, policies, attitudes, and barriers

Families are especially dependent on the availability and quality of the local service delivery system. Families benefit indirectly from improved services for their relative and directly from services for themselves. There is a good deal of variability in services across states, which may add considerably to the burden of family members whose relatives do not remain in a single location.[24] And stigma continues to brand people who have mental illness with a mark of shame, with adverse consequences for all concerned. One family member wrote about the stigma that pervades contemporary books, songs, and movies: "I like to read mysteries, but when I pick up a book at the store, read the jacket, and see that the book involves a 'psychotic' killer, I quickly lose interest."[25]

More positively, families can benefit from the buffering effects of social support.[26] Assistance may be available from the informal support network, which includes the nuclear family, the extended family, friends and acquaintances, neighbors, coworkers, and advocacy groups, such as NAMI. In addition, the formal support network is an important resource for families, who can receive assistance from professionals and other service providers, the local service delivery system, and state and federal programs, such as welfare and Social Security.

Coping Strategies

Although all families experience some burden, there are wide differences in their coping effectiveness. Figley has identified 11 characteristics of functional family coping: clear acceptance of the stressor, a family-centered locus of problem, solution-oriented problem solving, high tolerance, clear and direct expressions of commitment and affection, open and effective communication, high family cohesion, flexible family roles, efficient resource utilization, absence of violence, and infrequent substance use.[27] All of these apply in the case of serious mental illness.

Many publications and training materials are available for practitioners who work with families. For example, a large body of literature addresses coping among children and adolescents, among adults, among people with mental illness, and among their family members.[28] In addition, many resources are available to assist family members themselves, including the educational programs and support groups that are offered through NAMI.

Other useful resources include coping skills workshops, such as those offered by Marilyn Meisel and Edie Mannion, and educational programs, such as the MESA model of family education developed in Virginia (see

Chapter 15). Several excellent books are available for professionals and for family members (see Notes).[29] These books contain a wealth of useful information, some of which is incorporated into the Family Action Plan discussed in Chapter 6.

Based on the suggestions of family members and professionals, here is a compendium of effective family coping strategies:

Cognitive Strategies

- Accepting the mental illness
- Acquiring relevant information
- Developing appropriate expectations
- Modifying unproductive patterns of thinking and behaving
- Reframing to focus on positive aspects

Behavioral Strategies

- Strengthening communication skills
- Developing stress management skills
- Acquiring illness management skills
- Improving problem-solving skills
- Striving to set limits

Emotional Strategies

- Resolving feelings of grief and loss
- Sharing feelings with others
- Re-allocating emotional energy
- Enhancing spirituality
- Seeking professional counseling

Social Strategies

- Joining a support group
- Expanding activities and relationships
- Participating in social, religious, or cultural organizations
- Working collaboratively with professionals
- Increasing advocacy efforts

Family Recovery

As LeRoy Spaniol and Anthony Zipple have pointed out, families as well as patients can experience recovery. They describe recovery as a process of self-discovery, self-renewal, and transformation that is characterized by changed attitudes, feelings, perceptions, beliefs, and behaviors. Encouraging professionals to understand how families react to the trauma of mental illness in a relative, they specify several general characteristics of recovery, noting that:

- Recovery is a growth process that transforms families and individuals.
- The particular impact of the illness differs for individual family members, each of whom recovers at his or her own rate.
- Each phase of recovery is marked by specific developmental tasks and by certain family responses, such as disbelief, grief, or coping.
- Because recovery is not linear, family members recycle through the phases as they gradually complete tasks that facilitate growth.
- During the recovery process, emotional responses, even intense ones, are natural reactions that do not imply dysfunction or pathology.

Spaniol and Zipple describe a final phase of the recovery process that often involves personal and political advocacy:

Family members say they feel differently about themselves. Even though the illness of their family member continues, they have changed. They blame themselves less. They let go of what they can't change or don't want to change and become more focused on efforts to bring about the changes they see as necessary.[30]

Many professionals have viewed family adaptation in terms of similar phases of adaptation.[31] In fact, when asked directly, a majority of family members say they have moved through a series of phases in coming to terms with the mental illness of their relative.[32] Their process generally conforms to the three-phase structure delineated by Theresa Rando in connection with bereavement:

- Avoidance, which is characterized by feelings of shock, denial, and disbelief
- Confrontation, which is characterized by intense feelings of grief and loss and by a wide range of negative emotions, including anger, helplessness, depression, withdrawal, guilt, and responsibility

- Re-establishment, which is characterized by understanding and acceptance of the mental illness and by reinvestment of energy in one's own life[33]

Each of these phases is examined in connection with mental illness. As already noted, however, from the perspective of professional practice, there is no single pattern or pace of adaptation for family members, nor is there a universal and time-limited series of sequential phases. Some family members experience little or no avoidance, but are instantly confronted with the full force of this traumatic event. Others may seem forever encapsulated in the confrontation phase. Moreover, the process of family adaptation is enormously complex and uneven, with reverses as well as gains.[34] For most family members, phase theories imply an implausible final harmony and an unreachable "emotional promised land."[35]

Nevertheless, the following phases provide a useful framework for understanding family adaptation to serious mental illness.

THE INITIAL ENCOUNTER

When they are first confronted with the mental illness of a close relative, many family members do exhibit the characteristics of the avoidance phase described by Rando, including feelings of shock, denial, disbelief, and confusion. In fact, the initial response of most family members to the onset of mental illness is often a paralyzing sense of shock and disbelief. Few family members have much understanding of mental illness or its meaning for their family. Initially, they may dismiss the behavior as a temporary aberration that will disappear with time.

Especially at the onset of the illness, it is important to remember that denial is a common response among family members that may serve a protective function:

Denial was the longest stage. In some ways denial was helpful. I was able to get on with my life in high school, not realizing that my brother's illness was serious. As an adult, I continued to run away from the situation. It was obviously not a healthy response, but I had my own separate issues.[36]

As time goes on, however, entrenched denial may prevent family members from coming to terms with the illness.

CONFRONTATION

Whatever their initial reactions to the onset of their relative's illness, eventually family members do become aware of the nature and proportions of this unnatural disaster. During the confrontation phase, many family members report the experiences mentioned by Rando, including feelings of "angry sadness"; a range of intense emotions, including anger, guilt, depression, and despair; preoccupation with the loss; and "grief attacks," which are acute surges in grief that may interfere with ongoing activities.

Conveying this anguish, one mother told me she felt as if her heart had been crushed; another declared, "The shock, disbelief, denial, and anger are what hit me first. It is depressing to see a life so drained and confused."[37] Young family members, too, are subject to this heartache, which may continue to shadow their lives:

I spent years hiding from my pain. It is difficult to let hurt flow; I want to continue to push it down. But I know that I can't be released from the pain until I acknowledge it, and let myself feel it. Only then can I grow from it. It will probably be a lifelong process for me.[38]

RESOLUTION

During the resolution phase, family members exhibit many of the features of Rando's re-establishment phase, including gradual decline of the intense feelings experienced earlier. Although they do not forget the loss, they are able to reinvest their emotional energy in new relationships and activities. As families confront the full force of mental illness, they gradually work through their painful emotions and are able to place the mental illness in perspective, as a single event in their lives. Along with their resolution, they may gain a new perspective on their family. Here is one mother's account:

As time went on, we all made adjustments to our daughter's illness. The last crisis was difficult for all of us because she seemed to be doing so well. But there was something else. I saw how well we were able to handle things as a family. We were able to show our love, respect, support, and commitment, and to decide as a unit how to handle things. We have done very well under the most difficult circumstances.[39]

POSTTRAUMATIC STRESS REACTIONS

Especially if they were very young when their relative developed mental illness, family members may experience symptoms of posttraumatic stress disorder. Children and adolescents can suffer posttraumatic stress reactions similar to those seen in adults. Symptoms may include sleep disturbance, loss of newly acquired developmental skills, raised levels of anxiety, and panic attacks triggered by particular environmental events.[40]

Likewise, adult family members may manifest the symptoms of post-traumatic stress disorder specified in *DSM-IV*, including re-experiencing the traumatic event (e.g., recurrent painful, intrusive recollections; recurrent dreams or nightmares); diminished responsiveness to the external world (e.g., psychic numbing or emotional anesthesia); and a variety of autonomic, dysphoric, or cognitive symptoms (e.g., hyperalertness, sleep disturbance, difficulty concentrating, depression, anxiety). One family member who was traumatized by the mental illness of her brother and sister continues to experience some of these symptoms as an adult:

Images are also a problem. They are set off by seemingly little things—walking by a homeless person on the street, watching a cop show on television—and it's like a slide projector switches on in my head. Images—of my brother walking the icy streets as he hunts for food and a place to sleep, of my sister being handcuffed and forced into a police car—flash by, each a twist of the knife in my gut. They come unannounced. They hurt. They're hard to switch off.[41]

As Aphrodite Matsakis discusses in her handbook for trauma survivors, family members may also experience "secondary wounding" if others respond to their distress with ignorance and insensitivity.[42] For instance, people outside the family may discount the magnitude of the trauma, blame them for their family problems, or judge them negatively because of their reactions. One sibling talked about an early encounter with the world outside her family:

I remember standing up in second grade and sharing the mental condition of my brother as my contribution to Show & Tell. I thought it was the most unique thing about my life and certainly better than any hamster! I still can see the awkward panic on my teacher's face as she hastily ushered me to my seat.[43]

Given the potentially traumatic impact of mental illness on family members, practitioners may find the trauma literature helpful, particularly when they offer psychotherapy to individual family members.[44]

RESILIENCE

The concept of family recovery implies something more than adaptation and effective coping. Indeed, as noted earlier, families have the potential for a resilient response to this catastrophic event. Individuals, too, can demonstrate what researchers have termed invulnerability, stress resistance, or resilience. In my research and practice with family members, I have been impressed with their capacity for personal resilience under challenging circumstances. Responding to our survey, one family member asserted, "I can now say that, like that old aluminum foil ad, I am 'oven-tempered for flexible strength.' "[45] Others described beneficial changes in self-concept and self-efficacy, in compassion and tolerance toward others, in contributions to society, in family relationships and social life, and in attitudes and priorities.

The popularity of the term *invulnerable* is unfortunate in some respects, because it seems to preclude suffering. In that sense, there are no invulnerable family members; all are vulnerable to this catastrophic stressor. Whatever their degree of resilience, family members also carry the scars of their encounter with mental illness. Consider, for example, the following account, which evokes thoughts of the invulnerable children who have received so much attention in the professional literature. One wonders how many of those children were like this young family member, whose competent public persona masked an inner world of anguish and turmoil:

I learned from a young age that I should act mature and self-reliant and not cause any waves. I did not want to hurt my parents after observing how much my sister had hurt them. I kept my difficulties to myself and kept up a good front in part because I didn't want my parents to be disappointed. I finally sought counseling at the age of 30.[46]

The concept of resilience—which always involves adversity—has important implications for professional practice. Frederick Flach has noted the potential for constructive reintegration following a state of disintegration ("falling apart"): "Resilience depends on our ability to recognize pain, acknowledge its purpose, tolerate it for a reasonable time until things begin to take shape, and resolve our conflict constructively."[47] Other writers have provided a vocabulary of resilient survivor strengths, such as insight, independence, initiative, creativity, and humor.[48] Still others have emphasized the art of self-renewal: "Our destiny is to journey on the river of change, and this calls for a capacity to adventure well—at all times, in all seasons."[49]

From Theory to Practice

This discussion of family appraisal, resources, and coping strategies provides a blueprint for practitioners who work with families. Each of these variables can be modified by effective intervention strategies, with substantial benefits for families. Namely, family adaptation is likely to be enhanced by constructive changes in family appraisal that result from greater understanding of mental illness; by services that increase resource availability and utilization, such as a support group or an educational or psychoeducational program; and by enhanced coping strategies, such as those learned in a coping skills workshop. In essence, services that alter family appraisal, resources, and coping strategies in affirmative ways are also likely to have a positive impact on family adaptation, recovery, and resilience.

The following family member charts her own recovery process, eloquently portraying her anguish as well as her progress:

My adolescent years were filled with a hollow dread. I felt somehow that I was responsible. I felt incredibly angry, resentful toward my mother, unable to escape, and very guilty. Gradually, I have come to see my mother's mental illness as just one part of my life. I have my own life, dreams, and goals. Her illness has caused me to develop tremendous strength, discipline, and personal stability.[50]

Turning now to the Horner family, how might Elizabeth Lewis translate her understanding of family adaptation into effective practice? Here is her initial meeting with the Horners:

PRACTITIONER: *Hello, I'm Elizabeth Lewis. I realize how upset you are about Patrick and appreciate your willingness to meet with me.*

MOTHER: *Actually, I'm not sure we should have come. The commitment hearing was one of the worst experiences of our lives. Patrick was drunk during the episode with the neighbors and doesn't remember much of what happened. When he heard our testimony, he felt angry and betrayed, yelling that he never wanted to see us again. Maybe that's best for all of us.*

FATHER: *I agree. We've been good parents. I've had enough. I can't imagine why Patrick would act like this.*

PRACTITIONER: *Almost all families share your feelings about the commitment process. It's so destructive for families to have to testify against their relative. I wish we had a better way to get professional help for someone who is experiencing psychotic symptoms, as Patrick was. I can understand your anger and frustration with his behavior. But during an episode like this, people with schizophrenia may have little awareness of their behavior and limited ability to control it. The symptoms are caused by schizophrenia, which is a brain disorder.*

FATHER: *I always thought schizophrenia meant a split personality. You mean it's an actual illness?*

PRACTITIONER: *Yes. It is a real illness like heart disease or diabetes, one that can be treated effectively. In fact, Patrick is beginning to respond to his medication, although we're still trying to find the right combination.*

MOTHER: *Someone told me that schizophrenia results from bad parenting. Is that the case?*

PRACTITIONER: *No, that's an old—and unfortunate—theory that has now been discarded. With our new technology, we have been able to get a much better understanding of mental disorders like schizophrenia. We now know that the illness is a brain disorder. Those older theories did a lot of harm to caring families. Here is some current information about schizophrenia. It should help you understand the illness.*

MOTHER: *I still feel so responsible. I keep wondering what I did wrong or could have done differently. Until the past year, Patrick seemed to be doing so well. I just don't know what happened.*

PRACTITIONER: *You sound like you feel guilty. It seems most mothers feel like you do. It's a terrible trauma to watch someone you love experience mental illness. But it's not your fault—and it's not Patrick's fault. Schizophrenia usually appears in late adolescence or early adulthood, as it did in his case.*

FATHER: *What about Patrick's drinking? Was that the reason this happened?*

PRACTITIONER: *Alcohol abuse doesn't cause schizophrenia, although it may trigger the symptoms in someone who is predisposed to develop the disorder. His drinking is one of the things we need to work on with Patrick, as he learns to manage his illness.*

MOTHER: *Well, I feel a little better knowing it's a real illness with real treatments. But, still, we're overwhelmed and exhausted. We can't deal with this. You can't imagine what we've been through.*

PRACTITIONER: *It has to be devastating for all of you. Actually, members of our family support group have shared many of your experiences. You might find it helpful to participate in the group. As difficult as this has been, there are ways to cope with mental illness. The group offers coping skills workshops you might find useful.*

MOTHER: *Oh, I couldn't talk about our experiences with a group. I'd be too embarrassed.*

PRACTITIONER: *Most family members feel embarrassed, especially in the beginning. Several of the mothers in the group have volunteered to speak to new family members. Would you be interested in talking with another mother?*

MOTHER: *I suppose so.*

PRACTITIONER: *I'll have someone get in touch with you. We also have an educational program for families that offers information about mental illness and about the services available for Patrick and for your family. Family members generally find the program very helpful.*

FATHER: *I don't know. I'm not interested in a support group. I don't like to talk about my feelings. But the educational program might be worth a try.*

PRACTITIONER: *I think you'll find it worthwhile. I realize you're over-whelmed right now. I'd like to schedule another appointment with you to discuss how we can work together to meet your needs. In the mean-time, I'll get both of you signed up for the educational program and also have another mother contact Mrs. Horner.*

MOTHER: *What about Patrick? How is he doing?*

PRACTITIONER: *He's exhausted from his ordeal, as both of you are. But he's starting to benefit from the medication and is also receiving education about schizophrenia. The symptoms of schizophrenia are often confus-ing and frightening. It helps to understand the symptoms are part of the disorder and to learn how to cope with them. But this takes time. When they are first hospitalized, most patients have difficulty accept-ing their mental illness. After all, we live in a society that ostracizes "crazy" people. Although 1 in 100 people suffers from schizophrenia, it's still difficult to accept that you're one of them. Of course, it's just as hard for family members.*

FATHER: *What about the voices? Patrick said he hears voices that tell him to harm himself. I keep telling him that's nonsense.*

PRACTITIONER: *Hearing voices is one of the common symptoms of schizo-phrenia. They're called auditory hallucinations, which seem very real to the person experiencing them. So he may get angry when you tell him the voices are nonsense, although with time he may understand that they are symptoms of the illness. Family members in our group put together some suggestions for coping with the symptoms of schizo-phrenia, including hallucinations. Why don't you look at the material. I can answer your questions next time we meet.*

MOTHER: *Do you think Patrick wants to see us?*

PRACTITIONER: *I told him you were scheduled to come in today. He said he would like to meet with you soon, so I think we can arrange that after our next session. By then, we should be seeing even more improvement.*

CHAPTER 6

Developing Family and Personal Action Plans

Social worker Douglas Bailey has been hired as a consultant by the administrator of the mental health and mental retardation program to train staff at the six county mental health centers to meet the needs of families of patients with serious mental illness. Over the past year, the administrator has received numerous complaints about one of the centers. Just last week, he received a call from Martin Cooper, an angry father who complained that he was given no assistance in coping with a son who has a dual diagnosis. Mr. Cooper said his son stayed up all night, was drunk or stoned most of the time, refused to take his lithium, and threatened to kill family members who asked him to leave. Concerned about his other children, this desperate father called the CMHC for assistance and was told there was nothing they could do. Mr. Cooper screamed at the administrator, "When will I get help—when he kills himself or someone else?" The embattled MH/MR administrator has asked Doug to offer an inservice program designed to train staff at the CMHCs in helping families like the Coopers to cope with crises and other serious problems. In planning the program, Doug wants to be sure he covers the most difficult problems faced by these families.

Until relatively recently, families of people with mental illness had few resources to assist them in coping with their relative's mental illness. That is no longer the case. NAMI has over 1,000 local affiliates in 50 states, so most families have access to its services, including educational programs and support groups. Other services may also be offered in local communities, such as the provider-based educational or psychoeducational programs discussed later. In addition, several excellent books are available (see Notes).[1] Each of these resources offers practical suggestions for families to assist them in coping with problems associated with mental illness.

A Family Action Plan

In our book, *Troubled Journey*,[2] we adapted suggestions from these and other resources to formulate a Family Action Plan (FAP) that targets specific problems. The FAP is expanded here as a resource that practitioners might wish to share with families or to use as a guide for family consultation.

Family education provides the foundation for developing a FAP. As discussed in Chapter 2, families need information regarding biological and psychosocial factors in serious mental illness, their links with symptoms and functional limitations, current approaches to treatment and rehabilitation, and effective coping skills and strategies. For instance, particularly during a relapse, patients may manifest limitations in concentration and attention, information processing, planning ability, problem solving, social awareness, or emotional modulation. These limitations add to the stress of daily living and require some adaptation on the part of families who wish to provide a supportive environment. Likewise, good communication and problem-solving skills can reduce the level of family stress. Figure 6.1 specifies the potential components of a FAP.

FIGURE 6.1
COMPONENTS OF A FAMILY ACTION PLAN

The Family Action Plan has been developed to assist families in coping with some specific challenges that accompany the serious mental illness of a close relative. The FAP addresses the following concerns: responding to a catastrophic stressor, providing a supportive environment, maintaining hope and heart, dealing with positive symptoms, dealing with negative symptoms, dealing with mood disorders, dealing with manic episodes, dealing with depressive episodes, coping with crises, managing potentially self-destructive behavior, managing potentially violent behavior, dealing with alcohol and drug abuse, and planning for the future.

RESPONDING TO A CATASTROPHIC STRESSOR

The mental illness of a close relative confronts all families with a challenge of enormous proportions. The initial response of most family members is often a paralyzing sense of disbelief, confusion, helplessness, and hopelessness. Yet your family already has some strengths for coping with this challenge. No one

(continued)

FIGURE 6.1 Continued

has a better understanding of your family or shares your lifetime commitment to your relative.

Under these circumstances your family also needs to obtain new knowledge about your relative's mental illness and its treatment, to acquire new skills for coping with the illness and the mental health system, and to find new sources of support.

Initially, it may be helpful to establish a family team that consists of all members of the family, including your relative, whose recovery will be enhanced by playing an active and informed role in decisions about treatment and rehabilitation. Young members of the family also need to feel they are part of the process.

Responsibilities of family members should reflect their particular roles, ages, concerns, and circumstances. For example, adult members of the family need to ensure that young family members do not move into "parentified" roles that involve adult responsibilities; young siblings and offspring need support for their own growth and development. At the same time, young family members need information in terms they can understand, opportunities to share their feelings and concerns, and assistance in coping.

It is essential for your family to work collaboratively with the professional team that is treating your relative. Professionals can help your family promote your relative's recovery, develop appropriate expectations, and respond to early warning signs of relapse. In addition, they can help your family cope with specific problems, such as medication adherence, substance abuse, or the risk of self-destructive or violent behavior.

Although crises demand an immediate and focused response, on a long-term basis your family should aim to maintain a normal lifestyle, re-establish family routines, and continue with customary activities. Your family can strive for a balance that meets the needs of all members of the family, that encourages their growth and development, and that improves their quality of life. This is often easier said than done!

PROVIDING A SUPPORTIVE ENVIRONMENT

Because of their brain abnormalities and related functional limitations, people with mental illness are unusually vulnerable to stress. Events that are barely noticed by others may overwhelm them. Thus, your relative can benefit from a low-key environment and an opportunity for a time-out when things get hectic.

Your relative may be especially sensitive to interpersonal friction. Avoid unnecessary criticism and conflict and learn to express your concerns in a non-judgmental way. Use "I Messages" ("I can't do my work when the music is so loud") rather than "You Messages" ("You are rude to play your music so loud").

Mental illness sometimes makes it difficult for your relative to communicate effectively. You can help by listening attentively, responding empathically, speaking clearly and directly, and keeping messages brief and straightforward.

Your family can benefit from good problem solving skills. In a given situation, these skills can help in defining and analyzing the problem, in generating and evaluating solutions, and in selecting and implementing a solution. If the chosen solution does not result in satisfactory resolution of the problem, the process may begin again.

FIGURE 6.1 Continued

Given the confusion and disorganization that often accompany mental illness, your relative can also benefit from an environment that offers structure, stability, and consistency. When change is necessary or desirable, it can be facilitated by open discussion, careful planning, and a pace that is comfortable for your relative.

A constructive atmosphere can improve your family's ability to cope with the mental illness. Such an atmosphere is characterized by open and direct communication, by mutual tolerance and respect, and by caring, commitment, and affection. Differences can then be resolved in a way that acknowledges the perspectives of all family members and results in a mutually acceptable solution.

MAINTAINING HOPE AND HEART

Maintain a realistic sense of hope for your relative and your family. With time, most people with mental illness achieve a meaningful degree of recovery. During the darkest periods, "look for the light" that can come with increased knowledge and skills and with professional assistance.[3]

Effective treatments are available for even the most severe and persistent mental disorders. With appropriate treatment, your relative can obtain relief from symptoms, learn to manage the illness, and construct a satisfying life. Finding the right combination of medication and psychosocial interventions may take considerable time and effort. Be patient and encourage your relative to persevere.

Many factors can promote recovery. Describing their recovery process, for instance, people with mental illness emphasize the value of their own determination, self-monitoring, education about the illness, meaningful work, a healthy lifestyle, spirituality, supportive friends, significant others, and family support. Families can encourage their relative to develop and make use of these resources.

Become familiar with current research findings regarding long-term outcomes. Studies indicate that a majority of people with serious mental illness achieve recovery or significant improvement. New medications and psychosocial interventions are likely to assist even more individuals in the future.

Encourage your relative to take responsibility for managing the illness. As with other severe health problems, people with mental illness need to obtain education about their illness, to make best use of professional services, and to maintain a healthy lifestyle. It's also important for them to control the level of psychosocial stress in their lives and to identify their symptom triggers. Other helpful strategies include charting symptoms and moods, using relaxation and stress management techniques, and increasing pleasurable activities.

Mental illness is often traumatic for all members of the family. Under these circumstances, it is normal for family members to have fears about the future. At the same time, your family should avoid remaining frozen in a crisis mode that places all of you under a cloud of anxiety and strips your lives of satisfaction.

Strive to "put mental illness in its place." The illness should not be allowed to define your relative or your family. Along with a mental illness, your relative has strengths and resources, as does your family. Maintain the integrity of your family, experiencing the joys as well as the sorrows. There is life after mental illness!

(continued)

Figure 6.1 Continued

Learning to Set Limits

Limit setting is important for all family members. No one should have to live in a dangerous or disturbing environment.

Certain behaviors are not acceptable and should not be tolerated. These include behavior that is abusive, self-destructive, harmful to others, damaging to property, or severely disruptive. You need to decide which behaviors are unacceptable, set clear limits, and impose consequences when those limits are exceeded.

It is also important to decide which behaviors can be ignored. For example, behavior that may harm your relative or others is more important than behavior that is merely annoying or embarrassing.

It is best to discuss these issues with your relative prior to a crisis. Many problems can be avoided through advance planning. It may be helpful to have a written contract that lists unacceptable behaviors and the actions that will be taken by family members if those behaviors occur.

Limits should be based on reasonable expectations for all members of the family. Those expectations should reflect their ages, their roles in the family, and their strengths and limitations.

Learn to set personal limits. Don't let the mental illness of your relative overpower your own needs and goals. The illness needs to be placed in perspective—as a single event in your entire life, which encompasses a wide range of experiences, relationships, challenges, and opportunities. Maintain a comfortable level of involvement in your relative's life that allows you to fully live your own life.

Dealing with Positive Symptoms

The symptoms of schizophrenia are sometimes divided into positive and negative symptoms. Positive (psychotic) symptoms involve exaggeration or distortion of normal functions. Examples include hallucinations (false perceptions), such as hearing voices; delusions (false beliefs), such as a conviction that one is being persecuted; disorganized thought and speech; and bizarre behavior.

It is useful to remember that people with mental illness experience hallucinations and delusions as real, although with time they may learn to recognize these experiences as symptoms of their disorder. It is not helpful to argue with them about the reality of their hallucinations and delusions. You are not likely to convince them they are wrong, and the conflict will be stressful for both of you.

It is best to respond in a way that respects their dignity without reinforcing their symptoms. You can remain nonjudgmental (avoid challenging their statement) while responding to your relative's concerns. For example, you may choose to acknowledge what you have heard ("That's very interesting"), to offer support ("I'm sure that must upset you"), to convey empathy ("I'd be worried too if I heard those voices"), to offer assistance ("Can I do anything to make you feel better?"), or to change the subject ("Let's go for a walk").

Remember that your relative may suffer considerably from the hallucinations and delusions that often accompany schizophrenia. What may be annoying for you can be horrifying for your relative. For instance, one woman wrote

FIGURE 6.1 Continued

that the phrase "interpersonal terror" was perhaps the most apt description of her experience of mental illness.[4]

Personal accounts of people who have experienced psychotic symptoms can offer insight into the subjective experience of schizophrenia. A consumer has written: "We struggle constantly with our raging fears and the brutality of our thoughts, and then we are subjected as well to the misunderstanding, distrust, and ongoing stigma we experience from the community."[5]

You may wish to consult with your relative's therapist or case manager regarding the best way to handle positive symptoms in his or her case.

DEALING WITH NEGATIVE SYMPTOMS

Negative symptoms involve a decrease in or loss of normal thoughts, experiences, and feelings. Such symptoms may include lack of motivation, inability to follow through on tasks, inability to experience pleasure and to enjoy relationships, inability to feel and express emotions, inability to focus on activities, and impoverished thought and speech.

Learn to recognize these symptoms as part of the illness and to develop realistic expectations for your relative. Struggling with mental illness may consume much of your relative's time and energy.

As difficult as it may be for you to observe the limitations of your relative's life, it is also difficult to live such a life, which may seem barren and meaningless. Patricia Deegan, who has since become a psychologist, talks about the early years of her illness:

> Giving up was not a problem, it was a solution. It was a solution because it protected me from wanting anything. If I didn't want anything, then it couldn't be taken away. If I didn't try, then I wouldn't have to undergo another failure. If I didn't care, then nothing could hurt me again. My heart became hardened.[6]

Offer your relative an opportunity to talk about his or her negative symptoms and discuss possible strategies for improving task performance. Rehabilitation may offer an opportunity to improve skills, functioning, and life satisfaction. In addition, some newer medications appear to lessen negative symptoms.

Encourage your relative to engage in new social activities. Many communities have drop-in centers and support groups for people with mental illness. As with the rest of the family, your relative may benefit from contact with others who have had similar experiences and who can offer hope and advice during difficult periods.

You may wish to consult with your relative's therapist or case manager regarding the best way to handle negative symptoms in his or her case.

DEALING WITH MOOD DISORDERS

Symptoms of mood disorders, such as mania and depression, are sometimes difficult to distinguish from normal emotions. It is important for your family to accept the reality of the disorder and to work with your relative to define what

(continued)

Figure 6.1 Continued

is part of the illness in his or her case. That will allow your family to respond to the earliest warning signs of impending episode and to obtain early treatment. It is easier to treat mood instability at its onset than when it has developed into a full-blown manic or depressive episode.

Your family also needs to define what *is not* a symptom of the disorder and will not be cause for alarm. That allows all of you to maintain the distinction between the person and the disorder and to avoid pathologizing normal emotions, such as natural mood swings. Such a distinction also avoids the hypervigilance that can occur when family members respond to intense or despondent feelings with excessive anxiety.

With effective treatment, most people with mood disorders recover, remain well for long periods of time, and lead productive and reasonably normal lives. Functional impairment is generally less than occurs with schizophrenia. Thus, a hopeful attitude is both appropriate and life-enhancing for your relative and your family.

Develop realistic expectations for a relative who is experiencing significant emotional symptoms. Especially when the symptoms are intense, people with mood disorders may have little control over their feelings and behavior. During a manic or depressive episode, it's important to ensure safety, to set appropriate limits, to facilitate treatment and medication adherence, and to redistribute essential role functions.

Following an episode, your family should strive to return to a normal lifestyle. Avoid a preoccupation with relapse that can undermine family relationships and satisfactions. It's also important for your family to talk openly about the illness, to empathize with your relative's feelings of loss and pain, and to look toward a more promising future.

Researchers have found that emotional symptoms exact a high toll among family members, who may feel personally targeted by their relative's hostility, withdrawal, or manipulation. Don't take it personally; view these behaviors as symptoms of the illness. At the same time, acknowledge your own needs, reach out to supportive family and friends, and make time for yourself.

Dealing with Manic Episodes

Over time, your family can learn to distinguish reasonably well between normal moods and the symptoms of mania. Recognize early warning signs of a manic episode, which may include insomnia, racing thoughts, or talking rapidly. Also identify the triggers, such as a high level of stress or conflict. However, your family needs to avoid inappropriately pathologizing your relative's good moods, ambitious plans, and creative activities.

A healthy lifestyle is very important in managing bipolar disorder. For example, disruptions of biological rhythms (including the sleep-wake cycle) can induce manic episodes. Likewise, a balanced diet, regular exercise, and increased exposure to light can stabilize moods and decrease the risk of an episode.[7]

Medication, even when effective in controlling symptoms, poses special problems in the treatment of bipolar disorder, which is often associated with periods of remarkable euphoria, creativity, and energy. People with this disorder may

FIGURE 6.1 Continued

---

feel less alive on medication, worry about diminished productivity, or miss "the high flights of mind and mood."[8] At the same time, failure to take medication can decrease the interval between episodes (the "kindling" effect).[9] Thus, it is important for your relative to find a medication that offers protection against recurrences of mania without sacrificing quality of life.

Family relationships can be profoundly affected by symptoms of mania, such as spending sprees, hypersexual periods, and grandiose business decisions. After an episode, family members may experience hurt, fear, and anger. It is important not to avoid painful discussion for fear of unsetting your relative and triggering relapse. Good communication and problem solving skills can help your family deal with these difficult issues and reduce future problems.

During periods of relative calm, your family can work to set limits and establish controls for minimizing problems in the future. For example, a given family might set restrictions on bank accounts or credit cards. Another family might decide to modify business policies and procedures, perhaps in consultation with business partners or associates.

After a relapse, your family will need to renegotiate roles and responsibilities and to reestablish trust. Learn to avoid the escalations may follow in the wake of a manic episode. Work with your relative to understand factors that may have triggered the episode and the changes that can reduce the risk of future episodes. This collaborative approach can reduce guilt and recriminations, channel energy constructively, and promote recovery.

DEALING WITH DEPRESSIVE EPISODES

Symptoms of depression are "contagious"—it's easy for family members to absorb some of the feelings of hopelessness and helplessness. Take care of yourself, learn how deal to deal with your own emotions, reach out for personal support, and obtain professional assistance as appropriate. Sometimes the best thing you can do is strengthen and nurture yourself.

Recognize that depression often involves a failure of will. It is not helpful to tell your relative to "snap out of it" or to "get moving" again. People with major depression often struggle heroically simply to get through the day—or even to get out of bed. Acknowledge your relative's efforts and courage.

Learn how to assist your relative by offering unqualified support, by simplifying life, and by providing concrete assistance with tasks and responsibilities that may seem overwhelming. Often, the best approach is to ask, "What can I do to help?" Your relative can usually let you know what is most helpful—a hug or an errand or simply a presence. As one person wrote, "Sometimes I just need someone to be there, so the dark isn't quite so big."[10] Avoid becoming impatient or angry, which may increase your relative's feelings of inadequacy or rejection.

As with mania, eventually your family can learn to distinguish fairly well between normal moods and the symptoms of depression. Recognize early warning signs of a depressive episode, such as fatigue, withdrawal, or difficulty getting up in the morning. At the same time, people with depression are subject to normal feelings of being unhappy and discouraged, which should

(continued)

FIGURE 6.1 Continued

not evoke consternation on the part of family members. Likewise, periods of solitude can serve a protective function; such periods shouldn't be equated with depressive withdrawal.

Your relative may have feelings about dependency on medication for symptom control. Most people have tried repeatedly—and sometimes desperately—to break out of an overpowering depression. Encourage your relative to take advantage of the many beneficial medications now available. Depression is a real illness with many effective treatments.

Your family can benefit from the personal accounts of people who have learned how to survive serious depression and to construct fulfilling lives. Describing his own depression in *Darkness Visible: A Memoir of Madness,* Pulitzer Prize-winning author William Styron has written of enduring "the despair beyond despair," yet returning from "the abyss" with his capacity for joy and serenity restored.[11]

COPING WITH CRISES

Learn the warning signs of impending crisis. Warning signs may include sudden changes in behavior, hallucinations or delusions, disorganized speech or thinking, bizarre behavior, verbal threats, changes in eating or sleeping patterns, or fluctuations in activity level or mood. Individuals often have their own unique warning signs. For instance, one mother said she knew a crisis was coming when her son called her by her first name.

Be prepared. Have contingency plans ready and keep emergency phone numbers available. You may find it helpful to discuss these plans with your relative in advance. Your plans should include a list of people who can offer assistance in a crisis. These may include other family members, friends, neighbors, case managers or other providers, members of your own support group, or the police.

During a crisis, your relative is likely to be confused, overwhelmed, and unfocused. Remain calm yourself and give your relative an opportunity to calm down. Your own behavior is likely to have a major impact on your relative during a crisis. Avoid threatening, shouting, criticizing, or arguing with other family members. Separate the person from the symptoms, which may include anger directed at you. Don't take it personally. A brief time-out may be best for everyone.

Approach the crisis in a firm, straightforward, loving, and respectful manner. Comply with reasonable requests that are not harmful to your relative or to others; this can increase your relative's sense of control and support. Attend to the physical environment. Encourage everyone to sit down (it is less threatening), minimize direct eye contact and physical contact with your relative (both can increase stress), and avoid cornering or restricting your relative (which can increase the risk of harm). Don't get cornered yourself, either.

Medication adherence is generally an essential part of treatment that is likely to reduce the risk of relapse and crisis. People with mental illness may refuse to take medication because they can't tolerate the side effects, don't accept their illness, or are experiencing symptoms that interfere with treatment. Consider using a Portable Medication Record that can track medication,

FIGURE 6.1 Continued

teach consumers and families about medication management, and serve as a history of medication usage in crises or for use in treatment.[12]

Calmly discuss these issues with your relative, offer relevant educational materials, and work with professionals in increasing the likelihood of medication adherence. Strategies include using injectables, the lowest effective dosage, and the medication most acceptable to your relative. Promising new medications have become available in recent years; others are currently in development.[13]

MANAGING POTENTIALLY SELF-DESTRUCTIVE BEHAVIOR

People who attempt suicide often show warning signs. These may include expressions of hopelessness or helplessness; changes in biological functions, such as eating or sleeping; severe mood changes; withdrawal from usual activities; final arrangements, such as giving away possessions or writing a will; suicidal threats, especially if there is a suicide plan; hallucinations that encourage a suicide attempt; or an expressed wish to die. Prior suicidal thoughts, gestures, or attempts increase the risk associated with any of these signs.

Do not ignore the signs of potentially self-destructive behavior. That may encourage this behavior, lead to further escalation, or increase the likelihood of harm to your relative. Stay calm, show concern and empathy, and remain available to talk.

Ask your relative if he or she is thinking about suicide. Such an approach may offer the opportunity to better understand your relative's state of mind, to prevent self-destructive behavior, and to obtain professional assistance. Also ask if your relative has a suicide plan, which is considered a significant risk factor.

Encourage your relative to get professional help. If necessary, seek professional assistance yourself. Contact a mental health professional, a suicide prevention center, or the police.

Consider using an advance directive if there has been prior self-destructive behavior. An advance directive allows your relative to specify preferred treatment decisions if he or she is not capable of making an informed choice. Petition for an involuntary commitment if your relative has committed any self-destructive acts and you cannot get assistance in any other way.

Someone who is determined to die may ultimately be successful. You cannot always prevent suicide and should not feel responsible if you are faced with this tragic loss. The consequences of a relative's suicide are devastating for family members. Help is available through specialized support groups that focus on suicide or bereavement, other family-focused programs, and professional counseling.

MANAGING POTENTIALLY VIOLENT BEHAVIOR

Learn the warning signs of potentially violent behavior. These may include expressions of hostility; harmful threats, especially if there is a violent plan; hallucinations that encourage violence; or a paranoid delusion that one is being watched, persecuted, or attacked. The best predictor of future violence is a history of violence, which increases the risk associated with any of these signs.

(continued)

FIGURE 6.1 Continued

Do not ignore the signs of potentially violent behavior. Such a stance may encourage the behavior, lead to further escalation, or increase the likelihood of harm to your relative or others. Whatever your inner turmoil, try to respond in a calm, accepting, and respectful manner. Offer concrete suggestions that can defuse the situation.

Tell your relative that his or her behavior is frightening you. Sometimes this can lessen the risk of harm and help your relative understand the impact of his or her behavior on other people.

Avoid lectures, criticism, verbal threats, and hostile remarks. These are likely to further upset your relative and increase the risk of harm.

Leave the scene immediately if you feel in danger. Have an escape route available. Get assistance from the police or other appropriate parties.

Consider using an advance directive if there has been prior violent behavior. Petition for an involuntary commitment if your relative has committed any violent acts and you cannot get assistance in any other way.

DEALING WITH ALCOHOL AND DRUG ABUSE

Alcohol and drug abuse are frequent problems among people with mental illness. For example, at some point in their lives almost 50% of people who have schizophrenia also develop a substance abuse disorder, as do 30% of those with major depression, manic depression, or other mood disorders. When a person suffers from both mental illness and substance abuse, it is called a dual diagnosis.[14]

Family members face special challenges when their relative carries a dual diagnosis. For all people with a substance abuse problem, there are harmful effects on health, relationships, and work. When a mental illness is present, substance abuse can result in exacerbation of symptoms and increase the risk of relapse and hospitalization. Even when your relative is receiving substance abuse treatment, the risk of relapse is high and recovery often involves repeated efforts and long-term treatment.

Learn about your relative's use of alcohol and drugs. People with mental illness generally abuse substances for three reasons: (a) to temporarily reduce symptoms or side effects of medication through self-medication with alcohol or drugs; (b) to enhance their social life and reduce their feelings of isolation; and (c) to increase pleasant feelings (or at least reduce unpleasant ones) as an antidote to the anguish and loss associated with mental illness. In severe cases, substances are used to prevent withdrawal symptoms or cravings. These are all powerful reinforcers.

Keep the channel of communication open with your relative. When you are not in the midst of a crisis, discuss the substance abuse calmly, nonjudgmentally, and compassionately. Talk about the advantages and disadvantages of substance use. Express your concern and try to understand your relative's perspective.

On a long-term basis, try to persuade your relative that the substance abuse is a problem (denial is common). Encourage your relative to get help and to find better ways of meeting his or her needs. These might include participation in structured activities, involvement in a self-help group (such as a mental health consumer group or Alcoholics Anonymous), or professional substance abuse treatment. Ultimately, however, these steps must be taken by your relative.

FIGURE 6.1 Continued

You may wish to consult with your relative's therapist or case manager to develop a plan that meets the needs of all members of the family. Establish household rules (for example, no substance abuse in the home) and consider alternative living arrangements if your relative cannot conform to the rules. Develop a list of resources for your relative with names and phone numbers, such as an intensive case manager, another family member or consumer who is willing to serve as a resource, a consumer self-help group, or a member of Alcoholics Anonymous.

PLANNING FOR THE FUTURE

By definition, serious mental illness involves the possibility of severe and persistent disabilities in multiple areas of functioning. People with these disabilities often need long-term support, which in turn requires long-term planning.[15] Thus, it is essential for families to have an open and continuing dialogue regarding plans for their relative and to consult with experts who can assist them. Your relative should play an active role in decisions that affect his or her future.

People with serious mental illness are generally eligible for a range of benefits, including Social Security Disability Insurance (SSDI), Supplementary Security Income (SSI), and public assistance (welfare), as well as associated health care and other benefits. Contact your local Social Security office or department of public welfare for further information. Your family needs to ensure that long-term plans do not jeopardize eligibility for these benefits.

Community resources are an essential component of your family plan. A local case manager can serve as your relative's advocate, coordinate mental health and other important services, and keep your family informed about residential living arrangements in your community. Sometimes these functions are performed by family members, such as parents of an adult son or daughter who resides at home. As they age, parents need to develop a community network that can meet the needs of their relative on a continuing basis. Such a network is essential for siblings who do not reside locally.

Long-term planning also involves family resources. Contact a lawyer who is knowledgeable about estate planning for people with mental illness and who can meet periodically with your family. If your family wishes to provide for your relative's future without jeopardizing his or her eligibility for benefits, you may wish to establish a trust fund and appoint a trustee to administer the trust. The trustee, either an individual or financial institution, distributes funds based on the specific provisions of the trust.

Your family can also benefit from other resources, both locally and nationally. For instance, NAMI can provide information about the Planned Lifetime Assistance Network (PLAN).

Finally, depending on the age and capacities of your relative, your family may need to become familiar with procedures for establishing health care proxy (concerned with treatment decisions) and durable power of attorney (concerned with legal and financial matters); and for appointment of a guardian (with authority over personal and financial decisions) or conservator (with authority over property and money issues).

Developing a FAP for Individual Families

Although the FAP addresses many family concerns, each family has its own set of experiences, needs, and concerns. Following family assessment, practitioners will be able to modify the FAP to address the needs of specific families. Some families may identify one of more components of the FAP as pressing concerns, such as suicide potential or substance abuse. Targeting these concerns, professionals can help families develop a detailed written plan that specifies roles and responsibilities of individual family members, emergency numbers, organizations or individuals who can offer assistance, and other pertinent information. For families who are dealing with troublesome behavior at home, a written contract might cite acceptable and unacceptable behaviors, as well as consequences for the latter. In both of these instances, all family members, including the patient, should be involved in developing these plans.

Families who want to enhance their coping skills are likely to benefit from pertinent reading material and from role playing and feedback. For example, family members might wish to learn how to communicate more effectively in dealing with a relative who is unusually vulnerable to stress, to respond to their relative's positive or negative symptoms, to defuse volatile situations, or to discuss concerns about suicide or substance abuse. These are all challenging circumstances; unless properly handled, they can increase the level of family stress, with adverse consequences for everyone.

Other components of the FAP, such as long-term planning, require families to learn about local, state, and national resources and to consult with other professionals, such as an attorney knowledgeable about mental health and disability issues. Practitioners can make appropriate referrals and encourage families to include all members in the planning process. Referrals may also be needed for families that include an elderly member with mental illness. Clinicians can assist these families in understanding and responding to the changing needs of their aging relative and in developing new coping skills and strategies.

For a particular family, the FAP may not address their most urgent concern, such as homelessness or incarceration. Indeed, families whose relatives attract the attention of police officers, attorneys, and judges may find these personnel poorly trained to deal with people who are suicidal, threatening, or disruptive. As June Husted has pointed out, such personnel rarely receive satisfactory training about serious mental illness and may not even recognize blatantly psychotic symptoms as indicative of the illness.[16] Consequently, people with mental illness may receive substandard treatment—or no treatment at all—in an environment that is likely to exacerbate their symptoms and to increase their vulnerability.

In my original interviews, I listened horrified to one mother's account of her son's incarceration. By the time she was able to get her son hospitalized, he had not eaten for 16 days, was dehydrated, and had lost approximately 70 pounds. Shackled with a ball and chain, this psychotic, frightened, and debilitated young man was released in the custody of three deputies.

Developing a Personal Action Plan

In *Troubled Journey*, we also developed a Personal Action Plan (PAP) to assist individual family members (Figure 6.2). As with the FAP, practitioners may choose to share this material with family members or to incorporate some of these suggestions into their overall service plan.[17]

FIGURE 6.2
COMPONENTS OF A PERSONAL ACTION PLAN

A Personal Action Plan

The Personal Action Plan (PAP) is designed to assist family members of people with serious mental illness in meeting their own needs. The PAP offers suggestions for taking care of yourself, taking charge of your life, accepting what you cannot change, maintaining a hopeful attitude, cultivating your personal garden, learning about mental illness, improving your coping skills, and strengthening your personal support network.

TAKING CARE OF YOURSELF

Practice good self-care. If you're like many family members, you may be so involved in meeting the needs of others that you sometimes forget to take care of yourself. Develop healthy habits for daily living that meet your needs for sleep, nutrition, exercise, and relaxation. Also do something special for yourself on a regular basis.

Strive to maintain a normal lifestyle. Expand activities and relationships outside your family. Aim for reasonable stability and a comfortable rhythm of daily life. Avoid assuming a crisis mode that keeps you anticipating the next emergency even when things are calm.

Maintain a satisfactory balance in your life. Find ways to fulfill your commitments to others without neglecting your own needs. Remember that caregiving is only one of your roles; don't let it define your relationships.

Enhance your ability to love, to work, and to play. Seek out people who value and care for you. Find meaningful work that showcases your talents. Take time to unwind in pleasurable activities; build in brief getaways.

Mourn your losses. Grieving is a necessary, normal, and natural process. Acknowledge your losses, give yourself time and space to mourn, and then move on.

(continued)

Figure 6.2 Continued

Seek professional counseling if appropriate. If you remain consumed by your family circumstances and unable to derive much pleasure from your own life, consider counseling a wise investment.

Taking Charge of Your Life

Place the mental illness in perspective, as a single event in your life. Apply a wide-angle lens that captures your other experiences, relationships, and opportunities, and your future as well as your past.

Separate yourself from the mental illness in your family. Also separate your family from the illness, which is only one family event, and your relative from the illness, never losing sight of the human being behind the symptoms.

Learn from the past. Free yourself from earlier maladaptive patterns and choices. Every day offers the opportunity to make new choices and to pursue new goals.

Accept and appreciate yourself. Be honest with yourself, set realistic goals, and acknowledge your limits. Accept your best as good enough; don't aim for perfection. For yourself and others, focus on strengths rather than shortcomings.

Be willing to take risks. Changing familiar patterns can be frightening. Decide upon a course of change, prepare yourself for action, and gradually translate your plan into reality.

Learn to set limits. Don't let the mental illness of your relative take over your life. You can live only one life—make sure it is the one you choose.

Accepting What You Cannot Change

Accept your family circumstances. The mental illness is etched on your family slate, leaving an indelible mark on all your lives. You cannot alter that reality.

Accept the pain in your family. Your family has suffered irrevocable losses. You cannot change that fact or compensate them for their suffering.

Accept your relative's mental illness. Your relative has also suffered major losses. You cannot will those losses to disappear.

Accept your own sorrow. You too have experienced significant losses in the past. Acknowledge and grieve your losses; they are woven into the fabric of your life.

Accept the legacy for your current life. You carry the weight of your family experience, which is likely to influence your thoughts, feelings, and behavior in the present.

Accept the meaning of mental illness for your future. The illness has affected not only your past and your present. It also colors your future, leaving a residue of uncertainty for your relative, your family, and yourself. At the same time, the future offers hope for improvement.

Maintaining a Hopeful Attitude

Strive for a positive attitude. Reframe to emphasize strengths as well as limitations, gains as well as losses, and hope as well as despair. Preserve your sense of humor.

FIGURE 6.2 Continued

Revise your family experience of mental illness. Along with their experience of mental illness, your family shares an intricate tapestry woven of common bonds, memories, rituals, celebrations, losses, and myths.

Reconsider your relative's experience of mental illness. Along with the limitations that result from the illness, your relative has the potential for recovery and for an improved quality of life.

Review your past. Along with your anguish, your experience with mental illness may have given you increased understanding, enhanced tolerance and compassion, and greater appreciation of life's treasures.

Invest in your current life. Whatever your past experiences, you have an opportunity in the present to gain insight, to achieve resolution, to reclaim your territory, and to reallocate your energy.

Plan for your future. Whatever your past choices, you have an opportunity in the future to make new choices, to pursue new goals, to rebuild current relationships, and to form new ones.

CULTIVATING YOUR PERSONAL GARDEN

Nourish your talents. Promote your talents as a writer, artist, actor, dancer, or musician. Develop new talents.

Explore your interests. Expand your interests in gardening, hiking, cooking, camping, crafts, or exercise. Develop new interests.

Reconsider your occupation. People typically make four major career changes in their lives, including time spent at home. Consider changing your career or pursuing education or training that can unlock new opportunities.

Expand your emotional, intellectual, and spiritual horizons. Seek out new people, experiences, and activities.

Enlarge your geographical boundaries. Travel by land, sea, and air. Visit new terrains, regions, and countries.

Hear the call to service. Contribute your gifts to others. Volunteer your energy to a valued cause or group.

LEARNING ABOUT MENTAL ILLNESS

Learn about mental illness and its treatment. Many resources are available to assist you in learning more about the illness and family issues.

Learn about the mental health system and community resources. Contact professionals or a local family support group.

Learn about the family experience of mental illness. Read the publications by professionals and by family members themselves.

Learn about the impact on individual members of the family, such as parents, spouses, siblings, and offspring.

Learn about your relative's experience of mental illness. Connect with the person behind the illness. Ask about his or her symptoms, struggle, coping strategies, and hopes for the future.

Learn about the experiences of the rest of your family. Ask them about their experiences, concerns, and needs. Share feelings and coping strategies.

(continued)

FIGURE 6.2 Continued

IMPROVING YOUR COPING SKILLS

Be prepared. Anticipate your challenges, develop useful knowledge and skills, marshal your allies, and take action when necessary.

Avoid ineffective coping strategies. Each of the following offers short-term gains: denial, withdrawal, alcohol and drugs, and negative emotions, such as anger and resentment. However, these strategies all undermine your coping efforts in the long term.

Improve your communication skills. Effective listening is active, nonjudgmental, responsive, and empathic. Effective expression is clear, complete, direct, and supportive.

Refine your problem solving and conflict management skills. Aim for a win-win solution that respects the interests of all parties and results in a mutually acceptable option. Create an atmosphere of mutual tolerance and respect.

Develop your stress management skills. Understand the nature of stress, as well as the kinds and sources of stress in your life. When possible, avoid stressful situations or reduce the level of stress. When stress is inevitable, learn to manage it more effectively.

Enhance your assertiveness skills. Learn to stand up for your legitimate rights, to refuse to let others take advantage of you, and to meet your own needs without violating the rights of others. Speak up and let others know how your feel.

STRENGTHENING YOUR PERSONAL SUPPORT NETWORK

Build lifelines to other people. They are your most important resource. Share your story with them and listen to theirs.

Cherish any viable relationships with your family, partner, friends, and colleagues. Develop new relationships that can nurture and console you.

Seek out others who have shared the family experience of mental illness. They can validate your experience, share your anguish, and offer practical advice.

Contact professionals and other service providers. They can inform you about mental illness, the service delivery system, and community resources.

Join a support group for family members. Organize a group if none is available in your community.

Become active in an advocacy group. Family advocacy organizations, such as NAMI, have already had a significant impact on state and national levels. As an advocate on the local level, you can improve the lives of people with mental illness in your community.

From Theory to Practice

Returning to Douglas Bailey, as requested by the country MH/MR administrator, he has scheduled inservice training for staff at the six community mental health centers. The initial 6-hour training program includes the following:

- A unit on current thinking about serious mental illness and its treatment
- A unit on family experiences, needs, and concerns
- Copies of the Family Action Plan that staff can share with families
- A list of resources that can be used by staff and families, including pertinent books, articles, and audiovisual materials[18]
- A discussion of confidentiality and strategies for resolving potential conflicts
- A panel of family members who tell their stories, share their insights, and offer suggestions to staff

Doug also plans an ongoing series of initiatives designed to strengthen the community support network for patients and to encourage the involvement of families, who will be invited to the remaining sessions. Plans include:

- Appointment of a family advisory board for each of the CMHCs, charged with developing a plan for enhancing family-provider communication and recommending specific family-focused services
- Inclusion of family members on the treatment team when appropriate
- Needs assessment to identify areas of particular interest and concern among families, patients, and staff at each of the CMHCs
- A future program with representatives of the full array of services needed by patients with mental illness, including medical, educational, rehabilitation, social, recreational, residential, and family support services
- A future program with local advocacy organizations, such as affiliates of NAMI
- A future program with personnel from the criminal justice and social service systems

PART THREE

Family Interventions

CHAPTER 7

Family Intervention Strategies: Family Consultation

Family therapist Sharon Vaccaro participates in a multidisciplinary group practice, which has recently contracted with a managed behavioral health care program to provide treatment and rehabilitation services for patients with serious mental illness. The services will include a family program that Sharon has been asked to design and implement. An experienced practitioner, she wonders why the families she has approached show little interest in traditional clinical services. Sharon consults with another member of the group, social worker Tom Cohen, who has a brother with schizophrenia. Tom shares his family's frustration with a system that has often been insensitive to the needs of families. As in the case of his parents, when services are provided, such as family therapy, they may have little relationship to the actual needs and desires of families. Tom suggests that Sharon begin with a consultative approach designed to address the expressed needs of particular families and to assist them in making an informed choice about their use of other available services. Familiarizing herself with the literature on family consultation, Sharon begins to revise her plans for the new program, expecting to have more success in encouraging the involvement of families and in developing individualized service plans.

As in the case of Sharon Vaccaro, practitioners are likely to find family consultation an effective approach in working with families. How does this mode differ from traditional therapy? And how might clinicians translate this mode into professional practice? This chapter answers these questions and assists practitioners in developing individualized service plans for families. Topics include features of family consultation, dimensions of family consultation, and variations in family consultation, as well as an example of a consultative session.

Features of Family Consultation

Consultation is offered by a wide range of professionals, including lawyers, accountants, and health care professionals. The consultative process involves a discussion between two or more parties designed to clarify a situation, to reach a decision, to solve a problem, or to accomplish an objective. As delineated by Kayla Bernheim and by Lyman Wynne, Timothy Weber, and Susan McDaniel, consultation offers a useful family intervention in the area of serious mental illness.[1, 2]

Family consultants offer expert knowledge, skills, and advice to family members, who maintain primary responsibility for determining their own goals, for deciding whether to accept professional recommendations, and for implementing decisions. Consultation can result in a range of outcomes, including a decision to continue the consultative relationship, to pursue other services, or to decline further services. Family satisfaction is a central outcome variable in consultation, along with enhanced family competence and confidence. Family consultation offers a number of advantages for practitioners. A consultative approach fosters collaborative relationships with families, offers an objective and systems-oriented assessment of their concerns, emphasizes family strengths and resources, and facilitates the shift to alternative professional roles as appropriate.

It is important to distinguish between family consultation and traditional clinical services, such as family therapy. In fact, the distinction between the two family interventions is captured in their dictionary definitions. Consultation is defined as asking the advice or opinion of an expert and as deliberating together. Therapy (or more properly psychotherapy) involves the treatment of mental or emotional disorders by psychological means.

In professional practice, there is some overlap between the two. For instance, psychotherapy often involves deliberation and advice. In contrast, consultation never involves treatment or implies pathology. Thus, in working with families who may have been pathologized in the past, professionals should be clear about the distinction between family consultation and family therapy. On the other hand, assuming an initial role as family consultants, practitioners may recommend other services, including family therapy, to meet the requirements of a given family.

Moreover, although the conceptual distinction between family consultation and family therapy is meaningful, the difference is sometimes less clear in practice. Christopher Amenson, an experienced family practitioner, has observed that the same presenting problem can have different—and even multiple—sources.[3] In asking for assistance, one couple might report, "Our son refuses to take medication." Consultation may be helpful for these parents, perhaps supplemented by family education or psychoeducation. In another case, parents might state, "We could never agree on parenting, but now that our son has schizophrenia, it is much worse." These parents are raising a family systems issue, which is an appropriate target of intervention. As Amenson points out, these latter parents can at least be *offered* therapy designed to improve their relationship and consistency.

In practice, Amenson has found that families often present with both consultative and therapeutic issues. For instance, a given set of parents might express concern about their son's refusal to take medication and also about their longstanding inability to agree on child rearing. These parents might be asked, "Do you want to work on medication adherence using your current limited ability to agree? *Or* do you want to work on improving your ability to agree?" Amenson told me he often spends half a session discussing what each of these options would mean in terms of time, cost, methods, probability of success, demands on the family, and so forth. He then sends the parents home to consider their options, proceeding based on their choice when they return.

In spite of this clinical complexity, practitioners need to be familiar with the distinctions between family consultation and family therapy so they can recommend the optimal intervention for a particular family. Some important differences between the interventions are specified in Table 7.1,

TABLE 7.1
DIFFERENCES BETWEEN FAMILY CONSULTATION AND FAMILY THERAPY

	Family Consultation	Family Therapy
Paradigm:	Family competence	Family dysfunction
Professional Role:	Consultant	Therapist
Family Role:	Consultee	Client
Mode:	Collaborative	Authoritarian
Focus of Intervention:	Family agenda	Family system
Goal:	Enhanced coping	Reduced dysfunction
Outcome Measure:	Family satisfaction	Patient improvement
Communication:	Open, direct, and complete	Often partially concealed
Family Status:	Member of treatment team	Focus of treatment plan
Place in Family Service Plan:	Component of service plan	Often sole family service

with emphasis on their use with families that include a member with serious mental illness.[4] First, family consultation is based on a competence paradigm that emphasizes the strengths, resources, and contributions of families. No a priori dysfunction is assumed to exist; rather, the family is presumed to be competent but lacking in knowledge and skills. In contrast, family therapy presupposes the presence of family pathology or relational dysfunction and, by implication, the potential for harm to the patient.

Second, family consultants offer their expert knowledge, skills, and advice to families, who are assisted in setting and attaining goals. Consultation is at the request of the family and should not be imposed by the consultant or the program. Family therapists seek to reduce family dysfunction and to improve family interactions. Such therapy may be strongly recommended as part of the patient's treatment plan or even required by a particular agency.

Third, as consultees, family members determine the nature and scope of the consultative contract and, following the consultation, decide upon a course of action. The autonomy of families is assumed, as is their freedom to accept or reject consultative recommendations. As clients, although the therapeutic contract is also negotiated, families are expected to be receptive to therapeutic recommendations. In the absence of agreement, practitioners may decide to terminate the therapeutic relationship or to make a referral to another clinician.

Fourth, family consultants work collaboratively with families, share knowledge and power with them, and acknowledge their expertise. As Bernheim has expressed it, family consultation implies a "doing with" rather than a "doing to" or even a "doing for."[5] Conversely, family therapists are more likely to assume an authoritarian stance based on their superior knowledge, expertise, and power.

Fifth, the focus of family consultation is the agenda of families themselves, who are coping with a catastrophic stressor. Along with their need to support their relative's treatment and rehabilitation, families have important needs of their own that are reflected in the individualized family service plan. In contrast, family therapy in mental illness generally focuses on the family system. For example, patients are expected to benefit from improvements in family communication and problem solving, which are commonly targeted in family interventions in serious mental illness (see Chapter 8).

Sixth, the goal of family consultation is to enhance the ability of families to cope with mental illness and to meet their own needs under challenging circumstances. The primary goal of family therapy in serious mental illness is typically to facilitate the patient's treatment by decreasing family dysfunction and improving family interactions.

Seventh, a central outcome measure in family consultation is family satisfaction with services designed to address their expressed needs. Other measures are also important, such as those related to family effectiveness. In family therapy, outcome measures usually include patient rate of relapse or rehospitalization. In the past, when family outcomes were assessed, such as family knowledge, skills, or interactions, it was chiefly because these variables were assumed to influence the course of the patient's illness. Reflecting an increased interest in the needs of families themselves, however, recent studies are more likely to include measures of family burden.

Eighth, family consultants communicate openly, directly, and completely with families so as to accomplish the consultative goals. In family therapy, it would be unusual for clinicians to fully inform families about the nature of the therapy and the problems they present for treatment. Moreover, family therapists may have specific, unstated goals, such as decreasing the dependence of the patient on the family.

Ninth, in family consultation, families are seen as formal or informal members of the treatment team who contribute their expertise as essential members of the patient's support system and who expect to play a role in decisions that affect their family. In family therapy, families are viewed as recipients of services, which are typically included in the patient's treatment plan.

Finally, family consultation is only part of a family service plan, which also includes services for the patient and may include other services for families, such as a support group or educational program. Conversely, family therapy is often the sole service offered to families.

The competencies required for family consultation are largely those specified in Chapter 2. In addition to knowledge of serious mental illness and of family concerns, as Bernheim indicates, family consultants need good pedagogical skills: the ability to simplify and synthesize, to organize material and communicate clearly, to tailor teaching pace and techniques as necessary, and to check frequently that what is being taught is what is being learned.[6] Comparing consultative skills to those of a good clinical supervisor, she observes that family consultants need to adapt the amount of direction and the blend of task orientation/emotional support in response to the needs of the consultee.

Family consultation also requires the ability to interact with families in an appropriate manner. Bernheim maintains that a compassionate, engaging, and active style is generally preferable to a distant, formal, and reserved manner. Families have suffered an assault on their self-confidence, self-esteem, and coping effectiveness. They may also have had encounters with professionals who have intensified these problems.

Likewise, families are prone to demoralization and guilt; they can easily misinterpret ambiguous professional behavior as blaming or demeaning. Thus, consultants need to be able to demonstrate warmth, empathy, and support in their effort to gain family trust and to repair their damaged sense of self-efficacy.

Furthermore, consultants need to respect the autonomy of families, who might choose not to follow a recommended course of action. As one practitioner observed, because mental illness is often severe and persistent, it is important to "hang in there for the long haul" with these families.

Dimensions of Family Consultation

Given the diversity among families and provider settings, consultation requires a flexible approach to professional practice. Regardless of its variations, however, family consultation serves two general purposes: to provide direct service to families regarding a wide range of illness-related concerns; and to assist them in making an informed choice regarding their use of other available services. Working directly with families, consultants can offer education about mental illness and its treatment, about caregiving and management issues, and about the mental health system and community resources.

Consultants can also assist families regarding their use of additional services. Describing a particular intervention, practitioners can mention its expected cost, effort, duration, and benefits, which allows families to make a truly informed choice regarding their use of services. The locus of decision making resides with families, who may decide to decline services or defer their use of services; to receive a single service, such as family consultation; or to pursue complementary services, such as an educational or psychoeducational program led by professionals and a family-facilitated support group in the community. In some cases, with the knowledge and consent of the family, family consultants may shift to an alternative role, such as psychotherapist.

Modifying the consultative approach to meet the requirements of individual families, practitioners should consider their needs, resources, and wishes; their life cycle and adaptational phases; and the goals of the specific consultation. Given the severity and persistence of serious mental illness, family consultation is best viewed as an ongoing resource for families that can be tailored to their changing circumstances.

Variables that merit consideration in family consultation include format, frequency, and setting.

FORMAT

The format of family consultation determines the number of family members who are present. Consultative sessions may be provided to the entire family, including the patient; to two or more family members who share a goal or concern; or to an individual member with specific issues and needs. Presence of the entire family might be appropriate when the consultative goal is to learn about the patient's mental illness or treatment plan, to establish household rules, or to develop long-term plans. Family sessions should not be held when the patient is experiencing severe psychotic symptoms or will have difficulty participating in the family dialogue. On the other hand, especially if they are residing at home, patients should be involved in family decisions and plans as fully as possible. For example, patients who are involved in establishing household rules are far more likely to accept and conform to them.

Particularly if they are serving as primary caregivers, parents of an adult child with mental illness may benefit from regular consultative sessions that address their changing needs and concerns. During the early years, parents may profit from a consultative focus on education, skills, and support. In subsequent years, they may have general questions about their role in treatment or specific questions about such matters as symptom management or living arrangements. Aging parents might choose to consult about long-term financial and psychosocial planning that ensures continuity of caregiving for their son or daughter.

Individual family members may also benefit from family consultation, which may offer a welcome opportunity to express feelings or raise personal concerns. As discussed later, spouses, siblings, and offspring have specific issues of their own that may not be addressed in general services for families, which tend to focus on parents.

One family includes two siblings who had not been involved in their sister's care for 3 decades. Following their mother's death, they wanted to play a more active role in her life and attended a family consultation session. The consultant helped them develop a family service plan that reflected the current and long-term needs of their sister, the physical decline of their aging father, and their own responsibilities as siblings who resided outside the area. When I recently spoke with the patient, she commented on the "wonderful" support she was receiving from her family.

One task of family consultants is to assist families in assigning roles to individual members, in reassigning responsibilities as their circumstances change, and in making best use their sessions. In a given family, for instance, a single member—typically a caregiving mother—might meet with the consultant and keep other family members informed, perhaps supplemented by occasional sessions with one or more additional family members.

FREQUENCY

As Amenson has discussed, the frequency of family consultations is highly variable.[7] Single-session consultations might occur when there has been a request for a second opinion about the diagnosis or treatment recommendations, or when a family requires assistance with a specific problem or needs reassurance that they are acting appropriately. Based on his extensive experience as a consultant, he observes that many families repeatedly but infrequently use single-session consultations as issues arise over time.

Some consultations involve several sessions that focus on one or a few goals or that provide supervised practice as the family develops a new skill or pattern of dealing with their relative. The frequency and duration of these consultations need to fit the family's concerns as well as their learning style and pace. Amenson cautions that the request for frequent family sessions (e.g., weekly sessions for more than 2 months) may indicate that the boundary between consultation and treatment has been crossed. As he indicates, this shift in roles and methods should be done only with the understanding and consent of the family.

Given the severity and persistence of serious mental illness, family consultation is generally best offered on an ongoing and as-needed basis. Following the initial diagnosis or during periods of crisis or inpatient treatment, families may make greater use of this service. Once families have learned to cope effectively with the mental illness, they may request single or multiple sessions to deal with targeted problems or with long-term concerns. The availability of a continuing relationship with an informed and empathic practitioner can be an enormously valuable resource for families under these circumstances.

SETTING

Family consultation may vary somewhat across provider settings. Families that are seen in inpatient settings may be dealing with the initial hospitalization and diagnosis or with a rehospitalization following a relapse or crisis. In either case, the family's distress is likely to be significant, which will in turn focus the consultative session on their emotional needs. In contrast, families that receive consultation in conjunction with the patient's day treatment, outpatient, rehabilitation, or case management services are more likely to be dealing with ongoing concerns, with knowledge and skills development, with specific problems, or with long-term planning. Having weathered their earlier crises and resolved some of their feelings of grief and loss, these families may be able to articulate their needs and to set their agenda with greater clarity. Thus, in comparison with families whose services are tied to the patient's inpatient treatment, consultations with these families are likely to differ in both content and process.

Similarly, the roles of family consultants will vary depending on whether they offer family services as a member of the patient's treatment team at an agency or as an independent practitioner, and on whether the services are home-based or provider-based. As Bernheim has discussed, agency-based consultants often assume multiple roles as treatment team members, as family advocates, and perhaps as consultants to other agencies.[8] These practitioners need to establish the nature of their consultative relationship with the family and to assist them in deciding who will participate in developing the family service plan, who will represent the family in communicating with the treatment team, and when to include the patient.

Bernheim considers the family consultant to be an ombudsman or advocate for the family, whose opinions may otherwise be neither sought nor seriously considered by the patient's treatment team. Consequently, consultants may need to encourage the team to consider the needs, wishes, and priorities of the family in treatment planning. These professionals may also be involved in deciding when to offer multifamily group sessions, when to provide home-based rather than agency-based services, and how family services will be funded.

Although independent practitioners deal with fewer systemic concerns, they may also assume different professional roles and responsibilities. For example, they may offer family consultation as sole practitioners or as a members of multidisciplinary group; and they may offer consultation to families as primary clients or in conjunction with their relative's treatment.

Variations in Family Consultation

Let us consider four approaches to family consultation: family-oriented consultation, patient-oriented consultation, and two agency-based approaches. In addition to consultation, all of the following providers offer a range of other services. All also have frequent contact with families through their work as advocates and members of NAMI, which serves as a source of referrals.

FAMILY-ORIENTED CONSULTATION

June Husted is a psychologist who has served both as a clinician/administrator for an outpatient psychiatric program at a Department of Veterans Affairs medical center and as an independent practitioner.[9] Based on her experience with both agency-based and independent family consultation, Husted considers the former to be far more effective. For example, the agency staff becomes well acquainted with patients and can discuss with them the benefits of having their families involved. Rarely in her 24 years at the medical center did she have a patient refuse to sign a release form permitting the staff to share information with the family.

In addition, working with both patients and families increases the information available to staff and provides a more thorough picture of patient's history and illness and of the family's needs and concerns. Furthermore, important information regarding the patient's changing condition can be incorporated into the treatment and rehabilitation plan. Families might reveal reactions to medication, problems with treatment adherence, family stressors that affect the patient, or unacceptable behaviors that might benefit from intervention.

Finally, the needs of families themselves can also be addressed. At the V.A. center, families were regularly invited to meet with their relative and the staff throughout the patient's treatment, were referred to local NAMI affiliates, and were sometimes offered family education classes. Illustrating her work as an agency-based consultant, Husted shared the following encounter:

The parents came into my office with frustrated, angry looks on their faces, escorting their decompensating son. "It's been hell living with him these past 20 years," his mother exclaimed, as if it were his fault. I acknowledged how horrible it is for the patient and the family to live with this brain disorder and educated them about schizophrenia. The mother looked stunned by the realization that many of his behaviors were symptoms of the illness, not volitional behaviors. The change in the family's response to him, as well as a modification of his medication suggested by their description of the pattern of his illness, had a major impact on his improvement. In later months, I learned that their family relationships had improved significantly and that their son was now included in family dinners and celebrations.[10]

In contrast to agency-based consultation, an independent practitioner may see a family member under two different circumstances. In the first situation, family members seek therapy for personal problems but may be unaware of the role of the illness in these problems or its impact on other aspects of their lives. Citing adult siblings and offspring, Husted remarks that these clients may benefit from education about the familial consequences of mental illness and from an opportunity to resolve some of the unfinished business that remains.

In the second situation, the role of the family consultant is often more difficult, because the family is likely to seek a special appointment under the most extreme circumstances. It is also more frustrating, because the consultant is likely to have no input into treatment decisions. Moreover, given the time-limited focus of most consultations, independent practitioners may not learn the outcome of the consultation. In spite of these limitations, however, independent consultation offers significant benefits for families, as Husted's cases illustrate:

Family 1. *I met with aging parents who strongly disagreed about moving their daughter (who had schizophrenia) out of their home, despite her unwillingness or inability to comply with household rules. The parents were faced with their daughter's unkempt grooming, messy surroundings, and uncooperativeness, but feared for her well-being if they did not meet her basic needs. Their daughter's psychiatrist would not speak with them or offer alternative solutions or medications. As a consultant, I helped them see the pros and cons of different actions, educated them about the benefits available to their daughter, discussed with them the probable advantages of her participation in a rehabilitation program, and clarified their fears and frustrations. But the choices were theirs, and they seemed locked in the status quo.*

Family 2. *I also offered consultation to a father and sister of a man who was currently hospitalized. Both family members had been attacked at different times by their relative. The mother had died (possibly related to the stress of being the caregiver); the family was without financial resources; and the patient refused to take medication. Yet these family members still felt an obligation to keep their relative in their home and to placate him by complying with his every wish. I educated the father and sister regarding the benefits available to the patient. I also painstakingly outlined the process they should follow to ensure that the department of mental health took responsibility for assigning a public guardian, selecting a group home placement, and securing Supplemental Security Insurance (SSI) benefits for the patient.*

The well sibling appeared on the verge of collapse herself, both financially and emotionally, and I was concerned that she would be unable to take any action. The next day, after mailing a summary of the procedures we had discussed, I phoned to alert her that the summary was coming and was relieved to learn she had followed through. She had already visited the hospital and insisted on a public guardian for her brother as well as a placement following his discharge. The sibling also started attending a local NAMI group to get some personal support.

Family 3. I met several times with a family in which the father had a difficult time accepting his son's schizophrenia and was constantly pressuring the son to do more to obtain regular employment. I educated the family about the limitations that resulted from the illness, taught the father some ways he could positively reinforce his son's efforts and progress, and resolved some areas of family conflict. There was no feedback on the resolution of these issues, but a year later I was pleased to see the family participating in a special reception for a job program for people with serious mental illness. The son was a successful participant.

Family 4. In another case, I received a call from a psychologist whose son had been diagnosed with schizophrenia. The son persistently declined medication and was extremely paranoid. Because the psychologist lived an hour away, I offered consultation by telephone, discussing the patient's symptoms, his lack of adherence to treatment recommendations, and his response to prior medications. I also sent informational brochures on schizophrenia and on the newer medications, suggesting that the material be shared with her son and that he be involved in treatment decisions. The son agreed to try one of the new medication. On Christmas day, I had a message from the psychologist: "Thank you! I feel like I have my son back!"

PATIENT-ORIENTED CONSULTATION

Martin Willick is a psychiatrist and psychoanalyst who has an independent practice as well as an affiliation with the College of Physicians and Surgeons at Columbia University.[11] He brings a wide range of experience to his practice, including expertise regarding the role of psychotherapy in the treatment of schizophrenia. As a matter of course, he recommends that practitioners involve the family in the treatment process, as long as they have the patient's consent. He acknowledges that some patients insist that their therapist not speak to the family for various reasons, ranging from legitimate fears of intrusion to paranoid ideas about parents and siblings. In most cases, however, patients are willing to have their families involved.

Working with the families of his patients, Willick assists them in navigating illness-related problems and conflicts and in understanding what mental illness is, what its symptoms are, and what they can do to reduce the possibilities of relapse. Illustrating his patient-oriented approach to consultation, he described his ongoing work with one patient over a period of 7 years. At the onset of treatment, the patient had recently been hospitalized following a suicide attempt. He was living at home with his parents and working at odd jobs, although not always holding them. He was beset with psychotic symptoms, including auditory hallucinations and ideas of reference; responded to stressful situations with extraordinary fatigue; was unable to concentrate or even to read a few paragraphs in a music magazine, an area of interest; and could hardly play his guitar, which used to afford him pleasure.

During the course of therapy, the patient has been stabilized on clozaril and lithium, experiencing considerable functional improvement in the quality of his life. For the past 4 years, he has held a job at an office supply retail store; he has gradually received raises but has been unable to move into a supervisory capacity. Three years ago, he moved to his own apartment. After two unsuccessful relationships, he has been married for a year to a woman who seems reasonably healthy and stable. In spite of this progress, significant residual difficulties remain, including problems in concentration, exceptional fatigue in response to stress, and chronic worry that other people will get angry with him.

Recounting his roles in this case, Willick notes that he has been his patient's beacon of reality, his concrete helper, his reliable physician, his understanding and sympathetic friend, and someone his patient has called almost every day for a reality check. During the course of treatment, he has also offered consultation to the patient's mother and stepfather, and more recently, to his wife. At the beginning, he educated them (as he had his patient) about schizophrenia and offered concrete assistance with their concerns: how much they should expect of their relative, how much they should demand, what they could expect for his future. Sometimes, the patient was included in family sessions designed to work out positive ways for dealing with family interactions.

Thus, although his primary professional relationship was with his patient, Willick established an ongoing consultative relationship with the family designed to address their concerns and to assist them in supporting their relative's treatment and recovery.

Agency-Based Consultation: A Multimodal Program

Christopher Amenson is a psychologist who serves as Director of Pacific Clinics Institute, the professional and family education division of Pacific Clinics, a community mental health center in the San Gabriel Valley (suburban Los Angeles).[12] His program offers a wide array of services to both patients and families. A provider of family education since 1981, Amenson has developed a range of outstanding resources for family practitioners, including a family education curriculum series with accompanying handbooks, a lecture series, written materials, and videotapes. Several direct services are offered to families, including consultation, education, psychoeducation, and psychotherapy. Thus, in addition to consultation, the agency also offers many of the family services described in Chapters 8 and 9.

Limited resources and strong community need have led Amenson to a hierarchical approach to educating families. All families are initially referred to a 7-week basic class or to written material or videotapes. This class, "Surviving and Thriving When a Family Member has a Mental Illness," focuses on schizophrenia and covers the following topics: schizophrenia, a brain disease; research into causes, courses, and treatment; medication and compliance; preventing and managing crises; helpful family roles and skills; psychosocial rehabilitation; and motivation toward realistic goals. Two additional sessions focus on controlling major depressive and bipolar disorders.

Amenson compares his hierarchical approach to clinical training. A few natural therapists take clinical courses and immediately implement the techniques with great skill. Most clinicians require supervised practice over time; and a few require extra supervision. Likewise, the basic class may be sufficient for those families (approximately one-fifth) who already have good interpersonal and problem solving skills but need assistance in applying these skills to serious mental illness. A majority of families (more than three-fourths) also receive supervised practice in the specific coping skills associated with positive outcomes for the entire family, which they can obtain in a 6- to-12-month seminar.

In light of their continuing problems, a minority of these families (about one-fifth) subsequently participate in individual family psychoeducation. A small number of families (around 5%) manifest significant dysfunction that represents a threat to the patient's recovery. Because their needs are not met through group or individual family education, these families are referred for individual, marital, or family therapy when appropriate. This program of training is supplemented by individual family consultation, which is offered as needed for families who are dealing with a recent onset or current crisis.

In addition to direct services to families, Amenson offers extensive professional training concerned with family-focused services. These services and a wide range of professional issues are described in *Education, Consultation, and Treatment of Families of the Mentally Ill.* The manual includes 26 chapters that cover introductory material; processes involved in family intervention (e.g., education, support, consultation, family therapy); contents (e.g., information, skills, attitudes); special populations (e.g., mood disorders, dual diagnosis); and professional and family reading lists.

Among Amenson's continuing education programs for professionals is a 3-day schizophrenia conference that covers treatment, recovery, and family interventions. He has developed materials for family education courses. His curriculum, *Schizophrenia: A Family Education Curriculum,* consists of 159 slides and a page of lecture notes to accompany each slide. The curriculum is paired with a handbook, *Schizophrenia: Family Education Methods,* that includes four sections: introduction, research and theoretical bases, structure and process considerations, and issues and exercises for a basic class. A second curriculum focuses on family skills and skill training methods.

Amenson also offers courses for professionals who provide family education. The curriculum consists of three levels of courses that are offered sequentially. Level I consists of a 7-week basic skills course that covers the knowledge and skills needed to approach families in a constructive manner and that provides an overview of education, skills training, and consultation. Level II involves a six-session biweekly application seminar that provides the intermediate-level skills required to teach family educational classes. Trainees are expected to develop and teach a family class during the session, based on this family education curriculum for schizophrenia.

Level III consists of a six-session biweekly technical assistance seminar that teaches advanced individual and group family psychoeducational interventions. Participants are expected to teach an advanced family psychoeducational class based on Amenson's curriculum and skill training methods. A series of advanced curricula for multifamily courses is being developed to deal with specific family concerns, including treatment adherence, dual diagnosis (substance abuse), relapse prevention, persistent symptoms, family relationships, and motivation for recovery.

AGENCY-BASED CONSULTATION: A TEAM APPROACH

Working at the Training and Consultation (T. E. C.) Network in Philadelphia, family therapist Edie Mannion and family member Marilyn Meisel regularly offer general coping skills workshops for family members, as well as specialized workshops for spouses (see Chapter 15).[13] In conjunction with their workshops, they have been offering individual consultative sessions to families of adults with mental illness for the past 10 years. Their approach to consultation is embodied in "The Three Fs":

- FEELINGS (providing empathy and emotional support)
- FOCUSING (clarifying the family's current agenda)
- FINDING (facilitating the family's current agenda)

During the FEELINGS phase, consultants-in-training are encouraged to empathize with family consultees in a very specific way. Namely, the consultative goal is to *normalize and support* the emotional responses of families. In contrast to reflective listening ("You sound angry"), consultants are coached to make responses such as "I'd be angry too if that happened to me"; "It must have been awful when that happened"; or "It's only natural to feel the way you're feeling." The objective is to increase the likelihood that family members will feel understood and respected by the consultant.

Mannion and Meisel have found that families are often overwhelmed with questions and concerns by the time they speak to a family consultant. During the FOCUSING phase, consultants can help families to organize their agenda by prioritizing their needs. For example, a consultant might say: "There are so many issues that need to be addressed. You've mentioned [list concerns]. Which of these would you like to focus on first?" The consultant can express an opinion about the relative importance or urgency of various concerns, while making it clear that the priorities of the family will determine which issue is pursued first. Once the family agrees on a top priority (and this may require mediation if family members are not in agreement), the consultant needs to learn *how* or *why* that particular problem is significant. For example, in prioritizing their son's refusal to continue in his day program, one set of parents explained that this behavior has been an early sign of relapse in the past.

The FINDING phase includes any strategy that might address or resolve the top concern. Consultants should ask about the family's prior efforts to address the concern in order to learn more about any underlying issues, such as unacknowledged grief, and to avoid repeating unsuccessful strategies. FINDING can involve many activities, including (a) providing relevant information; (b) brainstorming about possible solutions with the family; (c) developing and role playing family and personal action plans; (d) providing grief counseling; (e) offering mediation to resolve problems with providers, their relative, or other family members; (f) referring the family to a specialized person, agency, or support group that can address their particular need; and (g) referring or contracting for therapy if the consultant is convinced that more intensive intervention is required.

Their consultation service is available to families on an as-needed basis through telephone or face-to-face appointments. The former can be provided more quickly, an advantage during a crisis. There is much variability among families in their use of the service. Some families, particularly those in crisis or new to the diagnosis, may request regular weekly or biweekly sessions for a period of time; months or years later, they may return when faced with a new crisis or concern. Other families may use only one or two consultations before moving on to access other resources. Mannion and Meisel stress the importance of continuity, flexibility, and accessibility in working with these families. There is evidence that this consultative approach enhances feelings of self-efficacy among family members, who report increased confidence in their ability to understand and manage the mental illness of their relative.[14]

The T. E. C. Network is a funded program, which has allowed Mannion and Meisel to offer family consultation to a large number of families. Agencies that are dependent on insurance reimbursement from managed care organizations face several challenges in providing this family intervention. Typically, providers are reimbursed for only a limited number of family sessions, which must be billed as family therapy. In light of the distinctions between family consultation and family therapy noted earlier, this requirement may misrepresent the content and process of intervention. Additional problems include low annual behavioral health care benefits and lifetime limits, as well as the requirement of face-to-face sessions. Until these challenges are overcome, providers and family members will need to be creative in negotiating these barriers to the accessibility of family consultation.

In spite of their differences, all four approaches to family consultation offer an initial intervention that is likely to be appropriate for most families who are coping with serious mental illness. Provided on an ongoing and as-needed basis, this intervention may be sufficient for some families. Other families may benefit from additional services, either singly or in combination, such as a family support group, a family educational or psychoeducational program, or psychotherapy for one or more members. These family interventions are discussed in the following two chapters.

From Theory to Practice

Let's return now to Sharon Vaccaro, as she develops and implements a family consultation program for her multidisciplinary group practice. Initially, she works to establish consultative relationships with families, ensuring that they understand the distinction between family consultation and family therapy. Next, she meets with each family to determine the appropriate format, frequency, and setting for their consultative sessions; to formulate an individualized family service plan that prioritizes and addresses their needs; and to establish procedures for periodically reviewing and modifying their service plan.

Shifting to the actual sessions, Sharon must to be prepared to deal with the concerns likely to arise in professional practice with these families. In his training manual, Amenson lists family ratings in order of their educational priorities.[15] The top 15 (in rank order) are: helping the patient develop realistic goals, motivating the patient, communicating with the patient, making the home environment therapeutic, getting the patient to accept medication and treatment, pursuing realistic employment possibilities, coping with substance abuse, predicting and preventing relapse, increasing acceptance of the illness by family and friends, dealing with their own anger and frustration, deciding how protective to be, helping the patient manage stress, financing living expenses and treatment, and designing a rehabilitation program at home. It is noteworthy that families also mentioned many other concerns related to their relative's symptoms, their own reactions to the illness, and the mental health system. Thus, a wide range of consultative foci may arise in professional practice.

One common concern is the need to set reasonable limits for a patient with mental illness. Consider, for example, the parents of a woman with bipolar disorder who, during a manic phase, spends money beyond her means. In the past, her parents have always "bailed out" their daughter. Although the parents recognize that their rescue efforts might prevent their daughter from assuming responsibility for her illness, they are concerned that she will end up on the street, in jail, or worse. Following family consultation, these parents might decide to set reasonable limits (e.g., no longer rescuing their daughter), and to discuss alternatives with her, such as cancelling all charge cards and having a bank establish a limited-access account that restricts the amount of money available on a weekly basis. Once that money has been spent, the parents might provide food and other essentials, but not cash.

Residential arrangements are also a frequent focus of family consultation. This issue has been addressed by Kim Mueser and Susan Gingerich in *Coping with Schizophrenia* and by Rebecca Woolis in *When Someone You Love has a Mental Illness*.[16] As both books point out, there is no single answer to the question of whether an adult son or daughter with mental illness should reside at home. Many families and professionals have found that all members of the family do best when the relative with mental illness resides separately and the family continues to have contact and offer support. Given their particular circumstances, however, each family must decide what is best.

Here is a consultative session with Frank and Nancy McDermit, whose daughter Linda has resided at home since her schizophrenia was diagnosed more than a decade ago:

PRACTITIONER: *Hello, I'm Sharon Vaccaro. Based on your phone call, I imagine you're under considerable stress. Living with an adult son or daughter who has schizophrenia can be enormously draining for parents. How can I be helpful?*

FATHER: *Things have really gotten out of control at home. Linda has been living with us all of her life, except for a brief period when she lived away at college just before her first hospitalization. Until this year, at least she was going to her day program and taking her medication. But now she often refuses to go, and I'm sure she has stopped taking her pills. And she's drinking again, both at the local bars and even at home. I can't live like this.*

MOTHER: *I agree with Frank—it's become intolerable at home. It feels like we have no life at all. When we try to talk to Linda, she just screams at us and locks herself in her room. But I don't want to put her out on the street. Who knows what might happen to her. What can we do?*

PRACTITIONER: *Sounds as if you've both been pushed to your limit. Often, when parents are caring for a son or daughter with mental illness, the issue of living arrangements comes up. It's frequently hard to know what's best. We can start with the question of what's best for Linda and for both of you.*

MOTHER: *Our present situation isn't good for any of us! Certainly, Linda isn't getting any better. And we're both on the verge of collapse. Often she's up all night—sometimes I'm almost too tired to go to work.*

FATHER: *Linda doesn't seem to have any friends except the people she sees at the local bars. And that can't be good for her.*

PRACTITIONER: *No, I'm sure that isn't helpful. Alcohol usually makes the symptoms of schizophrenia worse. And it may trigger a relapse. Have you tried to talk to Linda about her drinking?*

MOTHER: *Not recently—it's just too stressful. She won't listen to us at all and responds with anger. It's easier to avoid talking about it.*

FATHER: *When we do try to talk with Linda, all of us end up more upset. It's not worth it. We really need to find another place for her to live.*

PRACTITIONER: *It does sound that way. I'll do my best to help you. Initially, we need to determine what community resources are available for Linda, such as case management or supported housing.*

FATHER: *I'm not sure about community resources. Linda receives disability payments and does have a case manager, although I don't think she has much contact with him. I don't even know who he is. And I have no idea what other housing is available.*

PRACTITIONER: *Given Linda's situation, there may be several possibilities for her. For example, she may be eligible for supported housing, such as a group home or supervised apartment. I'll learn more about these programs before we meet again.*

MOTHER: *We both work and have some money saved for our retirement. So we can help out a bit. But we don't have a lot of money. Is that a problem?*

PRACTITIONER: *I don't think so. Because Linda receives disability payments, she should be eligible for these programs without cost.*

FATHER: *That's a relief. We were worried we'd have to use up all of our savings, which really don't amount to much.*

PRACTITIONER: *With careful planning, your savings shouldn't be at risk. But we need to learn more about the best financial arrangements for your family. Here is the name of a contact person in the county who can give you some information on Linda's eligibility for services. Then we can see how you want to proceed regarding housing.*

MOTHER: *You know, the more I think about it, the more convinced I am that Linda should live on her own. We're not going to be around forever. What will she do after we're gone?*

PRACTITIONER: *That's a realistic question. Often, the best guarantee of a secure future for an adult with mental illness is a history of independent living in the community before aging parents become unable to provide caregiving.*

FATHER: *That makes sense. We hope you can help us make other arrangements. I'm not sure how long I can take this.*

PRACTITIONER: *Nancy, how do you feel?*

MOTHER: *I agree with Frank. But I do worry about Linda. She's not going to like moving. And I know she's going to be upset—I don't want to see her back in the hospital.*

PRACTITIONER: *I can understand your concern. Change is difficult for all of us, but especially for someone with mental illness. Sounds as if you've decided what you want to do, so let's develop a plan. I can work with you as we proceed. As soon as we learn about the available, we can talk about the best way to present your decision to Linda. It's important to explain your reasons and to make it clear that the decision is not negotiable, while listening sympathetically to Linda's concerns and assuring her of your continued support. It's likely to be an extremely demanding meeting for all of you.*

MOTHER: *I have no idea how Linda will react. In spite of our problems, we've really been her only source of support. And I don't want to abandon her.*

PRACTITIONER: *Yes, you have been her major resource. And, whatever your decision, it's important to assure Linda that she has your love and support. It's also important to give her time to adjust to your decision and to become involved in planning for other living arrangements. After you have told Linda of your decision, it may be best to plan for a second family meeting to give her time to adjust to the idea of moving out.*

FATHER: *Actually, I'm not sure we can handle this without help. What if she's been drinking or starts screaming at us?*

PRACTITIONER: *Those are reasonable questions. I can offer to meet with the three of you if you think that would be helpful. We can also consult* with members of Linda's treatment team, who may able to offer suggestions and support your decision. And I have another suggestion. There is a local chapter of NAMI, the mental health organization for families. It might be helpful for you to talk with other families who have been through the same situation. Their support and advice may be very useful under these circumstances.

MOTHER: *I've heard of NAMI, but we've never contacted them. This might be a good time.*

PRACTITIONER: *Most families find the organization helpful. Our time is nearly up, so let's begin as follows. I'll obtain more information about community housing before we meet next week. You can follow up on Linda's eligibility for other services and the financial implications for your family. In the meantime, you can think more about your decision and how to present it to Linda. When we meet, we can decide what to do next.*

CHAPTER 8

Family Intervention Strategies: Information, Skills, and Support

Anna Wang is an advanced practice psychiatric nurse who plans to establish her own comprehensive center for the treatment and rehabilitation of patients with serious mental illness. The center will offer a range of services for patients and their family members. Planning the specific kinds of family-focused services that should be included, she thinks of the diverse families she has known over the years. Anna recalls the Webers, a strong and effective family that chose to participate in a family support and advocacy group; the Riveras, a close, working-class family that benefited from family education; the Murphys, a volatile family that was helped by family psychoeducation; and Ellen Raimondo, a widowed parent of an adult son with mental illness, who was able to work though her paralyzing feelings of grief and loss in individual therapy. Thinking of both their common and diverse needs, Anna plans to include a range of consultative, supportive, educational, psychoeducational, and psychotherapeutic services in her new program. But first she needs to learn more about the most effective family interventions.

Anna is aware that a comprehensive treatment and rehabilitation center should offer an array of interventions for both patients and families that can be tailored to their specific needs, desires, and resources. This chapter describes a range of family interventions that provide potential benefits for families.

As Phyllis Solomon has observed, over the past 2 decades, interventions for families of adults with serious mental illness, particularly schizophrenia, have proliferated.[1] Several factors that have stimulated this development, including concerns about the minimal effect of psychotropic medication on negative symptoms and social functioning;

research evidence that the course of schizophrenia is influenced by the patient's social environment; and—most important—the fact that families became de facto caregivers for adults with mental illness but lacked the requisite knowledge, skills, and resources for this role.

Following a review of some general considerations, three family interventions are considered: family support and advocacy groups, family education, and family psychoeducation. These supportive and educational services are the initial interventions of choice for most families. Some family members may also benefit from more intensive intervention, including psychotherapy, which is discussed in Chapter 9.

General Considerations

The family interventions to be explored reflect a shift in perspective from the family as a cause of mental illness to the family as a source of support. Acknowledging the supportive role of families, practitioners can intervene to assist them in carrying out their caregiving functions, which will in turn enhance the recovery of the patient. In fact, many family interventions focus largely or exclusively on this caregiving role. For caring families, improvements in their relative's functioning and quality of life are likely to have a commensurate impact on their own lives.

In addition to their need for effective caregiving, however, families have needs of their own. They need to resolve their emotional burden, to preserve the integrity of their own lives, and to fulfill their personal hopes and dreams. Family interventions that focus primarily on their supportive role may ignore other important individual and family needs. From a family systems perspective, the goal is to assist families in strengthening their family unit and in finding a balance that can meet the needs of all family members. Certainly, over the long term, this goal cannot be met by a narrow patient-oriented focus.

Each of the family interventions to be considered has particular strengths and calls for different skills and resources, although they share a number of common features.[2]

COMMON FEATURES

Effective family interventions incorporate the principles of professional practice with families already discussed. These include approaching families with respect, compassion, and sensitivity to the catastrophic impact of serious mental illness; maintaining a family systems perspective designed to address the needs of all members of the family; applying a competency paradigm that acknowledges their strengths and resources; developing a collaborative partnership that builds on the expertise and contributions of patients, families, and professionals; and encouraging a sense of hopefulness for the future.

Family interventions should also reflect current thinking regarding serious mental illness and family interventions. For example, it is essential for practitioners to:

- Avoid assuming that the family environment is implicated in the etiology of mental illness
- Reduce destructive family blame and guilt, thus freeing family energy for adaptation
- Incorporate research findings concerned with family needs, family perception of services, and family interventions
- Aim for an individualized family service plan that provides an appropriate mix of consultation, support, education, skills training, and therapy
- Focus initially on current issues and concerns, while avoiding intensive exploration of individual or family dynamics
- Titrate family services over time to simultaneously provide necessary assistance and foster family autonomy

The ultimate goal is to assist families in acquiring the knowledge, skills, and resources that will enable them to meet their own needs.

MEETING FAMILY NEEDS

Family interventions are not likely to be effective—or used—unless they address the expressed needs of families. Researchers have consistently found that the central needs of families are for information, skills, and support. Table 8.1 presents results of research with a large national sample of NAMI members who were asked to identify the frequency with which they used particular resources and to evaluate the relative value of each resource.[3] Consistent with other research findings, utilization and evaluation were highest for those resources that address family needs for information (e.g., lectures and books), skills (e.g., coping skills workshops), and support (e.g., a support group).[4]

Accordingly, all effective interventions satisfy—in varying degrees—the needs of families for information, skills, support, and resolution of their emotional burden. A wide range of services may benefit families, including educational programs, skills-oriented workshops, support groups,

TABLE 8.1
FAMILY EVALUATION OF RESOURCES ($N = 3099$)

Resource	Percent Using the Resource	Percent Perceiving Some or Great Value
Lectures and books	75%	96%
Classes/workshops	21	96
Support group	76	95
Friends	71	90
Relatives	72	84
Individual therapy	61	77
Group therapy	35	68
Family therapy	33	61
Clergy	42	58

and advocacy opportunities, along with resource libraries, written materials, videotapes, and newsletters. For example, in one study researchers conducted telephone interviews with 778 family members whose relatives were receiving publicly funded services for serious mental illness. A lower level of psychological distress was reported by family caregivers who developed collaborative relationships with their relative's providers, who received information and advice from professionals, and whose relatives received more mental health services.[5]

Involving families in the design, implementation, and evaluation of services increases the likelihood that families will find these services responsive to their needs and will choose to participate. Moreover, services can benefit from the involvement of family members as consultants, facilitators, or presenters, either alone or in collaboration with professionals.

Supportive and educational family interventions offer substantial benefits for families and for patients. Benefits for families include increased understanding and acceptance of mental illness, more realistic expectations, improved family relationships, enhanced coping effectiveness, reduced stigma and isolation, and a greater sense of hopefulness. Similarly, patients may benefit from a more constructive family environment, increased knowledge of available resources, family support of the treatment and rehabilitation plan, reduced risk of relapse, and improvements in the mental health system.

As the initial interventions of choice, supportive and educational services are likely to meet the needs of most families. Given the diversity among family members, however, some may also benefit from traditional clinical services, including individual, marital, or family therapy. Thus, the family interventions discussed in this chapter might be considered as necessary for all families, but insufficient for some.

DIFFERENCES AMONG FAMILY INTERVENTIONS

Although sharing many common features, effective family interventions also differ in some important respects.[6] These include:

- Their relative emphasis on support, information, and skills
- Their format, which may involve individual families or multifamily groups
- Their inclusion or exclusion of patients
- Their mode of facilitation or presentation, which may involve professionals, family members, or a professional-family team
- Their setting, which may be the family's home, a mental health agency, or a community organization
- Their frequency, duration, and intensity
- The patient's phase of illness at the onset of the program
- The family's phase of adaptation

For some families, these differences may be of particular importance. For example, a given family may strongly prefer to meet individually with a practitioner, may require home-based services, may be unable to participate in frequent or prolonged interventions, or may have particular developmental concerns, such as continuity of caregiving among aging parents. An initial consultative session can allow practitioners to respond to these requirements.[7]

THE INTERVENTION PROCESS

As Christopher Amenson has pointed out, families often require time and practice to master the range of necessary skills.[8] He cautions practitioners to remember that families do not choose to learn these skills, that the skills do not necessarily fit their basic talents, and that the illness creates tremendous family stress, which in turn can impede new learning. From an adaptational perspective, families can be helped to understand the catastrophic impact of mental illness on families, to relinquish or modify their unsuccessful coping efforts, and to develop more effective skills and strategies.

Amenson recommends that the principles of adult education inform family interventions. As they proceed to a new level of competence, adult learners often go through a period of relative incompetence during which they discard established attitudes and behaviors. Practitioners can assist families in maintaining their overall sense of competence as they experiment with new skills. Using a nutrition analogy, Amenson encourages practitioners to provide a balanced diet of consultation, support, education, skill building, and therapy, mixing these ingredients in creative ways to match an endless variety of circumstances.

Illustrating these general principles of professional practice, three family interventions are discussed: family support and advocacy groups, family education, and family psychoeducation. There is some empirical support for all of these interventions, particularly family psychoeducation.[9] Representative examples of each are presented.

Family Support and Advocacy Groups

Making use of community resources, practitioners can regularly make referrals to advocacy organizations such as NAMI or one of its more than 1,000 local affiliates. Especially at the onset of their relative's mental illness, families are burdened and distressed, at a loss for information, and greatly in need of support. NAMI was created by families to respond to these needs. Family support and advocacy groups serve three important functions.

1. They provide essential support to families through member-facilitated group sessions and informal networking. Contacts with others foster the normalization of family experiences and offer opportunities to learn from experienced family members, to obtain practical suggestions for daily coping, and to enhance self-esteem through helping others.

2. These groups offer educational programs through local NAMI affiliates and at state and national conventions. In many communities, NAMI chapters provide the Family-to-Family Education Program (formerly Journey of Hope), a comprehensive family education and support program that has now reached thousands of families.

3. Family groups encourage advocacy, as members join forces to work for improved services, expanded research, and new social priorities and policies. Harriet Lefley has observed that advocacy activities can be an extremely therapeutic intervention for depressed or demoralized

family members. Once their essential needs for information, skills, and support have been largely satisfied, families may want to assume advocacy roles:

They want to do something—to eradicate mental illness, to change the system, to provide needed services, to fight stigma, to obtain a better quality of life for their loved ones. It is at this level that participation in an advocacy movement often becomes personally therapeutic as well as socially constructive. Action gives meaning and validity to families formerly preoccupied with tragedy. It changes the central core of their lives from one of misery to one of mission and purpose.[10]

In addition to advocacy opportunities, family-facilitated services have a number of advantages. Such services are likely to be relatively inexpensive, because they are usually offered by volunteers; to be responsive to the needs of families, because they are family-driven; and to enhance the sense of family empowerment, because such groups often have a strong advocacy component. Evaluating the 12-week NAMI Family-to-Family Education Program, one participant wrote:

It was a stroke of genius to use people as teachers who have mentally ill family members. Not only could they contribute ideas and knowledge from their own experience, but they could understand what class members were going through. All that plus their training made them ideal for leading the course.[11]

Similarly affirming the value of a NAMI support group, a family member wrote: "The group has been like a beacon, providing me with information, support, and understanding."[12]

Family Education

Families have a compelling need for information about mental illness and its treatment, about caregiving and management issues, and about the mental health system and community resources. Working with multiple families, practitioners can meet their educational needs through a variety of formats.[13] For example, Carol Anderson and her colleagues have designed a day-long Survival Skills Workshop that includes information on the nature of serious mental illness (etiology, prevalence, course, personal experience); on pharmacological and psychosocial treatment; on the family and mental illness (family reactions to the illness, needs of the patient and the family); and on family coping skills and strategies.[14]

More extended educational programs for families can also be offered by family members (as in the Family-to-Family Education Program), by professionals, or by a professional-family member team. The 10-week educational program in Table 8.2 is appropriate for family members whose relatives have recently received a diagnosis of schizophrenia or a mood disorder.[15] The format can easily be modified to meet the requirements of different providers, settings, and diagnostic groups.

Weekly sessions lasting 1½ hours can include a mix of didactic material, videotapes, and handouts, as well as an opportunity for social interaction. For example, a session might be structured as follows: welcome and overview (10 min.); formal presentation (30 min.); questions, discussion, and applications (30 min.); and socializing (20 min.).

TABLE 8.2
10-WEEK FAMILY EDUCATION PROGRAM

A Family Education Program

Week 1. Nature and Purpose of Program
Introductions; overview of program; written survey of family members

Week 2. Family-Professional Relationships
Collaboration; roles and responsibilities; channels of communication

Week 3. Mental Illness I
Schizophrenia (etiology, symptoms, treatment, prognosis)

Week 4. Mental Illness II
Bipolar disorder and major depression (etiology, symptoms, treatment, prognosis)

Week 5. The Family Experience
Family burden and needs; life span perspectives; family roles

Week 6. Stress, Coping, and Adaptation
A catastrophic stressor; family adaptation; coping resources and strategies

Week 7. Enhancing Personal and Family Effectiveness I
Communication; problem solving; illness management; relapse prevention; health maintenance

Week 8. Enhancing Personal and Family Effectiveness II
Stress management; assertiveness; balancing personal and family needs; self-care

Week 9. Dealing with Specific Problems
Positive and negative symptoms; manic and depressive episodes; self-destructive and violent behavior; substance abuse; other concerns

Week 10. A Comprehensive System of Community-Based Care
Services, providers, and resources; family support; referrals

Complementing educational programs are self-help books that offer guidance for patients and families who are coping with schizophrenia, bipolar disorder, depression, obsessive-compulsive disorder, and other severe and persistent disorders.[16] Whatever the format, family education offers many benefits for families.[17] As one family member remarked, "Family education enabled us to be a help rather than a hinderance."[18]

The professional literature provides many descriptions of educational programs for families, as well as some empirical support for their value. Summarizing results of her review of five rigorously designed evaluations of family education programs, Solomon concludes that although no consistent outcomes have been reported, there is limited evidence suggesting that interventions of more than one session are effective.[19] For example, following participation in educational programs, family members have reported increased knowledge and satisfaction with mental health treatment; decreased burden, distress, and anxiety; and improved self-efficacy and coping behaviors.

Family Psychoeducation

Although the terms education and psychoeducation are sometimes used interchangeably, there are important differences between the two interventions. As noted, educational programs are designed to meet the needs of families for information about mental illness and its treatment, about caregiving and management issues, and about the mental health system and community resources. Such programs are variable in format, typically ranging from a 1-day workshop to a 10- or 12-week series.

In contrast, family psychoeducation includes education but goes beyond, with the objectives of enhancing the family's ability to cope with the serious mental illness of a member and to reduce the patient's risk of relapse. In the early 1970s, researchers in England discovered that certain family behaviors were related to increased relapse rates for patients with schizophrenia. These behaviors—criticism, hostility, and overinvolvement—have been termed *expressed emotion*. Programs designed to lower an initially high level of expressed emotion in families have been successful in reducing the risk of relapse.

Subsequent controlled studies of the family psychoeducation model confirmed the earlier findings, and a substantial body of literature is now available regarding this form of intervention for the treatment of schizophrenia, as well as a range of other disorders. These findings are important in highlighting the adverse impact of overstimulating or high-demand environments for individuals who have the core information-processing deficits of schizophrenia.[20]

FEATURES OF FAMILY PSYCHOEDUCATION

Psychoeducational programs generally include both patient and family components. Patient interventions consist of education about mental illness and its management, emphasis on medication adherence, and training in social skills. Family interventions typically involve the following: (a) an empathic, validating, nonblaming, task-oriented alliance with the family; (b) education about mental illness and its management; (c) training in coping skills, such as communication and problem solving; and (d) social support, especially through contact with other families.

Following their review of research concerned with psychoeducation, Lisa Dixon and Anthony Lehman concluded that there is substantial evidence that these family interventions reduce the rate of patient relapse; and that there is suggestive, though not conclusive, evidence that these interventions improve patient functioning and family well-being.[21] They also maintain that education alone is less effective than interventions that provide support, problem solving, and crisis intervention; and that dynamic approaches are ineffective. In their view, interventions of at least 9 months duration may be necessary to see effects. In fact, many psychoeducational interventions continue for a year or more.[22]

Family psychoeducation is in many respects a constructive development, since it encourages family-professional collaboration and meets many family needs. The strong empirical support for family psychoeducation argues for the availability of this intervention for all families who are involved with their relatives. Certainly, if the goal of intervention is the reduction of relapse rates, this intervention is the preferred strategy. On the other hand, psychoeducation is primarily offered by a professional team over a relatively long period, which may limit this intervention to certain settings and families. Moreover, especially if it is offered as the sole (or major) family intervention, psychoeducation may be inconsistent with the needs, desires, and resources of particular families or family members.

Two exemplary psychoeducational programs will be considered: behavioral family therapy, which is usually provided to individual families, and multiple family psychoeducation, which is designed for groups of families. Both family interventions are strongly supported by research findings and have useful manuals available for practitioners. In addition, because both programs have most often been used in the treatment of schizophrenia, family psychoeducation in bipolar disorder will also be considered.

BEHAVIORAL FAMILY THERAPY

Originally developed by Ian Falloon and his colleagues for the treatment of schizophrenia, behavioral family therapy (BFT) is one of the most widely studied models of family intervention.[23] It has since been adapted to a broad range of psychiatric disorders, as detailed by Kim Mueser and Shirley Glynn in their book, *Behavioral Family Therapy for Psychiatric Disorders*.[24] The book offers a wealth of practical information for practitioners who work with families, as well as handouts concerned with BFT and its strategies, the vulnerability-stress model, specific mental disorders, and communication and problem-solving skills.

BFT emphasizes the value of collaboration between families and professionals, with long-term objectives of minimizing relapses and hospitalizations and of optimizing social outcomes in a cost-effective manner. This approach is guided by three general goals: to improve the quality of life for the patient, to improve the quality of life for family members, and to improve communication and problem-solving skills as a means of reducing ambient stress.

Generally provided to individual families on a declining-contact basis, BFT proceeds from weekly sessions that are offered for approximately 3 months, to biweekly sessions for another 3 to 6 months, and then to monthly sessions for at least 3 more months. Although originally designed as a home-based intervention, research findings indicate BFT is equally effective when provided in a clinical setting. A combination of home- and clinic-based sessions is often optimal, with home-based sessions offered at the beginning of treatment to facilitate family engagement.

This intervention is provided to those family members most involved in caregiving, with the patient included whenever possible. The BFT model includes five sequential stages, with a recycling of each stage as needed. The stages include:

1. *Assessment* of family and individual strengths and limitations, based on interviews with the family unit and each individual member, as well as joint problem-solving discussions

2. *Education*, which consists of two to four sessions that cover the mental illness, medication, and the vulnerability-stress model

3. *Communication skills training*, which consists of four to eight sessions designed to apply the principles of social skills training in teaching family members to facilitate nonstressful communication and problem solving

4. *Problem-solving training*, which focuses on helping family members learn a structured approach to discussing and resolving individual and family problems

5. *Special problems*, which targets those areas still in need of improvement and which may involve the use of clinical methods, such as cognitive-behavioral strategies

In addition to *Behavioral Family Therapy for Psychiatric Disorders,* practitioners who wish to offer BFT will benefit from reading *Coping with Schizophrenia: A Guide for Families.* Written by Mueser and Susan Gingerich, the guide offers much useful information and practical advice.[25]

MULTIFAMILY PSYCHOEDUCATIONAL GROUPS

William McFarlane has developed and evaluated a multifamily approach to psychoeducation.[26] Using a large and representative sample, he and his colleagues compared psychoeducational single-family therapy (SFT) and multiple-family groups (MFG) during a 2-year period at six public hospitals in New York state. Both SFT and MFG interventions were designed to: (a) engage key members of the family within 7 days of an acute admission; (b) provide information about the biological aspects of schizophrenia and the treatment process, using a standardized videotape, lectures, and written coping guidelines; (c) intervene early in impending relapse; (d) provide ongoing support and formal clinical problem solving for at least 2 years; and (e) expand the family's social network.

In the MFG program, each family is assigned to a family clinician, who is a regular member of the social work, psychology, or nursing staff at the site hospital. The clinician is expected to act as the patient's primary case coordinator and therapist during inpatient and outpatient treatment, the family's educator and consultant, a leader of the MFG sessions, and the principal liaison to the treating psychiatrist and rehabilitation agencies. At each site, a full-time psychiatrist provides pharmacologic treatment for the entire subsample.

This approach includes four sequential phases. Phase 1 involves family engagement, usually at the time of an acute psychotic decompensation. Each of two family clinicians meets separately with three families for three weekly single-family sessions. Phase 2 consists of an educational workshop presented by the clinicians to these six families, using a standard videotape and coping guidelines (e.g., "GO SLOW. Recovery takes time, rest is important. Things will get better in their own time.")

Phases 3 and 4 are re-entry and rehabilitation phases, which focus respectively on stabilizing the patient out of the hospital and on slowly improving the patient's level of functioning. Cofacilitated by the same two clinicians, the six-family MFG begins to meet biweekly, now joined by the patients. These meetings are organized around a formal problem-solving procedure designed to develop individualized coping methods based on suggestions of group members. Lasting approximately 1½ hours, the sessions are structured as follows: socializing with families and patients (15 min.); a review of the week's events and scheduled topics (20 min.); selection of a single problem (5 min.); formal problem solving (45 min.); and socializing with families and patients (5 min.). The biweekly sessions are held for at least 12 months.

Results of the study provided strong support for the value of the MFG approach to psychoeducation. The MFGs yielded significantly lower 2-year cumulative relapse rates than did the SFT; moreover, relapse rates for both MFG and SFT were less than half the expected rate for standard interventions. In both interventions, rehospitalization rates and psychotic symptoms decreased significantly; medication adherence was high. McFarlane and his colleagues concluded that psychoeducational multiple-family groups were more effective than single-family treatment in extending remission, especially in patients at higher risk for relapse.

In discussing the greater effectiveness of MFG sessions, McFarlane suggests several possible explanations. In comparison with SFT, for instance, MFGs expand the patient's and family's social network. Other studies have found a relationship between size and density of the patient's social network and various outcome measures, especially relapse and rehospitalization. In addition, families in the multifamily group may enhance their problem solving capacity through exposure to other families, may learn to reduce their emotional overinvolvement in the supportive environment, and may benefit from the humor and warmth that often characterize MFG sessions. Thus, multiple-family psychoeducational groups offer a family intervention that is both beneficial and cost effective.

FAMILY PSYCHOEDUCATION IN BIPOLAR DISORDER

Most psychoeducational programs have been designed to assist patients and families in coping with schizophrenia. With modification, however, this intervention can also be helpful for families that include a member with bipolar disorder. In *Bipolar Disorder: A Family-Focused Treatment Approach,* David Miklowitz and Michael Goldstein have described their rationale for applying the psychoeducational approach to the treatment of bipolar disorder. They were impressed with research findings demonstrating that family psychoeducation is effective in treating schizophrenia; that many individuals with bipolar disorder have lasting residual symptoms and persistent deficits in social functioning; that the disorder has a major impact on families; and that a high-stress family environment is associated with increased risk of relapse.

As they point out, bipolar disorder is a relapsing and remitting illness. Even patients receiving optimal medication are likely to have multiple recurrences and to have difficulty holding jobs and maintaining relationships:

The behavioral and emotional experiences of the person with bipolar disorder af-
fect everyone—the patient's parents, spouse, siblings, and children. In fact, as
hospitalizations have become shorter and shorter, and as patients are discharged
in quite unstable clinical states, the burden on the family has become quite con-
siderable. In this milieu, family members need support, education, and advice in
coping with the ups and downs of their relative's condition.[27]

An additional reason for viewing bipolar disorder as a family problem
stems from the effects of the family environment on the course of the
disorder.

Building on family psychoeducation in schizophrenia, Miklowitz and
Goldstein found that this intervention had to be revised substantially for
patients with bipolar disorder and their families. First, these patients appeared to be more verbally assertive, higher in social and job functioning,
and more able to benefit from exploratory psychological interventions than
patients with schizophrenia. Second, patients with bipolar disorder were
more often married and had substantial relationship conflicts related to
their disorder. Third, their persistent denial of the disorder and resistance
to accepting necessary medication, combined with the emotional reactions
of family members to these stances, stood out as key features of the ongoing struggles of these patients and their families.

Miklowitz and Goldstein specify six objectives of their approach to treatment. These include assisting the patient and family to integrate the experiences associated with episodes of bipolar disorder, to accept the notion of
a vulnerability to future episodes, to accept a dependency on psychotropic
medication for symptom control, to distinguish between the patient's personality and his or her bipolar disorder, and to recognize and learn to cope
with stressful life events that trigger recurrences of bipolar disorder. In addition, the family is helped to reestablish functional relationships after a
manic or depressive episode.

Family-Focused Treatment (FFT) includes three relatively distinct
treatment phases or modules:

1. A psychoeducational phase that covers symptoms and course, etiology, treatment, family issues, self-management, and relapse
2. A communication enhancement training phase
3. A problem-solving training phase

These treatment modules are usually delivered in 12 weekly, 6 biweekly, and 3 monthly sessions spread over a 9-month outpatient period
following a manic or depressive episode. The book includes guidelines
for conducting FFT during each of these phases. There is also useful

information regarding the first encounter, the functional assessment, denial and resistance, managing crises, and termination. Initial data suggest that FFT benefits both patients and families. For example, patients are likely to remain in treatment; and their families demonstrate enhanced communication and problem-solving skills.

Additional Resources

Many other resources are available for practitioners who plan to offer educational or psychoeducational services for families. Working at Boston University Center for Psychiatric Rehabilitation, LeRoy Spaniol and his colleagues have developed several useful publications for professionals.[28] These include a practical manual, *The Role of the Family in Psychiatric Rehabilitation: A Workbook.* The manual includes 10 chapters that cover family experiences, needs, roles, and diversity; family coping, adaptation, and recovery; and family-professional relationships. Each chapter includes an overview of the topic, exercises, discussion questions, and summaries suitable for transparencies. Providing the content and structure for a 10-week program, the manual is accompanied by a trainer's guide and a supplementary book of readings.

Other useful books are also available. These include *Families Coping with Schizophrenia: A Practitioner's Guide to Family Groups* by Jacqueline Atkinson and Denise Coia; *Working with Families of the Mentally Ill* by Kayla Bernheim and Anthony Lehman; *Educating Patients and Families About Mental Illness: A Practical Guide* by Cynthia Bisbee; *Family Education* by Agnes Hatfield; *Family Interventions in Mental Illness*, edited by Agnes Hatfield; and *Helping Families Cope with Mental Illness*, edited by Harriet Lefley and Mona Wasow.[29]

From Theory to Practice

In preparation for her role as director of the comprehensive treatment and rehabilitation center, Anna Wang and her staff took advantage of several of the programs and resources described in this chapter. Now that her center is open, she offers each family an individual session designed to inform them about the center's consultative, supportive, educational, psychoeducational, and psychotherapeutic services, and to initiate a family service plan adapted to their specific requirements.

Here is staff social worker, Tom Granger, meeting with the Tussaud family for the initial consultative session. The Tussauds are a multigenerational

African American family that includes 28-year-old Robert, who was recently hospitalized for bipolar disorder; his 27-year-old wife, Kathleen; their two young children; Robert's mother, Maude; and his grandmother, Nellie. Robert and Kathleen live in a home not far from the apartment shared by Maude and Nellie.

PRACTITIONER: *Thank you for coming. This must be a very difficult time for the entire family.*

MOTHER: *We appreciate your scheduling the appointment in the evening. Kathleen and I can't miss any more work. But you're right about the family—I think we're all still in shock. During the past few months, we could see that Robert had some problems, but we figured it was his new job. Kathleen said he was sometimes up all night, talking nonstop and pacing. She and the children are exhausted. Nellie watches them after school until Kathleen gets home from work.*

GRANDMOTHER: *Those poor kids don't understand what happened to their father. I keep reassuring them that everything's going to be okay, but I'm not sure they believe me.*

PRACTITIONER: *Even with loving reassurance, a parent's mental illness is upsetting for children. I'll come back to their needs in a few minutes. How about you, Kathleen? It must be enormously difficult to cope simultaneously with your husband's illness, your children and home, and your job.*

SPOUSE: *Frankly, I'm not sure I'm coping all that well right now. I constantly worry about Robert and the children—and also about the future. We've worked so hard to get where we are. We have mortgage and car payments and a pile of other bills. When do you think Robert can go back to work? His employer has been understanding so far, but I worry about what might happen.*

PRACTITIONER: *Your concern about the future is understandable. We can't be sure at this point, but there are a number of hopeful signs. Robert has a good work history and is responding well to his medication. His moods have stabilized, and he's learning how to cope with his illness. We also want to help you manage the illness.*

MOTHER: *I'm sure we've been doing some things wrong. None of us even knew what bipolar disorder was before Robert was hospitalized. And knowing that it's a mood disorder doesn't tell what to do about it.*

PRACTITIONER: *That's true, a diagnosis doesn't tell you how to cope. Especially at the time of the initial diagnosis, most families feel unsettled and helpless. Here is some written material about bipolar disorder and related family concerns, as well as the services that can help you learn about Robert's mental illness and develop the coping skills you need. I* can also refer you to the local family support and advocacy group, which offers many programs for families.

MOTHER: *I'll be honest with you. I'm not sure I want to participate in an all-white organization. Do they have any African American members?*

PRACTITIONER: *I presented a program for the group last month and met several African American mothers. Would you like me to see if one of them is willing to contact you? Then you can get a better sense of whether you want to join the organization or participate in their programs.*

MOTHER: *I suppose so.*

PRACTITIONER: *Kathleen, they even have a special support group for spouses and partners.*

SPOUSE: *Thanks, but I'm not sure I can find the time. I just received a promotion at work. With Robert on disability leave and the future uncertain, I need to make sure my job is secure. But maybe at some later time.*

GRANDMOTHER: *You know, especially with the children, none of us have much time to run around attending meetings.*

PRACTITIONER: *I can understand how you feel. If you prefer, I can meet with you once a week in the evening to answer your questions and assist you in managing Robert's illness. The center has child care services, so you can bring the children if necessary. Once we've met several times, you can decide whether you want to receive any other services.*

MOTHER: *That sounds good to me. What do you think, Kathleen?*

SPOUSE: *I guess so. I'm still worried about all my responsibilities.*

MOTHER: *Well, if need be, I can come alone and then share information with you. Nellie, do you want to come with me?*

GRANDMOTHER: *Yes, I want to help as much as I can. After all, Robert's my grandson.*

MOTHER: *I would also like to hear from one of the African American mothers you mentioned.*

PRACTITIONER: *I'll see what I can do and let you know. Family members share a common bond under these circumstances. Do you have any other concerns before we set up another appointment?*

SPOUSE: *Yes, I'm worried about my children. What do I tell them? And how do I tell them? They're very close to their father. Both of the kids are having trouble sleeping and seem irritable. Do you think they need help too?*

PRACTITIONER: *I appreciate your concern. It's normal for children to experience distress when a parent develops mental illness. It's important to explain Robert's illness in a way they can understand—and to assure them they are not at fault. If you like, after this meeting, I'll set up an appointment for you with our child psychologist, who can consult with* you about your children. The psychologist may want to meet with them, just to get a sense of how they're doing.

MOTHER: *That sounds good. Nellie and I can take care of the kids while you meet with the psychologist. Then you can let us know what we can do to help.*

PRACTITIONER: *Okay, that's a start. We'll take it a step at a time. Let's set up another appointment for next week. If you can't all make it, I'll work with your family so you can each get the information you need. Here's my card; call me if you have any questions. Now, Kathleen, let's set up an appointment with our child psychologist so you can get some suggestions for your children.*

CHAPTER 9

Family Interventions: Psychotherapy

As director of family services at the psychiatric unit of a large university-affiliated medical center, psychologist Ron Caplan and his staff have developed a range of family-focused services. These include initial and as-needed consultative sessions with all families of current patients, an ongoing support group facilitated by members of a local NAMI chapter, a 1-day educational workshop copresented by a family member and a staff psychologist, and a 9-month psychoeducational program offered by team of professionals affiliated with the medical center. Both families and staff speak enthusiastically about the program, which meets the needs of most families. However, some family members continue to experience significant problems even after their supportive and educational needs have been met. Ron recalls a recent supervisory session with a young social worker, Ann Hampton, who described continuing conflict that threatened the marriage of Margaret and Hector Gonzales, middle-aged parents of an 18-year-old son with a dual diagnosis of bipolar disorder and substance abuse. Their discussion raised several questions. When, for instance, should family members be referred for psychotherapy? What are the most effective strategies and techniques with these families? What are the risks of negative treatment effects?

Like Ron Caplan and his professional staff, practitioners who work with families are likely to find that the needs of most families can be met through some combination of consultative, supportive, and educational services. These are the initial interventions of choice for family members, whose primary needs are for information, skills, and support. If these interventions are not sufficient, other services may also be appropriate, including psychotherapy, the topic of the present chapter.

176

Psychotherapy: Professional Issues

Psychotherapy offers a valuable resource for some family members, who may benefit from intervention designed to assist them in dealing with pre-existing mental health problems that may have been exacerbated by current stress or in resolving problems that are reactive to their relative's mental illness. The following family member attests to some of the possible gains:

I did not explore therapy until age 35. Professionals can be a wonderful vehicle to bring out repressed pain and guilt. It's hard to move forward without opening up blocked tears. Once I allowed myself to really cry, I unburdened more than I ever thought I could carry. Besides making me feel relieved, I felt human—a healthy human for the first time.[1]

POTENTIAL BENEFITS

As documented in a vast professional literature, psychotherapy offers many potential benefits, including improvements in interpersonal functioning, in self-esteem and self-confidence, in satisfaction, in mastery and competency, and in level of distress.[2] Similarly, in the popular literature, based on a survey of their readers, an article in *Consumer Reports* concluded that clients profited significantly from psychotherapy.[3]

In addition to these general benefits, therapy may offer family members an opportunity to achieve:

- Understanding of the family experience of mental illness
- Insight into its impact on their own lives
- An opportunity to resolve feelings of grief and loss
- Assistance in establishing more constructive relationships
- More effective coping skills and strategies
- More positive feelings about themselves and their future

In recommending psychotherapy for family members, practitioners need to address several questions, including when therapy is—and is not—an appropriate intervention. More technical concerns include appropriate strategies, techniques, duration, and frequency, as well as the risk of negative treatment effects.[4] Each of these issues will be examined.

MAKING A REFERRAL FOR PSYCHOTHERAPY

Given the limitations of family, professional, and social resources, it is reasonable for practitioners to begin with the question of when clinical intervention is *not* appropriate. Applying the principle of least intervention,[5] psychotherapy is generally not recommended when the needs of families can be addressed through the supportive and educational interventions already discussed. Moreover, therapy should not be recommended when family members are at risk for a negative response to treatment or when treatment is not likely to be effective.[6]

Illustrating some of these considerations, one of the mothers told me she felt it had been a mistake to become involved with psychotherapy, remarking that she "was not mentally ill and did not need treatment or analysis." She complained that the therapeutic process seemed to emphasize her vulnerability and to drain her energy, proclaiming, "The last thing I needed was to be treated as if I were the problem instead of my daughter."[7]

On the other hand, clinical intervention *is* likely to be appropriate under two general circumstances: when significant individual or family problems are present and when family members prefer to meet their needs through psychotherapy. Sometimes the problems of family members are apparent during their initial contacts with practitioners, who can incorporate a recommendation for therapy when formulating the initial service plan. In other cases, family members might continue to experience significant difficulties even after their supportive and educational needs have been satisfied. With the knowledge and consent of the family, a consultant might then recommend a shift to individual, marital, or family therapy, instead of or in addition to other family interventions.

Consistent with general standards of clinical practice, consultants should consider a referral for professional services when there is evidence of persistent depression, marked mood swings, significant anxiety, substance abuse, or other symptoms of mental disorders. In fact, given the genetic risks associated with serious mental illness, some family members are subject to mental illness themselves. Given the intense distress that is often experienced by family members, however, caution should be exercised when conducting individual and family assessments.

Especially at the onset of the illness, family members may look clinically disturbed when in fact they are informationally and sleep deprived, which is likely to increase their level of stress and confusion. Likewise, in the midst of a crisis, distressed families are more in need of satisfactory services for their relative than for therapy. In the words of an old proverb: "Hearing hoofbeats, we might assume it is a horse, when, in fact, it is a zebra." It is prudent to defer a family assessment until the situation has stabilized and the family can be evaluated more objectively.

Still, some family members do experience illness-related concerns that are appropriate therapeutic foci. For instance, individual family members may experience an unresolved grieving process, incapacitating feelings of guilt and responsibility, or inappropriate anger directed at the relative, other family members, or people outside the family. Other problems might include an exclusive focus on the person with mental illness that prevents the family from meeting the needs of other members or persistent conflict regarding the treatment and rehabilitation plan.

On the other hand, some family members may manifest none of these problems but nevertheless prefer to meet their needs within the context of a confidential therapeutic relationship. An individual family member might welcome the opportunity to deal with issues of loss and grief in a protected forum; a couple might prefer to resolve illness-related conflicts with the assistance of a marital therapist; or a family might wish more individualized attention than is afforded in a multifamily group. Under these circumstances, psychotherapy may offer a viable alternative.

Conceptualizing the Change Process

Kenneth Howard and his colleagues have conceptualized the change process that occurs in psychotherapy in terms of three phases: remoralization, remediation, and rehabilitation.[8] Namely, the objectives of therapy are to reduce feelings of demoralization, to decrease symptoms, and to improve adaptive functioning. Their formulation is helpful in evaluating the potential usefulness of therapy for family members. They observe that some individuals seeking therapy are so overwhelmed that they become demoralized, which may severely disrupt their ability to mobilize their coping resources and result in feelings of hopelessness and desperation.

The first phase of remoralization is usually accomplished in a few sessions, based on an outcome criterion of subjective well-being. The second phase is focused on remediation of symptoms that led to the decision to seek treatment and perhaps to demoralization. During this phase, treatment is concerned with refocusing the client's coping skills in a way that brings symptomatic relief. The outcome criterion for the second phase is symptomatic improvement, which may involve gradual change and repeated sessions.

The third phase of treatment is rehabilitation, which is focused on unlearning troublesome, maladaptive, and habitual behaviors, and on establishing new ways of dealing with various aspects of life. This phase again involves gradual change and repeated sessions, depending upon the severity of symptoms and the particular area of problematic functioning, such as relationships, work, or personal attitudes. The outcome criterion for this phase is life functioning.

Applying this model to clinical practice with family members, the phases of remoralization and symptomatic improvement may well take place in response to the consultative, supportive, and educational interventions already discussed. Indeed, family members who receive these less intensive interventions often report improvements in subjective well-being and coping effectiveness. It is during the third rehabilitative phase that psychotherapy offers the greatest potential benefits for family members, including those who are experiencing problematic functioning in areas of their lives unrelated to the illness and those whose lives are held hostage by the illness:

I was so depressed and lonely. I even thought of suicide. For many years, I looked for answers for my brother's problems, never realizing I had to find myself first. I had to leave home to survive. I have—being in therapy, learning I'm okay. I'm now married and successful in my job as an elementary guidance counselor. I am what I wanted to be—a caring, nurturing person.[9]

Formulating a Treatment Plan

In their initial contacts with professionals, families who are appropriate candidates for psychotherapeutic services may manifest significant vulnerability and defensiveness. Consumed with feelings of grief and loss and overwhelmed by the demands of the illness, they may also be reeling from prior contacts with professionals. Thus, practitioners need to make special efforts to engage these families and to avoid the application of conceptual approaches that pathologize families, intensify their feelings of guilt, and create a climate of blame that undermines family relationships.

In contrast, family members are likely to respond positively to therapeutic services that incorporate new competency-based models and collaborative modes.[10] Several treatment goals are typically appropriate for family members, including provision of support, expression and resolution of the emotional burden, enhancement of coping effectiveness, and reframing of personal and familial experience. The unique requirements of particular families and individual family members also merit consideration.

Our research findings suggest that adult siblings and offspring may particularly benefit from individual therapy.[11] Over three-quarters (77%) of our survey participants indicated they had received therapy themselves. The percentage was even higher (90%) among those who were both a sibling and offspring and among those who were age 10 or younger at the onset of their relative's mental illness. Almost all rated the therapy as helpful, although one participant cited the "very poor grasp of serious mental illness" among clinicians.

It is important to note, however, that few of these siblings and off-spring had other services available to them as they were growing up. Had their concerns been addressed during their childhood and adolescence, perhaps their need for therapy in adulthood would have been less compelling. Nevertheless, their personal accounts of therapy argue strongly for its potential value, as the following woman affirms:

It wasn't until I sought therapy for anxiety upon my divorce that I began to understand some of the dynamics of my family and myself. I have missed much, have just begun to recognize what has been lost or even never realized. It has taken me a long time to finally face the original problem. Therapy opened doors to my self and answered many puzzling questions.[12]

FORMAT

Alternative formats include individual therapy, marital or couple therapy, family therapy, and group therapy. Format determines the number of individuals who will be present and the nature of the interpersonal context. Given the diversity among family members, each of these formats has potential value and poses certain risks.

Individual therapy may be appropriate for family members who desire the privacy and intimacy of a confidential relationship, are experiencing intrapsychic conflict, are having difficulty resolving their emotional burden, or are dealing with issues of separation and autonomy. Whatever their value in reducing patient relapse and rehospitalization, multifamily groups are unlikely to offer much help in dealing with these issues.

Marital therapy may offer assistance in resolving illness-related conflicts or other relational problems. Especially at the onset of the illness, there is often confusion about diagnostic and treatment issues, and individual family members may differ in their acceptance of the illness. Consider the Gonzales family described in the opening vignette. The entire family will benefit if the parents can resolve their conflicts and work as an effective team. Otherwise, their marital conflicts may play out in the family arena, with adverse consequences for all concerned.

In light of the interpersonal legacy they often carry into adulthood (see Chapters 13 and 14), adult siblings and offspring may also be appropriate candidates for marital therapy. The following woman grew up with a father who had major depression:

I related to my husband as I had related to my father. I rarely communicated my feelings to him and I felt responsible for his. I pulled away from him when things became difficult and built up a wall that would keep potential pain at bay. Fortunately, recognizing these discoveries, understanding them, and working toward changing them has made the difference in our relationship.[13]

Family therapy may be beneficial when there are pre-existing problems in communication or conflict management, the family is unable to cope adequately with the mental illness, or successful treatment of an individual requires the involvement of other family members. Group therapy offers a relatively economical format that is similar in many respects to a support group. This format is likely to reduce the feelings of isolation often experienced by family members and, depending on group structure, may also meet their informational and skills needs.

There are risks associated with each of these formats. Individual therapy may result in isolation, distortion, and scapegoating, as well as failure to address important marital or family problems. Potential risks of marital or family therapy include reduced autonomy, increased family disruption, loss of privacy, and deflection from individual problems and concerns.

Family therapy appears to pose particular risks under these circumstances. In several studies designed to evaluate the comparative helpfulness of various resources, both family members and consumers have rated this format relatively low.[14] For example, in our study of consumer experiences, needs, and coping resources, survey participants ranked family therapy as the least helpful of 15 potential resources, with a mean rating of 1.48 (1 = Not helpful at all).[15] One consumer explained his low rating by declaring that he had little enough time with his therapist; he wanted to spend it dealing with his *own* issues, not family concerns.

Similarly, in our survey of adult siblings and offspring, several mentioned negative experiences in family therapy, including the frustration of attending sessions when their relative was exhibiting psychotic symptoms. One sibling remarked, "Every time we tried to get some direction on how to deal with this as a unit, my sister would stand up, threatening violence at times. There wasn't much good that came out of that experience."[16] As this case illustrates, psychotherapy with these families is unlikely to be effective unless clinicians have expertise in working with patients who have mental illness as well as an understanding of family issues.

STRATEGIES AND TECHNIQUES

Strategies and techniques are the technical interventions used to produce change. The orientations of therapists often influence their approach to therapy. Some important approaches include:

- Psychodynamic and psychoanalytic therapy, which emphasize the role of early childhood experience and inner conflict
- Cognitive-behavioral therapy, which addresses relationships among present emotions, thoughts, and behaviors, as well as the strategies that can modify maladaptive patterns of thinking and behaving
- Client-centered therapy, which underscores support, validation, and the innate potential of human beings for self-actualization
- Existential therapy, which highlights questions of meaning and value, and the importance of personal responsibility
- Expressive therapy, which makes use of painting, music, dance, writing, and other media
- Gestalt therapy, which features present circumstances, the use of role playing, and a holistic conception of personality
- Interpersonal therapy, which focuses on current and past relationships

All of these strategies offer potential benefits for family members, who may profit from an opportunity to explore their early childhood, to resolve their feelings of grief and loss, to change maladaptive patterns of thinking and behavior, to receive support and validation, to understand the personal meaning of the mental illness, to channel their feelings through expressive therapy, and to examine their experiences and relationships. Given the pervasive impact of mental illness, family members may benefit from an integrative or eclectic approach that can address their multiple concerns.

Therapeutic strategies and techniques should be tailored to the needs of individual family members. For instance, psychodynamic strategies are likely to be useful in addressing issues of loss and mourning, in working through issues pertaining to earlier losses that have been resurrected, and in resolving intrapsychic conflict. Siblings and offspring may particularly profit from an opportunity to come to terms with the meaning of their relative's mental illness for their own lives.

Cognitive-behavioral strategies offer an effective means of treating the depression that is a salient component of the subjective burden and of meeting the informational and skills needs of families.[17] In light of their anguish, family members may also benefit from an experiential-humanistic approach that provides an empathic and validating therapeutic milieu, encourages the expression and resolution of the intense emotions often evoked under these circumstances, and provides opportunities for reframing and reassurance.

Regardless of the orientation espoused, past and current relationships are likely to require considerable therapeutic attention. Likewise, issues of grief and loss are commonly an important focus, as the following family member affirms:

A big part of my problem was unresolved feelings of grief and loss. Our family has lost so much as the result of Mom's illness, but it has happened a little at a time, so there hasn't really been an opportunity to grieve. Eventually I realized I had been deprived of the opportunity to mourn my losses. . . . I wanted to give the scared little boy inside me every opportunity to mourn.[18]

Complementing the personal accounts of family members are some excellent professional publications concerned with familial grief.[19] As several writers have noted, family members are subject not only to a powerful grieving process and the risk of unresolved grief, but also to "disenfranchised grief" when their loss is not acknowledged, publicly mourned, and socially supported. Moreover, in the absence of social validation, professionals may misinterpret, ignore, or pathologize family grief, interpreting their anguish as personal or family dysfunction.

DURATION AND FREQUENCY

Ideally, the duration and frequency of psychotherapy should reflect the circumstances of particular family members. A brief course of supportive therapy is suggested by satisfactory prior and current functioning, by the relatively poor match between the expressed needs of families and ambitious treatment goals, and by the likelihood of poor motivation for extended therapy among families whose resources are depleted by the demands of the illness. This mother's comments suggest that a brief course of supportive therapy would have better met her needs:

I was both helped and hurt by therapy. I needed an opportunity to unburden my soul, and my therapist was a caring and empathic listener. But that is all that I needed. When my own goals were met, and I was ready to terminate, I was talked into remaining in therapy. . . . As a result, I spent another year in therapy that didn't benefit me in any way that I can see and that added significantly to my problems.[20]

On the other hand, long-term psychotherapy may be appropriate for family members who have mental illness themselves or who are experiencing severe problems in several areas of their lives, as was the case for this adult offspring:

I sank into an 8-year depression. My mother's illness completely interrupted my life. Her illness progressed, and I found myself isolated and powerless in dealing

*with it. The establishment repeatedly told me that there was nothing they could do
unless my mother wished help. My mother would not agree to see a doctor. I've
been in therapy for 11 years now. That's the only good result I can see coming out
of this tragedy.*[21]

In addition to—and sometimes in conflict with—these clinical considerations are the limitations imposed by the behavioral health care system.
Managed care organizations and capitated practitioners both earn profits
by withholding services or by substituting less expensive for more costly
care. Services to family members may also be affected by the concept of
medical necessity, which may restrict the range of services available; and
by an acute care focus, which limits the potential to deliver long-term treatment. Accordingly, practitioners who work with families may find themselves limited to a few sessions of problem-focused therapy.

With careful planning, these sessions can be very helpful to family
members. Six sessions, for instance, can include consultation, referrals to
community resources, an opportunity for expression and resolution of
powerful emotions, family education and skills training, and some long-
term planning. As valuable as this short-term assistance may be, practitioners also need to discuss the limitations of brief therapy and assist
families in meeting their long-term needs. Given the constraints of the
mental health marketplace, family support and advocacy groups offer a
cost-effective way of expanding limited professional resources.

Negative Treatment Effects

Along with the potential benefits of psychotherapy for family members,
clinical intervention also carries some risks, including negative treatment
effects. Negative effects can result from general problems, including defi-
cient training and skill on the part of the therapist; low motivation on the
part of the client; problems in the therapist-client relationship, such as poor
communication or absence of rapport; or inappropriate decisions regarding
treatment format, strategies, or duration. There are also specific risks associated with the family experience of mental illness.[22]

It is important not to overprescribe therapy for problems that family
members can resolve on their own or through a support group or educational program.[23] Under these circumstances, intensive therapy may add
to their feelings of helplessness and result in a substantial investment of
time, energy, and money that cannot be justified. Additional risks are associated with failure to obtain informed consent from all members of the
family, which sometimes occurs when family therapy is mandated as part
of the patient's treatment plan.

Then, there is the risk that universal family issues will be defined as personal, marital, or family problems, intensifying the feelings of responsibility among family members and further eroding their shaken self-esteem. Moreover, the intensity of their emotional response may leave family members with questions about their own mental health. Often, what they need is reassurance that they are experiencing a normal response—however anguished—to an abnormal family event.

Additional risks are associated with general prescriptions of family therapy that are based on assumptions of family dysfunction or pathogenesis. Such therapy is likely to increase the feelings of guilt frequently experienced by family members and add significantly to their burden, as the following mother attests:

I felt so battered after my experiences with professionals. When my daughter was hospitalized, we were placed in family therapy, . . . something we neither needed nor wanted. And the comments of various professionals suggested that they held us responsible for our daughter's problems, adding to our feelings of guilt and responsibility. . . . We needed understanding and support during that period. Instead, our experiences with professionals added to our problems.[24]

Especially if they were exposed to traumatic events as young children, family members may have buried painful memories and feelings that can resurface in therapy with an intensity that leaves them feeling overwhelmed and immobilized (see the personal account in the following section). When dealing with trauma, practitioners need to provide a controlled confrontation in a safe setting, as memories and feelings are reconnected with the original event. Even with careful attention to the risk of emotional flooding, these clients may experience considerable distress during therapy. Confronting his painful feelings in therapy, one family member wrote, "Right now, what I mostly see is pain all around me. Every time I rub up against reality I feel like crying."[25]

Finally, many clinicians do not have expertise concerned with serious mental illness or with the experiences and needs of family members. Thus, there is the risk that family members will feel misunderstood by their therapist and find therapy unproductive. One family member talks about his unsatisfactory experiences in therapy:

Over the years, I have spent time with several different individual and group therapists. My attempts at therapy have been largely disappointing. Little was done for me. It was frustrating. So much wasted time, money, and energy. This can only add to your despair.[26]

Psychotherapy: A Personal Account

With her generous permission, I am sharing the personal account of Diane Ammons, who grew up with a mother who had serious mental illness.[27] During her decades-long struggle to understand and recover from her traumatic childhood and adolescence, Diane benefited significantly from psychotherapy. We originally met as mental health advocates and have since worked together on several projects, including presentations and publications concerned with adult siblings and offspring. In one of our collaborative publications, Diane wrote about the devastating impact of her mother's mental illness on her own life. At my request, she adapted her powerful account for this book, imploring me to educate professionals about the traumatic impact of parental illness on offspring.

I have struggled all my life with the memories surrounding my mother's mental illness and with my lack of emotional connectedness to the years after her illness worsened. Her depressive episodes began during her pregnancy with me. In the years to follow, she would periodically become extremely withdrawn and disappear to a "sanitarium" for months.

As early as 6, I knew never to ask about her illness, learning coping strategies that were carried—with many adverse consequences—into my adult life. During my early years, I just accepted her symptoms and her absences as a normal part of my life.

Approaching adolescence, however, I silently began to question. When I was 12, my mother's illness transformed my life. Following my father's retirement, we moved to a farm far from other family members. I arrived home from my first day at school to find my mother hospitalized—the first of many such incidents during those years.

Our home portrayed all the "don'ts" connected to mental illness. Don't talk about it. Don't think for yourself; "they" know best. Don't trust anyone. Don't feel. And one more: Don't change anything! *I learned those strategies well, probably too well.*

I never told anyone what was happening, nor did anyone ask. I learned not to express emotion, but that did not keep me from feeling. I felt fear of what I didn't understand. I felt anger at what had been stolen from my life: the mother whom I had never really known and who became increasingly distant during my adolescence. I spent many hours alone with my mother; talking to unknown persons, she often didn't know I was present. I felt fear and guilt that I might cause or had caused an episode by my actions. I tried to be stable, constant, never changing. But I was changing; after all, I was an adolescent. I tried not to judge. But I hurt! I was angry! And I was alone!

But I couldn't let anyone know how I felt. The emotions became buried. I created an escapist world of images to get my own needs met. I invented a woman who would join me on the hillside, who would sit beside me, and who knew my hurt and my pain. The hillside was the only place I could allow myself to feel. I didn't dare feel around others—the "rules" were in place.

I froze emotionally at age 14. Turning to God, I struggled with the commandment: Thou shalt love thy father and thy mother. *Loving them but hating what was happening in my life, I was sometimes unable to tell the difference between the emotions. I was scared. What was wrong with me? Why couldn't I be like others seemed to be? On the outside, I tried to look like them, but I couldn't let anyone get close to me. They might learn the "truth" about me. I left home at 16 for work, school, and later for college.*

By 20, I could allow myself to feel the old painful emotions only in the school chapel at night, temporarily becoming "the girl in the chapel." I felt so alone, and I was alone. I could tell no one about our family or about my feelings. The fear of being "locked away" for being different was embedded in me. I spent more and more hours in that chapel, but my prayers for understanding and for release from pain went seemingly unanswered. For me, "the girl" never left that chapel; a part of me was left behind. As I learned later, I had dissociated from my pain and my anger. I had to survive!

When I was 23, the unthinkable happened. I had always yearned for acknowledgment from mother for my awards and accomplishments. This time it was a state recognition. Surely, this time I would hear words of praise from my mother, now hospitalized again. Her only response to my letter was to comment on a misspelled word. Unable to separate her from the illness, I reacted with intense anger and stopped writing altogether. I now allowed myself to hate my mother. It was my first act of rebellion.

She got even with me: She took her own life! In response to unbearable anguish, I dissociated again. The ability to feel, in any form, was gone—even the memories of what the feeling words meant.

The years passed. Outwardly, my life looked normal. But I continued to feel no emotions. I copied those around me to know how to act and respond, my responses always a second or so behind everyone else's.

By my mid-30s, I knew I needed help. I had built a successful career but I was burning out. My marriage was troubled. I didn't know how to nurture my young son; after all, I had never been nurtured myself.

Simply wanting "it" to be over, I sought therapy. I was beginning to get in touch with my emotions again. Supportive psychotherapy helped me understand my past and relax my perfectionistic tendencies and need for control. But I still had what I now know were "flashbacks" to the early adolescent years. I was unable to anticipate the flashbacks, which could be triggered by a thought or by a comment or action of another. Sometimes I had to resort to emotional blockage to stop the pain. I could go into blockage instantly; it took much longer—hours, days, sometimes weeks—to recover my ability to feel and to think clearly.

Having heard that some offspring suffered from posttraumatic stress disorder, I began looking in this direction for relief and contacted a psychologist who specialized in working with trauma victims. During our sessions, I felt as if I were watching a movie in my mind. But the events in the movie were connected to my emotions, including the painful emotional cascades I experienced as a teenager in response to my mother's worsening condition. During the sessions, I learned in my mind how to walk away—to disconnect—from my mother in her ill state. The emotional cascades stopped instantly. I felt as if a part of my mind had been found.

I was able to visit "the girl in the chapel," recovering that part of myself. That proved to be a very painful reconnection, since I had left a great deal of pain and anger embodied in her. But I am now in touch with that pain and anger and have proceeded to heal it. I have also been able to access the separate ego state created at the time of my mother's suicide. That process of reconnection and healing has been especially painful and complicated.

Working through my early trauma was enormously difficult. At times my therapy was almost too rapid and disruptive. Occasionally, in response to my emotional flooding, I resorted to the earlier survival techniques that allowed me to function at all costs. With my therapist's help, I was able to work through these problems and achieve some resolution.

My daily emotions have slowed down. The painful emotional cascades are gone! I can look back, and my life feels continuous. I have begun to reconnect with the well of emotions that were lost at the time of my mother's suicide. I am aware of how far I have come. I have confronted my traumatic experiences, worked through a large part of my emotional legacy, and achieved a degree of peace. The search for emotional connection and relief, for forgiveness of self and others, and for inner peace and understanding will continue to be lifelong goals.

But I am also angry. What happened to me didn't have to happen!!! What could have made a difference? Age-appropriate information and support; validation of my emotions—that they were a normal response to a very abnormal situation; some kind of explanation about my mother's treatment and hospitalizations. The illness was kept a total mystery, forcing me to develop unhealthy coping mechanisms that allowed me to survive my childhood but that interfered with my adult life.

What would I recommend for professionals? Reach out as early as possible to children who are growing up with mental illness in their family. Educate them about mental illness in a way they can understand. Teach them effective coping skills. Provide support and help them develop their own support network. Offer personal counseling if they are experiencing significant problems. Assure them that their parent's mental illness is not their fault. Encourage them to live their own lives—and not to feel guilty about it!

From Theory to Practice

After her supervisory session with Ron Caplan, social worker Ann Hampton feels confident that her recommendation of marital therapy is appropriate for Margaret and Hector Gonzales, a middle-aged couple who are experiencing considerable conflict and distress in connection with the dual diagnosis of their 18-year-old son, John. Recently diagnosed with bipolar disorder, John has been abusing alcohol and marijuana for several years. Almost lost in the family's embroilment are the needs of two younger teenagers, Ron and Carol, who are alternately immobilized and angry in response to the family situation. In light of their deteriorating marital and family problems, Ann is hopeful that Mr. and Mrs. Gonzales will accept her recommendation for therapy.

PRACTITIONER: *Good evening. I'm glad we could rearrange our meeting to accommodate your new shift at the factory.*

FATHER: *Actually, we were ready to cancel our appointment. With all the stress at home, the last thing we need is more meetings at the clinic. As it is, I'm having trouble concentrating at work. And I arrive home to nothing but trouble. Margaret starts on me about spending more time with John, who acts like he's angry with the world—and especially with me. What's the matter with that kid? After all we've tried to do for him, he shows no respect or appreciation. And his mother always takes his side. It feels like an armed camp.*

PRACTITIONER: *From what you've described, I can imagine how embattled all of you feel. What about you, Mrs. Gonzales?*

MOTHER: *It's been a nightmare. During the day I have constant headaches; at night I have trouble sleeping. I get no help from Hector, even when he's around, which isn't much these days. He has no idea what I go through with John. And the younger children seem out of control, too. I can't take any more.*

PRACTITIONER: *It sounds like you're all hurting. I have been concerned about the continuing family conflict and stress. Yesterday, I spoke with my supervisor, Ron Caplan, about your family situation. As you know, having a teenager with a dual diagnosis places a tremendous burden on all members of the family.*

FATHER: *I'll say. I never bargained for this when we got married. But at least I expected Margaret to support me. We don't seem to have any marriage at all any more. Our home life is nothing but problems—not enough money, not enough time, not any pleasure at all. And, of course, there's John.*

MOTHER: *Well, I don't like it any more than you do. I can't remember when we had any real time for ourselves. And when we are together, we do nothing but argue. Ron said he doesn't want to bring friends home anymore. And Carol is worried the family will fall apart. So am I.*

PRACTITIONER: *Listening to both of you, I wonder if our center can't offer more assistance. We scheduled these sessions to assist you in managing John's illness and his substance abuse. But now we seem to be spending all our time on your marital problems.*

MOTHER: *You know, that's true. We did find the educational program helpful, along with your suggestions during our first few sessions. But right now our marriage seems to be more of a problem. I'm not sure I want to go on.*

FATHER: *You're not the only one. The only happiness I have right now is with my friends after work. And then you complain that I'm drinking too much and avoiding you.*

MOTHER: *It does feel that way. This is the most difficult period of my life, and I feel all alone. I often find my self crying and wondering what will happen to us.*

FATHER: *I don't want you to feel abandoned, but I don't know how to help. It's just too much.*

PRACTITIONER: *Let me make a suggestion. I think we may be able to help you work on some of your problems. You know, with John's illness and the younger children, it's essential for you to work together. All of your children need parents who can work as a team. And John's illness seems to have erased the enjoyment in your marriage and in your family. If you are open to the possibility of marriage counseling, I think we can help you strengthen your marriage, resolve some of your problems, and regain some of the satisfactions in your family life.*

MOTHER: *At this point, I'd be willing to try anything. We are all suffering and seem to strike out at each other. We both need support.*

PRACTITIONER: *I agree. No family could deal with all of your problems without hardships. But when the marriage is in trouble, it makes things much more difficult. What about you, Mr. Gonzales? Are you willing to consider some marriage counseling to help you get through this difficult period?*

FATHER: *I'm not ready to give up on our marriage, but I'm not sure what anybody can do. You can't cure John's illness, can you?*

PRACTITIONER: *No, we can't cure John's bipolar disorder, which tends to be long term. But we can treat the illness effectively, and he is already responding to medication. We can also help you deal with the problems that have resulted from John's illness. And, if you are open to the possibility, we can work together to help you rebuild your marriage.*

FATHER: *Okay, I'm willing to give it a try, but only for a few sessions. I'm too busy to waste my time. Will we continue to meet with you or will we have to deal with someone new?*

PRACTITIONER: *Either way is fine. If you prefer to continue with me, we can change the focus of our sessions to your marital problems. Or if you like, I can refer you to another of our therapists.*

FATHER: *Well, you understand our problems pretty well. I don't feel like starting over again with someone else.*

PRACTITIONER: *Mrs. Gonzales?*

MOTHER: *I agree with Hector. I'm not willing to give up on our marriage. Let's plan to work with you. After a few sessions, we can see whether it makes any sense to continue. We've had a lot of good years, really until John's problems started a couple of years ago. Maybe we can regain some of the good times. I want to try.*

PRACTITIONER: *I hope I can help. Let me schedule an appointment for next week. In the meantime, why don't you think about issues that seem most important at this time, as well as the changes that would make the most difference in your lives. We can begin with those concerns.*

CHAPTER 10

Coping with Challenges

As clinical director at a community mental health center, psychiatrist Claire Mulvihill opens the staff meeting with a case presentation of the Elliot family. Mr. Elliot refuses to accept the mental illness of his 22-year-old daughter, Heather. A heavy drinker for many years, he has recently begun to experience blackouts, to miss work, and to threaten his wife. Heather often disappears for long periods of time. Returning home disheveled and malnourished, she is subjected to an endless stream of criticism from her father. Mrs. Elliot seems frightened of her husband, enraged with Heather, and clinically depressed. Angry with each other, with professionals, and even with God, the Elliots finally agree to attend a single session at the inpatient unit where Heather is now hospitalized. In scheduling the appointment, Mrs. Elliot indignantly proclaims that it might be a good opportunity for them to spell out what's wrong with professionals. As Dr. Mulvihill anticipated, her presentation generates a number of reactions from staff, including a joking suggestion of early retirement. During the ensuring discussion, various staff members describe problems they have faced in working with families, such as entrenched denial of the illness that interferes with effective coping or family intrusiveness that undermines the patient's recovery process. Claire schedules an inservice program to discuss these and other challenges in family practice, asking several staff members to present hypothetical cases that illustrate maladaptive family patterns. She also invites members of the family advisory committee to participate in the program and to share their suggestions with staff.

Although practitioners rarely encounter the array of difficulties posed by the Elliots, it is best to be prepared for family patterns that may interfere with a collaborative and family-focused approach to professional practice. I recently offered a 2-day workshop for

193

case managers who provided services to patients with serious mental illness. One day of the workshop was devoted to family issues, including the challenges these front-line workers had experienced. Each participant wrote down some problems encountered in helping families understand and cope with the mental illness of their relative. We then listed the major problems and spent the remainder of the time on strategies for their resolution.

Some of the family patterns they listed have already been addressed, including confidentiality; limited family understanding of mental illness, its treatment, and its management; failure to recognize the limitations imposed by the illness, such as parents who believed their son could "pull himself up by his bootstraps"; unrealistic expectations for the patient, the family, and the case manager; and specific concerns, such as those experienced by elderly family members. The educational and supportive family interventions already discussed are likely to be helpful in resolving these problems.

Other family patterns may defy straightforward resolution. For instance, families were criticized for having "limited contact" or being "difficult to reach"; for "not accepting the diagnosis"; for "blaming the patient"; for "wanting to do everything"; for "becoming martyrs"; for responding with "polarizing anger"; and for "throwing up their hands" or "giving up—they don't want to cope anymore." Several case managers also commented on patient attitudes, such as not wanting families involved because "It's my problem and I can handle it."

Over time, practitioners who work with families are likely to encounter these and other challenges, which are the focus of the present chapter. Following a discussion of patient resistance, common maladaptive family patterns will be explored, including denial, anger, conflict, overinvolvement, demoralization, and disengagement.

Patient Resistance

Although most patients do not object to professional contact with their families, some do express strong reservations. Negative patient attitudes toward family involvement have many sources, including real mistreatment during the early years of life or paranoid symptoms that are directed toward those with whom they have the most contact. Another source is the healthy desire of patients for separation and autonomy. Because serious mental illness often has its onset in late adolescence or early adulthood, the illness is likely to severely disrupt the developmental achievements of those phases, such as identity, sexuality, separation, autonomy, career plans, and intimacy.

As a result of this developmental disruption, the mental illness may leave a residue of unfinished business for patients whose illness consumes their energy and deflects them from age-appropriate concerns. When patients begin to recover, they are likely to resume their developmental course—however off-time—and to re-engage with their arrested tasks. The awakenings experienced by patients in response to the newer medications illustrate this developmental pattern, sometimes after many years spent in state hospitals, entangled in the revolving door of the community-based system, or encapsulated in psychotic symptoms.

Both patients and parents have commented to me regarding this sense of lost years and its Rip Van Winkle effect:

Consider, for example, a 36-year-old woman, Cheryl, who developed schizophrenia at age 17. Failing to respond to an earlier generation of antipsychotic medications, Cheryl spent almost 2 decades in the public mental health system. In response to clozapine, one of the newer atypical antipsychotic medications, her symptoms are significantly improved.

Now living independently in the community, Cheryl is ready to resume her life. While rejoicing at her daughter's progress, her mother tells me that Cheryl still seems like a teenager in many respects, asking about her high school friends and reading the magazines she enjoyed during that period. Cheryl herself recognizes that she seems to be "stuck" in adolescence, whereas the friends from those years have moved on. Now approaching middle age and contemplating these lost years with new-found lucidity, Cheryl wonders if she will ever catch up.

The developmental course of families offers many parallels. The period of the initial diagnosis is typically disruptive for parents as well as patients, and may pose genuine risks of harm. Often, desperate parents have struggled for many months or even years to obtain treatment for their son or daughter, leaving them with enduring feelings of anxiety and a compelling need to ensure his or her safety. The vigilance and protectiveness of this early period may continue to define family attitudes even when they are no longer appropriate. For instance, the tenacious intrusiveness or overprotectiveness of parents may conflict with the needs of recovering patients to manage their illness, to take risks and learn from their mistakes, to enlarge their social network, and to revive earlier vocational plans.

This conflict between the desire of families to ensure the safety of their relative and the need of patients to achieve separation and autonomy can escalate to the point of estrangement. I have spoken with patients who feel increasingly resentful and smothered by the interference of their parents. Meeting with their parents, I have heard their anguished concern that their son or daughter will end up on the streets or in jail, will again spiral downward into psychosis, or will attempt suicide.

Practitioners can play a constructive role in resolving such conflicts, assisting patients and parents in understanding each other's legitimate concerns, in assuring parents that other supports are now available for their son or daughter, and in helping both parties to develop new attitudes, skills, and behaviors that can foster recovery. Especially if they reside with their parents, most patients can understand the value of having educated and supportive families.

Similarly, most parents can recognize the importance of independence and autonomy. Indeed, offered satisfactory alternatives, most would welcome the opportunity to relinquish some of their caregiving responsibilities and to reinvest their energy in their own lives. Working with both parties, clinicians can help them establish appropriate boundaries and negotiate a comfortable level of contact and family involvement. New adaptations may require time and patience on the part of patients, families, and practitioners. As with all developmental change, transitional periods have an inherent quality of upheaval and disruption that may interact with the stress associated with mental illness. At the same time, these periods offer opportunities for personal and family renewal, as existing patterns are reevaluated and modified in the face of changing circumstances.

On the other hand, some patients—often late adolescents or young adults—may adamantly refuse to have families involved in their treatment, perhaps threatening to terminate treatment if their wishes are not honored. Because their top priority is generally to obtain treatment for their son or daughter, parents are likely to respect a professional recommendation that their involvement is clinically unwise, at least for the present. Over time, some accommodation can usually be reached; in other cases, alternative living arrangements may be required. When it is best for the therapist to avoid personal contact, parents should receive an explanation for the policy and a referral to other resources.

In contrast to these developmental issues, patient resistance may be an appropriate response to a family environment that poses significant risks for the patient and perhaps for other members of the family. Examples include families that manifest domestic violence or abuse, frequent substance abuse, unrelenting hostility toward the patient, or an inadequate level of functioning that places the family at risk. In such cases of potential—or actual—harm, practitioners are often required to take protective action. In one situation, each time a hospitalized patient returned from a home visit with a perpetually chaotic family, he suffered symptom exacerbation that prolonged his inpatient stay. With the patient's agreement (and the family's concurrence), the therapist began planning for his eventual release to a community residence, where the weekend visits proceeded without incident.

Maladaptive Family Patterns

Other family patterns may also pose significant challenges for practitioners, including family denial, anger, conflict, overinvolvement, demoralization, and disengagement. In some cases, these patterns are unrelated to the
mental illness. In other cases, the patterns can be understood as exaggerated manifestations of the family experience of mental illness. During the
course of family adaptation and recovery, for instance, many family members experience a sense of disbelief, intense negative emotions, and family
strife; they often oscillate between overinvolvement and disengagement;
and, especially during periods of crisis or relapse, they are subject to feelings of demoralization. Although understandable, these patterns can pose
significant problems when they persist, when they seriously undermine
family functioning, and when they interfere with patient recovery.

The family interventions already discussed may assist some of these
troubled families to modify their attitudes and behaviors in constructive
ways, although their adaptational course is typically slow and uneven.
Each of these family patterns will be examined, with emphasis on the experiential context and the implications for professional practice.

DENIAL

Robert Gottfried's parents refuse to believe their son has schizophrenia.
His father, Rudolf, insists that Robert could solve his problems if he simply
started taking responsibility for his life. His mother, Gertrude, insists that
it is impossible that one of *her* children could have mental illness. They present a united—and tenacious—front in the face of the treatment team,
which is attempting to educate them about Robert's mental illness and
about its treatment and management. What is a practitioner to do?

Initially, it is important to recognize that denial and disbelief are common responses during the beginning phase of family adaptation. In fact,
these defense mechanisms often serve an essential protective function that
shields family members from the full force of this catastrophic stressor and
allows them to adapt at their own pace. When these protective mechanisms
persist, however, they can prevent families from coming to terms with the
illness.

Denial is most frequent during the initial psychotic episode. As Kayla
Bernheim and Anthony Lehman have counseled, family members should
not be pushed into giving up their denial prematurely (or entirely); they
can be helped to adapt in spite of their need to protect themselves from
the harsh reality of serious mental illness.[1] In fact, as family members develop an accurate understanding about mental illness, they may find that
reality is not as bad as they assumed. On the other hand, some family

members may never fully accept the mental illness; others may require an extended period of time before relinquishing their early denial and disbelief. A given family may include members with varying degrees of acceptance.

In the case of the Gottfried family, their entrenched pattern of denial is likely to redouble if confronted directly. Recognizing the protective function of their adaptation, family therapist Joyce Guerlain allows the family to set their own pace and agenda. Beginning with relatively unstructured home-based sessions, she listens to their stories and patiently encourages them to acquire pertinent knowledge and skills. With time and support, she is able to engage the family, to increase their understanding, and to enlist their support for Robert. Acceptance is particularly difficult for Mr. Gottfied, but eventually he, too, is able to acknowledge the illness and to begin to play a constructive role in his son's life. Ultimately, Joyce's goal is to assist the family to find an appropriate balance between denying and overemphasizing the illness.[2]

Anger

Even as her paranoia subsides in response to medication, 18-year-old Janet Paulson remains livid with her mother, Lateva, who served as a petitioner at the hearing resulting in her daughter's involuntary commitment. In turn, Lateva is furious with Janet for adding to her problems as a single parent of three teenagers. Having struggled for years to create a stable and religious home for her children in a crime-ridden inner-city neighborhood, she is outraged at her daughter's destructive and bizarre behavior, experiencing it as a personal affront. Lateva refuses to believe Janet is not fully responsible for her behavior. After her mother's visits, which escalate their joint anger, Janet's symptoms frequently intensify.

Families who have suffered through an involuntary commitment commonly experience considerable anger in its wake. More generally, anger is inextricably woven into the family experience of mental illness; it derives from many sources, assumes many forms, and focuses on many objects. When experienced in connection with intense feelings of grief and loss, anger may define a particular phase of the grieving process or erupt periodically as a manifestation of chronic sorrow. Family members may direct the anger at God or fate for the injustice visited on their family, at the patient for symptomatic behavior or for failing to get better, at other relatives for real or imagined transgressions, at themselves for actual mistakes or human fallibility, or at professionals for genuine deficiencies or a shortage of miracles.

Sometimes the anger masks other aspects of the subjective burden, serving to deflect unbearable feelings of hopelessness. As one mother explained, "Anger is sometimes a protection against helplessness and emptiness. It makes me feel temporarily less vulnerable—at least for a little while."[3] Often, these sources of anger are cumulative. When it predominates and persists, anger subverts patient recovery, family relationships, and family-professional alliances.

This accumulating anger may intersect with—and potentiate—the anger associated with particular family circumstances, as in the case of Janet and Lateva Paulson. Faced with such intense anger, it is sensible for practitioners to meet separately with family members and with patients, allowing them to express their feelings of frustration. Responding with compassion and tolerance, professionals can educate family members regarding the symptoms and limitations associated with mental illness, and assist them in developing more realistic expectations for all members of the family.

Likewise, clinicians can assist patients to understand the attitudes and behaviors of their family members, who are often struggling to do their best under formidable circumstances. Both parties can be helped to understand the roots of their anger, to express their feelings in more appropriate ways, and to channel some of their anger more productively. For instance, advocacy efforts benefit significantly from a "fire in the belly."

CONFLICT

The parents of Peter Lang have been arguing about their son's mental illness since the time of his admission, their vociferous disputes attracting considerable attention from the unit's patients, staff, and visitors. Mr. Lang repeatedly screams at his wife for being "too easy" on their son and for "turning him into a sissy." His wife responds in kind, yelling that her husband is too busy visiting the local bars to know what has been going on at home. Two younger siblings seem paralyzed by their brother's illness and by the family conflict.

As noted earlier, mental illness creates fertile ground for conflict. Especially at the onset of the illness, family members may disagree about the diagnosis, the treatment and rehabilitation plan, the roles and responsibilities of particular family members, the best ways of managing the illness, and their relationships with professionals. Given the stress and disruption associated with mental illness, any pre-existing conflicts are likely to be exacerbated under these circumstances, siphoning energy that is needed for effective family functioning, undermining family relationships, eroding the family's quality of life, and interfering with the patient's recovery.

Working with the Lang family, psychiatric nurse Theresa Hampton schedules an initial meeting with the parents to allow them to express their feelings and to assist them in understanding each other's views. She validates each of their perspectives, indicating that it is indeed important for Peter to assume responsibility for managing his illness, as his father believes, and that family support is also essential, as his mother asserts. At the same time, Theresa encourages the parents to work together to support Peter's recovery and to meet the needs of their younger children.

Enlisting the family's natural support network, Theresa assists them in involving members of the extended family who reside nearby, as well as supportive neighbors and members of their church. Once family conflict has diminished, she can meet with the entire family—and perhaps other members of their support network—to educate them about Peter's mental illness and his vulnerability to stress. Continuing sessions might assist the family to enhance communication and problem-solving skills, to resolve disagreements in a less contentious manner, and to develop a workable family plan that can address their present and future needs.

OVERINVOLVEMENT

The irate parents of Antonio Torres have arrived at the treatment center where their son is hospitalized. The first member of his family to attend college, Antonio received a full scholarship to attend a university an hour away from home. His parents strongly resisted his plans to live away from home, although his own wishes ultimately prevailed. Antonio experienced his first psychotic episode several months ago, at the beginning of his sophomore year. His parents received a call from the dean, who described Antonio's symptoms and recommended hospitalization at a nearby medical center. Rejecting the recommendation, the parents insisted on bringing their son home and attempted to provide care.

After Antonio's condition deteriorated further, however, they brought him to a local emergency room, which transferred him to the inpatient unit of their mental health center. Although his parents initially approved their son's hospitalization, they now insist that they want Antonio released immediately to their care, resisting all recommendations of the treatment team and expressing outrage at this intrusion into what they consider a family matter.

Overinvolvement is an understandable response, especially among family members who serve as primary caregivers or informal case managers for their relatives, often with little professional support and guidance. Over the course of the illness, they may have experienced repeated crises, frightening psychotic episodes, difficulty accessing appropriate treatment, and perhaps homelessness, suicide attempts, violence, or incarceration. Mindful of these potential hazards, families may circle the wagons in an effort to protect their relative's safety and perhaps his or her life.

Frozen into a centripetal mode of functioning, the family's posture may hinder the patient's recovery as well as the autonomy of other family members.

What appears to be a pattern of family overinvolvement may have many sources, including the cultural patterns of ethnic minority families, whose extended network often serves as a great resource and protector during period of stress. Frequently, separation from the family is not desired, expected, or easily accepted. Yet this culturally normative pattern of close family ties may be viewed as family enmeshment or interference. Other sources of family overinvolvement may be more personal, such as the need of a parent to feel important and needed, to avoid loneliness or emptiness, or to atone for presumed sins of the past.[4]

At the same time, a high level of family involvement is not always inappropriate. A diagnosis of serious mental illness carries genuine risks of harm to the patient and perhaps to others. Family members often complain about the absence of professional assistance when they are forced to deal with these risks. Thus, practitioners need to apprehend the family's subjective reality before drawing conclusions. Likewise, although it conflicts with the Western value of personal autonomy, a comfortable pattern of interdependence may be a reasonable accommodation for a given family. When a counterproductive pattern of overinvolvement does exist, after gaining an understanding of its cultural and dynamic origins, practitioners can assist families to respond more appropriately to their relative while simultaneously meeting their own needs.

Working with the Torres family, psychologist Steve Thomas recognizes the value of Antonio's extensive support network, at least over the long term. The immediate goal, however, is to help his parents understand his mental illness and the importance of treatment. Meeting with the parents, Steve affirms the significance of the family in helping Antonio recover. He also begins to educate the family about the illness, especially emphasizing the benefits of providing a low-stress environment for Antonio in the hospital and following his release.

Assured that Antonio's illness is truly a family matter and that their involvement is essential for his recovery, his parents gradually become more receptive to the suggestions of the treatment team. Responding to medication, Antonio himself encourages his parents to work with the team as they plan for his release.

DEMORALIZATION

The Wu family arrives at the inpatient unit to visit their son Charlie, who has been hospitalized repeatedly for schizophrenia over the past 2 years.

His symptoms are partially responsive to medication, but he frequently misses appointments. Emigrating from Taiwan 20 years ago, the Wus now own a small grocery store, which requires long hours of work. Struggling to ensure their children a better life, they remain confused about Charlie's illness and despondent about their family's future. Their feelings of hopelessness and helplessness have been internalized by Charlie, an only son who feels he has failed to satisfy his parents' expectations, and whose missed appointments—and frequent relapses—are closely tied to his struggle with role demands he can no longer fulfill.

The experience of demoralization is a familiar one to many families. Reeling from the family burden, family members may struggle with intense feelings of grief and loss, recurrent crises and relapses, symptomatic behavior, caregiving responsibilities, limitations of the service delivery system, and social stigma. Faced with these long-term and sometimes lifetime burdens, it is no wonder that most families occasionally appear disheartened and debilitated. For some families, however, demoralization calcifies into a constant state that renders them paralyzed by their anguish and unable to move on with their lives.

Meeting with the Wus for the first time, social worker Joan Morelli encourages them to talk about their feelings. Acknowledging the difficulty of discussing such "private" concerns with someone outside their family, Mr. and Mrs. Wu gradually begin to share their shattered hopes and expectations. Educating them about the illness, Joan explains that schizophrenia is a real illness for which there are effective treatments. Comparing the illness to diabetes, which is familiar to the family, she talks about Charlie's biological vulnerability, the importance of obtaining appropriate treatment, and the possibility of his recovery.

Patiently, Joan assists them in developing realistic expectations for Charlie and other members of the family. Mobilizing their family's considerable resources, the Wus begin to come to terms with the mental illness, to reach out to their son, and to reinvest in their family's future.

DISENGAGEMENT

Following their daughter Rosa's involuntary commitment, Mr. and Mrs. Carsella have told the treatment team they no longer wish to have contact with her. The past few months have been a nightmare for the family, as they witnessed 20-year-old Rosa swing from manic highs to immobilizing lows, threaten suicide, spend family money that is needed for food, abuse alcohol, and embarrass the family by becoming sexually involved with several men. Feeling violated and betrayed, these Catholic parents have decided they can only protect their younger children by severing their relationship with Rosa. With little recollection of her manic episodes and now stabilized on lithium, Rosa feels abandoned by her family.

It is not difficult to empathize with families like the Carsellas and to understand their feelings of violation and betrayal. Witnessing their relative's bizarre, inappropriate, or destructive behavior, families may assume the behavior is both willful and hostile. Feeling drained and helpless, they may consider their very survival dependent on terminating their relationship. For instance, following a brutalizing involuntary commitment process, I was consulted by an out-of-state sibling. He believed that his elderly mother required protection from the devastation wrought by his brother's mental illness. For many years, this widowed mother had served as a primary caregiver for her son; now in declining health, she was no longer able to fulfill that role.

Yet, taking a course of action they considered unavoidable, this caring mother and sibling were consumed with feelings of guilt as they contemplated their "divorce" (the term they used) from their relative. With professional assistance, the family was able to develop a plan that allowed them to meet the needs of the patient, who is now living in a community residence with the support of a case manager; of the sibling, who regularly consults with his brother's case manager and plays a more active role in his life; and of the mother, who is assured that she can honor her commitment to her son in spite of declining health.

Understanding and respecting the sentiments of the Carsellas, counselor Tim Goulding offers to make a home visit to listen to their concerns. Gradually gaining a better understanding of Rosa's bipolar disorder, the Carsellas begin to separate their daughter from her illness, to view her troublesome symptoms in a less personal way, and to acknowledge her efforts to cope with her illness. After receiving home-based services for several weeks, the Carsellas are willing to receive services at the agency, including some joint sessions with Rosa. Now working together, the family is slowly learning to communicate more effectively, to resolve their disputes, and to manage the illness.

Meeting Challenges: Issues and Strategies

Although understandable from the perspective of family burden, the family patterns just discussed nevertheless pose significant risks for patients, for families, and for family-professional relationships. Most families do want to play a constructive role in their relative's life, but may have little sense of what that role might be. Assured that they need not sacrifice the integrity of their own lives to the illness, family members may welcome an opportunity to sustain family bonds in some form and to maintain a "loving distance."[5]

In fact, with time and appropriate interventions, most problems do show improvement. Encountering these family patterns, practitioners can increase the likelihood of constructive change by:

- Fostering family engagement
- Focusing on the concerns of families themselves
- Serving as a cornerstone of their support system
- Reframing these patterns from the family's perspective
- Addressing the essential needs of families
- Initiating a process of successive approximation
- Employing a flexible and creative approach
- Encouraging a sense of hopefulness
- Joining forces with families as advocates for system change

Each of these suggestions is discussed briefly. First, it is critical to *foster family engagement,* which may require substantial patience, energy, tolerance, and compassion. However maladaptive their responses may appear, most families struggle to do their best under daunting circumstances. Often, these families are aware of negative professional judgments regarding their attitudes and behaviors, which only serve to consolidate their resistance. Thus, practitioners need to understand each family's history and current situation, to accept each family on its own terms, and to respect their unique adaptations and responses.

Second, especially in their initial contacts, clinicians should *focus on the concerns of families themselves.* An important source of family anger and disengagement is the failure of providers—both individuals and agencies—to acknowledge the experiences and needs of families, to establish channels of communication with them, and to involve them in decisions that affect them. Practitioners can offer families an opportunity to ventilate about their previous encounters with providers and assure them of a genuine interest in addressing their needs. As Bernheim and Lehman have indicated, the attitude "What can we do *for you?"* works much better than "What are *you going to do* for the patient?"[6] The more hostile and defensive the family, the more important it is to assume a consultative mode and to serve as a family advisor, educator, and collaborator.

Third, practitioners can *serve as a cornerstone of the support system* of these embattled and enervated families. As Susan McDaniel and her colleagues have affirmed, such families have a need for the communion found in emotional bonds, which can be all but sundered by illness. Defining communion as a restoration of human connections, they encourage practitioners to counteract the collective isolation imposed by the illness and to assist families in recapturing their affection, humor, common interests, and mutual respect:

Family members may be stuck together in a tight clump of single-minded preoccupation with the illness and its costs, while at the same time feeling deeply isolated from one another. Their love and concern for one another can become fused with guilt, anguish, resentment and depression that completely distort the quality of family life.[7]

The more disorganized and inadequate the family, the more important it is to enlist community resources on their behalf. These may include case managers, home aides, respite services, church volunteers, extended family, and other potential sources of support.

Fourth, it is important to *reframe these patterns from the family's perspective,* which can offer practitioners insight into their current adaptations. As Harriet Lefley has discussed, families may manifest aggression as a means of meeting their needs; anger in response to a long history of being sloughed off or ignored; defensive humility in response to their treatment as pariahs; acting out in response to provider expectations; guilt as a strategy for controlling the illness (if they have caused the illness, perhaps they can cure it); sabotage in response to inappropriate interventions or to unresolved hostilities that may surface in the patient's therapy; and fear of recovery in response to a history of dashed expectations.[8] Understanding possible sources of these family responses can facilitate their modification.

Fifth, practitioners need to *offer families a forum* for telling their stories and expressing their feelings. Families may experience guilt or fear about their relative's illness, resistance to accepting its severe and persistent nature, anger regarding prior negative experiences with the mental health system, and despair about their family circumstances. It is often helpful to bring these feelings out in the open and place them in the context of the family experience of mental illness.[9] In turn, this open expression of feelings allows practitioners to help family members come to terms with the illness, resolve their subjective burden, and learn how to meet their needs.

Sixth, practitioners should strive to *address the essential needs of families* for information, skills, and support. Whatever their unique circumstances, virtually all families that have contact with their relatives can benefit from current information about mental illness, skills for managing the illness, and social support. With better understanding of mental illness and its symptoms, family members are likely to develop compassion and tolerance for relatives who may sometimes have little control over their behavior and equally little awareness of its impact on others. Likewise, effective coping skills can lessen the family's feelings of vulnerability, reduce their level of ambient stress, and enhance their sense of self-confidence and self-efficacy. Social support can serve as a buffer against high levels of stress and reduce family isolation and alienation.

Seventh, beginning with the family's current adaptation, practitioners can *initiate a process of successive approximation* that can assist families in reaching appropriate goals in a step-by-step fashion. With professional support, the defensiveness and rigidity of families are likely to decrease, which in turn offers an opportunity for beneficial change. Allowing families to set their own pace and agenda, practitioners can encourage them to gradually alter their attitudes, expectations, and behaviors. An initial step might involve a willingness to meet with a consultant for a single session, to attend a 1-day workshop, to consider re-establishing contact with their relative, or to support a change in residence.

Eighth, practitioners need to *employ a flexible and creative approach* in working with these families. For example, within a given family, members are likely to vary in their degree of acceptance, their coping effectiveness, and their desire and ability to provide support to their relative. Some members may never be able to play a constructive role in their relative's life; others may require an extended period of time before relinquishing their earlier maladaptive patterns. Establishing a workable alliance with selected individuals, clinicians can encourage them to assist their less functional and accessible family members. Similarly, professionals might work creatively with a given family to develop a nontraditional family network of close friends, neighbors, and church members.[10]

Ninth, it is essential to *encourage a sense hopefulness* regarding the future. In *The Psychology of Hope: You Can Get There from Here*, C. Snyder[11] specifies the three essential elements of hope: a meaningful goal; willpower, which is the reservoir of determination and commitment that drives us toward our goal; and waypower, defined as the pathways—our mental maps or road plans—that guide us toward our goal. Practitioners can offer invaluable assistance to families who need support in clarifying their goals, in replenishing their depleted reservoir of willpower, and in finding the pathways to family renewal.

Finally, recognizing the limitations of the current service delivery system, practitioners can *join forces with families* as advocates for system change.[12] Salutary changes include increasing family access to providers, including family members on treatment teams, educating staff regarding family experiences and needs, training professionals regarding consultative and collaborative modes of working with families, and developing family-focused programs. At the same time, as Agnes Hatfield has cautioned, the availability of effective family interventions should not imply that families are solely responsible for the care of people with mental illness.[13] The ultimate responsibility should be shared with society and the mental health system.

Not all families are willing or able to modify their maladaptive patterns or to play a constructive role in the patient's life. In such cases, treatment planning should reflect these limitations. For example, where family hostility and conflict remain entrenched, the patient may need alternative living arrangements and sources of social support. As Bernheim and Lehman have written, "Every family deserves a chance, and every clinician has the right and responsibility to say 'enough is enough.'"[14] Indeed, practitioners need to protect themselves by recognizing their own limitations, making necessary referrals, consulting with knowledgeable colleagues, and cultivating their personal support network.

From Theory to Practice

Along with these suggestions for resolving family problems, several family interventions have now been discussed, including consultation, family support and advocacy groups, family education, family psychoeducation, and psychotherapy. Each of these interventions offers potential benefits—and poses potential risks—for particular families and individual family members. What is the best way to proceed?

The following sequential model can assist practitioners in achieving an optimal service match for particular families and settings. Incorporating the guidelines already discussed, the model encourages a competency-based and collaborative mode of working with families and an individualized approach to family service planning. Regardless of the potential value of various interventions, however, there is no way to know in advance which services will be most helpful for a particular family at a given point in time.

A Three-Step Model for Family Intervention

The model includes three sequential steps: (a) offering an initial family consultation session; (b) assisting families to select and access a combination of consultative, supportive, and educational services; and (c) recommending psychotherapy for those families who continue to experience significant problems.

Step 1

At the onset of the illness, family consultation offers a useful means of engaging families and of assisting them in identifying and prioritizing their needs, in dealing with illness-related concerns, in making an informed choice about their use of other available services, and in formulating a family service plan. As already noted, consultation may be sufficient for some families, especially if it is offered at the time of the initial diagnosis and thereafter on an as-needed basis, such as during crises, periods of inpatient treatment, or life span transitions.

Step 2

Virtually all families share certain essential needs, including their needs for information, skills, and support. In a given community, a variety of services may help families address these needs, including a local family support and advocacy organization, such as NAMI, which may offer a family support group and a variety of educational programs. Professional services may also be helpful, such as a provider-based support group, educational workshops or programs, or a more intensive psychoeducational program. When they are integrated into an individualized family service plan, Steps 1 and 2 are likely to meet the needs of most families.

Step 3

Family members who continue to manifest significant problems may be appropriate candidates for individual, marital, or family therapy, either singly or in combination. For instance, individual therapy can assist family members in resolving issues of grief, loss, guilt, and responsibility; marital therapy can help couples resolve illness-related conflicts and other relational problems; and family therapy can foster improvements in communication, problem solving, conflict resolution, and illness management skills.

The model requires practitioners to evaluate the potential value of various services with respect to the requirements of a given family. The following tables may offer some assistance.

COMPARING FAMILY INTERVENTIONS

Tables 10.1 and 10.2 summarize material presented thus far for the five family interventions: consultation, support and advocacy groups (NAMI), education, psychoeducation, and psychotherapy.[15] Table 10.1 presents four dimensions of family interventions: provider, components, format, and duration.

TABLE 10.1
DIMENSIONS OF FAMILY INTERVENTIONS

Family Intervention	Provider	Components	Format	Duration
Consultation	Professional	Support Education Skills	Family: Single Patient: Variable	Initially and as needed
Support and Advocacy Group (NAMI)	Family	Support Education Skills Advocacy	Family: Multiple Patient: Variable	Ongoing 12 weeks Ongoing Ongoing
Education	Family Professional Family- professional team	Support Education Skills	Family: Multiple Patient: Variable	1 day to 12 weeks
Psycho- education	Professional	Support Education Skills Treatment	Family: Variable Patient: Variable	9 months to 2 years
Psychotherapy	Professional	Treatment	Individual Marital Family Group	Variable

Provider

Professionals serve as providers for consultation, psychoeducation, and psychotherapy, whereas support and advocacy groups are run by families. Educational programs may be offered by family members, by professionals, or by a family-professional team.

Components

Consultation, support and advocacy groups, education, and psychoeducation all target family support, information, and skills, although their relative emphasis differs, partly as a function of duration. A 1-day educational workshop is largely informational; a 12-week educational program can offer some skills training; and a 9-month psychoeducational program can provide individualized practice and feedback. In addition to these shared components, support and advocacy groups also offer

TABLE 10.2
FAMILY INTERVENTIONS: PROFESSIONAL ISSUES

Family Intervention	Services Model	Conceptual Basis	Outcome Variables	Empirical Support
Consultation	Advisory & collaborative	Professional expertise	Family satisfaction Family competence & confidence	Insufficient research
Support and Advocacy Group (NAMI)	Self- & mutual-help	Family empowerment	Family burden, knowledge, skills, & quality of life System change	Insufficient research
Education	Instructional & developmental	Coping & adaptation Family stress Social support	Family burden, knowledge, skills, & quality of life	Insufficient research
Psycho-education	Medical & authoritarian	Vulnerability-stress	Patient relapse & rehospitalization Family burden	Strong
Psychotherapy	Medical & authoritarian	Professional expertise	Functioning Satisfaction Distress	Mixed

opportunities for advocacy; psychoeducation may include a treatment component. Psychotherapy primarily offers treatment, which may—but does not necessarily—involve support, education, and skills training.

Format

Consultation is offered to single families, with patients sometimes included in sessions. NAMI generally offers separate educational and support services to families and to consumers (although some programs include both groups), with joint participation in advocacy activities. Education is typically offered to multiple family groups, with patient participation variable. Psychoeducation may be offered to single or multiple families, again with patient participation variable. Psychotherapy may be provided to individual family members, to couples, or to single or multiple families (with or without patients).

Duration

Consultation is best offered initially and then on an as-needed basis. NAMI provides most services on an ongoing basis; however, their popular Family-to-Family Education Program lasts 12 weeks. Educational programs typically vary from a 1-day workshop to a 12-week program. Psychoeducation requires the longest duration, generally ranging from 9 months to 2 years or more. Although the duration of psychotherapy is flexible, the mandates of managed care organizations have increased the likelihood of relatively brief, problem-focused approaches.

Table 10.2 compares the family interventions with respect to four important professional issues: services model, conceptual basis, outcome variables, and empirical support.

Services Model

Consultation assumes an advisory and collaborative services model; support and advocacy groups are guided by the principles of self- and mutual-help; and education offers an instructional and developmental approach to intervention. Both psychoeducation and psychotherapy largely reflect a medical model and an authoritarian mode.

Conceptual Basis

The conceptual basis of both consultation and psychotherapy is professional expertise. In contrast, family empowerment provides the conceptual foundation for support and advocacy groups. Family education draws on several conceptual models, including coping and adaptation, family stress, and social support. Psychoeducation is based primarily on the vulnerability-stress model of serious mental illness, with emphasis on the value of medication, education, and skills training.

Outcome Variables

The primary outcome variable for consultation is family satisfaction; family competence and confidence are also important. Several outcome variables are important both in support and advocacy groups and in education: family burden, knowledge, skills, and quality of life. By virtue of their advocacy role, the family groups also target system change. Earlier psychoeducational programs typically focused on patient relapse and rehospitalization; current programs are more likely to give equal weight to measures of family burden. Outcomes in psychotherapy consist of such variables as levels of functioning, satisfaction, and distress.

Empirical Support

Strongest support is available for psychoeducation and psychotherapy, although the latter support is not specifically concerned with families of people with mental illness. In fact, in responding to surveys, family members consistently rate educational and supportive resources as more helpful than therapy. Empirical support is limited for consultation, support and advocacy groups, and education, reflecting a shortage of relevant research rather than negative results.

The few controlled studies *do* suggest that these interventions offer benefits for families. For example, based on their evaluation of the 12-week Family-to-Family Education Program offered by NAMI, Susan Pickett and her colleagues found that participants reported increased knowledge of mental illness and its treatment, better understanding of symptoms and their management, and increased awareness of mental health programs and advocacy strategies.[16] In addition, families developed more realistic expectations and an improved relationship with their relative. They also reported diminished feelings of guilt and isolation and described themselves as more empowered, better able to take care of themselves, and having a happier outlook on life.

IMPLEMENTING THE MODEL

Summarizing material presented thus far, several considerations should guide the application of this model in working with families. First, the available *professional and community resources* will largely determine the services that can be provided. For instance, although NAMI has more than 1,000 local affiliates, the distance may be prohibitive for some family members. Solo or group practitioners may be limited to family consultation, family support groups, family education, and psychotherapy. Agency-based clinicians may be able to provide the full array of family interventions, including family psychoeducation.

Second, *family involvement* in the development of services will enhance the likelihood that families will actually participate in them and find them responsive to their needs. Going a step further, family members might participate as copresenters of an educational program or as cofacilitators of an ongoing support group. Thus, agency-based services can benefit from family consultation as services are designed, implemented, and evaluated.

Third, as is the case with patients, *an individualized service plan* should be developed for particular families. During the initial consultative session, practitioners can ascertain the family's comparative needs for support, information, skills, resolution, and advocacy; their preference for an individual or multifamily format; the most appropriate setting for service provision (e.g., home-based or provider-based); the optimal duration and intensity (e.g., an educational workshop, family psychoeducation, or psychotherapy); and their developmental phase (e.g., the initial diagnosis, a relapse or rehospitalization, or continuity of caregiving).

Fourth, *a differentiated approach* to family-oriented services is needed. Because the experiences, needs, and coping resources of family members differ as a function of their role, practitioners can offer services not only to parents, but also to spouses, siblings, and offspring (see Chapters 11 through 15). Thus, during the initial consultative phase, clinicians should explore the needs of all members of the family, including those who are not present.

Fifth, during the consultative process, practitioners need to conduct *cost-benefit and risk-benefit analyses* of alternative services and to share this analysis with families. The objective is to recommend the combination of interventions that provide the most benefits for the lowest cost and with the fewest risks. Thus, for example, in accordance with the principle of least intervention, professionals can make a referral to family-facilitated services in the community, which are commonly offered without charge.[17] Likewise, consultants should recommend psychotherapy only when less intensive services have not been sufficient.[18]

At the same time, research support for various interventions should receive consideration, including the strong evidence that family psychoeducation can reduce the risk of relapse or rehospitalization. When making recommendations to particular families, consultants should share their rationale, offer an opportunity for discussion, and respect the right of families to decide upon their use of services.

Sixth, as Solomon remarks, reforms in behavioral health care require *time-limited, efficient, and cost-effective interventions.*[19] Although family interventions have the potential to meet these criteria, many unanswered questions remain. For example, what is the optimal length of these interventions? Does it matter who is the service provider? What is the most effective combination of interventions? Is there a preferable sequencing of interventions? Additional research is needed to answer these questions.

Finally, regardless of the potential value of family interventions, some families may decline all services or may terminate their participation prematurely. Requesting *feedback from families,* practitioners can gain insight into their reasons for declining or terminating services, which may include lack of time or insurance coverage, alienation from the mental health system, family disengagement, or various personal, family, or cultural considerations. Such feedback can assist professionals in tailoring service plans for individual families and in developing more satisfactory and responsive family-focused services.

PART FOUR

Working with Individual Family Members

CHAPTER 11

Working with Parents

Social worker Jeffrey Blume has scheduled an appointment for marital therapy with Marsha and Harold Rosenthal, whose 19-year-old son Andrew was diagnosed with schizophrenia a year ago. In her telephone call, Marsha said her son's mental illness has had a devastating effect on the entire family. Requesting marital therapy, Marsha remarked that she and her husband seem unable to discuss their son's illness without conflict; she is unsure the marriage will survive. She is also worried about the impact of their family stress and marital problems on her younger sons, 16-year-old twins Kevin and Rick. As the parent of teenagers himself, Jeffrey reflects on the meaning of a child's mental illness for parents who are living through what is already a turbulent period for most families.

Contemplating his appointment with the Rosenthals, Jeffrey Blume mentally reviews his understanding of the family experience of mental illness. He wonders why so much of the literature seems to focus on the family unit, as if its members were indistinguishable. In his own contacts with family members, he has been impressed not only with their diversity but also with the importance of various family roles. Individual family members have unique experiences, needs, and concerns in their role as parent, spouse, sibling, or offspring.

Jeffrey thinks of Joseph Brown, a 43-year-old patient with bipolar disorder who was recently hospitalized following a relapse. During Joseph's inpatient treatment, the staff had contact with various members of his family. Although these family members shared a commitment to Joseph, each also had personal concerns. In poor health herself, his widowed 68-year-old mother was concerned about continuity of caregiving for her son following her death, his 41-year-old wife about the impact of her husband's hospitalization on their teenage children, his 48-year-old sister about balancing her commitments to her brother and her own family, and his 19-year-old son about future caregiving responsibilities for his father.

Recognizing both the shared and unique concerns of family members, Jeffrey offers consultation and education to single families and multifamily groups, as well as services to individual family members upon request. He is pleased to see that the professional literature has increasingly focused on the needs of all members of the family, including spouses, siblings, offspring, grandparents, and other extended family members. For example, in *The Skipping Stone: Ripple Effects of Mental Illness on the Family*, Mona Wasow has explored each of these roles.[1]

Capturing some of their essential differences in her chapter titles, Wasow writes of spouses who cope with "The No-Casserole Illness" in the absence of social validation and support (or even the casseroles typically offered when a husband or wife has a severe medical condition); of siblings who beseech "Please Hear Me" in a world where the mental illness of their brother or sister seems to garner all the attention; of offspring who plaintively cry "Help Me" in the face of pressure to grow up quickly in response to forces over which they have so little control; of grandparents who experience "The Triple Whammy" of losses for themselves, their adult child, and their grandchild; and of extended family members who are often aware of the mental illness in their family but curious about "What Is Going On?"

Chapters 11 through 14 explore parental, spousal, sibling, and offspring roles. These nuclear family members are most likely to be affected by their relative's mental illness, to assume caregiving roles, and to interact with practitioners. In a given family, however, grandparents or other extended family members may fulfill important functions. Professionals should routinely inquire whether there is anyone else in the family who might benefit from contact with practitioners or who might offer support to the patient or primary caregiver.

In one family, following the unexpected death of the patient's mother, who had served as his primary caregiver for over three decades, a first cousin and his wife helped the fragile family unit regroup. During a transitional time, these extended family members represented the family in their contacts with professionals, helped the family make necessary legal and clinical decisions, attended meetings with the treatment team, and assisted the family to develop long-term plans for the patient and other family members. The children of this couple (the patient's second cousins) have also been affected by the mental illness of someone who lives in the same community and has been a regular presence in their lives.

Many families have extended family members like these. Some may have worried about their relative from a distance; perhaps they have questions or concerns. Others might welcome an opportunity to play a more active role in their relative's life but have little sense of what that role might be. In the absence of professional overtures, their distress will remain unacknowledged, their questions unanswered, and their contributions to the family unrealized.

In fact, whatever the formal role of individual family members, their functional role may be analogous to those discussed in these four chapters, with similar implications for professional practice. Often, a grandmother or aunt will function as a parent, or a cousin as a sibling. In addition, many families have nonbiological surrogate members who participate in the life of the family, perform important functions, and offer invaluable support. Thus, while these chapters deal specifically with parents, spouses, siblings, and offspring, the material also applies to other individuals who fulfill similar roles and who serve as an important family resource.

Because most of what has been written about families of people with mental illness focuses on parents, there is greatest understanding of their experiences and of the interventions that can address their needs. Indeed, much of the material covered thus far in this book depicts the parental experience of mental illness, or at least the experience of parents who have had contact with researchers and clinicians. There is less understanding of other members of the family, although they, too, are often deeply affected by their relative's mental illness. In reaching out to extended family members, practitioners increase the likelihood that all members of the family will play a constructive role in the lives of their relative and the nuclear family.

The earlier discussion of diversity provides an essential context for understanding the needs of parents, spouses, siblings, and offspring, whose experiences are defined in important respects by their gender, culture, ethnicity, and social status. These variables are likely to influence their family ties, relationships, and caregiving responsibilities; their experience of family burden; the availability of social support; their perception of mental illness and its management; and their encounter with the mental health system. However, certain themes are likely to be associated with each family role.

This, the first of these role-oriented chapters, focuses appropriately on parents, who are most likely to serve as primary caregivers and to have contact with professionals and other service providers. Topics include the parental experience of mental illness, particular themes that distinguish that experience, the needs of parents, and intervention strategies for parents.

The Parental Experience

What does it mean to be a parent of a child with serious mental illness? Parents are subject to a subjective burden, which consists of a powerful grieving process, symbolic losses that pertain to hopes and expectations, chronic sorrow that is woven into the familial fabric on a continuing basis, an emotional roller coaster in response to alternating periods of remission and relapse, and empathic pain for the continuing losses experienced by their child. Parents must also deal with an onerous objective burden, which is the daily problems and challenges associated with mental illness: the symptoms of the illness, caregiving responsibilities, family disruption and stress, financial problems, limitations of the service delivery system, and social stigma.

As with other family members, parents have essential needs for information, skills, and support; they undergo a process of adaptation and recovery; and they can benefit from a range of interventions, including family support and advocacy groups, consultation, education, psychoeducation, and psychotherapy. Thus, general material concerned with the family experience of mental illness provides a solid foundation for professional practice with parents. There are nevertheless a number of distinct themes likely to arise in working with these family members.

Parental Themes

Practitioners who work with parents and listen to their stories will find that certain issues and concerns arise repeatedly and with much force. This section explores salient themes that practitioners encounter in working with mothers and fathers as individuals or as a couple. In contacts with parents, practitioners might use this discussion as a basis for exploring the experiences of individual parents, who may be so consumed with their caregiving role that they overlook their own needs and concerns.

Many of these parental themes suggest anguish, loss, and—at best— challenge. Yet it is essential to be cognizant of the potential for parental resilience. Most parents do manage to cope with the mental illness of their child, to sustain their family, and to achieve a balance that meets the needs of all family members. This woman was 7 years old when her older sister developed schizophrenia. Yet her parents were able to meet the needs of their other children, and she felt loved and cherished as she was growing up:

Amazingly, despite the presence of this horrible illness in our lives, my childhood was, in many ways, a normal one. I took piano lessons, went to camp. My parents took us on vacations and out to dinner. They attended all of the important milestones in my childhood. I never doubted their love for me.[2]

GRIEF AND LOSS

Feelings of grief and loss are typically at the center of the parental experience. Indeed, parents may mourn for the loss of the well child for whom there was so much potential, for the loss of their normal family, and for the loss of their own hopes and dreams. In the words of one mother, "The sense of what might have been is overwhelming."[3]

As Theresa Rando has discussed, bereavement is especially intense when the loss involves a child.[4] Children embody many things to parents: promise, aspirations, dreams, fantasies, and new beginnings. With the loss of a son or daughter, parents have lost parts of themselves, each other, their family, and their future. These intense feelings of loss are captured in the personal accounts of parents, such as *Tell Me I'm Here* by Anne Deveson and *Conquering Schizophrenia* by Peter Wyden.[5]

When discussing the mental illness of a beloved son or daughter, parents often describe their experiences in terms of grief and loss, as mothers did during my interviews. One mother remarked, "You do grieve, not only for what your child has lost but for the many changes and demands that are made for yourself. I don't think you ever really quit grieving." Another mother, who had experienced the death of one child and the mental illness of another, told me, "I've lost a child to death. This is worse, because death is final." With mental illness, she clarified, "I have to continue to see him suffer. To see a handsome, young, bright life destroyed."[6] When I asked directly whether they had experienced a kind of mourning, 75 percent of the mothers responded affirmatively; an identical proportion described their grief as chronic.

Fathers, too, share in the parental grieving process. One father told me about his intense sense of loss in the wake of his son's mental illness and suicide attempt. "After that, every day you worried when the phone rang. At night we were thankful that our son had lived another day. . . . Little by little, you learn to live with it."[7] Even as some resolution is achieved by fathers, a residue of grief often remains: "We loved our son and had grown to understand him as he was, not as we wanted him to be. But we continued to grieve, grieve for the injustices in society, the exploitation of the weak by the strong, and intolerance of people who are different."[8]

Although many parents do experience intense feelings of grief and loss, it is important to note the contrast with the biological death of a child. A child's death is an actual loss that is tangible and permanent, that receives social validation, and that offers parents an opportunity for closure. In contrast, a child's mental illness is a loss that involves someone who is very much alive, with the potential for full recovery; that receives little social validation and support; and that may continue for a lifetime.

As one mother has written, although the recovery process of their family was similar to that experienced following a biological death, the process did not lead to the acceptance of a death, but to the acceptance of a life—a transformed life and a person who was far different from the daughter they knew before the illness.[9] Erma Bombeck, the late humorist, has described children as kites. "You spend a lifetime trying to get them off the ground," she has written, running with them "until you're both breathless." When they crash, you add a longer tail:

Finally they are airborne, but they need more string so you keep letting it out. With each twist of the ball of twine there is a sadness that goes with the joy, because the kite becomes more distant, and somehow you know it won't be long before that beautiful creature will snap the lifeline that bound you together and soar as it was meant to soar—free and alone.[10]

Bombeck's passage is likely to evoke a piercing sense of loss among parents, who may never see their own beautiful creature soar free and alone.

This sense of symbolic loss is at the core of the parental experience of mental illness.[11] Mental illness does not generally involve the loss of life itself, but of the potential for a meaningful and productive life; nor the loss of physical existence, but of hopes and dreams and expectations. Our hopes and dreams, and our individual and family myths and illusions, are what distinguish us as uniquely human. Their loss represents an irreparable narcissistic blow.

PRIMARY CAREGIVING

One of the most prominent parental themes is that of primary caregiving, which may become the central event of their lives. Whatever their current level of involvement, as the first and last resort for their child, parents may hear the call to caregiving at any time. There can be no escape from caregiving responsibilities for a child who may never quite grow up.[12]

Throughout history, the burden of caregiving for people with mental illness has been overwhelmingly a female one. Often, the personal price is very high, sometimes exceedingly so. One mother told me about her efforts to cope both with a son whose mental illness jeopardized his life and with a husband who was devastated by his son's illness: "So I had to be strong. My feelings were kept inside because I know, first of all I have to help my son, and then I have to help my husband."[13] Her energy spent in caregiving for her son and husband, she remarked that there was little energy left to meet her own needs—adding ironically, if she could only remember what they were.

Fathers may share caregiving responsibilities along with concern about their child's future following their own death or incapacitation. One of the older mothers I interviewed tearfully expressed this concern. Her repetitive questions echo her obsessive concern with her son's future: "What is going to become of our son when my husband and I are no longer here? What is going to become of him?. . . I do worry. Because what happens? What happens when we're no longer here? What happens to our son? I don't know what the answer is."[14]

GUILT AND RESPONSIBILITY

Although common among all family members, feelings of guilt and responsibility are experienced with a special intensity by mothers and fathers. At the time of the initial diagnosis, there is an almost reflexive response among parents, who insistently ask themselves what they have done wrong. Given our universal human fallibility, this desperate search for understanding and coherence may result in an assignment of responsibility that intensifies parental anguish. In fact, when asked whether they had experienced feelings of guilt and responsibility, a large majority (87%) of the mothers I interviewed responded positively.

The tendency of parents to feel responsible for their child's mental illness partly reflects the cultural edict: If there is a troubled child, there must be troubled parents. Internalized by mothers, this edict adds considerably to their burden:

And of course you don't have to have somebody start to tell you it's your fault. You've already started in your mind saying, "What did I do when she was this age and this age?". . . And I'd think "Was that the reason that this happened? Should I have not said that? Should I have not done this?" You relive or try to relive every situation you can think of to see where you make a mistake, what you have done wrong. I don't think you ever get over it.[15]

Another mother sought the cause of her son's mental illness in her personal circumstances: "I'm a single parent. Maybe if my son had another mother, he would have been all right."[16] As in the case of these women, the sense of guilt and responsibility experienced by mothers may cast a general shadow over their parenthood.

INTRUSIONS INTO THE FAMILY LIFE SPACE

When a child is diagnosed with serious mental illness, parents are likely to feel aggrieved, overwhelmed, and distraught. What they need most of all is satisfactory services for their son or daughter, as well as a period of respite that allows them to regain their equilibrium. What they often get instead is an insensitive intrusion into their family life space. In an egregious—and unethical—example of intrusive practices, Evelyn McElroy has described her feelings of rage upon learning that an emotional family session had been witnessed without their knowledge or permission by a team of professionals behind a one-way mirror.[17]

During an initial hospitalization, parents are typically asked a barrage of questions, many of them of designed to elicit information about private family matters. One mother told me she felt violated by the professionals who seemed to feel entitled to all manner of information about her family, her marriage, and her personal life, as if she were a creature on display. She felt pushed, prodded, and debased: a curious object rather than a human being in pain. In retrospect, she can understand that practitioners were simply trying to do their jobs; but she wonders if the process needs to be so dehumanizing for parents.

Intrusions into the family life space are even more insistent when parents are involved with the criminal justice system or in legal proceedings concerning their child. Participating in an involuntary commitment procedure, one mother described it "as hell for any parent," noting that she and her husband watched in horror as police removed their nonviolent son from their home in handcuffs and shackles. Recalling that traumatic experience during our interview, this mother was overcome with emotion: "That was the worst ordeal. Even after all these years, it hurts, it hurts inside."[18]

GENDER ROLES

For all of the epochal changes affecting gender roles in recent years, female identity nevertheless remains precariously dependent on mothering: on whether it is done, rendering those who do not become mothers somehow incomplete; and on how well it is done, as judged by the success of their children. Through all of history, motherhood has been imbued with a sense of the primordial and momentous. As Simone de Beauvoir has observed, a woman experiencing motherhood is fulfilling her destiny: "She is the incarnation of the species, she represents the promise of life, of eternity."[19] Or as Rachel proclaimed in the Book of Genesis, "Give me children or else I die."[20]

Other family members do not share quite the same vulnerability with respect to identity. Whatever their commitment to their family, fathers continue to define themselves largely in terms of their work; spouses have reached adulthood with a well-established sense of identity by the time they confront the mental illness of a partner; and siblings and offspring grow up to have lives of their own, however their early experiences may imprint those lives.

It is mothers whose identity is tied inextricably to their parenting, mothers who are held—who hold themselves—accountable when their children fall short. Moreover, women tend to define themselves in terms of relationships, with emphasis on their ability to nurture and support their family members.[21] As a result, they are likely to be profoundly shaken when they witness the anguish of their family; and shaken anew, when that anguish persists in spite of their best efforts.

Different issues—and vulnerabilities—attend paternal roles. In the past, fathers were largely ignored or treated as "biological necessities."[22] The traditional father was expected to assume the roles of provider and protector, to play a limited role in nurturing and emotional tasks, and to encourage achievement. In contrast, the "new father" is involved in active parenting, shares equally in instrumental and expressive roles, and relates to his children with warmth and sensitivity.

Most fathers today are likely to have internalized both role constellations. When a child develops serious mental illness, each constellation carries risks. Traditional fathers are likely to fail in their protective role and to have problems confronting the powerful emotions evoked under these circumstances. At the same time, the expressive and nurturant roles of contemporary fathers may increase their emotional and caregiving burden. In reality, most fathers are subject to all of these risks.

Hence, both gender roles are fraught with problems when a child has mental illness. Mothers are likely to be buffeted by expectations regarding caregiving, accountability, the emotional life of the family, and the quality of family relationships. Fathers are likely to struggle with a restrictive role that requires them to serve as stalwart protectors in the face of this relentless attack on their family. Whether the role obligations of parents are shouldered individually or jointly, their duties will be difficult to fulfill under these circumstances, especially at the onset of the illness.

SOCIAL ROLES

A child's mental illness also results in social role transformations both for parents and for the family unit. As the most basic unit of social structure, roles define expected behaviors, influence our feelings about ourselves, and determine our range of social experiences. Prior to the illness, parents may have assumed such valued roles as capable parent and normal family member. Involuntarily relinquishing these roles, they may find they have assumed caregiving roles in the family, pathogenic roles in the mental health system, and deviant roles in society.

Family roles may also have shifted: from functional to dysfunctional, from respectable to shameful, and from ordinary to aberrant. Cultural expectations are relatively clear for families, who are judged by their ability to produce competent and autonomous children. Almost by definition, then, families that include a child with a disability of any kind are doomed to fail at this cardinal task. Thus, along with other losses, parents may suffer the unwelcome loss of personal and family roles that have been satisfying and esteemed.

Some of the role transformations experienced by family members occur along the lines of social class, gender, and age.[23] Namely, those who are poor, female, and elderly are often faced with caregiving responsibilities in light of the disproportionate presence of serious mental illness among families in lower socioeconomic strata, the traditional role of women as caregivers, and the necessity for aging parents to assume caregiving roles for their adult children.

As difficult as these initial role transformations are, eventually parental and family roles may be redefined in constructive ways. For instance, parents may assume roles as effective advocates for their family and as architects of a more responsive and humane system of care. Participating in their child's recovery process, they may regain their sense of themselves as competent and successful parents. But at the onset of the illness, often there is only a profound sense of loss for who they once were as individuals, as a couple, and as a family.

LIFE SPAN ISSUES

In Chapter 4, John Rolland's essential developmental question was paraphrased as follows: What life plans have family members had to cancel, postpone, or alter as a result of their relative's mental illness?[24] Because serious mental illness is most often diagnosed in late adolescence or early adulthood, parents are most likely to be dealing initially with the developmental tasks of middle adulthood and, as the illness progresses, with the tasks of late adulthood.

Midlife brings an opportunity for parents to renegotiate their earlier personal, interpersonal, and vocational commitments. This phase is characterized by the launching of children, which results in a return to a narrower family structure along with increased parental time and energy. Faced with the mental illness of a child, midlife parents may experience neither the launching of their child nor the opportunity to close the gap between their earlier hopes and current achievements.

One mother told of relinquishing her lifetime goal: "I had begun my life's dream of starting college when my daughter became ill. I don't foresee having enough mental energy to take college on again."[25] Another spoke more generally about this developmental disruption:

My daughter's mental illness would have been devastating at any time, but the timing was a cruel twist of fate, just as she was leaving for college. My husband and I were feeling good about our parenting and ready to put more energy into our marriage and careers. And instead of being able to move on in our lives, we were forced back in time. Her mental illness pushed us back into parenting of the most demanding kind, probably for the rest of our lives.[26]

Fathers of adult children with mental illness also confront developmental disarray. One father who had recently retired told me with a mix of exhilaration and exhaustion that he found himself far busier in his work as a mental health advocate than he had ever been in his former job. Initially serving as an advocate for his son, he had gradually expanded his role to become active on county and state levels. As in the case of this father, foreclosed from their anticipated course, parents may move in unexpected directions and enter uncharted waters. "I have found this period exceptionally difficult," one mother wrote, "but to my surprise I have emerged strengthened and even renewed, with exciting possibilities for the future. In a real sense, of necessity we have all created new lives."[27]

During late adulthood, parents typically adapt to more restricted vocational, financial, and social circumstances, restrictions that may be exacerbated by the mental illness of an adult son or daughter. One mother shared her resentment about the limitations imposed by her daughter's mental illness, remarking that she had looked forward to the time when her children would be grown and she would have more freedom: "But we just have to face the fact that she does have an illness and she'll always be dependent."[28]

Aging parents also confront the imminence of their own mortality and strive to achieve a sense of meaning and coherence in their lives. More positively, they may embark on a period of successful aging marked by growth, vitality, and creativity. For parents who serve as primary caregivers, however, these developmental tasks may be pushed to the periphery as they contemplate a far more pressing issue: Who will provide caregiving for their child?

Personal Issues

In addition to the shared family burden, each family member bears a personal burden. In fact, researchers have consistently documented the price paid by parents when a child has a mental illness. In my survey of mothers, for instance, a majority of participants reported adverse effects on their mental health (65%), their physical health (52%), and their social life (61%). Almost all (96%) of these mothers reported feelings of depression. In the words of one mother, "Many people tell me I am strong, but actually, I feel my heart has been crushed."[29] A majority (73%) also experienced feelings of withdrawal. "I just want to be by myself most of the time," a mother remarked, "I can't associate with people."[30]

For most mothers, these painful feelings diminish with time and adaptation, as in the case of the following mother:

I can remember thinking that it felt as if my internal territory had been shaken up by a blender, that everything inside of me was in a state of chaos. I was in my 40s when my daughter became mentally ill, and my adult life had been fairly stable until then. All of a sudden, everything that had been secure and comfortable was in turmoil. There was a sense that things would never be the same again. My internal territory is different now, and there is painful territory now that didn't exist before. The pain is just as intense sometimes, but the territory is smaller than it was, and it leaves room for the rest of my life.[31]

The personal consequences for caring fathers are also considerable, with the added burden of the masculine imperative to suppress feelings. In spite of less restrictive gender roles, men in our society often continue to have difficulty dealing with their emotional lives, which are likely to assume central importance under these circumstances. Terrence Real has explored what Thoreau called men's "quiet desperation."[32] Men have difficulty talking about their suffering, he observes, because the suffering itself is so fraught with shame. As long as feelings are associated with women, depression is seen as unmanly; thus, men tend to hide their pain from themselves and from others, a silencing that can have adverse personal and marital consequences.

MARITAL ISSUES

Especially at the onset of the illness, parents may experience significant marital distress as they struggle to deal with the mental health system and to understand the meaning of mental illness for their child, their family, and themselves. One mother lamented, "My daughter has ripped our family apart, ripped us apart, given us so much grief . . . The vibrations in the house are so tense that you can cut them with a knife."[33]

Helen Featherstone has described how the disability of a child attacks the fabric of a marriage: It elicits powerful emotions in both parents that may erode the margin of happiness and undermine communication; it may serve as a dispiriting symptom of shared failure, since "at the magical and metaphorical level where so much of the emotional life is lived, a child's disability calls the union into question"; it alters the structural organization of the family and changes alignments within the family as well as around it; and it creates fertile ground for conflict.[34] One mother declared that her family "lived in fear"; another wrote, "The tension takes all that is good out of life and marriage."[35]

Although parents may be responding to shared personal and family tragedy, their cadence may differ in beat, time, and measure. Mothers may be more likely to assume a nurturant stance in responding to their troubled child, to become enmeshed in the vortex of caregiving, and to reach out for affective sharing with their partner. Simultaneously, fathers may be more likely to promote independence and autonomy, to become detached from clamorous family demands, and to aim for suppression of unmanageable emotions.

The mental illness of a child poses formidable challenges for the marital relationship. Indeed, whatever the eventual outcome, the marriage contract is inevitably renegotiated. Sometimes the mental illness becomes forbidden territory, a seething cauldron to be avoided as much as possible; sometimes the marriage is reconstructed in fulfilling ways; and sometimes the marriage does not endure. My interviews provided examples of each of these outcomes. Recounting her husband's gradual disengagement during their son's hospitalization, one mother finished her story: "My husband of 25 years became involved with another woman, and we wound up divorced."

Another described a different result: "We've been married over 30 years. I think it's made our marriage stronger because we've shared the grief and we've shared the joys."[36] Still another had experienced both a divorce and a remarriage. At the onset, she told me, her husband could not accept their daughter's mental illness and spent his time in local bars with his friends. "I began to realize that this was his way of coping," she explained, and "now that I understand, I try to be more supportive. And he's trying to deal with it. At this point, our marriage is strengthened by our problems."[37]

SOCIAL ISSUES

Researchers have repeatedly documented the adverse social consequences of a child's mental illness for parents. Parents report that their social life is restricted by their caregiving responsibilities; that they feel isolated and alienated from those outside the family; and that they are stigmatized by an illness that continues to be denigrated. In fact, in one study, researchers found that anxiety about social concerns was associated with problems in physical health.[38]

Even brief contact with parents is likely to elicit their comments about social limitations and alienation: "It's very difficult to have friends"; "I didn't want to tell anybody"; "There is a stigma involved with it." One father declared: "I have to boycott the church because they shut their doors on the mentally ill. You talk about no room at the inn—that's the way they treat the mentally ill."[39]

PROFESSIONAL ISSUES

Given the severity and persistence of serious mental illness, parent-professional encounters assume much importance. In the past, parental encounters with professionals were often neglectful, adversarial, or intrusive, thus intensifying their burden. Reflecting the tenor of an earlier era, one article described the "mal de mere" ideology that generated a seemingly endless list of pejorative terms commonly used by mental health professionals to describe mothers of children with mental illness, placing them in the role of "the enemy, the culprit."[40]

My interviews with mothers who had been involved with the system for many years highlighted some of these problems. One older mother wondered how her family could possibly be helped by professionals who seemed to believe that her son "lived in an unholy environment."[41] Another commented tersely, "Experience with professionals has been the most devastating part of this illness."[42] Although less frequently espoused in our collaborative era, the "mal de mere" ideology sometimes continues to inform professional encounters with mothers, with potentially devastating consequences:

My son's therapist told me that his early relationship with me was the central problem—at the same time I was told that his prognosis was poor and he might need institutional care. . . . I needed support during the most difficult period of my life. Instead, my pain was intensified by someone who passed judgment without taking the time to understand our family.[43]

Several mothers remarked on the "mother-blaming" they found in the professional literature.[44] Informed that her daughter's diagnosis was borderline personality disorder, for instance, one mother asked how she could learn more about the disorder. She was given the title of a professional book, which she purchased and read. This mother described the book as an indictment of her parenting, wondering how the author could hold her accountable for her daughter's illness without even meeting her. She added, "The profile of the mother does not fit me at all, but this is what they go by."[45]

Fortunately, there is evidence that professional attitudes toward mothers have been changing, particularly in recent years. One mother shared her helpful experience with a social worker: "She explained the illness at the family group meetings. She gave us a lot of input and told us which way to go. They had a really good family support system there."[46] Another commented on the improvement in her contacts with mental health professionals over the years, using a rating scale of 1 to 5: "At the beginning, we would have rated our contacts with a 1"; 14 years later, she rated her contacts a 4.[47]

Given the frequent visibility of mothers as primary caregivers, fathers face their own challenges in working with professionals, who may cast them into a peripheral role. Yet as full partners in the parenting enterprise, fathers may share in primary caregiving and its associated burden. These fathers are equally entitled to play a role in decisions that affect their family.

System Issues

There is ample documentation in the professional literature of parental frustration with the mental health system. Parents complain about unsatisfactory handling of crises and emergencies, fragmentation and gaps in community-based services, and insufficient involvement of families in treatment planning. In light of their child's dependence on the system, these shortcomings often result in substantial parental distress. As one mother remarked, "Many family members and clients are underserved, and others are bobbing around on a sea of frustration and helplessness."[48]

An incensed mother told me about her daughter's accelerating decompensation, which was marked by command hallucinations. Arriving at the local community mental health center, the family was informed that no beds were available. Following their return home, the daughter jumped in the car with her two young children and announced that, like God, she was going to have to sacrifice one of her sons. The desperate parents again called to secure a bed at the center but were told by staff that there was still none available, although they were trying. The mother's response: "You know if you don't soon find one bed, you're going to be finding a half a dozen because there's not too much more we can tolerate at this point."[49]

Fortunately, especially in recent years, parental evaluations of the system are more likely to be positive. One mother related, "When I went to the hospital out there, it was really a different system. It was wonderful to have some doctor call me in and tell me about my son's illness, explain everything, give me choices, and tell me what he thought was the best, all the whys and ifs."[50] Another praised the case management services in her community that had funded residential, educational, and vocational services for her son.

Needs of Parents

Each of these four chapters covers the needs and intervention strategies associated with the respective roles of parent, spouse, sibling, and offspring. Compared to the other chapters, the material on parental needs and intervention strategies is relatively brief. In fact, because the family literature focuses largely on parents, these topics have already been addressed earlier in the book. For example, the essential family needs were specified as follows:

- A truly comprehensive and humane system of care that can support their relative in the community
- Information about serious mental illness and available resources
- Skills to cope with the illness and its sequelae for families
- Support for themselves
- Meaningful involvement in decisions that affect them

This compendium of needs is shared by virtually all caring parents and provides a sound basis for designing services for these family members.

In addition to these generic needs, specific parents may have other personal or interpersonal needs. For instance, a given parent may have difficulty resolving his or her emotional burden, maintaining a low-stress family environment, or managing conflicts with other family members. Thus, when working with parents, practitioners should always conduct an initial family assessment to determine the relative importance of each of the generic family needs, the adequacy of parental coping strategies and resources, and the requirements of individual parents.

Intervention Strategies for Parents

The family interventions discussed in Chapters 7 through 10 were primarily designed to address the needs of parents, the most frequent participants in family-focused programs. Thus, the three-step model already presented is usually appropriate in working with parents. Applying the model, Step 1 involves family consultation, which offers a useful means of engaging parents and of assisting them in identifying and prioritizing their needs, in dealing with illness-related concerns, and in making an informed choice about their use of other available services.

In Step 2, practitioners work with parents to develop an individualized family service plan. The objective is to achieve an optimal match between the available services and their particular needs and desires. For instance, parents might choose to participate in a family support and advocacy organization, in educational workshops, in a more intensive psychoeducational program, or in a provider-based support group, either singly or in combination.

Step 3 consists of a referral for psychotherapy, which may vary in format (individual, marital, family, or group); in strategies and techniques; and in duration, frequency, and intensity. The distinction is sometime made between counseling, which refers to briefer, less intensive, and more supportive forms of treatment, and psychotherapy, which is appropriate for severe and deep-seated problems. Some parents may be appropriate candidates for individual counseling or psychotherapy, including those who continue to manifest significant problems after their informational and supportive needs have been met. Other parents may benefit from marital therapy to deal with illness-related conflicts or other relational problems; or from family therapy to address pre-existing problems in communication or conflict management.

Maintaining an individualized and flexible approach, professionals need to be alert to any unusual parental concerns or problems that merit special consideration. These might include concerns about harm to their child or to someone else, significant personal or marital distress, or the risk of family demoralization or disengagement. Offering immediate assistance, practitioners can help parents to identify and manage these problems.

From Theory to Practice

Social worker Jeffrey Blume introduces himself to Marsha and Harold Rosenthal, who have arrived for their first session of marital therapy. After discussing his office policies and procedures, Jeffrey begins the session:

> PRACTITIONER: *Marsha, when you called to schedule the appointment, you said Andrew's schizophrenia has had a devastating impact on your entire family. I'd like to learn more.*

MOTHER: *It's been a nightmare. Andrew has withdrawn from the family to live in his own world. He talks to his voices, accuses us of poisoning his food, and often refuses to take care of his basic needs. It's a struggle to get him to his appointments, which in any case don't seem to be doing much good. I've never felt so helpless in my entire life.*

PRACTITIONER: *It has to be horrible to watch helplessly as a child descends into mental illness, yet refuses your assistance.*

FATHER: *It's more than that—he seems to feel we are the enemy. He tells me the voices say we can't be trusted. Sometimes I wonder if he's making this up just to get attention. It's extremely upsetting to try and communicate with him. I tell him the voices are not real, but he simply won't listen.*

PRACTITIONER: *I'm sure it is frustrating for you, as it would be for most parents. As you learned in the educational program at the hospital, however, the symptoms of schizophrenia include delusions, which are false beliefs, and hallucinations, which are false perceptions, such as hearing voices or seeing things that are not actually present. But these experiences seem very real to people who experience them. Arguing with them doesn't usually convince them they're not real. With appropriate treatment, Andrew may be less susceptible to these symptoms. But let's talk about how is this affecting each of you. Marsha?*

MOTHER: *I seem to be anxious and depressed most of the time. I have trouble sleeping and difficulty concentrating at work. I lose my temper at home, which just makes matters worse. Although I'm getting from day to day, I just feel paralyzed—overwhelmed with feelings of grief for all of us. I know it sounds strange, but I almost feel as if Andrew had died.*

PRACTITIONER: *Actually, it's not strange at all. As painful as they are, your feelings are normal under these circumstances. In fact, several articles written by mothers like yourself have focused on their experience of grief and loss. Would you like to have copies?*

MOTHER: *Yes, I think it would be helpful. I feel so depressed I have begun wondering about my own mental health. Hearing that my feelings are normal makes me feel a little better.*

FATHER: *You know, Marsha, I didn't realize you were feeling so depressed. You seem to be so efficient: managing the twins, getting Andrew to his appointments, handling your job and the household. I thought I was the one falling apart. Mostly what I feel is anger—at Andrew for causing so much trouble, I suppose, but mostly just anger. I want to strike out; it all seems so unfair. I'm afraid much of my anger has landed on you. Then I get upset with myself and withdraw from the family.*

MOTHER: *It's been hard to tolerate your anger. I need your help in dealing with this. But I feel so alone.*

FATHER: *I would help if I knew how. But I guess I share your sense of help-lessness. Things just keep getting worse. And I keep getting more frus-trated.*

PRACTITIONER: *You know, under the circumstances, both of your reactions are understandable. A sense of unfairness is almost always experi-enced by parents when a child develops a mental illness. And along with the feelings of grief and loss come a wide range of other feelings, including anger. So the real problem isn't your feelings, but the impact they're having on your relationship.*

FATHER: *That's probably true. But a part of me has just given up. I don't feel like trying anymore. Nothing seems to make any difference.*

PRACTITIONER: *Right now, I'm sure it does look that way. And it may take time for Andrew to accept and respond to treatment. So your problems may continue. At the same time, his illness seems to have swallowed up your entire family, as if there's nothing else.*

MOTHER: *Yes, it does seem that way. In the year since Andrew became ill, I can't think of a single happy moment.*

FATHER: *That's for sure.*

PRACTITIONER: *Well, perhaps we can begin to separate the illness from the rest of your family life, like your relationship.*

FATHER: *To be honest, our relationship has become painful, too. We can't discuss Andrew's illness without arguing. And we don't seem to talk about anything else.*

MOTHER: *I find I avoid talking to Harold about Andrew. I just can't take any more.*

PRACTITIONER: *Under these circumstances, any discussion of Andrew is likely to add to your distress. But perhaps I can help you find ways of talking about the illness that avoid some of the conflict. Then at least your discussions won't add to your problems.*

MOTHER: *That might be helpful.*

PRACTITIONER: *How about you, Harold? Are you interested in learning some communication skills that might help you resolve some of your problems?*

FATHER: *I suppose so. I realize we need to work together on this.*

PRACTITIONER: *You're dealing with an enormously difficult situation, and your usual coping strategies may not be enough. There are so many powerful emotions involved when a child has mental illness; they can so easily spill over.*

MOTHER: *What do you have in mind?*

PRACTITIONER: *Let's begin with some materials on communication skills, which you can review at home. Then next week we can work on some systematic skills training. In the meantime, it might be helpful if you could get a little time for yourselves—without talking about Andrew's illness.*

FATHER: *I can't remember when we last went out to dinner. It would be a welcome break—if we can manage to avoid arguing about Andrew.*

MOTHER: *I sure could use a break. And I promise not to discuss Andrew. I need to have a life apart from all the pain.*

PRACTITIONER: *I think you both do. You need to take some time for yourselves and for each other. If you don't take care of yourselves, you won't be able to take care of anyone else.*

FATHER: *That makes sense. Let's give it a try. We'll go out to dinner on Friday—with no discussion of Andrew. And we'll read your material before we come in next week.*

PRACTITIONER: *I realize this is just a start, but I'm impressed with your willingness to reach out to each other and to learn skills that may help you cope more effectively. So we can get a sense of what we need to accomplish over the next few weeks, what would you like to cover?*

MOTHER: *I'm worried about our twins, Kevin and Rick. They seem so angry and confused. I'm not sure how to help them. And, of course, they're 16, so they don't want me fussing over them.*

PRACTITIONER: *We can talk about their needs at our next session. The local mental health center has a support group for teenagers who have a sibling or parent with mental illness. I'll find out more about the group. And I'm open to meeting with them if they are interested. Sometimes it's easier for adolescents to talk with someone outside the family. Anything else?*

FATHER: *I would like to learn more about Andrew's illness. I don't know if Marsha told you, but my mother spent some time in a mental hospital. My family never talked about it, so I'm not sure what her diagnosis was, and she died a decade ago. But her symptoms seemed similar to the ones Andrew has.*

MOTHER: *I would also like to know how we can be helpful to Andrew. Or isn't there anything we can do?*

PRACTITIONER: *I'm glad to work with you on these issues. Harold, here are some handouts on schizophrenia. At our next session, I can answer your questions and give you additional material if you like. And, yes, there are many ways you can help Andrew. We can discuss some things you can do when we meet next week. How about the same time?*

MOTHER: *That sounds fine.*

FATHER: *For me as well.*

PRACTITIONER: *Good. I look forward to seeing you both next week.*

CHAPTER 12

Working with Spouses

At the psychiatric unit of a community hospital where she works as a family therapist, Carole Montague is scheduled to meet with Jane Ravansky, a 26-year-old mother of two young children. After several tumultuous months of extreme mood swings, sleepless nights, and excessive spending, Jane's husband, Don, has been hospitalized with a diagnosis of bipolar disorder. Married right after high school, Jane remained at home after the children arrived and has always depended on Don to provide for the family, which includes 6-year-old Amy and 8-year-old Heather. For the past year, however, Jane has been working as a teacher's aide. During their brief telephone call, Jane tearfully told Carole that she feels overwhelmed by her family situation and uncertain how to meet the needs of her husband and children. Jane added that she had been waiting until the girls were in school to begin taking college classes part time at night to earn a degree in elementary education. Now she wonders how she can fulfill her own hopes and dreams and still honor her commitment to her family. Although Carole has considerable experience working with parents of adult children with mental illness, she has had less contact with other family members, such as spouses. How can she be most helpful to Jane?

Given her work with parents, Carole already has a solid foundation for working with spouses such as Jane. Spouses share the subjective and objective burden of other family members, as well as their essential needs and potential coping resources. Because they are living with a partner who has mental illness, however, these family members also have additional needs that merit the attention of practitioners.

The title of this chapter refers only to spouses, although others may also seek professional services to cope with the mental illness of someone with whom they share a long-term commitment. Certainly, couple therapy is not restricted only to those who have formalized their relationship in marriage. Other couples who may seek professional services include those who are contemplating marriage; are cohabiting; have chosen not to formalize a long-term commitment; or are involved in gay, lesbian, and bisexual relationships.

Nevertheless, the challenge of building a fulfilling life with someone who has serious mental illness may be substantial, particularly if there is a severe level of impairment. Those who choose to sustain the relationship and to assume a caregiving role are a select group. Along with an enduring commitment and strong family values, they are likely to have exchanged marriage vows. Thus, although others may share the experiences, needs, and concerns discussed in this chapter, practitioners are most likely to be working with spouses. For ease of communication, I use the term *spouse* to refer to the well husband or wife, as well as other life companions; the term *partner* refers to the person with serious mental illness.

As is the case for parents, the personal and family circumstances of spouses are important in defining their experience of mental illness, including their culture, ethnicity, and social status. For example, there are cultural difference in the experience, presentation, course, and outcome of schizophrenia, major depression, and bipolar disorder.[1] In turn, the spousal experience may vary considerably across culture and ethnicity.

In addition, diagnosis and gender are important variables for spouses. In the case of schizophrenia, for example, although males and females are affected in roughly equal numbers, the disorder most often appears in the early to mid-20s for males and in the late 20s for females. As a result, women are more likely to marry and have children before the onset of the illness. The prognosis is better for women with schizophrenia than for men, although both groups are likely to experience persistent functional limitations, which require accommodations on the part of spouses.

Gender is also important in major depression, which is estimated to occur twice as frequently in women as in men. Bipolar I Disorder (manic or both manic and depressive episodes) is considered to be equally common in men and women, although Bipolar II Disorder (recurrent major depressive episodes with hypomanic episodes) may be more common in women. Thus, although many people with mood disorders marry and have children, their spouses are more likely to be men in the case of major depression and perhaps hypomania.

For all of these disorders, caregiving responsibilities are often substantial for spouses, who may additionally find their lives circumscribed by the constraints of gender, particularly if they are female and poor. The caregiving role of women is accorded little value in modern societies and may conflict with their personal agenda.[2] Indeed, their caregiving role may come to define their sense of personal identity. Several spouses reviewed an early draft of this chapter and provided comments and suggestions. One wife offered the following advice to practitioners: "Help spouses learn again who they are and regain an identity. A spouse gets totally LOST in the wants and needs of the ill partner. It is a very lonely, isolating experience. There is so much self-doubt experienced."[3]

The Spousal Experience

In contrast to parents, spouses have received relatively little attention in the professional literature. Several studies have focused on the spousal burden, but more often these family members have been included in larger samples consisting primarily of parents.[4] Moreover, spouses are frequently neglected by service providers.[5] Yet it is estimated that 35% to 40% of people hospitalized for mental illness are discharged to live with spouses. At least half a million people with serious mental illness reside with a husband or wife; some estimates place the figure considerably higher.[6] For most spouses, their partner's mental illness is a major presence in their lives. As one woman remarked, "My husband's schizophrenia is like a third member in our marriage. It is always there. Even with medication, we still deal with his paranoia, his isolation, and his need for my full attention on a daily basis."[7]

Although attention to spouses is far less than their numbers warrant, some descriptions of the spousal experience of mental illness are available.[8] In her book, *Crazy Love*, Phyllis Naylor offers a moving account of the spousal experience. Recounting the early years of her husbands' mental illness, Naylor writes that it did not occur to her to leave him: "I still clung to the belief that if I could just get him in treatment somewhere with a skillful psychiatrist, there might be a breakthrough. Leaving him would have been like walking out on a frightened though belligerent child." She "nourished the fantasy that some day when he was well, the doctors would tell him all that had happened, and he would look at me with grateful, misty eyes and love me forever and ever because of my loyalty." Ultimately, Naylor did choose to leave a relationship in which "love and trust had been replaced by suspicion." But it was an ambivalent departure:

No matter how thoroughly one insists that a relationship is over, it is never quite ended. No matter how much one wants to begin life anew, the past is never quite forgotten. No matter how strongly I had promised to remain detached, my heart cried out when I saw him, wept for him and for all that he might have been, for what we could have had together.[9]

In her memoir, *Personal History,* Katharine Graham, publisher of *The Washington Post,* describes many of the major journalistic events of the century. She also offers an eloquent description of life with her husband, the gifted and mercurial Philip Graham, who had bipolar disorder and ultimately committed suicide. Graham charts many landmarks of the spousal experience, including the onus of serving as the sole resource for someone whose life is unraveling; of being excluded from her husband's treatment (and even his diagnosis); and of witnessing her children's distress during their father's illness and following his suicide, when "in effect, they lost both parents at once."[10]

Increasingly, spouses are speaking openly about their experiences to professional audiences. One spouse began her presentation as follows: "I lay wrapped in my husband's arms last night. . . . We shared the moment in quiet pleasure. It felt good just to be with each other. It was so comforting to feel his nearness. To love and to feel loved."[11] She added that it had not always been so. Her husband's first hospitalization occurred after 23 years of marriage, ending the marriage "as we had known it." In the beginning, the couple struggled to come to terms with conflicting diagnoses (including schizophrenia, bipolar disorder, and major depression) and with destructive professional accusations (her husband was told that had it not been for his wife's "enabling," he would never have "broken down"). "Our marriage very nearly ended there."

Fortunately, subsequent practitioners have been far more helpful. A collaborative relationship was established with the psychiatrist who was treating her husband, a social worker who met with the couple both individually and jointly, and the couple themselves. Early on, this spouse particularly benefited from individual sessions that allowed her to talk about her feelings of abandonment, the despair of not having her husband available to her emotionally, and the daily pain of watching him struggle to complete even simple tasks when fighting depression. Their marital sessions permitted the couple to address and resolve problems in their relationship. Encouraging other professionals to work in partnership with spouses, she testifies to the value of her own involvement: "As a result, we aren't just married; we are building a good working, loving relationship."

Edie Mannion has described spouses as "the ultimate acrobats."[12] While walking a high wire of moral dilemmas, they are juggling a host of roles, feelings, and questions. If they contemplate divorce, spouses worry that they may risk their partner's suicide, violence, homelessness, imprisonment, or institutionalization, and perhaps a custody battle or step down on the socioeconomic ladder. If they remain in the relationship, they can risk losing themselves in the everyday struggle with mental illness and subjecting their children to the adverse consequences of their family circumstances. Struggling to remain aloft during their high-wire act, spouses are propelled by the knowledge that if they lose their balance, the whole family may plummet with them.

Often ignored by practitioners, spouses have been organizing their own support groups, primarily through NAMI, and the number of such groups has been increasing. Kathleen Bayes, a pioneer in the development of spouse support groups, has generously shared material used in her group and commented on this chapter.[13] Other spouses have also been involved in developing specialized services for spouses, including Rita Packard, who annually cofacilitates the Spouse Coping Skills Workshop with Mannion (see Chapter 15). With her husband, Fred, a psychologist who has schizophrenia, Penny Frese has produced a videotape that portrays his life as someone with serious mental illness and hers as a spouse (described as a "realistic view of what it's like to love someone with schizophrenia").[14]

Even when there is a positive outcome, the challenges that accompany the spousal role may be considerable. In addition to the shared family burden, spouses are faced with increased responsibility for parenting and other aspects of family life; and they often struggle to balance their own needs with those of other family members. In addition, spouses may feel that they are no longer married to the same individual, lamenting their lost opportunity to share intimacy, financial responsibility, parenting, confidences, decision making, and household tasks. Spouses are subject to intense feelings of grief, anger, depression, frustration, and exhaustion, as well as disruption of normal social life. Moreover, well husbands and wives may experience substantial conflict and guilt if they consider separation or divorce.

In my contacts with spouses, I have heard of the arduous daily responsibilities they must assume to ensure continuation of their family. Yet, under daunting circumstances, many spouses manage to honor their commitments and to become the "super copers" described by Harriet Lefley.[15] Indeed, some manage to create lives of vitality, joy, and creativity, embodying Bayes' advice to members of her spouse support group: "Bloom where you are planted." During the ensuing discussion of the spousal experience, practitioners need to remain cognizant of these positive outcomes, which are captured in the words of one woman who grew up in such a family: "At heart, my mother was a lovely, gentle person. My father loved her for 57 years."[16]

Spousal Themes

Many of the following themes have been introduced earlier in the book, although they arise with a distinctive texture in the spousal experience of mental illness. Other themes are unique to the experience, including the "difficult choices" faced by spouses and the "single parenting" that often results when a partner has mental illness. Furthermore, unlike other family relationships, the spousal relationship usually requires physical proximity. Thus, even when caregiving threatens to exceed their physical, emotional, or financial resources, spouses may have little respite.[17]

GRIEF AND LOSS

The spousal experience of mental illness is similar in many respects to that of spousal bereavement. In both instances, the experience is usually accompanied by the loss of emotional, social, and economic support; increased vulnerability to physical and mental disorders; stigmatization; identity problems; and loneliness.[18] Spouses may experience intense feelings of loss for the preillness spouse, for the suffering of their partner, for companionship and intimacy, for major changes in lifestyle and altered plans for the future, for a sense of self that is consumed with caregiving, and for the "luxury" of having one's own needs met.[19] "I feel such great sorrow towards my wife of 25 years," one spouse remarked. "The person I knew died in 1985. I try to grieve, but it's complicated by the body that keeps reappearing. It looks like her, but it's not."[20]

Gender may mediate some of these spousal reactions. For example, the vulnerability of wives may be increased by their tendency to depend on others for many of their identity, status, and economic needs.[21] On the other hand, husbands may be less comfortable with the emotional expression of grief and more likely to require assistance with daily living, especially if there are children.[22] As one of the male spouses who reviewed this chapter observed, however, others may have less stereotypical reactions.

As with the spousal experience of biological death, the experience of mental illness varies considerably among individuals and for a given spouse over time. Thus, practitioners need to be sensitive to the diversity among these family members. In contrast to most of the published material, for example, Penny Frese offers a more positive view. She met Fred in graduate school and was immediately attracted to his wit, gentlemanly charm, and keen mind. Prior to their marriage, they spent many hours talking about Fred's schizophrenia and considering their future.

Married more than 2 decades ago, both Freses completed their doctorates, welcomed the arrival of three children, and channeled energy into their family and careers. Over the years, they worked to create a quiet, supportive environment at home; to avoid rigid structures, accusatory statements, and overcontrol; and to place high priority on flexibility, encouragement of each others' talents, and mutual cooperation. "Being mere mortals, we don't always succeed," Penny has written. She continues:

Living with a mentally ill person can be a very intense experience. It can condition our responses, drain our energy, eat us up. But, in the large picture, it is only a small part of life. In our family we must give it its place, and we must go on . . . We can find many things that will enrich us and give our lives fullness and grace despite, and in some cases because of, this illness.[23]

DIFFICULT CHOICES

Unlike parent-child and sibling relationships, our culture permits us to choose a spouse with whom to face the complex demands of adulthood.[24] Our spousal relationship also permits later choices regarding continuation of the relationship or its termination through separation or divorce. Thus, compared with other family relationships, a qualitatively different kind of commitment is involved in the spousal relationship, one that may be profoundly ambivalent.

Several studies point to a significantly higher divorce rate among these couples than among the general population.[25] Not surprisingly, the dissolution of a marriage under these circumstances can provoke intense feelings of anxiety and guilt. Six years after his divorce, an exspouse commented, "I'm still in love with her, and that's very confusing. I can't get over having abandoned her."[26] The spouse may be presented with a menu of unsatisfying choices, particularly when children are involved.[27]

On one hand, spouses may find themselves bound to a relationship that drains their emotional and financial resources and to a partner who may also experience dissatisfaction in the marriage, perhaps attributing illness-related problems to the marriage or resenting the dependency that has developed in the relationship. On the other hand, spouses have made a commitment to someone they have vowed to love, honor, and cherish, in sickness and in health. Many spouses are truly on the horns of a dilemma.

Much of the literature concerned with spouses presumes the mental illness of their partner developed or was diagnosed after the marriage commenced. But spouses may choose to marry someone with mental illness for all of the reasons that any of us marry. Responding to the person beyond the illness, they have chosen to formalize their commitment and perhaps to have children. Yet in the wake of mental illness, these spouses may feel they betrayed their children by knowingly bringing them into a family with so many built-in psychological complexities.[28]

Faced with these complexities, spouses may struggle to find the best course. Some spouses choose to remain in their marriage. Packard has described her decision as follows:

Many parents of mentally ill children have told me how lucky I am because I can just leave my husband. Would that it were so easy! I took my marriage vows very seriously. My husband didn't ask for mental illness, and I would hope that if the tables were turned, he'd be there for me. I also feel that I have a responsibility to teach my children the seriousness of a committed relationship. . . . Probably the deepest of my reasons for staying is the fear of his committing suicide if I leave. Worse than that is the fear of my children suffering from the aftershocks of such a tragedy.[29]

I also heard from another spouse who was recently divorced after decades of marriage to a husband with a dual diagnosis of major depression and substance abuse.[30] This longtime mental health advocate has had frequent contact with other spouses over the years and has witnessed a wide spectrum of relationships and choices. In her view, it is the overall quality of the relationship that matters, rather than the mental illness per se. Ultimately, she divorced to protect her financial security in response to her husband's multiple drunk driving episodes. But she added that her own marriage had never really been satisfactory, stating that she and her husband had married for the wrong reasons, had remained married largely because of their children, and were now both better off following the divorce.

Remarking that there are usually multiple reasons for divorce, this woman also shared the experiences of several of other spouses she has known. She wrote that one wife had "had tried *everything* to remain married, but finally gave up" when the relationship had deteriorated to the point where only a caregiver role remained and her husband was unwilling to support her in any way. My divorced friend also mentioned two marriages that have remained strong and gratifying in spite of the mental illness. She contrasted these latter marriages with her own, noting that these women are very much in love with their husbands, who meet many of their own needs. When there are illness-related problems, these wives place them in the larger context of relationships they value and want to preserve.

The discussion thus far assumes the freedom of spouses to make choices about their marriage. In reality, many spouses will tell you they do not feel free to choose because there seem to be *no* good choices. Indeed, whatever their choices, there can be substantial stress and trauma for all members of the family. Spouses face not only the haunting moral dilemma of leaving or staying, but also more subtle dilemmas that arise in daily life, such as coping strategies that work in some ways and backfire in others. For instance, emotional distancing may provide safety but also engender strong feelings of loss.

In working with spouses who find both their current status and divorce untenable, Mannion suggests a third alternative: "staying in a different way."[31] Namely, some spouses may be able to renegotiate the marital relationship, to redefine their own role in the relationship, and to restructure their lives outside the family. A given spouse might redistribute roles and responsibilities within the marriage, make different personal choices, or seek more autonomy. As a result, a marital relationship that has seemed intolerable may become more comfortable and even satisfying.

SINGLE PARENTING

The theme of single parenting is prominent among discussions of spouses and in the professional literature. One spouse complained, for instance, that she was "doing the roles of mother, wife, and father."[32] Packard has written of suddenly becoming a single parent, with the additional responsibility of caring for a partner with mental illness.[33] "You need to work hard at not treating this person like a child" in spite of the difficulty partners may have in carrying their "own weight, let alone the weight of partner and parent." Yet parents with mental illness are a diverse group. Their ability to manage parenting and other responsibilities varies among partners with mental illness and perhaps for a given partner at different developmental phases, as the following spouse indicated: "He's been a good father. He could only briefly handle the kids when they were small, but now he is 'Mr. Mom' while I am working."[34]

"Single parenting" poses special obligations when children have a parent with mental illness. As discussed in Chapter 14, these offspring have compelling needs of their own. They share essential needs for information about the mental illness, age-appropriate coping skills, and support for themselves, along with a reasonable degree of security and predictability. Often, however, the needs of the parent with mental illness take precedence, sometimes leaving their children feeling neglected, resentful, or even abandoned. Moreover, many spouses are confused about mental illness, which limits their ability to provide explanations to their children. Packard has written of the difficulty of describing an illness that you yourself don't understand; and of explaining why a parent can't or won't do the things he used to do, such as taking children to the playground, staying at their birthday parties, attending school functions, or helping with school or scout projects.[35]

Thus, along with all of the usual parental responsibilities, spouses are required to help their children deal with the mental illness. Bayes and Mannion have both observed that children often imagine things are worse than they are; accurate information can correct their perceptions and assist them in coping.[36] Furthermore, being honest with children about the illness helps them to trust their well parent and to view the parent who has mental illness with empathy and respect. An understanding of mental illness may also reduce some of their anger and guilt about what is happening in their family, as well as mistrust if they are left to discover the family situation on their own.

In addition, spouses typically worry considerably about the genetic and psychosocial risks for their children. Listening to a panel of family members discuss their experiences, I heard one spouse remark that the preceding presentation of an adult offspring had "terrified" her in underscoring the risks faced by her own children. Dealing with all these concerns would be a tall order for even the most competent and energetic parent. Yet many spouses do an admirable job with their children, somehow finding the strength, as one spouse affirmed, "to be a father in the truest sense of the word."[37]

FINANCIAL DISTRESS

Financial problems have already been discussed as a frequent component of the objective burden. The mental illness of a partner, especially a primary wage earner, often compromises the economic security of the family. A partner's mental illness may result in job loss, a leave of absence, loss of opportunities for advancement, reduced benefits for retirement, and loss of insurance coverage and other benefits.[38] Furthermore, if the partner is unable to fulfill duties at home, the spouse may be faced with additional expenses for car maintenance and repair, house maintenance, and child care.

These financial problems are compounded by the ineligibility of married individuals with mental disabilities for some benefits available to those who are single. Furthermore, given the disparity between the earnings of males and females, if the spouse is a wife who becomes the sole wage earner, family income is likely to decrease. The spending sprees associated with bipolar disorder may further increase the financial problems faced by the family. The following spouse describes a poignant episode from her life with a husband who has bipolar disorder:

When one of the collection agency representatives called to threaten me with imprisonment if I didn't make a payment on our credit card, I told the man my spouse has a mental illness and that I would give anything to go to jail where I could get some rest and somebody to cook for me. They stopped calling.[39]

When spouses do attempt to protect their family from the financial ravages of spending sprees, their actions may threaten the marital relationship:

*Taking control of our bills and checkbook helps me feel more secure, but my hus-
band calls me a control freak, and says I'm undermining what little self-esteem he
has left. I try to explain it's that I can't trust his illness, but it's like choosing between our survival and our marriage.*[40]

CRUSHING RESPONSIBILITIES

An onerous burden typically accompanies the spousal role. While dealing
with their own feelings of grief and loss, many spouses must learn to manage the mental illness of their partner, to meet the needs of their children,
to maintain full-time employment and fulfill household responsibilities,
and to deal with continuing family disruption and stress. Moreover, many
spouses must shoulder this burden without much assistance from an adult
partner.

Under these circumstances, exhaustion and burnout are virtually inevitable, at least occasionally and sometimes unremittingly. As is well
documented, such a level of stress places individuals at risk for a wide
range of physical and psychological problems. The spouses who serve as
advocates and resources for other spouses (and who have contributed to
this chapter) are an exceptional group who have managed to create fulfilling lives for their families and to reach out to other spouses. But one
wonders about the legions of spouses who struggle alone, with fewer supports and resources, under this extraordinary burden. Professional services might make a significant difference in their lives.

A FRAGILE EQUILIBRIUM

Maintaining equilibrium is often difficult when a partner has mental illness. The illness may unbalance the marital relationship in several ways.
First, at least periodically, the illness is likely to impose limitations that
prevent the partner from fulfilling his or her roles and duties, thus requiring the spouse to compensate. A commensurate reallocation of power is
likely to result when one spouse must assume primary responsibility for
the family. Along with the risk of resentment on the part of a spouse who
feels unfairly burdened, a partner may feel devalued and disenfranchised.

An additional source of imbalance is the symptoms of mental illness,
which may prevent the partner from engaging in a fully reciprocal relationship distinguished by sharing of parenting, decision making, empathy, and companionship. Imbalance can also result from cycles of relapse
and remission, which can preclude the couple from achieving a stable
adaptation. An accommodation developed during a period of remission

may be unworkable following a relapse. Recovery may further imbalance the marital relationship if the partner is able to return to roles and responsibilities that were earlier relinquished.

It is a remarkable couple that can manage these oscillations without some distress. In some cases, a comfortable accommodation can be achieved, as the following spouse related: "My husband and I simply reversed traditional family roles. I furnished financial support, working as a medical technologist, while he did the shopping and the cooking."[41] In other cases, the persistent limitations of a partner may require the spouse to remain in charge. In the words of one wife, "The ill spouse must accept the fact that control vests with the well spouse. That's just the way it is."[42]

LIFE SPAN ISSUES

For many individuals in our culture, the marital relationship provides the context for adult development. As a result, the tasks of early, middle, and late adulthood are most likely to be affected by the mental illness of a partner. If mental illness is present at the time of marriage or develops soon thereafter, the tasks of young adulthood may be disrupted for both husband and wife, with an adverse impact on intimacy and the marital relationship, on the early years of parenthood, and on vocational plans.

Midlife spouses may have little energy available for renegotiating earlier personal, interpersonal, and vocational commitments. Indeed, struggling to ensure the survival of their family, these spouses may feel they have few choices at all. Likewise, the period of late adulthood may pose hardships. Already dealing with limited vocational, financial, and social circumstances, spouses may face further limitations as they confront their retirement, the increasing risk of medical problems in old age, and the need to plan for an uncertain future.

At the same time, late adulthood may bring real satisfactions for a couple that has managed to navigate the shoals of this challenging relationship successfully. For instance, later years may bring new relationships with their adult children and their grandchildren that validate their commitment. Coming to terms with their own life review, spouses may enjoy the sense of having prevailed in the face of enormously difficult circumstances.

In fact, over the course of their lives, many couples that include a partner with mental illness undergo a process of adaptation as they learn to manage the illness and to build a rewarding family life. In one survey, 83% of spouses attested to such a process, most often citing their personal qualities as facilitating positive change. One wife wrote of her relationship with a partner who had mental illness: "It was reciprocal. He gave me adaptability and I gave him social and financial stability. I believe we were the making of each other."[43]

PERSONAL ISSUES

Although the spousal role is not without its potential satisfactions, these family members must deal with a wide range of personal concerns. Along with other family members, spouses experience a subjective burden that consists of a range of powerful emotions, including grief, loss, shock, disbelief, anger, despair, guilt, anxiety, and shame. Moreover, there is some evidence that spouses themselves experience an increased rate of minor mood disorders.[44]

Finding time and energy to deal with personal issues may seem impossible for spouses who feel responsible for a partner with mental illness, for children with compelling needs, and even for an extended family that may have little understanding of the illness. Yet it is imperative for spouses to acknowledge their own concerns. As one spouse wrote, these issues are the "crux of the problem":

I had a desperate need to address issues like: Who am I? How did I get myself in this fix? What choices do I have? Why am I doing what I am doing? Are my perceptions of reality correct? Is what I'm feeling and experiencing real? In other words, I desperately need the focus to be on ME instead of the ill spouse, the children, the extended family, the family "burden," etc. I had to rediscover myself.[45]

MARITAL ISSUES

A number of researchers have documented the marital problems that may occur when a partner has mental illness. These include marital dissatisfaction and disruption, accountability, an absence of reciprocity, the need to deal with symptoms of the illness, role distortions, problems in sexual relations, and the need to set limits.

Marital Dissatisfaction and Disruption

Researchers have found that there is a high rate of marital discord among these couples, that 50% of spouses married to partners with major mood disorders would not have married had they known more about the illness, and that a similar proportion have seriously considered separation or divorce. In virtually all investigations, spouses have reported feelings of frustration, isolation, exhaustion, and depression.[46]

Accountability

A central marital issue is whether the partner is able to "own" the mental illness: to acknowledge its existence, to adhere to the treatment and rehabilitation plan, and to assume responsibility for managing the illness and protecting the family.[47] Coming to terms with the illness is likely to require time and courage. Nevertheless, whatever a family's particular circumstances, the partner's degree of accountability may be the most important factor in determining the quality and status of the marriage. For example, marital bonds may be damaged beyond repair when the partner abuses substances or refuses to take medication in spite of the destructive consequences of the illness for the family.

Absence of Reciprocity

A partner with mental illness may be too self-involved to offer assurance that the spouse is important, valued, or loved.[48] As a result, spouses may need to accept a relationship that is not fully—or even largely—reciprocal. Reciprocity is distinguished by mutual sharing, experiencing, and demonstrating. Yet serious mental illness may limit a partner's ability to share intimacy and responsibilities, to experience feelings and events in a similar manner, and to demonstrate regard, affection, and love. Even when spouses are sensitive to the limitations imposed by the illness, they may sometimes feel profoundly alone. As Bayes has written:

My husband suffers from a serious mental illness. This illness has robbed us both of peace, security, love, companionship, the intimacy and partnership of marriage. I have no peace because I'm afraid and isolated. I have no security because he has difficulty holding a job, and medical expenses may ultimately wipe out our finances. I do not have his love and companionship because he is unable to relate to me consistently at any other level than as an adult child to a caretaker. There are many days when he just isn't "there" for me.[49]

These problems have not prevented Bayes from seeing her husband apart from his illness: "I admire his courage greatly. When he is there for me, I like him a lot. He is a very caring, generous, kind, thoughtful, intelligent man. Unconditional love is something you do daily, even when the going gets tough."

Symptoms

Another area of potential difficulty is the symptomotology of serious mental illness, which may result in impaired thinking and significant functional limitations. Several studies have documented the distress experienced by spouses in response to the positive symptoms of schizophrenia, such as hallucinations and delusions. As one wife commented, such symptoms can "suck the spouse into the paranoia."[50] Yet most family members have more difficulty dealing with negative symptoms, such as lack of interest, passivity, and withdrawal.[51] In a marital relationship, positive symptoms may be more easily understood as caused by the illness, whereas negative symptoms may be experienced more personally.

Similarly, when a partner has a mood disorder, spouses may be faced with their partner's severely depressed mood, unusually elevated mood, or extreme mood swings. As already noted, these symptoms can be "contagious"; for instance, contact with someone who is depressed is a very depressing experience. Other troubling symptoms may include potentially harmful or self-destructive behavior, socially inappropriate or disruptive behavior, or poor daily living habits. As difficult as it may be for spouses to deal with these symptoms, it is even more troubling when the partner's behavior harms the children.

Role Distortions

A central marital problem is the perception of spouses that their partners are in some respects like another child; that they have relinquished a spousal relationship for a parental one. In the words of one woman, "I feel like I've lost a partner and gained a problem child."[52] The contrast between spousal and parental roles may generate considerable conflict for a spouse who alternates between the two roles and for a partner who responds with feelings of dependency and resentment.

Sexual Problems

Their sexual relationship may also pose problems for spouses and partners. Potential sources of sexual problems include medication, which may cause impotence and decreased desire; symptoms of depression, which may include diminished interest in sexual relations; and symptoms of mania, which may include excessive sexual demands. Over time, a given partner may manifest all of these patterns, requiring the spouse to respond to changing expectations and desires. Buffeted by forces inside and outside their marriage, spouses may find their own depleted energy and resentment contribute to the couple's sexual problems.

Commenting on an early draft of this chapter, one spouse asserted that "this issue needs more than a passing thought":

The partner may place blame for physical inadequacies on the well spouse, which results in the spouse feeling guilty for a less than ideal physical relationship. Also, therapists tell well spouses to set their own wants and desires aside in deference to the ill partner. Then, when or if there is an improvement, guilt is again experienced when the well spouse has little or no desire to be intimate after setting personal desire for intimacy on the shelf for so long.[53]

She added that the partner typically has little understanding or sensitivity when the couple's sexual needs are incompatible.

Setting Limits

Limit setting is important for all family members; no one should have to live in a dangerous or disturbing environment. When there are children, spouses have a special obligation to ensure the safety and security of the family environment. Some behaviors are not acceptable and should not be tolerated, including behavior that is abusive, self-destructive, harmful to others, damaging to property, or severely disruptive. Spouses need to decide which behaviors are unacceptable, set clear limits, and impose consequences when those limits are exceeded.

As Bayes has discussed, before establishing the "boundaries" that are vital to the survival of the family, spouses need to know themselves and what they can live with, to be prepared to enforce consequences, and to obtain support for themselves and their family.[54] Once reasonable limits have been established, it is important for spouses to acknowledge and expand the satisfactions in the marriage. As she has noted, working with their partner, spouses need to build joint self-esteem, to have friends and go places, to work together on parenting and household responsibilities, to fight together in managing the system and the illness, to play together, and to turn the tables through advocacy.

Diversity

Although the marital issues mentioned here embody a common theme among spouses, it is again important to recognize that some couples do not experience this level of marital distress. In a study of spouse resilience, for instance, a wife offered the following description of her husband: "He is a loving, caring person and meets my needs in that area of my life."[55] In fact, like all long-term relationships, the intricate tapestry of these marriages is undoubtedly woven of a varied palate of memories, rituals, celebrations, joys, and sorrows.

Upon reading about the hardships experienced by many spouses, one wife who reviewed this chapter observed that this simply does not ring true to her. She said that her husband brings much to their marriage and their family life: "Despite his illness, he is a source of strength, comfort, and support. We are learning together how to accommodate to the illness and to minimize its intrusion into our lives." "I wonder," she wrote, "how unique our situation is."[56]

Given the limited literature concerned with the spousal experience of mental illness, there is no way to know how unique her marriage is. What is certain, however, is the potential for practitioners to ease the burden of these spouses and to strengthen their families. As this spouse asserted:

It would be great to be invited to come to sessions and to be seen as part of the treatment team. It would certainly help to strengthen the marriage to feel that I had some part in helping my husband get better, as well as some idea of symptoms, medications, and prognosis.

SOCIAL ISSUES

Almost universally, spouses report feelings of isolation and significant limitations in social life.[57] Some of these limitations reflect exhaustion and burnout among spouses who are serving as primary wage earner for their family, primary parent for their children, and primary caregiver for their partner. Social activities may seem like a luxury, an impossibility, or even, as one spouse commented, another chore. When they do participate in social events, these couples may feel they do not fit in. Medication may also affect social life:

The schizophrenia plays a role in every activity in which we participate. Due to medication stupor, my husband isn't functional until 10:30 A.M. Every event is planned around his illness, his ability to cope with the event, how long we can stay, and whether it is at a time of the day that he can participate without drawing attention to his illness (evening events are a problem if he takes his meds before dinner).[58]

Other factors also have an adverse impact on social life, including the stigma associated with mental illness, the embarrassment of their partner's symptoms, and the absence of understanding among extended family and friends. Social activities may simply add to the burden of spouses who prefer not to deal with the misunderstanding and stigma. Concealing the illness from people outside the family, spouses may also avoid sharing personal feelings with a vulnerable partner. Thus, dealing with exceptionally stressful circumstances, spouses may have little personal support.

Professional Issues

Researchers have consistently found a high level of frustration with professionals among spouses. Spouses complain that practitioners fail to provide information and advice regarding their partner's mental illness, to include them in treatment planning, to offer assistance with the legal system, or to help them in meeting the needs of their children. As with other family members, spouses often feel either ignored or blamed by professionals. In the words of one spouse, "They see us as the enemy."[59] In particular, spouses complain about confidentiality, which they view as a barrier to their family's well-being.

As Mona Wasow has discussed, professionals sometimes put spouses in a double-bind, no-win situation: If these family members want to know what is happening in treatment, some practitioners may see their questions as encroaching on the limits set out by confidentiality laws.[60] If spouses say nothing, on the other hand, clinicians may perceive them as uncaring. Many family members end up immobilized, not knowing in which direction to move. In the end, everyone loses.

System Issues

What spouses perceive as problems with professionals are often actually problems with the service delivery system. Indeed, professional attitudes and behaviors are strongly influenced by a system that frequently fails to provide satisfactory services for the partner with mental illness, to acknowledge the legitimate rights and needs of spouses, or to address the needs of children who are growing up in these families. The following spouse has captured some of these problems:

Upon hospitalization of their partners, spouses are required to sign hospital documents that will hold them responsible for bills incurred during their partner's stay that are not covered by insurance. This creates a rare situation in that spouses are expected to be responsible for paying for services they cannot see, and for treatment from which they are excluded and about which they have no right to question professionals.[61]

Needs of Spouses

Spouses share the essential needs of all family members. Accordingly, they need satisfactory services for their partner with serious mental illness, information about the illness and available resources, skills to manage the illness, support for themselves, and meaningful involvement in decisions that affect their family. In light of their particular role, however, spouses have additional marital, parental, and personal needs.[62]

MARITAL NEEDS

Because they are dealing with the serious mental illness of a partner, spouses might benefit from assistance in:

- Coming to terms with a marriage to a partner who has mental illness
- Acknowledging and enhancing the positive aspects of the marriage
- Distinguishing between behaviors that are attributable to the illness and those that are not
- Ensuring that a spousal relationship is not reduced solely to a caregiving one
- Dealing with specific concerns that affect their marital relationship, such as sexual relations
- Managing symptoms that affect their family, such as the spending sprees of a partner with hypomania or mania
- Setting reasonable limits that can preserve the emotional, physical, and financial security of the family
- Finding realistic ways their partner can contribute to the household
- Encouraging their partner to engage in meaningful vocational and social activities outside the home
- If appropriate, assisting them to make and implement decisions about remaining in the marriage

PARENTAL NEEDS

Spouses also need support in meeting the needs of their children, such as:

- Learning how to explain mental illness to their children
- Assuring them that they are not to blame
- Encouraging them to discuss their feelings and concerns
- Reinforcing their participation in activities outside the family
- Providing special comfort to children in distress
- Helping their children cope with illness-related issues
- Offering suggestions for answering questions from peers and others outside the family

- Promoting compassion and respect for the parent with mental illness
- Deciding when professional counseling is appropriate
- Keeping their children on a normal developmental course

Personal Needs

In addition, spouses may need assistance in maintaining the integrity of their own lives. In fact, one spouse commented that these needs "should be the primary focal point" of professional practice.[63] Important personal needs include:

- Recognizing that their own feelings and needs matter
- Preserving a sense of personal identity in a family that is often focused on the needs of the partner
- Finding sources of companionship and support outside the family
- Maintaining a sense of mastery and control
- Achieving a balance that meets the needs of all members of the family
- Managing high levels of family stress
- Developing their own interests and potential
- Pursuing a more lucrative or satisfying career
- Providing assurance about their own mental health
- Keeping hope alive

From the perspective of professional practice with spouses, clinicians need to be sensitive to their unique experiences, needs, and concerns. An initial consultative session can clarify the salient issues for a particular husband or wife.

Intervention Strategies for Spouses

Services for spouses are a cost-effective means of strengthening the family and meeting the needs of individual members. Responsive services have the potential to reduce the patient's risk of relapse and hospitalization, to educate and support the overwhelmed spouse, to address the needs of their high-risk children, and to stabilize their family life.[64] Unfortunately, specialized services for spouses are rarely available. Moreover, family services that are available are typically designed for parents of adult children with mental illness, whose needs may differ significantly from those of spouses.

One of the model programs described in Chapter 15 is the T.E.C. Network Coping Skills Workshop developed by family therapist Edie Mannion and family member Marilyn Meisel. Although the program is very well received by parents, these family educators found that spouses had the highest dropout rate among participants in the general workshops. In fact, over a 3-year period, 34 of 36 spouses did not complete the program. Spouses also reported a high degree of dissatisfaction with the general program in comments on anonymous evaluation forms and during follow-up calls. Similar spousal dissatisfaction has been observed by facilitators of NAMI support groups comprised largely of parents. (Commenting on this chapter, one spouse asserted, "If spouses go to parent-oriented groups, rest assured that they *will not* return, as there is nothing for them!")[65]

Based on her substantial experience in working with spouses, Mannion has generously offered some suggestions for this section.[66] Discussing the dissatisfaction of spouses with generic programs, she notes that these groups are typically oriented to the needs of parents. For instance, these groups might focus on parental concern about continuity of caregiving for their son or daughter following their own death or decline. In contrast, spouses may need immediate assistance in compensating for their partner's impaired functioning, protecting themselves and their children during a partner's manic episodes, or preventing personal financial ruin due to the legal liabilities of marriage.

In addition, Mannion points out that certain coping skills for parents may be inappropriate for spouses. For example, parents are often the "head of the household" with the right to set and enforce "house rules" when their adult child resides at home. This strategy is often inappropriate for spouses who have co-signed a mortgage or lease with their partner. As a result, if spouses attend support groups or educational programs that are primarily attended by and directed at parents, they may find the benefits do not offset the inconvenience of arranging child care or sacrificing precious time from their extremely busy schedules. Furthermore, programs or groups that require a long-term commitment may not be feasible for spouses who are juggling jobs and multiple caregiving responsibilities.

Because the needs and concerns of spouses are so different from those of parents, siblings, and offspring, the three-step model already discussed requires some modifications when applied to professional practice with spouses.

THE THREE-STEP MODEL

Step 1 consists of family consultation, which is well suited to working with these family members. Spouses can benefit from an opportunity to identify and prioritize their marital, parental, and personal needs, to deal with illness-related concerns, and to make an informed choice about their use of other services.

Step 2 involves working with spouses to develop an individualized family service plan. The plan might include a referral to a local support group or educational program. Sometimes these programs involve professionals, but more often they are affiliates of national advocacy organizations such as NAMI or the National Depressive and Manic Depressive Association (NDMDA). Unfortunately, the parent orientation of most programs may reduce their applicability to the concerns of spouses. Nevertheless, spouses generally find NAMI's 12-week Family-to-Family Education Program very helpful. In addition, some NAMI affiliates have specialized services for spouses, such as spouse support groups, which are highly praised by participants.

Attrition rates of spouses in generic family support groups and educational programs can be high, particularly if there is not a substantial subgroup of spouses in attendance who can offer mutual support. Practitioners can address this challenge by trying to locate specialized programs that cater to spouses. If none can be found, as is often the case, spouse support groups and educational workshops can be adapted from already existing models, such as the Spouse Coping Skills Workshop developed by Mannion and Meisel (see Chapter 15). This specialized program has significantly reduced the high attrition rate of spouses. Moreover, there is evidence that participation in the group results in increased knowledge of mental illness and coping strategies, and in decreased personal distress and negative attitudes toward the partner.[67]

Step 3 involves a referral to psychotherapy for those spouses who are experiencing significant difficulty even after their educational and supportive needs have been addressed. Given the overall level of stress experienced by spouses, practitioners should be sensitive to their financial and time constraints during the referral process. Nevertheless, spouses may benefit significantly from therapy designed to address their personal, marital, and family concerns.

Individual Counseling or Psychotherapy

A brief course of supportive therapy may be helpful for spouses, particularly if they have few other resources available or are unable to manage the circumstances of their lives. In response to my recommendation of supportive counseling in an early draft of this chapter, one spouse wrote in the margin: "Yes, yes, yes." In fact, several spouses affirmed the value of individual counseling. Noting that life with a partner who has mental illness can be "crazy-making" for spouses, another asserted, "Supportive therapy is essential and does not have to be long term. Spouses must have acknowledgement from a professional that they are okay; that it is the mentally ill partner who is *not* okay." She added:

I think the most important aspect of my own "recovery" was to find myself. Well spouses struggle so hard to maintain some semblance of control in the chaos that they may lose their own identity. The therapist can help well spouses find themselves again.[68]

In addition to identity concerns, an important therapeutic focus is likely to be the marital relationship. Some spouses may struggle to understand their current situation, as in the case of one woman who grew up with a mother who had mental illness and committed suicide:

I have no idea what marriage to a healthy individual would be like. I ask myself why I am here. Is it because I am subconsciously making up for what I couldn't do for my mother? That I can provide my husband with that sense of stability and happiness in life that my mother never had? Is it because when I met him, he was loving and caring but was too heavily involved in living his own life to really see my problems and my inability to share at an intimate level. I really don't know.[69]

Other spouses may have a compelling need to deal with the question of remaining in the marriage. Unless there is risk of harm, it is important for therapists to remain relatively neutral as spouses deal with this issue. Some spouses may need help to remain in the marriage; others may need assistance to depart. As with other personal issues that arise in therapy, practitioners can assist spouses to clarify their options, to consider the consequences of each option, to arrive at a decision, to implement the decision, and to manage the aftermath. What they do *not* need, one spouse asserts, is criticism of what is ultimately their own decision. Speaking of her spouse support group, Bayes wrote:

Every single one of our spouses has been told by psychiatrists and therapists that we should get a divorce. If we don't get a divorce, there must be something wrong with us. We must be codependent or on a power trip, etc. That is painfully common. What therapists don't realize is that the high cost of faithfulness to a mentally ill spouse is surpassed by the higher cost of denying one's fundamental values.[70]

Couple Therapy

Based on her experience with spouses, Mannion cautions that couple therapy can be destructive if certain conditions are not met.[71] For example, couple therapy is not likely to be effective unless (a) the partner's illness is stabilized; (b) the partner acknowledges the illness; (c) both members of the couple are committed to trying couple therapy; and (d) the therapist has special expertise in mental illness. In one case, a couple saw four different therapists before the husband's behavior was correctly identified as a hypomanic episode and he received a medication adjustment that brought his symptoms under control.

When these conditions are met, couple therapy can be very helpful. For instance, therapy can help the couple "get reacquainted" after the trauma of an acute episode of mental illness. In addition, when a partner becomes physically aggressive, accusatory, or threatening, or attacks the spouse's character and intentions, spouses are often left wondering how much to attribute such behavior to symptoms. They may question whether these behaviors are expressions of what their partner *really* feels about them, how their partner *really* perceives them, or who their partner really *is*. Similarly, a partner may interpret a spouse's caregiving or self-protective behavior as attempts to control, criticize, or "rain on my parade," in the words of one partner.

A partner may often be too self-absorbed with the illness to even notice or acknowledge all the spouse is doing to keep the family going, which further alienates the spouse. Self-doubt, loss of self-esteem, mutual anger, mistrust, fear, grief, depression, and marital distress can worsen if the couple cannot communicate about these central issues. Couple therapy can be a safe place for them to discuss these sensitive areas, reassess each other, and appraise the viability of the marriage.

Similarly, a therapist who is knowledgeable about mental illness can help the couple sort out the symptoms of the partner's mental illness, such as paranoia, depression, or the aggressiveness of hypomania or mania, so that these behaviors are not personalized by the spouse. Sessions can also offer an opportunity to explore spouse behavior that the partner perceives as controlling, degrading, or intrusive, such as asking, "Did you take your medication today?" Once identified, such behavior can be reframed as attempts to help or cope and perhaps altered in ways that the partner will not find offensive. As trust is re-established, dialogue can continue about what the husband and wife need from each other to unite against the illness.

Regardless of the available services, practitioners should make an effort to reach out to spouses, to address their unique concerns, and to help them make contact with one another. They can also encourage the development of specialized programs, such as spouse support groups and coping skills workshops.

From Theory to Practice

Family therapist Carole Montague introduces herself to Jane Ravansky, the wife of a patient who has just been admitted to the psychiatric unit with a diagnosis of bipolar disorder. After Carole has described hospital policies and procedures, she explains her role in working with families.

PRACTITIONER: *During Don's hospitalization, I see my role as assisting you and your children in any way that I can. This has to be extremely difficult for all of you.*

SPOUSE: *I feel overwhelmed by Don's hospitalization—and exhausted after the last few months. From day to day I never knew what to expect. Sometimes Don paced through the night and talked like a tape that was played on fast forward. Then all of a sudden he would crash, staying in bed for days at a time. I felt so helpless—not knowing what to say or do. Nothing seemed to help.*

PRACTITIONER: *Anyone would feel overwhelmed under these circumstances. Often, nothing does seem to help until patients receive appropriate treatment, including medication, which often helps control the symptoms of bipolar disorder, such as the highs and the lows you witnessed. When Don was hospitalized for the first time last year, did the staff provide information about his illness?*

SPOUSE: *Don was only hospitalized for a few days. And no one would talk to me. They said it was because of confidentiality. I wasn't told what the diagnosis was or what to expect. Then suddenly they released Don, who didn't seem much better. I don't think they told him much, either. And he doesn't want to talk about it, almost as if his problems would go away if we ignored them.*

PRACTITIONER: *I'm sorry to hear about your earlier experience. I often hear from family members who say they feel ignored when their relative is hospitalized. We have a different approach here. We believe in working closely with families. A strong and informed family is the best resource a patient can have.*

SPOUSE: *It has been much better during this hospitalization. I've really felt that you cared about our family. Still, I'm not sure if anything will make a difference for us. It almost seems as if the person I married has somehow been replaced by a stranger.*

PRACTITIONER: *Your sense of being married to a stranger is often experienced when a husband or wife develops mental illness. After all, you were married for a number of years before Don developed symptoms of mental illness. So in many ways, you are adjusting to a different person, or at least to a person who has become different in some important respects.*

SPOUSE: *It's not just Don. I feel like all my hopes and dreams for the future have been destroyed. We were high school sweethearts and married right after we graduated. It felt like a dream come true. When I was younger, all I ever really wanted was to marry and have children. I know this sounds old-fashioned, but I felt I had everything I wanted in life: a man I loved and two beautiful daughters. But as the children have gotten older, I have begun planning for a career as a teacher. Last year, I started working as a teacher's aide and expected to begin college part time in the fall. Now, everything has changed. It just feels so unfair. To be honest, I feel depressed myself.*

PRACTITIONER: *Mental illness is unfair. All of you must feel as if you've lost so much—through no fault of your own. So your feeling of unfairness is understandable. And so is your depression. After all, Don is someone you love and depend on. But in spite of your feelings, you're doing very well. You're managing to take care of your children, to support Don, and to handle your job and the household. Sometimes it's enough to get from day to day.*

SPOUSE: *I suppose I am taking care of the basics. But I feel empty inside, as if all the pleasure is gone and I'm just going through the motions. I keep thinking of those awful weeks before Don was hospitalized. It's strange, but in the middle of something else, all of a sudden I'll get an image of some earlier incident. All of my emotions come rushing back, almost as if I'm living through it again. And I've lost weight and am having trouble sleeping.*

PRACTITIONER: *This has been a traumatic event for all of you. In some ways, it's like living through a tornado or hurricane. Just like these natural disasters, mental illness is a catastrophic event for families. An experience like that shakes up your entire life. Even the world seems different, as if it's no longer a predictable and stable place. What you've described— the sense of reliving the frightening episodes—are called flashbacks. People who have been through a traumatic experience, as you have, sometimes experience flashbacks like these, as well as the other problems you mentioned, such as difficulty eating and sleeping. But understanding that these reactions are normal doesn't make it any easier.*

SPOUSE: *Well, it is helpful to have you explain it. Mental illness really does feel like a catastrophe for our family. I can't imagine that a hurricane could be any worse. At least a hurricane ends; this seems to go on and on. And the girls seem so confused. I feel so tired, yet I need to be strong for them.*

PRACTITIONER: *It sounds as if you are overwhelmed. But I think you have been strong. You are doing your best under extremely difficult* circumstances. That doesn't mean you can't feel upset and depressed sometimes. Almost anyone would under these circumstances.

SPOUSE: *Sometimes what I feel most is anger. And then, of course, I feel guilty, because Don is suffering so much. He didn't ask to have this illness. We're both frightened. And he's been a wonderful husband and father. I know he worries about me and the girls. I don't know how to reassure them when I'm so worried and confused myself.*

PRACTITIONER: *It's hard to know what to tell young children when a parent has mental illness. What have you told them so far?*

SPOUSE: *Not much. I don't know what to say. I'd never heard of bipolar illness before Don was hospitalized this time. I now understand it's the same as manic depression, although I don't know much about that either.*

PRACTITIONER: *Here's some written material about bipolar disorder. Why don't you look it over. Then I can answer your questions when we meet again. You don't have to learn everything at once. The most important thing for you and the girls to understand is that this is a real illness just like heart disease or diabetes and that there are many effective treatments. The material I gave you has some suggestions for explaining mental illness to children, who often need reassurance that the illness is not their fault.*

SPOUSE: *It's so difficult to talk about mental illness with the family. Even our parents react as if mental illness is something to be ashamed of. Everyone seems to back off, as if they don't want to talk about it. In fact, my mother-in-law told me not to tell anyone about Don's mental illness, almost as if it would brand him for life.*

PRACTITIONER: *Unfortunately, lots of people feel like your mother-in-law. Mental illness is still surrounded by stigma and ignorance, which makes it so much harder for patients and families. Once families become educated about mental illness, they're usually able to begin dealing with it.*

SPOUSE: *To be honest, at this point, it seems like more than I can handle. And I worry, too, about our future. With Don on medical leave, we're still getting most of his salary. But what if he can't return to his job? Right now, he doesn't seem able to handle anything.*

PRACTITIONER: *I'm sure Don shares your concern. He's exhausted after the last few months. But he's already responding to lithium. And many people with bipolar disorder do return to their jobs, although it may take some time.*

SPOUSE: *Don's psychiatrist told me the same thing, although it's hard to believe right now. I realize I can't rush things. But in the meantime, I need to take care of the children. My job helps, although I don't make much money as a teacher's aide. And what about my plan to begin college classes in the fall? Everybody else's needs seem to take precedence over mine.*

PRACTITIONER: *It must seem like that, especially right now. But it's essential for you to take care of yourself. Your hopes and dreams matter as well. I know the local college has special programs for nontraditional students, including a weekend college and an external studies program that limits classroom time. They even allow you to take courses and exams at your own pace. Why don't you contact the college to get more information on their programs and services.*

SPOUSE: *I definitely will. I was beginning to give up on my goal of a teaching degree. Maybe I can still fulfill my dream.*

PRACTITIONER: *It's important for you to pursue your own agenda, even if it requires some juggling. We can talk more about your plans next time we meet. Do you have other problems you want to discuss?*

SPOUSE: *I'm really concerned about money. Before Don was hospitalized, he went on spending sprees and ran up all our charge accounts. I don't know how I'm going to pay the bills. Don has always been so conservative about money. Is this something I need to worry about in the future?*

PRACTITIONER: *Excessive spending is one of the symptoms of bipolar disorder, so it is related to the illness. As Don learns to manage his illness, there will be fewer symptom-related problems, such as spending sprees. If you like, I can work with you on a plan that can help you and Don avoid future problems. There are ways to set up bank accounts and charge accounts to minimize problems. In the meantime, maybe I can offer some suggestions regarding your current financial situation when we meet next time.*

SPOUSE: *I'd appreciate that. But right now I'd really like some help with the girls. I don't know how to explain an illness that I don't really understand myself.*

PRACTITIONER: *I'd be glad to meet with the girls if you think that would be helpful.*

SPOUSE: *I'd really like that. There's a lot I don't understand yet. And they might be more open with you. I know they're upset, but they keep telling me they're fine.*

PRACTITIONER: *Let's set up an appointment. And from what you've said, your entire family might benefit from an educational program that's offered by the local affiliate of NAMI, which is a family advocacy organization. Here's some information about their programs along with their phone number. They also have a special support group for spouses.*

SPOUSE: *Thanks. I'll share that with Don's parents and with mine. I'm still feeling overwhelmed, but at least I don't feel so alone any more.*

PRACTITIONER: *As difficult as this is, Jane, you aren't alone. There are lots of resources that can assist your family. I'll help you find them.*

CHAPTER 13

Working with Siblings

To his surprise, advanced practice psychiatric nurse Carl Velden re-
ceived a call from the out-of-town sibling of one of his patients, Charles
Hogan, who has schizophrenia. Charles has always resided with his par-
ents, who have provided caregiving for more than 3 decades and are
now in their 70s. In requesting the appointment, Larry Hogan said that
he and his sister, Roberta, wanted to meet to discuss how they could
become more involved in their brother's care. The entire family, includ-
ing Charles, has discussed the situation and agreed that Larry and
Roberta should take a more active role. Both siblings live some distance
from their parents, however, and their last contact with professionals
was during Charles's initial hospitalization when the three were
teenagers. In their brief telephone conversation, Larry told Carl that his
adolescence was one of the most difficult periods of his life, remarking
that he wondered about his own sanity as he watched his admired older
brother become enveloped in psychosis. Larry added that he and his sis-
ter have long anticipated the time when they would assume the caregiv-
ing mantle of their parents. How can Carl assist these long-distance
siblings?

Anticipating his appointment with these siblings, Carl thinks of
his periodic contacts with Mr. and Mrs. Hogan over the years,
trying to recall what they have said about their other children.
But, in fact, their consultative sessions have focused almost exclusively on
Charles and on their immediate concerns, almost as if there were no other
children in the family. Yet it is clear from Larry's telephone call that these
siblings have been deeply affected by their brother's mental illness.

This chapter explores the sibling experience of mental illness. Along
with offspring, whose experiences are examined in the next chapter, siblings have grown up in the presence of mental illness. Often, the illness

265

becomes the defining event of their childhood or adolescence, imprinting their lives in the most profound way. In contrast to adult members of the family, because of their development status siblings and offspring experience mental illness in a more fundamental way. Namely, the illness is woven into their very sense of self, becoming *part* of them rather than something that happens to their family. This developmental context is essential in understanding the consequences of mental illness for young family members.

Young Family Members

Young family members are especially vulnerable to any disruptive or traumatic event, such as the mental illness of a close relative. More easily overwhelmed than adults, children and adolescents have fewer coping skills and psychological defenses. They are also more limited in their ability to understand mental illness and to verbalize their painful feelings. Moreover, children are more dependent on other people, which is a precarious position when a parent or older sibling suffers from mental illness.

All of these considerations are important in understanding the experiences of young family members. Indeed, research with adult siblings and offspring highlights the central importance of their age at the onset of their relative's mental illness.[1] In essence, the younger they are, the greater the potential impact of the illness, which is likely to reverberate through their entire lives:

I am just learning, at age 49, that I can be me. I have only just begun to identify what I want and who I really am. I adapted my behavior at home totally in the interest of keeping the equilibrium in the family. I felt responsible for making everyone happy. I took on emotions of others as something I had to fix. I developed a pattern of putting others before myself, lost my identity in relationships.[2]

As a result of their developmental status, siblings and offspring share an array of illness-related risks and concerns, both as children and as adults. In fact, sometimes they share both roles as well: 25% of our survey participants were both siblings and offspring. Rex Dickens, my collaborator on two books concerned with siblings and offspring, has experienced the mental illness of his mother and three siblings.[3] He has written evocatively of the difference between the roles, describing siblings as "frozen souls" who are struggling with ongoing trauma and with loss and grief, sometimes cutting off or compartmentalizing painful feelings in their effort to survive. Dickens views offspring as "hollowed souls" who are dealing with primal issues of self, their early experience with parental mental illness often leaving a void at their core.

Shared Risks

Researchers have provided substantial documentation of the risks for individuals who have a first-degree relative with mental illness, such as siblings and offspring. Investigations of family members have been designed to determine their risk of developing mental illness, to establish shared biological abnormalities or markers, to investigate the presence of psychosocial problems, to identify the vulnerability and protective factors that may mediate the impact of the illness, and to offer preventive and other appropriate services.[4]

Based on the results of these studies, first-degree relatives (parents, offspring, and siblings) carry an increased risk of developing mental illness themselves. In contrast to a 1% incidence of schizophrenia in the general population, for example, the risk of developing the disorder has been estimated at 9% for siblings and 13% for offspring. The risk of developing bipolar disorder among first-degree relatives is about 1 in 12 (8%); increased risk is also associated with major depression. The risk increases when the family includes more than one person with mental illness; thus, a referral for genetic counseling may be appropriate.[5] Young family members are also subject to a range of cognitive, social, emotional, behavioral, academic, and developmental problems.[6]

In spite of these risks, it is equally clear that many individual, familial, and extrafamilial variables mediate the risks for particular siblings and offspring.[7] Some of these variables may serve as predisposing or exacerbating factors, increasing the likelihood of clinical, developmental, and psychosocial problems. Other variables may serve as protectors that decrease the risks for these family members. Thus, many outcomes are possible for siblings and offspring, who remain a diverse group throughout their lives. Indeed, many do very well under challenging circumstances:

My husband once asked me how it was possible that I evolved unscathed from my upbringing with a mentally ill brother. It never occurred to me that as a family we should have fallen apart. To me my brother's illness was just a fact, like Daddy went to work on Monday mornings. It was okay for him to be that way, and it was okay for us to be happy. It was simple—you love your family, you care for each individual, you respect each other. It always felt solid, it felt right.[8]

Even when there are positive outcomes, however, siblings and offspring share a wide range of illness-related concerns.

Shared Concerns

In our research with adult siblings and offspring, we asked them about their concerns as family members. As indicated in Table 13.1, some of these concerns reflect the subjective and objective burden already discussed, including caregiving responsibilities, family disruption, difficulty balancing personal and family needs, and feelings of grief and loss. Other concerns are more closely tied to their developmental status, including their sense that their own needs had not been met as they were growing up or that they had grown up too fast. Our survey participants also reported a range of personal concerns, such as poor self-esteem and psychic numbing; of interpersonal concerns, such as problems with trust and intimacy; and of vocational concerns, such as a sense of unfulfilled potential.

Plainly, siblings and offspring live under a cloud of potential problems as a result of the mental illness in their families. At the same time, practitioners need to remain sensitive to the diversity among these family members and to their potential for personal resilience.

TABLE 13.1
SHARED CONCERNS OF ADULT SIBLINGS AND OFFSPRING

- Caregiving for their relative (94%)
- Family disruption (83%)
- Difficulty balancing personal and family needs (81%)
- Sense that their own needs had not been met (79%)
- Feelings of helplessness and hopelessness (75%)
- Poor self-esteem (75%)
- Guilt feelings (74%)
- Psychic numbing (70%)
- Problems trusting (69%)
- Problems with intimacy (69%)
- Sense of growing up too fast (67%)
- Personal depression (66%)
- Chronic sorrow (64%)
- Sense of unfulfilled potential (64%)
- Need to be perfect (63%)
- Grieving process (63%)
- Sense of abandonment (61%)
- Identity problems (59%)
- Fear of violence (57%)
- Social isolation (54%)
- Fear of suicide (52%)
- Effect on personal choices (51%)
- Difficulty separating from their family (51%)

Note: From D. T. Marsh and R. M. Dickens, 1997, pp. 61–62. Percentages refer to the number of participants who experienced this illness-related concern at least sometimes. Reprinted with permission of the authors.

SHARED RESILIENCE

When asked if they had experienced any positive consequences as a result of the mental illness in their families, a large majority (86%) answered affirmatively, citing the following:

- Personal growth and development, such as increased tolerance, empathy, compassion, and understanding
- Better self-concept, including a sense of greater strength, discipline, and personal stability
- Enhanced skills for coping with the mental illness and other challenges
- Significant contributions to other people and to society
- Effective advocacy for improvements in the mental health system
- Better family and social life, such as special closeness within their family
- Healthier perspective and priorities, such as a clearer sense of what is important
- Greater appreciation of life and of personal mental health

Reflecting this potential for personal resilience, one sibling remarked, "It's made me more compassionate toward those who don't have the abilities I have. I've become more cognizant of my blessings. I feel a responsibility to become involved with the mental health movement in some way."[9] As noted earlier, however, resilience often exacts a high personal price.

In addition to the experiences they share with other family members, siblings also have unique experiences as a result of their role in the family.

The Sibling Experience

More than 80% of children in the United States are siblings—brothers and sisters who share a special bond.[10] For example, siblings often:

- Know us like no one else
- Spend more time with us than other family members
- Strongly influence our personality and relationships
- Meet important needs for us

- Influence us throughout our lives
- Are partners in our longest relationship[11]

When one sibling develops a mental illness, it has a profound impact on the sibling bond. For example, siblings may feel they have experienced the dual losses of their brother or sister and of their parents, whose energy may be consumed by the mental illness. They may also feel that their needs are neglected or may try to compensate their anguished parents:

I became the perfect child to spare my parents more grief. I was forced to become responsible. In many ways it forced me to accomplish things in my life I might not have otherwise done. But I have spent my life trying to run away from this problem. Feeling guilty and helpless, the unending sorrow for not being able to help. I have not felt entitled to be happy most of my adult life.[12]

In addition, siblings of all ages often feel alienated from the "normal" world outside their beleaguered family, struggling to be heard when everyone seems to be fixated on the mental illness of their brother or sister. In response to all of these forces, siblings often lose sight of their own needs.

Nevertheless, even when a brother or sister has a mental illness, sibling pairs continue to share in the potential risks and gratifications that accompany all of our intimate relationships. The following siblings bear witness to both poles of the sibling bond. The first wrote that her brother's pain had taken its toll on their family: "I feel so helpless and filled with such sorrow for him. When I look into his eyes (and sometimes I can't even do that), I know he'll never be the same." But another sibling spoke of her brother's warm relationship with her daughter and his "divergent way of thinking": "He's fun, interesting, and entertaining—he makes me smile."[13] Over the course of a lifetime, siblings are likely to experience both poles of this central and intricate relationship.

Professionals who work with siblings need to be sensitive to the universal characteristics of the sibling bond, to its transformation by mental illness, and to the many potential outcomes for individual siblings. There is an expanding literature concerned with all of these topics.[14] For example, several powerful personal accounts by siblings are now available, including *My Sister's Keeper: Learning to Cope with a Sibling's Mental Illness* by Margaret Moorman; *Imagining Robert: My Brother, Madness, and Survival: A Memoir* by Jay Neugeboren; *Mad House: Growing Up in the Shadow of Mentally Ill Siblings* by Clea Simon; and *The Four of Us* by Elizabeth Swados.[15]

Interweaving strands of personal, family, and social history, Neugeboren's eloquent memoir tells the story of his brother Robert, an extraordinarily witty, intelligent man whose life has been ravaged by serious

mental illness for more than 3 decades.[16] "It is as if," Neugeboren has
written, "the very history of the ways in which our century has dealt with
those it calls mentally ill has, for more than 30 years now, been passing
through my brother's mind and body." Capturing a central theme of the
sibling experience, he often felt as if:

*The brother I grew up with had died, and now another brother had taken his
place—a brother who looked very much like my first brother, and who shared
many things with him—a history, a wonderfully idiosyncratic sense of humor, a
love of books, movies, and art, a sweet generosity of spirit, memories, feelings, desires. . . . but who seemed, sadly, a very different person, with a much grimmer,
narrower life.*

Throughout his life, Neugeboren has struggled with a sense that "that
any success or happiness I achieved had been earned, somehow, at the
price of his failure and misery." Yet after all these years, the brothers continue to talk with each other almost every day; and they see each other
often, sharing their lives in a sustained and constant way.

Simon's book portrays her life growing up with two siblings who had
schizophrenia. Leaving home for college, she tried unsuccessfully to close
the door on her traumatic early years:

*It would be another ten years before I realized that, far from having escaped my
family's problems, I was buried in them. The illness that had taken control of my
siblings' lives had made an indelible mark on my own, and denying the impact of
their illness simply kept me from seeing, and countering, its effects.[17]*

In addition to these memoirs, many other publications describe the
sibling experience of mental illness, including the two books I have published with Rex Dickens: *Anguished Voices,* a collection of personal accounts by adult siblings and offspring; and *Troubled Journey: Coming to
Terms with the Mental Illness of a Sibling or Parent.*[18] Other useful publications include a special sibling issue of *The JOURNAL,* a number of books
designed for the general public, and both early and more recent professional articles and books.[19] As is the case for other family members, the
experience of individual siblings is affected by the wide range of personal, family, and social variables specified earlier. For example, their
gender, birth order, and chronological proximity to their brother or sister
may affect their caregiving responsibilities and tendency to identify with
their relative.

Of particular importance is their age at the onset of the mental illness.
Although mental illness most often begins during late adolescence or

early adulthood, the illness can in fact strike at any age. The consequences of the illness for siblings may vary considerably depending on their own developmental phase. For example, if the illness occurs during their childhood, siblings may grow up with an illness that defines their family—and themselves—in fundamental ways. If they are teenagers at the onset of the illness, siblings are subject to profound feelings of loss for the brother or sister they have known and loved prior to the illness. If they are adults when their relative's illness develops, siblings may have less involvement in their relative's life.

Whatever their personal circumstances, however, it is clear that siblings are profoundly affected by the mental illness of a brother or sister. Along with the shared family burden, the sibling experience of mental illness is distinguished by numerous unique landmarks.

Sibling Themes

As is the case for parents, spouses, and offspring, some of the following themes are shared with other family members but experienced in a singular way by siblings; other themes, such as the "replacement child syndrome," are unique to the sibling role.

GRIEF AND LOSS

Because serious mental illness is often diagnosed in late adolescence or early adulthood, siblings have often experienced their brother or sister in a very different way: as a high-functioning person with the potential for an unbounded future. In the wake of mental illness, siblings may experience the multiple losses of love, comfort, entertainment, companionship, admiration, and protection. In many respects, the feelings of siblings are similar to those that accompany the biological death of a brother or sister.[20]

Siblings who are dealing with mental illness may mourn for their well brother or sister, for a shared past now shadowed by a painful present, and for an anticipated future with a healthy relative. As a sibling expressed it, "To me, it was a death. The person whom I knew and was so much like me in so many ways had died, and I didn't know this person who was living in the house any more."[21] Unlike a biological death, however, siblings need to adapt to a changed relationship, which can be surpassingly difficult. As one sibling wrote, "I have found it almost impossible to let go of what our relationship once was and accept what our relationship has become."[22]

If siblings are young children at the onset of the illness, their losses take on a different character. Indeed, they may grieve for the loss of a normal childhood and family life. If siblings are adults at the time, they may reexamine their earlier years, wondering "what if" their relative had received an earlier diagnosis and treatment. Compounding these feelings are additional losses involving other members of the family. For instance, siblings may experience the loss of their parents, who may be consumed by their own grief, or of their well siblings, who may have responded to this family tragedy with anger or disengagement.[23] As Neugeboren has written, there are an infinite number of ways in which the presence of mental illness "exhausts, strains, and informs *all* the moments and relations of a family's life."[24]

FORGOTTEN FAMILY MEMBERS

The sense of being a forgotten family member reverberates throughout the personal accounts of siblings. One wrote that when her sister developed mental illness, "my family turned inside out":

Until then, I had been the star of the family and got the bulk of the attention. Suddenly, both my brother and I felt there was no time for us; everyone was consumed by what was going on with my sister. We no longer mattered.[25]

Outside of the family, siblings may feel alienated from the world of their peers and ignored by a mental health system that seems impervious to their distress and their concerns. Capturing some of these feelings, Simon has written that well siblings are often doubly wounded: first by their family experiences and then by the lack of comprehension—in themselves as well as others—of the reasons for their hurt, anger, and disconnection: "As 'healthy' siblings we have wondered if our experience even counts; after all, we are not suffering the tragic and inexplicable illnesses of our brothers and sisters. But we, too, have come through tragedies."[26]

SURVIVOR'S GUILT

At its most basic level, survivor's guilt is experienced by siblings simply because they have been spared mental illness themselves. Through neither of their faults, one sibling has remained well; the other endures mental illness. The tragic unfairness of this reality is likely to cast a pall over the life of the well sibling, who may shoulder an irrational sense of culpability: that somehow the health of one sibling has been achieved at the expense of the other. This guilt may be intensified by normal feelings of sibling rivalry; for how does one compete fairly with a brother or sister who has been ravaged by mental illness.

Plagued by survivor's guilt, siblings may be reticent to embrace the riches of their own lives—the adventures, opportunities, relationships, and accomplishments that derive from a life fully lived. Sensitive to the disparities between the two lives, they may have difficulty enjoying the pleasures denied to a brother or sister.

The guilt that you feel can be debilitating. A lot of times you don't want to have success. You cover up your success because the ill family member is missing so many good things in life. And you feel bad about getting those yourself. If you have a girlfriend or fiancée, you want to play that down.[27]

Survivor's guilt may also incline siblings to ignore their own problems. After all, how can they complain about a life that is so much better than that of their brother or sister?[28]

REPLACEMENT CHILD SYNDROME

Siblings who have lost a brother or sister to biological death may place themselves in the role of a "replacement child" who must gratify the needs of their devastated parents.[29] A similar reaction may occur among siblings who are dealing with mental retardation or mental illness.[30] Striving to be perfect children or modeling themselves after an idealized brother or sister, siblings may accommodate parents who seek a substitute for their stricken child or may deny themselves opportunities for healthy rebellion. As one sibling remarked, "I never felt safe enough to rebel."[31]

Struggling to offset the dashed hopes of their parents, siblings my create a flawless public persona that contrasts with the emptiness within. Yet the need to function as a surrogate may occasion considerable resentment, as it did for this sibling:

The change in my status within my family has been difficult. After all, my brother was the genius with enormous potential. Now, with his illness, by default I am the star in the family. My parents, their hopes miserably shattered by my brother, now rise and fall with me through my every peak and valley. That is the load I carry now, and I hate it.[32]

As in this family, siblings sometimes respond to parental pressure to serve in a replacement role; in other cases, siblings themselves may feel compelled to assume such a role. An adolescent sibling I worked with in therapy told me she planned to change her career to the one formerly planned by her older brother. The anticipated change had little to do with her own aptitudes or interests; she felt it had to be done for her parents. Fortunately, in a joint session, her parents were able to assure her that they valued her for herself and wanted her to pursue her *own* goals. Thus liberated from her surrogate role, this sibling reconnected with her own hopes and plans.

ACADEMIC AND VOCATIONAL ISSUES

Adult siblings often observe that their encounter with mental illness has affected their academic life—both negatively and positively. During their early years, some siblings may find that their family circumstances drain energy needed for school work. Others may channel their energy into school work, becoming superachievers whose accomplishments belie their inner turmoil. In fact, academic achievement can offer a constructive avenue for growth and satisfaction even as it serves as an escape from their family circumstances: "I became an overachiever at school and withdrew emotionally from my family. I grew increasingly dependent on scholastic and then business achievements at the expense of a rich personal life."[33]

Extracurricular activities may be affected in similar ways. Such activities offer many opportunities for siblings to enhance their skills and self-esteem, to expand activities and relationships outside their family, to obtain reinforcement for normal developmental experiences and goals, and to identify with constructive role models. Yet their feelings of social isolation may keep some siblings from becoming involved.

As adolescents, siblings may feel constrained to remain close to their embattled family, at the risk of foreclosing their own academic and vocational opportunities. Wherever they reside, they may have difficult focusing on their own future in the face of their family's hardships. In the words of one sibling, "The pain and grief made it impossible for me to enjoy the 'best years' of my life."[34] As they decide on a career, siblings are often influenced by their earlier encounter with mental illness. On one hand, they may be drawn to a caregiving career in the fields of education, health care, or mental health, which offers an accustomed and satisfying role. Speaking for himself and an older brother, a sibling remarked, "We have gone toward human services like magnets because we can handle all this."[35] On the other hand, some siblings may pursue data-oriented careers that offer a welcome alternative to their earlier family roles.

Building a career, adult siblings may continue to find that their family circumstances siphon energy needed for further advancement. Her resources depleted by recurrent family crises, one sibling commented that she "couldn't find the energy to invest in my own life"; another wrote of feeling he "was working on only one or two cylinders out of four."[36]

IDENTITY AND ROLE ISSUES

Because mental illness appears in their family when they are growing up, siblings are likely to incorporate the illness into their sense of who they are and how they fit into the larger world. Sibling identity may be adversely affected by identification with an admired older brother or sister who manifests psychotic symptoms, by concerns about their own mental health, or by the corrosive stigma that continues to accompany a diagnosis of mental illness in our society. One sibling reported that her sister's mental illness had translated into "a pervasive sense of shame."[37]

Identity issues assume a special importance in certain relationships, such as twinship. A well twin described her experience of having a sister with schizophrenia: "It is especially difficult to look exactly like someone who behaves in ways that I would never dream of. And stigma is much harder to deal with because we are fused together in people's minds."[38] This twin said she experiences considerable anxiety when others confuse her with her sister or assume she has mental illness simply because her sister does.

Both inside and outside the family, sibling roles may be affected by mental illness. Inside the family, siblings may assume a parentified role to meet the needs of their overwhelmed family. Additional responsibilities can deflect siblings from pursuing their own life plans, leaving a legacy of resentment and unfulfilled dreams. One sibling declared that she lost out on her childhood: "I have always had to be responsible."[39] Outside the family, siblings may internalize the social role transformations imposed on their family, assuming that they too are dysfunctional, shameful, or deviant.

LIFE SPAN ISSUES

From the onset of their relative's illness, the life course of siblings is at risk for disruption. Thus, if the illness appears during their childhood, the tasks of this phase are most likely to be affected, including the development of attachment and basic trust, of the competencies needed for effective functioning, and of essential academic and interpersonal skills. Because mental illness typically develops in late adolescence or early adulthood, however, the illness is most likely to have initial repercussions during these developmental phases.

Adolescents are charged with forging a sense of personal identity, coming to terms with their emerging sexuality, charting a tentative career, and achieving separation from their family of origin. Siblings who are dealing with the mental illness of a brother or sister may find all of these tasks affected. One sibling continued to identify with an older brother who was no longer a constructive role model: "When he went crazy, I took drugs to be like him. I even moved into his bedroom when he was hospitalized." Losing sight of his own needs, this sibling wanted to rescue his brother—"to sacrifice myself to help him."[40]

During young adulthood, siblings often continue to find their developmental agenda unsettled. Tasks of this phase typically involve intimacy, marriage, parenthood, and career. Confronted with the mental illness of a brother or sister, siblings may avoid intimacy to prevent further losses, reconsider marriage in light of their troubled family history, weigh the genetic risks of mental illness when they contemplate having children, and find their career choices influenced by their earlier encounter with mental illness.

During middle and late adulthood, siblings may find their own tasks preempted by concerns about actual or potential caregiving responsibilities for their brother or sister. Under such circumstances, little energy may remain for renegotiating their earlier personal, interpersonal, and vocational commitments in midlife, or for confronting their own mortality in later years. Indeed, the tasks of these phases may evoke a renewed sense of loss, as was the case for one sibling who described the legacy he and his sister shared in the aftermath of their brother's mental illness. Neither he nor his sister had married: "With no children expected, our family line appears to be ending."[41]

PERSONAL ISSUES

Many of the personal issues facing siblings have already been noted, including the concerns listed in Table 13.1. Of particular importance is their fear of being an invisible family member: someone whose problems seem less serious, whose needs less pressing, whose dreams less compelling, whose life plans more dispensable. This sense of being pushed to the periphery of the family portrait may generate considerable anger and resentment.

In addition, siblings frequently report that the mental illness has an adverse impact on their self-esteem and self-concept:

The presence of this illness in my life had translated into low self-esteem . . . I was extremely sensitive to what others thought of me, ready to read in to their comments that they thought I was crazy, or at least inappropriate.[42]

Even when they have passed the period of greatest risk, siblings often worry that they will develop mental illness themselves. For example, the well twin mentioned earlier spoke of her anxiety when others confuse her with her sister or assume she has mental illness as well: "I am already watching myself like a hawk for any signs of a nervous breakdown. I don't need others to add to this."[43]

Interpersonal Issues

Well siblings often say their relationships have been affected by the mental illness. As they are growing up, siblings may feel estranged from peers who know little about mental illness, be reluctant to invite friends to visit an unpredictable home environment, and worry about the reactions of a boyfriend or girlfriend. A sibling captures some of these concerns:

I knew my sister was different. I was torn between loyalty to her and wanting to be accepted by my friends. The pain and sense of being different were already there. I felt unacceptable to my peers and restricted my friendships to a few people who accepted me and did not ask too many questions.[44]

Some siblings find it easier to avoid dealing with their social world. One said she kept so busy with a part-time job that "I didn't have time to think about how isolated I was from other people my age. I felt unattractive and unlovable in high school and didn't date."[45]

In adulthood, siblings describe an interpersonal legacy that is characterized by problems with trust and intimacy, fear of rejection or abandonment, and reluctance to make a long-term commitment. The following man grew up with a brother and sister who both had mental illness. His effort to shield himself from further pain as a teenager has had a pervasive impact on his adult relationships:

I remember at 18, I swore I would never trust anyone for the rest of my life. I went through a lot of therapy. I never had friends over and never told anyone that my brother and sister were psychotic. I was terribly ashamed of their illness. I was continually angry. I learned to develop a complete wall mentally to protect myself.[46]

Another sibling remarked on his difficulty in making a long-term commitment: "I have not had a relationship with a woman longer than 1 year. I withdrew socially, became very introverted, and had low self-esteem."[47]

An additional problem is the continuation of earlier attitudes or roles that interfere with mature adult relationships. For instance, siblings who have minimized their own needs as they were growing up may develop an excessive need to please others or lose sight of personal needs in relationships. As a sibling wrote, "I feel that I've denied my needs, interests, and goals. I have a hard time taking steps to focus on myself, making myself happy."[48] Likewise, adult siblings who inappropriately continue a caregiving role face the dual risks of choosing a troubled partner who needs their ministrations or alienating someone who prefers not to be parented. One sibling said she had cared for her brother since her 20s. Ensconced in this role, "I continued to treat men in a motherly way, not in a 'girlfriend' way."[49]

FAMILY ISSUES

As adults, siblings typically confront three kinds of family issues: concern about caregiving for their brother or sister, problems with their own spouse and children, and difficulty juggling commitments to their two families. Although siblings are comparatively free to define their caregiving role, some do shoulder caregiving responsibilities. One sibling reported that her sister often functions at a high level, maintaining her apartment and working for a major company. Yet every year or two, her sister has been hospitalized during a manic episode, most recently when she became convinced that a plane that she was traveling on was carrying a bomb. "I spent a week as her advocate," this sibling recounted, citing her contacts with lawyers, doctors, magistrates, and mental health workers. "This was the most intense and worst week of my life."[50]

Even when they are not currently involved in caregiving, siblings may experience apprehension about their future responsibilities. In the words of one sibling, "I worry about the present and future." Concerned about the burden of her parents, she wonders about herself and "the choices I can and will make. I have mixed feelings about whether I can and want to be a caregiver."[51] Another sibling experienced considerable distress as he contemplated the decline of his aging parents:

My brother, who is diagnosed with schizophrenia, lives in Florida near our parents, who are both now turning 80. I live a thousand miles away in Maine. I have a sister who lives in California. Over the years, my brother has received a lot of support from Mom and Dad. When they die, what do my sister and I do? What are our responsibilities? It's a deeply troubling question that cannot easily be avoided.[52]

In addition to concern about caregiving responsibilities, siblings may experience problems with their own spouse and children. For example, difficulties with trust and intimacy may undermine their relationship with their spouse, as may their fear of rejection or abandonment. Aware of the genetic risks associated with mental illness, siblings may also experience substantial anxiety about childbearing: "I will probably never have children. I have learned to deal with my sister's illness, but I don't think I could deal with it happening to my own child."[53]

If they do become parents, siblings may worry about the risk of mental illness in their children and assume a state of vigilance that heightens anxiety within their family. Ordinary problems and concerns may loom as a potential sign of mental illness in their children, who may internalize some of this free-floating anxiety.

Social Issues

The stigma that accompanies a diagnosis of mental illness is likely to have many deleterious consequences for siblings. If they are children or adolescents at the time of the diagnosis, they may grow up with a sense of social deviance that pervades their lives and leaves them feeling like outsiders in the world beyond their family. Internalizing negative social attitudes, siblings may also experience low self-esteem, a tendency toward self-stigmatization, and feelings of isolation and shame. Writing about the schizophrenia of her brother and sister, for instance, Simon remarks that her siblings "no longer inhabit my present life, but their illnesses haunt me, like ghosts." She continues, "Once people know my family's story—no matter how far I distance myself from my sister and brother, or how well I manage my life—they often treat me as if I am somehow damaged, too."[54]

If they are adults at the time of their relative's diagnosis, siblings may develop a pervasive sense of alienation from their own history as well as their current social world. Once mental illness has appeared, their entire family context—the patterns, myths, secrets, expectations, and attitudes that are transmitted from generation to generation—may seem fraudulent. In retrospect, siblings may feel the overarching event of their lives has been omitted from their family picture, rendering it fundamentally inaccurate. What they have "known" to be true—even who they have been—is open to question.

Professional Issues

Siblings have two kinds of contacts with professionals: as family members of people with serious mental illness and as clients who seek services for themselves, such as individual therapy. Their perceptions of professionals differ in the two roles. As family members, siblings often feel ignored by practitioners who fail to understand their experiences, address their needs, or acknowledge their concerns. Indeed, their sense of neglect within their own beleaguered families is likely to be compounded by their contacts with professionals. One sibling complained, "You don't get professional help and support. You're not given any guidance. You are left floundering."[55]

When they *do* receive family services, siblings tend to view them as unresponsive at best and harmful at worst. In her interviews, for example, Wasow heard from siblings who had been subject to "family bashing" that took place in family therapy, locked up in the hospital with the patient for therapy, videotaped in family therapy by a "show-off" therapist, and refused information under the guise of confidentiality.[56] My own contacts with siblings have elicited similar complaints:

Professionals seem to view siblings through the filters of their statistics and theories rather than listening and trying to understand the complexities of my relationship with my sister. Professionals did not communicate effectively with the family, and my opinions were ignored. While they seemed sympathetic at first to our stressed-out family, they seemed to blame my family for being "dysfunctional."[57]

In contrast, when describing their experiences as clients themselves, siblings generally view professionals more positively. As noted, many adult siblings who participated in our survey had sought personal therapy, which they usually found very helpful. As clients, siblings do get the attention of practitioners who hear their stories, strive to meet their needs, and respond with understanding and support.

Needs of Siblings

Throughout their lives, siblings have three kinds of needs: for their brother or sister with mental illness, for their family as a unit, and for themselves.

PATIENT NEEDS

Siblings need services that can support their relative in living a satisfying life. In fact, their own needs are likely to diminish in proportion to their relative's recovery. The following woman experienced a difficult adolescence marked by a sense that her "point of reference was gone" when her older sister developed schizophrenia. Twenty years later, her sister is living "an incredibly normal life":

She is happily married and holding a good computer job. There really is hope! She takes medication and is able to keep all the voices under control. Our relationship is great—we have the same sister feelings we had before her illness.[58]

Family Needs

Especially as young family members, siblings need services that can support and strengthen their family. Indeed, as they are growing up, a strong and effective family is their most important resource. Depending on their family circumstances, services might include the interventions that have been discussed, such as consultation, education, or psychoeducation; a home-based program that focuses on all members of the family; or respite care during periods of crisis.

Personal Needs

Siblings also have needs of their own for age-appropriate information, coping skills, and support. For example, children need simple and direct explanations of mental illness and practical suggestions for coping with what is often a frightening and confusing experience. Young siblings might benefit from individual attention from a grandparent or other extended family member, from participation in a support group for children or teenagers who have a relative with mental illness, or from individual sessions with a school psychologist or mental health professional.

Siblings often need assistance in maintaining the thrust of their own lives, including encouragement to do well in school, to develop constructive long-range plans, and to establish satisfactory relationships inside and outside their family. They may need reassurance that their needs matter and that they will be supported in achieving their goals. Siblings may also need assistance in finding a comfortable level of involvement in the life of their brother or sister. This level is likely to vary over the course of their lives.

There is research support for all of these needs. In our survey of adult siblings and offspring, we asked them to rate the importance of a range of needs during their childhood, adolescence, and adulthood. Participants assigned highest ratings to their needs for satisfactory services for their relative, and for information, coping skills, and support for themselves. They gave mixed ratings to their need for involvement in their relative's treatment. Some preferred to have no involvement; others wished to play a more active role.

We also explored their coping resources, including their personal qualities, their family, their friends, NAMI, a support group, mental health professionals, and clergy. These family members evaluated no resource as "helpful" during the first 10 years of their lives. As teenagers, they found just their personal qualities helpful. Only as adults do they have a range of coping resources available to them. Thus, during their period of greatest vulnerability, young siblings and offspring have fewest resources. In the words of one participant, "I don't think *anything* has helped."[59]

Responding to this remark, one practitioner wondered if anything *would* have helped under these circumstances. In fact, when asked what would have made a difference, an offspring asserted that communication is the key. "The one thing that can make a difference is someone reaching out, talking about the illness, letting these children know that their feelings are normal. Just someone to say, 'I care about you.' "[60]

Reflecting this sense of abandonment, a sibling wrote about her unrequited need for someone who "could have thrown out a lifeline" to her struggling family:

What siblings want is equal time and attention from parents. They want time with other siblings who have had similar experiences in dealing with the chaos of mental illness. They want to know that the illness is not their fault; and that it is okay to have transient angry feelings, or wishes that the ill family member were dead . . . They need help in expressing unexpressed emotions, and unspoken communications to their parents.[61]

Intervention Strategies for Siblings

Young family members have compelling needs from the moment that mental illness appears in their families. Accordingly, practitioners should reach out to young family members as early as possible: to acknowledge their anguish, to address their needs, and to assist them in coping with this catastrophic event. Likewise, services should be appropriate for their developmental level and responsive to their changing needs throughout their lives. In particular, professionals can encourage parents to devote time to their well children and to help them understand the illness.

CHILDHOOD

The developmental phases discussed earlier offer a framework that can guide the provision of services for young siblings and offspring. During early childhood, these family members need the presence of caregivers who can provide nurturing, commitment, and instruction. Thus, services should be designed to meet the needs of all adult members of the family and to assist them in supporting young family members.

Community support services may also be helpful, including home-based care for the family that includes home visits by providers, as well as respite care (temporary relief from caregiving responsibilities). Respite care generally includes community-based care for the patient, such as group day care (daytime activities) or group residential care (overnight care). Preschoolers might benefit from activities and programs outside the home and from the involvement of extended family members, such as grandparents. Young children who are experiencing significant problems might profit from a referral to a child therapist. For example, play therapy can be useful for preschoolers, who are likely to have difficulty expressing their concerns verbally.

During middle childhood, developmental tasks center on academic adjustment and peer relationships. Therefore, practitioners might find it helpful to work with the school system.[62] Guidance counselors may benefit from mental health consultation in designing a group for school children who are dealing with mental illness at home. Such a group can provide information about the illness in a form that children can comprehend, strengthen their coping skills, and offer understanding and support from counselors and other children. Programs to educate elementary children about mental illness may also be helpful, as may individual or group therapy for children who are experiencing significant difficulty at home or in school.

ADOLESCENCE

During adolescence, siblings who are coping with mental illness may profit from a range of services. Because peer relations are of central importance during this period, siblings may benefit from a group format that includes other teenagers who have a close relative with mental illness. Such groups are generally best offered separately for early adolescents (age 13 to 15) and late adolescents (16 to 18). Particularly with older adolescents, an experienced group member can serve as a peer counselor or cofacilitator. Groups might be offered through the school system, by a local NAMI chapter, or by an agency. Adolescents whose needs cannot be met through a support group or educational program may be candidates for individual or group therapy.

Although programs for young family members are relatively rare, two model programs are presented in Chapter 15: BART's (Bring All Relatives Together) Place, a provider-based program for children and adolescents who have parents with serious mental illness; and Project S. O. S. (Stamp Out Stigma of Mental Illness), a school-based program designed to educate students about mental illness. Regardless of service availability, individual practitioners can make a significant difference in the lives of children and adolescents who are growing up with mental illness in their families. Here are some suggestions:

1. Strengthen and support the family system as a whole. A wide range of resources and services may be helpful under these circumstances, including improved services for parents with mental illness, respite care during periods of crisis, education and support for adult family members, and special assistance for young family members.

2. Learn about the family experience of mental illness, the unique issues and concerns of siblings and offspring, effective coping skills and strategies, and beneficial services. Many useful resources are available.

3. Reach out as early as possible to young family members, who are profoundly affected by the mental illness of a beloved sibling or parent. Listen to their stories. Encourage them to ask questions and to share their feelings. Assure them that they are not to blame.

4. Meet the needs of young family members in an age-appropriate manner. As with other family members, children and adolescents need information about mental illness, skills for coping with the illness, and support for themselves. These needs can be met by adult members of the family, by caring people outside the family, or by professionals.

5. Provide services for siblings and offspring of all ages. Young children can benefit from provider-based programs designed to strengthen family relationships during crises or periods of hospitalization. Older siblings and offspring can profit from educational programs and support groups, which can be offered in a range of community settings. Adults can benefit from a referral to the local NAMI chapter, which may offer a specialized support group for adult siblings and offspring.

6. Offer professional counseling for siblings and offspring who are experiencing particular difficulty. More than three-fourths of our survey participants had received personal therapy. Almost all reported that it was beneficial.

7. Encourage educational programs in schools, which can increase understanding and reduce stigma among students. Such programs can also enlist the assistance of teachers, principals, guidance counselors, school nurses, and school psychologists, who can expand the support network of young family members.

8. Assist siblings and offspring of all ages in maintaining the integrity of their own lives and in developing constructive long-range plans.

They often need reassurance that their needs matter and that they will be supported in achieving their goals.

Adulthood

Although the family interventions discussed in Chapters 7 through 10 are primarily designed to address the needs of parents, with modifications they are also appropriate for adult siblings. Applying the three-step model, Step 1 involves family consultation, which offers a useful means of addressing the illness-related concerns of siblings and of informing them of other available services. Consultation may be particularly helpful for siblings who are serving as caregivers or informal case managers for their relatives or who are planning to increase their involvement.

In Step 2, practitioners can work with siblings in developing an individualized family service plan. Siblings who play an important role in their relative's life may benefit from a full range of services, including a family support and advocacy group such as NAMI. In fact, their popular Family-to-Family Education Program was developed by a sibling and psychologist, Joyce Burland. Support groups may also be life-enhancing, particularly if they include adult siblings and offspring. In our book *Troubled Journey*, Rex Dickens[63] offers suggestions for family members who plan to develop a support group for adult siblings and offspring. His discussion may also be helpful for practitioners who wish to encourage or facilitate a similar group.

Involved siblings may also benefit from provider-based support groups, family education, and family psychoeducation, either singly or in combination. On the other hand, siblings who reside elsewhere or are not involved in caregiving might prefer educational materials about mental illness and occasional telephone contact with practitioners. Over the course of their lives, these latter siblings may assume a more active role in their relative's life. Periodic contact with providers can provide some preparation for this role.

Step 3 consists of a referral for individual counseling or psychotherapy, which appears to be an important resource for some siblings. For example, 77% of the adult siblings and offspring who responded to our survey reported they had received personal therapy. A similarly high level of sibling participation in therapy was found in a later study.[64] Comments of siblings suggest they have benefited considerably from this intervention. The following sibling sought therapy to resolve her marital problems. During therapy, she discovered these problems were related to her family history:

My sister's illness had deeply affected me, and I'd never consciously realized it. Once I began to learn about schizophrenia, my life came into better focus, and I felt more in control. This crisis in our life was a new beginning for us. We began to reconstruct our marriage.[65]

As in the case of this woman, therapy may offer an opportunity to explore what has been called "the principle of the past in the present."[66]

When working with siblings, practitioners should to be sensitive to their needs at a given time. For example, what role do they play—or anticipate playing—in their relative's life? What do they know about their relative's mental illness and treatment history? What are the roles of other family members, such as parents or other well siblings? What are their personal circumstances and supports? What specific concerns do they have?

Often, practitioners can assist siblings to develop what Herbert Gravitz has called "the healing edge" between what is loving and responsible toward their relative and what is loving and responsible toward themselves; to learn what Al-Anon has termed "detaching with love."[67] Siblings repeatedly echo this theme when giving advice to other family members: Don't let the illness take over your whole life!

From Theory to Practice

Beginning his session with Larry and Roberta Hogan, Carl Velden discusses his office policies and procedures as well as other professional issues. He explains the confidential nature of his relationship with their brother Charles, who has signed a release form allowing Carl to speak with these out-of-town siblings about their family's future.

> PRACTITIONER: *I'm glad we could get together while you're in town. I know your brother values your support.*
>
> BROTHER: *We appreciate your taking the time to meet with us. It's difficult to know how to proceed. Our parents are in declining health and need to move to a smaller apartment. But they don't want to abandon Charles. It was really their idea that we call you.*
>
> PRACTITIONER: *Actually, Charles is aware of their changing circumstances and has been doing some thinking on his own. After so many years, change is difficult. But he's been spending more time at the psychosocial program in town and has spoken with other consumers about various residential options.*
>
> SISTER: *You know, that's interesting. Our parents were afraid to discuss their plans with Charles. They were concerned he would get upset and end up back in the hospital.*

PRACTITIONER: *I understand their concern, even though Charles has done very well with his outpatient treatment. It's been several years since he was last hospitalized. He's learned to manage his illness and to avoid things that exacerbate his symptoms. And his new medication is helpful as well. On the other hand, a change in residence would be stressful.*

BROTHER: *We came here today hoping to get some ideas about how to bring up the subject with Charles. But it sounds as if you have already begun working with him.*

PRACTITIONER: *We're just beginning to look at alternatives. In fact, Charles told me he wanted to play a role in any decisions about his future. He is open to a joint session if it would be helpful. After so many years of living with your parents, he is uneasy about living more independently.*

SISTER: *My mother has always tried to do everything for Charles. I've often thought he might do better on his own. And at this point, she really can't continue to take care of him.*

BROTHER: *I do feel a joint session would be helpful. Roberta and I share our parents' anxiety about upsetting Charles. Those chaotic early years are etched in my memory. Although we stay in touch, I'm not sure what Charles can handle. I'd appreciate your assistance as we make plans.*

PRACTITIONER: *Sounds as if you're unsure about what's best. I can give you some information on the residential possibilities for Charles, who also has this information. Then we can have a joint session to begin planning. It will be best if Charles is involved in the family plans from the beginning and if he has plenty of time to adjust to the move. Your parents might also wish to attend.*

SISTER: *I'll check with them. It might be best if they were present, just to reassure them that plans are under way. I also have a related concern. Larry and I both work and have families of our own. Even if we didn't live so far away, we couldn't take over our parents' role. Yet we want to support Charles.*

PRACTITIONER: *I understand your concern. It's difficult to juggle responsibilities even when you live in the same community. In the case of your family, Charles already receives case management services, which can be expanded as he secures other living arrangements. In fact, Charles has met with his case manager several times to explore employment possibilities. As you know, it's been many years since Charles worked a regular job. However, he's already working as a volunteer at the psychosocial program, which he seems to enjoy. So, along with his employment prospects, Charles's case manager can work with him on residential arrangements.*

BROTHER: *Our parents said Charles mentioned the possibility of employment. They are worried it might jeopardize his disability payments. Is that likely to happen?*

PRACTITIONER: *Not at the psychosocial program, which is largely staffed by volunteers. But it might be a problem in another job. That's something we can monitor when we see how Charles does in the program. It's a difficult issue. The opportunity to work brings many satisfactions, but I understand the concern of your parents about his benefits, especially in light of their declining health. They want to be sure Charles's needs are met.*

SISTER: *We feel the same way. To be honest, neither of our families has much money to spare, although we want to make sure Charles is taken care of.*

PRACTITIONER: *I understand how you feel. We can talk about that when we meet again. Here are some materials on the benefits available for people with psychiatric disabilities. The benefit programs may seem a bit complicated, so I can answer your questions during out next appointment.*

BROTHER: *We're only in town for a week. How can we best use the time? We'd both like to have some plans in place before we leave. I'm sure it would reassure our parents as well.*

PRACTITIONER: *I am scheduled to meet with Charles tomorrow morning. I can bring up some of the issues we've discussed today, including alternative residential arrangements and long-term financial planning. I'll meet with you both tomorrow afternoon if you're free. That will give you a chance to review the materials I've given you. Then we can schedule a joint session to initiate some plans. We may want to consult with Charles's case manager. We can work out a long-distance consultation arrangement if you like. How does that sound?*

BROTHER: *Actually, it sounds like an awful lot to accomplish in very little time!*

SISTER: *Frankly, I'm relieved that we can make some initial plans. I don't want to leave with our parents worried about the future. I realize this will take some time, but at least we have a start. I'm surprised that Charles is capable of making these decisions. I hadn't realized how well he was doing.*

PRACTITIONER: *He is doing very well. It's difficult to have a clear picture of his recovery when you live so far away. With an illness like schizophrenia, progress is sometimes painfully slow. However, Charles seems ready to make some changes in his life and is very hopeful about his future. Working together, I think we can develop a satisfactory plan for your family.*

CHAPTER 14

Working with Offspring

Donna Sauer, a 22-year-old nurse, called to schedule an appointment with psychologist Lynne Matthews. In her telephone call, Donna told Dr. Matthews that she was newly engaged to be married and wanted to discuss her concerns about her mother, Anita, who has major depression. An only child, Donna has served as her mother's caregiver since her parents' divorce 5 years ago, continuing to reside at home after she obtained her B.S.N. degree at a local college and began working full time. Donna said it has been years since her mother has worked as a secretary, adding that she monitors her mother's treatment and drives her to appointments, which consist largely of monthly medication checks. After their wedding, she and her new husband, Hugh, plan to reside in the area. However, Hugh anticipates a transfer within a year, and Donna wonders how her mother will manage if they relocate. Anticipating her future, she worries about balancing her commitments to her mother and her new husband. How can Lynne be most helpful to this adult offspring of a parent with mental illness?

Lynne Matthews thinks back to a similar period in her own life, more than 2 decades ago. She remembers feeling overwhelmed as she completed her doctoral degree, began a new job, and planned her forthcoming wedding. Yet Donna is dealing with all of these issues along with her mother's caregiving. Preparing for her appointment with Donna, Lynne contacts the county mental health office to learn about the services and programs that might be available for patients with serious mental illness, such as Donna's mother.

When major change is anticipated in a family that includes a member with mental illness, Lynne has generally found it best to meet with all members of the family, including the patient. Once they have relevant information about community resources, the family can consider alternatives and develop an initial plan. Lynne believes this approach might be helpful with Donna, who seems consumed with feelings of guilt and responsibility, almost as if she were abandoning her mother.

Indeed, such feelings of guilt and responsibility are universally experienced by offspring of parents with mental illness, regardless of their unique circumstances. The chapter explores the offspring experience of mental illness and charts its major themes.

The Offspring Experience

As is the case for siblings, offspring can only be fully understood within the larger context of family dynamics. After all, aside from their special onus, offspring are small human beings who are struggling to find their way in the world and to master their developmental tasks with the assistance of their parents. Among their many important functions, parents:

- Reside at the center of our earliest relationship
- Are essential for our survival
- Strongly influence our feelings about ourselves
- Function as agents of socialization who ease our way into society
- Act as role models and objects of identification
- Serve as a link to our ancestral history

Parental mental illness has a major impact on this parent-child bond. The risks for children of parents with mental illness are considerable. For instance, offspring may become enveloped in their parent's symptoms, such as paranoid delusions; may experience neglect as their parent struggles for survival; may assume a parentified role as caregivers; may mold themselves into perfect children in an effort to spare their parent more suffering; and may experience multiple losses that endure for a lifetime. In the words of one woman, "I have been burned to my very core."[1]

However, not all parents with mental illness are ineffective parents, nor are all of their offspring impaired or unable to cope.[2] In fact, these parents and their children are both heterogeneous groups who need to be described in terms of their strengths as well as their difficulties. Moreover, throughout their lives, the relationships between parents with mental illness and their offspring are likely to encompass the full spectrum of emotions and experiences.

The following woman, who grew up with a father who had major depression, discusses the consequences for her own life:

I recall clearly the feelings of guilt, fear, anger, grief, and mistrust. I now under-stand how they affected my life. Why did my father's mental illness affect me so? Because mental illness becomes a family illness, regardless of who carries its symptoms. It reaches out and scars the life of each family member. No one walks away unaffected.

Another adult offspring, this time a man whose mother has bipolar disor-der, provides a different perspective:

I feel that being a concerned family member has helped me become a better person in many ways. I learned to become self-sufficient at an early age. I am gratified that I helped my mother. I am a person who enjoys being alive despite having had the trauma of an adolescence with a severely mentally ill parent.[3]

As is the case for all family relationships, over the course of a lifetime, offspring are likely to experience both poles of this intricate parent-child bond.

In contrast to siblings, young offspring have received substantial atten-tion from professionals.[4] A number of reviews chart the impact of parental mental illness on children.[5] As noted in Chapter 13, these reviews have consistently documented the potentially negative consequences for off-spring, including their increased risk of developing mental illness them-selves, as well as a range of cognitive, social, emotional, behavioral, academic, and developmental problems.[6] These reviews also highlight the wide array of individual, marital, familial, and extrafamilial variables that can mediate the impact of parental mental illness; the importance of pre-vention and early treatment when problems do arise; and the opportuni-ties for professionals to strengthen families and to address the needs of these high-risk children.[7]

Although the long-term consequences of parental mental illness have received relatively little consideration, professionals are beginning to ex-plore this territory. Eva Brown (10) has described many dimensions of the offspring experience, including the risk of parentification when a child becomes a caregiver, of survivor's guilt in connection with leaving home, of stigma and isolation, and of difficulties in adult relationships.[8]

As is the case for siblings, several eloquent personal accounts of the off-spring experience are now available. These include *My Mother's Keeper: A Daughter's Memoir of Growing Up in the Shadow of Schizophrenia* by Tara Elgin Holley and Joe Holley; *The Liars' Club* by Mary Karr; *Daughter of the Queen of Sheba* by Jacki Lyden; *He Was Still My Daddy* by Laurie Samsel Olson; *Sweet Mystery: A Book of Remembering* by Judith Paterson; and *Searching for Mercy Street: My Journey Back to My Mother, Anne Sexton* by Linda Gray Sexton.[9]

All of these memoirs convey the intense losses that accompany parental mental illness. As a child, Olson tried to explain the impact of her father's mental illness to a friend:

It's like my dad left and, in his place, a stranger appeared. He looks like my dad. He sounds like my dad. He even walks like my dad. But he's not my dad. He's somebody I don't know, somebody I don't even want to know.

Even today, years after her father's death, Olson recalls the sentiment that reverberated through her early years: "My daddy's gone and I want him to come back real bad."[10]

In her compelling portrayal of life with the Queen of Sheba (one of her mother's identities), Lyden has similarly conveyed the desperation with which a child may search for a parent who seems lost to the forces of mental illness:

I longed to know my mother's secret language when she went mad. I yearned to know its passwords and frames of reference. . . . I have become obsessed with finding her in a chiaroscuro world where, despite every art of intimacy that I have ever learned, I am in high seas. She is lost. And I cannot follow.[11]

Lyden also portrays the intense ambivalence so often experienced by offspring: "When my mother was sick, the connection between us could not be contained in a simple word like love or hate."

An increasing number of publications deal specifically with offspring, including my books with Rex Dickens, *Anguished Voices* and *Troubled Journey.*[12] As this expanding body of literature demonstrates, parental mental illness has a profound impact on their children:

As a child, I tried desperately never to have a problem because our family had so many. So I became perfectionistic and hid my fears, concerns, and needs from everyone. On the outside, I always appeared strong and self-assured, able to handle anything. But I developed a lot of shame.[13]

Offspring Themes

Experienced with a fierce intensity by offspring, many of the following themes mark the experiences of parents and spouses, such as feelings of grief and loss, and with siblings, such as a sense of neglect or even abandonment. In particular, as young family members, offspring share the vulnerability of siblings that was discussed earlier. Other themes are uniquely associated with the offspring role, such as the high risk of parentification.

Grief and Loss

It is impossible to overstate the potential losses of offspring. These family members may mourn for their own loss of parents who struggle with the symptoms of mental illness; for their concomitant losses of love, comfort, guidance, companionship, validation, and protection; and for the losses experienced by their beloved parent.[14] One man reflected on the vitality that radiates from his mother's wedding picture, which is hung on a wall in his family home: "Before the illness struck she was a very beautiful adult woman. Presently, I am left with a feeling of sadness. The illness has robbed her of so much potential."[15]

In addition, offspring may mourn for their well parent, who may be overwhelmed by the illness of a partner and unable to meet their needs: "My dad also abandoned us, in the emotional sense, becoming so confused and devastated that he was oblivious to our feelings and unable to help us deal with them."[16] At the same time, spouses often manage to shoulder an extraordinary burden exceptionally well. A son wrote of his father, "I have learned many things from him, but most importantly he has loved my mother and has stuck with her all these years. He has taught me a great deal about commitment in personal relationships."[17]

Offspring may also mourn for a family that can no longer meet their essential needs or perhaps even survive as a unit. Accounts of children who are placed in foster care capture the intense losses associated with the rupture of parental and familial bonds.[18] Ultimately, offspring may mourn for the very loss of their childhood. In the words of one woman, "I can honestly say I have no idea what it is like to be a child."[19]

During their adulthood, the early losses of offspring may continue to have an amorphous jurisdiction over their lives:

I lost self-confidence. I lost a sense of knowing who I am, of what I wanted. I lost the ability to set my own agenda, to control my own life. I lost sight of my own needs. I lost the ability to care for myself properly. I feel out of sync with the normal developmental rhythms. I have been saddened in a chronic way.[20]

At any age, offspring may be faced with the loss of their parent as a result of suicide or other cause of death; of homelessness, incarceration, or prolonged hospitalization; or of dissolution of an oppressive bond. One woman described in searing detail the path that led her to terminate her relationship with a mother who had a "singular ability to tear me apart": "I said no to the pain, no to dealing for the second half of my life with your hatred, no to paying for your insanity with my sanity. I said no to mothering you."[21]

PARENTIFICATION

Perhaps the most salient theme of the offspring experience is that of parentification. Repeatedly, professionals and offspring alike note the frequency with which these family members assume a parental role as they are growing up, perhaps drawn into the role of "magic helper."[22] One adult offspring remarked with an air of inevitability, "I had to be the little mother, since I was the oldest girl."[23] Along with their parentified role, offspring often have a sense of having grown up too fast in response to circumstances over which they have little control: "I realize that I had to grow up fast as a child. I recognize that my mother's illness deprived me of having any sort of a carefree, normal childhood."[24]

SURVIVOR'S GUILT

As is the case for siblings, the survivor's guilt of offspring derives from their awareness of having been spared mental illness themselves. Yet the guilt of offspring rings with a special resonance, transfused as it is by the parent-child bond. One son remarked on his unending sadness at the thought that "a child would rack his brain over trying to find a way to get 'mommy' to feel happy again. The child, blaming himself, for lack of any other reason."[25] Similarly, a daughter captured the pervasive sense of guilt and responsibility that often afflicts offspring: "I could not understand why she wanted to die. I felt that if only I showed her enough love, did everything she wanted me to do, she would change and want to live." After all, wrote this adult offspring, "She was the mother who had given me life. Somehow, I thought to myself, I had to bring her happiness."[26]

CAREGIVING

Caregiving is a central theme for all family members. Yet parents and spouses assume caregiving roles only as adults, however onerous those roles may become. Siblings often worry about potential caregiving responsibilities in the wake of their parents' decline or death. However, offspring may assume caregiving roles from their earliest years; and they may remain in those roles for a lifetime. In our research with adult offspring, we heard of caregiving responsibilities at every phase of development.

After the death of her father, at the age of 8 one child became the sole caregiver for a mother with schizophrenia. By the time she was 12, this young offspring had hospitalized her mother for the first time. Dealing with her mother's recurrent breakdowns, for the next 6 years she battled the hospitals, the courts, and the landlords. Her mother died in a state hospital at the end of this turbulent period. "My whole childhood was spent taking care of others," she has written, "I was so competent and responsible"—and wholly unaware as a child that she had needs of her own. Only as an adult has she realized the price that was paid:

I have no idea what my life would have been like if my mother had been sane. I would not have the fear of going crazy. I would not feel responsible for the world. I would have a better developed sense of self.[27]

Another offspring (also a female) assumed a caregiving role as she embarked on her adult life:

When I was 18, I became my mother's caretaker. My mother lived with me until she died. I married, had children, and took care of Mother throughout my whole life. That placed our family under severe emotional stress. Every ordinarily stressful life experience precipitated a crisis in which Mother's hallucinations or delusions were exacerbated.[28]

Over the course of their lives, offspring may need to deal with the legal system as well as the mental health system. One woman was forced to seek permanent legal guardianship to protect her mother and to make decisions about her treatment. Remarking that she hopes a time will come when she is not so involved in her mother's care, this adult offspring wrote, "It is an awesome challenge to be faced with this role at my age and stage of life."[29]

Academic and Vocational Issues

Parental mental illness is also likely to have an impact on the academic and vocational lives of their children:

Very much of my young life was affected. I had trouble concentrating in school, was afraid Dad would appear at the school grounds when he was sick. I could not bring any school friends home for fear that they would not understand. Mom was busy working full time to make ends meet. Not much time was spent helping me get prepared for school.[30]

At the same time, the academic world can offer respite from a chaotic home environment, along with an opportunity to enhance self-esteem and to identify with constructive role models:

Education has always been an anchor for me. College enabled me to have a new identity, where I could not be constantly reminded of my depressing family situation. School was the one thing my parents couldn't mess up with their excesses and unpredictable behavior. Something positive when the rest of my life was in shambles.[31]

Choosing a tentative career path in adolescence, offspring continue to be influenced by their encounter with parental mental illness. As is the case for siblings, offspring may choose a career that replicates their earlier caregiving role:

I think my childhood experience led me into the mental health field because of my compassion for the people and their families and because I am comfortable with a certain amount of "craziness." It has made me very empathic and understanding.[32]

It is noteworthy that several of the vignettes in this chapter were taken from the accounts of adult offspring who have become mental health professionals.

Whatever their vocational path, adult offspring may have difficulty investing energy in their career, which may seem insignificant compared to their family drama. They may also have a sense of unfulfilled career potential, thus compounding their feelings of loss. Struggling to begin a career, one man felt that "most of the 'real' news in my life centered around the mental illness of my family members."[33] Another commented, "I had completely lost the thread of my own life."[34]

IDENTITY AND ROLE ISSUES

If they were exposed to parental mental illness during their early years, offspring are likely to weave the illness into their very sense of self. For example, they may identify with their parent or become enveloped in the psychotic system: "My mother has been sick practically my whole life. It is hard for me to decipher which of my experiences are 'normal' and which are not."[35] In the wake of parental mental illness, offspring may also have difficulty establishing a secure sense of self. One woman disclosed, "Most of my adult life has been spent 'constructing me.' My self-concept makes me work the hardest."[36]

The social role transformations imposed on the family inevitably affect offspring, who may internalize the stigma that encircles mental illness. Aware that others view them as growing up with a "crazy" parent and in a "dysfunctional" family, offspring may have little sense of normal family life. As one family member observed, "Community members, relatives, and friends retreat from a situation they do not understand."[37]

Many professionals have commented on the distorted roles that can follow in the wake of parental mental illness.[38] In addition to a parentified role, offspring may assume other roles that undermine healthy development. As a result of her mother's mental illness, for instance, one woman observed that she developed "a unique relationship" with her father, becoming "his confidant and fellow decision maker in the family." Growing up, she felt "this relationship was comforting, and I clung to it emotionally. Little did I realize how unhealthy it was, until as an adult I have had great difficulty in my relationships with men as a result."[39]

LIFE SPAN ISSUES

The entire developmental course of offspring is at risk for disruption by parental mental illness:

Since birth, I had been an emotional orphan, but I didn't know it. At some level, my parents could not relate to me, to each other, or to themselves. Like weeds along a roadside, my siblings and I grew up in random fashion, to a large degree untended and unminded. Navigating a path into adulthood would be difficult.[40]

Moreover, because early developmental accomplishments provide the foundation for later development, offspring may carry a legacy of interrupted, postponed, or cancelled tasks that increases with each subsequent phase.

During early childhood, for example, their sense of basic trust and security may be shaken by a parent whose own energy is consumed by mental illness, whose reality contact is sometimes impaired, or whose false beliefs and distorted perceptions are presented as real. One woman wrote of her own confusion in response to her mother's psychotic symptoms, "The crazy, paranoid attitudes and beliefs get incorporated so easily."[41] Young offspring may also have problems acquiring essential knowledge about their world and developing a healthy self-concept. In our research, a majority of adult siblings and offspring reported that they had been neglected when they were children. Speaking for many others, one woman declared, "My needs were not met when I was growing up."[42]

During middle childhood, offspring may have difficulty shifting from their home to the larger social arena and experience problems with academic adjustment and peer relationships. One adult offspring remembers sitting in class unable to concentrate, "all of my energy directed toward what was happening at home and what was going to become of our family."[43] As adolescents, offspring may struggle to forge a sense of personal identity, deal with their emerging sexuality, choose a tentative career path, and separate from a parent who has come to depend on them. When separation does occur, it may be accompanied by considerable guilt: "I had a hard time moving away. I felt guilty all the time. It was difficult to keep my mind on my studies in college."[44]

As young adults, offspring may have difficulty negotiating the shoals of intimacy, marriage, parenthood, and career. During middle and late adulthood, they may have little energy left for closing the gap between earlier dreams and current accomplishments or for dealing with personal mortality and life review. At each phase of development, the tasks of offspring may be deflected by their caregiving responsibilities, which may make clamorous demands on their time, energy, and spirit.

Personal Issues

Our research highlighted many of the personal concerns of offspring, as does this vignette:

I believe it has hardened me. I can't seem to love myself. I take care of others, but when I try to take care of me, I fail. I have become an angry person. A person who is afraid not to be liked by others. A person who fears close relationships but longs for them daily. A person who is afraid of change but who longs for adventure.[45]

Important personal issues for offspring include their feelings of helplessness and hopelessness, low self-esteem, psychic numbing, needs for perfectionism and control, and concern about their own mental health.

Given their early encounter with parental mental illness, it is not surprising that offspring often experience intense feelings of helplessness and hopelessness. As one man expressed it, "It was as if we were all passengers on a dangerous renegade train."[46] Becoming "enveloped in the depression when it settles on the household" and empathizing with their parent's suffering, offspring may find their own capacity for pleasure diminished.[47] One man remarked on his "propensity to take life too seriously and to live life with too much intensity. I have to work at having fun in my life."[48]

Offspring also report problems with low self-esteem. Consistent with the concept of the "looking-glass self," self-esteem is tied to the early appraisals of important people in our lives. Parents who are struggling with mental illness may have difficulty providing regular affirmation for their children, who in turn may have difficulty developing healthy self-regard, believing in their own capabilities, and expecting that they will succeed. Even when offspring have an impressive record of accomplishment, their sense of inadequacy may leave them feeling as if the facade might collapse at any moment. One adult offspring has written of herself as a child:

Ann knew she was a fraud. All show and no substance. Like one of those hollow wire mannequins in store windows, but with wire made of sawdust that might vaporize at any moment leaving fancy clothing and shiny accessories in a heap on the floor.[49]

Offspring commonly describe a pattern of psychic numbing, which is the legacy of childhood efforts to protect themselves from overwhelming feelings. In the words of one woman, "I lost the ability to feel for so many years. It was the only way I could protect myself and survive." Another wrote, "I shut down emotionally sometime in my youth, and this carried over into my adulthood."[50]

As children, offspring may have felt responsible for their parent's symptoms or relapses, which can induce a magical sense of power. Likewise, their early feelings of helplessness may engender strong needs for perfectionism and control. One woman described this pattern: "The burden of thinking anything I do or any mistake I make might result in the 'craziness' has made me feel insecure unless I can control the situation." She remarked that her early experience has "made me feel overly responsible for others, that I have an exaggerated power to cause others' behavior."

Finally, offspring worry about developing mental illness themselves. Even after they have passed the period of greatest risk, they may continue to experience considerable anxiety about their mental health. For some of these offspring, this fear becomes a reality:

My mother was hospitalized a total of 33 times in her life. I've probably always had a degree of depression as a result of her mental illness. When my father died, I suffered a major depression and went into therapy myself. On the positive side, I became a psychologist as a result of her illness, and I bring empathy and understanding to my work.[51]

INTERPERSONAL ISSUES

As is the case for siblings, offspring frequently develop qualities that endear them to others. Their tolerance, empathy, and compassion are likely to make them valued and sympathetic friends. These qualities also enhance their contributions as professional caregivers, along with their unusual sensitivity to the moods of others: "After a lifetime of tuning in to how things were with my mother, I have radar that can tune in to others' moods, to read between the lines."[52]

At the same time, offspring often report significant problems in their relationships, both as children and as adults. Early relationships within the family serve as a prototype for later relationships. When parental mental illness is present, children may have unsatisfactory models for later peer relationships. Along with their limited interpersonal skills, young offspring may feel tainted by the noxious effects of stigma and uncomfortable with friends who have little understanding of mental illness.

As adults, offspring commonly report interpersonal problems, including problems with trust and intimacy, inappropriate continuation of a caregiving role, and reluctance to make a long-term commitment:

I have spent the last 25 years trying to find confidence, love, and acceptance. I am extremely sensitive and weep easily. I avoid intimacy but crave it desperately. I want more friends but fear to trust.[53]

When they do develop close relationships, their low self-esteem may increase the likelihood of unsuitable partners. As one woman wrote, "I'm afraid people will reject me. I've been looking for love in inappropriate people and ways."[54]

Inability to trust and fear of abandonment may lead to avoidance of intimacy altogether. Although offering protection from hurtful or unhealthy relationships, this strategy exacts the intolerable price of enduring loneliness. As one woman wrote, "I never put myself in a position of needing anyone, because people I needed were never available. I had trouble trusting others and so became self-sufficient."[55]

FAMILY ISSUES

In addition to caregiving, offspring may experience family problems that center on their marriage, their children, and their multiple commitments. For instance, they may attempt to escape from their difficult family situation by entering into marriage before they have resolved their personal issues or have the maturity to choose an appropriate partner. One woman related, "I spent a lifetime in fantasy, waiting for my knight in shining armor to save me from all of this. And I clung to the very first person who came into my life—I married my first boyfriend."[56] Not surprisingly, the marriage did not survive.

Another woman recounted similar problems in establishing a constructive relationship:

For many years I thought that no one would really want me because I came from a "defective" family. So I married someone who didn't appreciate me, and then embarked on a series of shallow relationships based on sex. I still have a tendency to hold back in relationships for fear that I will be abandoned. Somehow I still feel like that little girl who had to take care of everything herself.[57]

When they do marry, adult offspring may find they are duplicating unhealthy patterns from the past. Noting his tendencies toward caregiving, one man stated, "I have married someone who needs to be taken care of." He added, "As a career, guess what—I'm a social worker."[58]

Compensating for their profound feelings of childhood loss, offspring may have a fervent need to create a new and more perfect family in the present. Although this need is likely to foster a strong commitment to marriage and parenthood, they may strive for a degree of togetherness that alienates a partner with a reasonable need for independence and that undermines the autonomy of their children. Ultimately realizing that she was "suffocating" her son and driving him away, one woman observed, "I was going to love him like my mother never loved me."[59]

In addition to marital problems, adult offspring may bring a wellspring of anxiety to their own parenting. Indeed, they may choose to avoid having children altogether. As an adult offspring wrote, "I was afraid to have children because I had a fear that they might be like my dad."[60] If they do choose to have children, they may worry about the risk of mental illness in the next generation.

As parents themselves, adult offspring may face additional hurdles. Our own parents serve as essential models and objects of identification, as we internalize their values and attitudes, their approach to discipline, their coping strategies, and their modes of communication. If our role models are inadequate, as is sometimes the case when a parent has mental illness, there may be few templates for adequate parenting. Following difficulties with her oldest son, a woman commented that she had to learn to become an effective parent, something she had not learned growing up: "My only role model was a schizophrenic mother."[61]

Even when they feel comfortable in their marital and parental roles, adult offspring almost universally struggle to balance their own needs with those of their families and to reach an equitable arrangement that honors all of their commitments. There is no easy resolution of a conflict that sometimes places personal and family commitments in painful opposition, which is likely to generate strong feelings of ambivalence:

At times I imagine what it would be like to sever ties with my family of origin. I will admit that the thought of being able to have a different life and not be involved in my mother's illness is inviting, but I have never taken action to distance myself.[62]

SOCIAL ISSUES

Both as children and as adults, offspring are likely to feel socially isolated and alienated, to respond with distress to the pervasive evidence of stigma and discrimination, and to have difficulty reconciling the disparate worlds inside and outside their family:

I worked very hard at being normal away from home, because I knew that what awaited me when I got home was more bizarre than anyone would believe. I felt best when I was normally active—working on the yearbook, biking with my friends, going on school trips, having fun with my friends, doing well in school. Being considered normal was my greatest salvation. Inside I felt like a total freak.[63]

In spite of her inner turmoil, this offspring managed to function effectively in the external world. Others are not so fortunate. One woman said that she and her brother had both been deeply affected by their mother's mental illness. Eventually she learned to feel more comfortable and secure around other people; however, her brother remains "completely withdrawn, a middle-aged man with no friends or relationships."[64]

PROFESSIONAL ISSUES

As with siblings, adult offspring perceive professionals differently in their roles as family members and as clients who receive services for themselves, such as psychotherapy. As family members, adult offspring frequently express frustration regarding their encounters with professionals and with the system as a whole. One man asserted that he and other offspring often feel twice abandoned, "first by your ill parent who *could not* meet your needs and next by a mental health system that *would not,* shoving you aside in its myopic obsession with your parent and its neglect of your family."[65]

Another adult offspring reflects on her family's experiences with the system:

The necessary information and resources have just not been available. It is no wonder offspring of parents with mental illness limp into adulthood searching for ways to heal from the trauma they have endured. . . . The mental health field provided me with no resources for coping. The professionals focused on my father's treatment as if he were an island, while my mother, my brothers, and myself suffered from invisibility.[66]

Often, adult offspring who are serving as caregivers feel they have been disenfranchised by the system: "The biggest problem I have had is getting people to listen to me, to take seriously what I had to say about my mother. To understand that I know her better than anyone."[67] Another proclaimed, "I hate social services for not helping me."[68] Still another lamented, "I endured a lot of unnecessary emotional pain. The impact still lingers on."[69] When they do receive services in connection with their parent's treatment, offspring often find these services unsatisfactory:

"We had one family therapy session behind a one-way mirror with people gawking at us. I just hated it."[70]

In contrast to their negative perceptions as family members, adult off-spring often have a positive appraisal of professionals when they are clients themselves. Indeed, they often find personal therapy very helpful:

It wasn't until I sought therapy for anxiety upon my divorce that I began to understand some of the dynamics of my family and myself. . . . Therapy opened doors to my self and answered many puzzling questions.[71]

Needs of Offspring

At each developmental phase, offspring have three kinds of needs: for their parent with mental illness, for their family unit, and for themselves.

PATIENT NEEDS

Offspring need treatment and rehabilitation services that promote the recovery of their parent with mental illness. As a parent recovers, an entire family benefits. Services that enhance effective parenting are also essential, such as support groups for parents with mental illness, supported housing for families, and parental role models and mentors. One adult offspring shares his loving recollections of a father with mental illness:

My father taught us to love each other—he was the best hugger I ever met. He loved my mom and all of us. He loved nature and taught us about trees, gardening, and caring for pets. He spent time with us going for walks, singing, playing cards, reading stories. He taught us songs. He was a happy, caring person who uplifted those who came in contact with him.[72]

Unfortunately, many families do not share this positive outcome. Several years ago, I facilitated a presentation by a panel of three people who described their experiences with mental illness, shared their coping strategies, and offered suggestions for family members and professionals. I have not forgotten the tearful account of a woman who described the earlier loss of her children. Now employed and doing very well, this mother had experienced recurrent hospitalizations during the early years of her illness. As a result, she had lost custody of her children to her husband, who had divorced her and remarried; her two daughters had grown up largely without her. That, she proclaimed, was the irreplaceable loss, one shared by her now-grown children.

Although many people with mental illness have children, few programs are targeted specifically to the needs of these parents. One survey found that only 16 state mental health authorities routinely asked if their adult patients had children.[73] As a result, these parents often struggle alone to fulfill their obligations to their children, who may suffer considerably. Satisfactory services for parents with mental illness could make a significant difference for all parties; yet such services are rarely available.

FAMILY NEEDS

Offspring also need an array of services that can strengthen their family. These might include a home-based program with services for offspring, respite care during periods of crisis, and an educational support group for their well parent. Many variables can influence the outcome for these families. These include the strengths of the parent with mental illness, of the well parent, and of the children; availability of other family resources, such as extended family members; availability of community resources, such as a family advocacy group or local church; and availability of professional services for all members of the family.

In particular, a strong and effective extended family can serve as a life-enhancing buffer for offspring. Vivian Spiese, the parent of a son with schizoaffective disorder, has described her role as a grandparent who provided essential support for her granddaughter during challenging times.[74] She offers suggestions for other extended family members: Protect children during the chaotic times; make sure their needs are met; educate them about the mental illness in understandable terms; provide stability; and assist them in seeing the affected parent as a *person* with the illness.

After many difficult years, both father and daughter are doing well. Supported by her extended family, at age 12 this young offspring declared that "those awful years are gone." Describing her many activities with her father, she adds simply, "I love him." She observes that "going through what I did made me grow up faster"; in her view, her early experiences "made me a wiser person, in the real world, than other kids."

PERSONAL NEEDS

Offspring need services for themselves that address their needs for information about their parent's mental illness, age-appropriate coping skills, and personal support. Affirming the importance of education, an adult offspring proclaimed, "Knowledge has kept me from the depths of hopelessness."[75] Even young children can understand that their parent has a real illness, that the illness has certain symptoms, and that it can be treated effectively. Children need reassurance that they have not caused the illness, that they are not responsible for their parent, and that they are not alone.

In addition, offspring need practical suggestions for dealing with the illness. Based on her research with adult siblings and offspring, Karen Kinsella, an adult offspring and family therapist, cites the following positive coping skills: employing constructive redirection through art, music, sports, or other activities; obtaining support from family members, peers, or others outside the family; objectifying the illness (separating the effects of the illness from the relative and from the self); acquiring information about mental illness; and maintaining spiritual faith.[76]

Kinsella also explored the negative coping skills of siblings and offspring, including their use of unhealthy escapes, such as denial of emotions, drug use, or dissociation; self-censoring through rigid self-control, hypervigilance, or the adoption of new roles and traits; and self-isolation. Demonstrating the potential for resilience, each of her participants reported they had developed some positive qualities or strengths, such as independence, creativity, and empathy.

Along with their needs for information, skills, and support, offspring often need assistance in finding a comfortable level of involvement in their parent's life. However they honor their commitment to their parent with mental illness, offspring need to be free to have lives of their own. One life should never be sacrificed to another; ultimately, such an arrangement is a recipe for disaster.

Consider the woman mentioned earlier in the chapter who said "no" to any further involvement in her mother's life. She felt she had sacrificed years of her life, a price she was no longer to pay. "I have forced a long and brutal chapter of my life as the child of a person with schizophrenia to end":

I have dealt with this illness and its effects throughout my life. I have done my best to secure the treatment she needs; I have tried desperately to help her. Unsupported by the medical community or the legal system, there is nothing more I can do.[77]

For this offspring, a satisfactory family support system might have avoided the sacrifice of her childhood; and it might have preserved her relationship with her mother in the present. For both of them, these are inestimable losses.

Intervention Strategies for Offspring

As children and adolescents, offspring as well as siblings can benefit from the services described in the previous chapter. Potential interventions include a variety of home-based, agency-based, school-based, and community-based services for offspring themselves. In addition, offspring can profit from services designed to promote the recovery of their parent with mental illness, to enhance parenting skills and parent-child relationships, to support their well parent, and to address other individual and family needs. There are some excellent programs for young offspring, such as BART's Place in Cleveland (see Chapter 15).

As adults, offspring can benefit from the family interventions discussed in Chapters 7 through 10, as long as services are responsive to their personal needs and concerns. With modifications, then, the three-step model can be applied to professional practice with offspring. During Step 1, consultation can be used to assist offspring in identifying and prioritizing their needs, in dealing with illness-related concerns, and in making an informed choice about their use of other available services. For offspring who are serving as primary caregivers or informal case managers for their parents, as-needed consultation can provide an essential resource over the long term.

In Step 2, practitioners can assist adult offspring to develop and implement an individualized family service plan. If they are serving in a caregiving role, that plan should include meaningful involvement in their parent's treatment and rehabilitation. Adult offspring may also benefit from participation in a family support and advocacy organization; in fact, some NAMI affiliates offer a specialized support group for adult siblings and offspring. In our book *Troubled Journey*, Rex Dickens offers suggestions for developing such a group.[78] Offspring may also profit from educational or psychoeducational programs, although such programs typically focus on parents.

Step 3 consists of a referral for personal counseling or psychotherapy. As is the case for siblings, personal therapy appears to be a valuable resource for some adult offspring. In our research, 77% of adult siblings and offspring reported they had participated in personal therapy; among those who were under age 10 at the onset of their relative's mental illness (primarily offspring), the level was 90%. A similarly high level of offspring participation in therapy was found in a later study.[79] Thus, in contrast to parents and spouses, offspring may be good candidates for therapy even when they appear to be functioning well. In fact, their outward resilience may mask an inner world of confusion and anguish. When their early trauma remains unresolved, its aftereffects may permeate all the crawl spaces of their adult lives.

Writing of the impact of parental mental illness on offspring, David Ogren observes that childhood trauma affects their view of the world.[80] Indeed, for these children, trauma can completely undermine any sense of the world as a safe and nurturing place and of themselves as architects of their lives. Ogren asserts that, with proper training, mental health professionals can assist offspring to cope with the effects of trauma, to heal, and to find meaning and purpose in life. Beyond listening hard, he encourages practitioners to arm themselves with a variety of therapeutic methods that can help traumatized children express the feelings and thoughts that haunt and shame them. Play, art, sand box, and other expressive therapies can prevent the current trauma from becoming a permanent part of the personality structure of the child.

When working with adults who suffered childhood trauma, practitioners first need to develop a safe therapeutic relationship. Deeply and firmly grounded in the safety of such a relationship, these adults can then allow themselves to revisit the past, touch and heal their deepest pain, and put the trauma into perspective. When trauma is resolved, clients can move from being haunted by the past to fully living in the present.

Recovery from trauma is often painfully slow. Commenting on her current therapy, one adult offspring wrote:

I suppose part of what is hurting me still is that I expected all this pain to be behind me by now. But here I am, 30 years old, fighting depression (still fighting) and being pierced by sadness. . . . What a mess I still am! I often don't know why I am crying. . . . Getting a handle on what my underlying psychological patterns are is difficult. They are elusive. How I wish some of them could have been prevented.[81]

As F. Robert Rodman has affirmed, therapists foster life over death "in the sense of lived over unlived life; the capacity to function, to realize potential, to flourish, over being thwarted, withdrawn, limited."[82] With offspring, as with all clients, the "ultimate criterion of termination" is not whether all problems have been solved but whether the client has resumed development, with a reasonable prospect for change in the future.

Virtually every professional article concerned with offspring recommends intensive and continuing intervention for these vulnerable family members. Yet this professional mandate is too rarely translated into clinical practice.[83] In one study, 30% to 50% of offspring who had parents with major affective disorders had developed a major depressive disorder by age 17; almost none of these offspring had either sought or received treatment.[84]

Practitioners need to address the concerns of such children, to offer services to them, and to acknowledge their often remarkable coping capacities.[85] In the words of one woman who grew up around mental illness, "There are many children out there who are suffering the way that my sisters and brother and I suffered. There has to be a way to reach them."[86]

From Theory to Practice

Psychologist Lynne Matthews introduces herself to Donna Sauer, who has requested an appointment to discuss the impact of her forthcoming marriage on her mother, Anita, who has major depression.

OFFSPRING: *I'm glad you could see me. I've thought about seeking some help for myself for many years. But somehow my problems didn't seem important in light of my mother's mental illness. It was really my fiancé, Hugh, who urged me to get some assistance.*

PRACTITIONER: *It's good that you were able to reach out. In your phone call, you said you had been taking care of your mother for the last few years. It's easy to get so caught up in a caregiving role that your own needs don't seem to matter. In my work with adolescent and adult offspring, I've found that to be a common theme.*

OFFSPRING: *That's reassuring, I suppose. My friends all joke about my caregiving tendencies. I always seem to be looking out for everybody else. But it's hard to let people know when I need support.*

PRACTITIONER: *That so often seems to be the case for offspring who have a parent with mental illness. It's an enormous burden, especially if you're serving in a caregiving role, as you have been. But you need support, too, and you also need to be free to live your own life.*

OFFSPRING: *Well, that's really why I'm here. I 'm getting married next summer and may even be moving from the area. I'm sure that will be difficult for my mother. She really has no one else. After the divorce, my father remarried and moved to another state. He always paid child support, but we haven't seen much of him.*

PRACTITIONER: *What about other members of your family?*

OFFSPRING: *There are my mother's brother and sister. Both have families of their own, but they stay in touch and live only a few miles away. And there's my grandmother, who has been an important part of my life, especially during my mother's hospitalizations. But it's as if no one can talk about my mother's mental illness—almost as if it's the family secret.*

PRACTITIONER: *That has to be difficult for you. Certainly, social stigma is a problem. People with mental illness are so often ridiculed and devalued. It's no wonder that many families feel ashamed. But when family members can't talk about the illness, it is so much more difficult to cope.*

OFFSPRING: *Since I've become engaged, we may actually be making some progress. My relatives have been encouraging me to move on with my life. They're proud of my nursing career and really like Hugh. In fact, my uncle said we needed to plan so that my mother's needs would be met after my marriage. But so far nothing has happened.*

PRACTITIONER: *Perhaps you and I can offer to meet with the rest of your family members.*

OFFSPRING: *That might be helpful. I know they all feel the professionals who have treated my mother have pretty much ignored them. They would like to know more about her illness and what to expect. The other day my grandmother said she wondered if my mother couldn't work, at least part time. After all, it's been several years since she was last hospitalized. Sometimes I feel resentful that I have to work so hard, first at school and now at the hospital, and still take care of my mother. Then, of course, I feel guilty. After all, she didn't ask to have mental illness.*

PRACTITIONER: *It's normal to feel some resentment. This is a lot to handle at your age—to say nothing of your earlier years. And the guilt is normal, too. You are probably well aware of all your mother has lost to this illness.*

OFFSPRING: *It's been such a terrible thing. I have seen pictures of my mother when she was young. She looked so vibrant, so hopeful about the future. After the divorce, she just seemed to give up on any kind of life at all. I feel so helpless.*

PRACTITIONER: *You know, Lynne, in many ways you are helpless—as we all are with respect to other people. The only life you can live is your own. Your mother is really the only one who can make changes in her life. And, aside from you, it doesn't sound like she's had much support.*

OFFSPRING: *No, I don't think she has. I know there are social and vocational programs for people with mental illness, but she's never participated. Just her regular med checks.*

PRACTITIONER: *How does your mother feel about this?*

OFFSPRING: *I'm not really sure. When I told her about my engagement to Hugh, she said maybe it was time for her to make some changes in her life. But it's scary for her, I think. And for me too. I worry about her getting worse and needing to be hospitalized again.*

PRACTITIONER: *Your worry is understandable. It's always risky to make changes, but especially if you're struggling with mental illness. Do you think she would be open to meeting with us?*

OFFSPRING: *Actually, I think she might be eager to come in. She knows about my appointment with you. And she really wants me to get married and have a full life. It just feels like such a vacuum at this point. Neither of us knows how to proceed.*

PRACTITIONER: *Anticipating our appointment, I contacted the county mental health office to find out what services might be available. In fact, there* are a wide range of services that might benefit your mother—and reassure you that her needs will be met. Why don't you see if your mother can join us for an appointment next week. Then, with her permission, I can contact her therapist. If your mother is interested, we can work with her therapist to develop a plan for your family. At some point, it might be helpful to meet with your aunt and uncle and your grandmother. It sounds as if they'd like to be helpful if they only knew how.

OFFSPRING: *I'm sure that's true. We've all felt so helpless.*

PRACTITIONER: I'm not surprised. So many family members share those feelings. Once we've met with your mother, we can decide how to proceed. We should be able to get some plans in place by the time of your wedding.

OFFSPRING: *I hope so. I know Hugh has been concerned about me. He's very understanding, and he and my mother get along well. But I think he worries that I'll be torn between my commitments to him and to my mother.*

PRACTITIONER: It sounds as if he's very supportive. And his feelings are understandable. Most husbands would feel that way.

OFFSPRING: *Sometimes I feel that caring for my mother has made it difficult in certain ways for me to relate to Hugh. He tells me I'm always trying to take care of him. He seems a little resentful, saying he wants to take care of me.*

PRACTITIONER: You've been a caregiver for so long, and you do it very well. That makes it natural to respond to others in the same way. Your compassion for others makes you a good friend—and a caring nurse. But most people are not as needy as your mother. It sounds as if Hugh is a pretty secure person who can meet his own needs.

OFFSPRING: *Yes, that's very true. His father died when he was young. He's always had some kind of job, all through high school and college. I'm just not always sure how to respond to him when he tries to take care of me. Often, I'm not even aware that I have needs of my own.*

PRACTITIONER: It's so easy to lose sight of your own needs when you're caring for a parent with mental illness. But acknowledging the problem is the first step in changing, although change is always difficult, even when you understand the source of the problem.

OFFSPRING: *You know, I wonder how much my mother's mental illness has affected me. I've never talked to a single person who grew up with a parent who had mental illness. It's hard to know what's normal.*

PRACTITIONER: I'm sure it is. It can be difficult to feel so isolated. Let me make a couple of suggestions. First, here is some reading material, including some personal accounts of other offspring. You'll see how *normal some of your feelings are. And you might find it helpful to talk with a member of a local support group for adult siblings and offspring.*

OFFSPRING: *That would be wonderful. I didn't know there was such a group. And the reading should be helpful, too.*

PRACTITIONER: *Our time's just about up. So let's plan on meeting next week. Please invite your mother to join us. Following our joint session, you and I can meet alone again. Then, if you are interested, we can begin dealing with any other concerns you might have.*

OFFSPRING: *I'll give you a call after I speak with my mother. And I think I'll follow up on that support group. I'm feeling better already.*

CHAPTER 15

Model Programs for Families

A n array of family-focused programs have been described in earlier chapters, including family support and advocacy groups, family consultation, family education, family psychoeducation, and psychotherapy. Many of the professionals who offer these services also provide consultation and training; others have developed useful materials for practitioners, including manuals and videotapes.[1]

Several additional programs are described in this chapter. Four of these are generic programs that offer a mix of family education, skills, and support. Three programs are specifically designed to address the needs of spouses, siblings, or offspring. The programs include:

- The Three R's Program, which is a comprehensive treatment program based on a wellness approach to the management of serious mental illness

- Supportive Family Training, which consists of a 12-week curriculum that focuses on family support, education, and advocacy

- The MESA model of family education, which offers a continuum of family-focused services

- The Training and Education Center (T.E.C.) Network, which offers a wide range of services for families

- The T.E.C. Network Spouse Coping Skills Workshops, which are planned specifically for spouses

- Project S.O.S. (Stamp Out Stigma of Mental Illness), which was developed to provide education about mental illness to students in elementary, middle, and high school

- BART's (Bring All Relatives Together) Place, which offers a program for children whose parents are receiving inpatient or outpatient treatment for serious mental illness

Some of these programs offer manuals for practitioners who wish to provide similar services. In addition, directors of the programs are available for training and consultation (additional information is provided in the Notes).

The Three R's Program

Developed by advanced psychiatric nurse practitioner Mary Moller, Chief Executive Officer of Psychiatric Rehabilitation Nurses, Inc., in Spokane, Washington, along with her colleague Milene Murphy, the Three R's Program is an interdisciplinary multiphasic program that incorporates a wellness approach to managing serious mental illness.[2] Objectives of the program are to enable people with mental illness to manage illness and stress, to access appropriate community services, to maintain wellness and self-care, to manage medications successfully, to manage symptoms in preventing relapse, and to achieve life and career goals. An unusual feature of the course is the inclusion of patients, family members, and mental health service providers. Building on shared knowledge and skills, the three groups can work collaboratively to enhance the recovery process.

Employing an educational approach to symptom management, the program incorporates three levels of wellness: unstable, stable, and actualized. At the unstable level, symptom triggers have reoccurred and current symptom management strategies are not successful, which leads to an intensification of symptoms. Relapse typically occurs when the unstable level persists for more than 24 hours. At the stable level, symptoms are present, but the individual is able to manage them and resume normal activities of daily living in a somewhat modified fashion. At the actualized level, symptoms are present but remain in the background. The patient is actively engaged in activities of daily living and pursuing desired life goals. These levels of wellness are tied to the three phases that structure the program.

THE RELAPSE PHASE

Relapse is defined as a return of symptoms severe enough to interfere with daily living activities. Successful outcomes during this phase include a decrease in intensity and frequency of symptoms, improved general health status, improved information processing, and a return to a stable level of wellness.

THE RECOVERY PHASE

Recovery is characterized by the achievement of a stable level of wellness. Successful outcomes during this phase consist of the ability to self-manage basic health, including rest, nutrition, and exercise; to utilize healthy coping mechanisms and improved interpersonal skills; to identify prodromal symptoms; to recognize relapse symptom triggers; and to evaluate lifestyle changes needed to maintain successful symptom management.

A 12-session course, "Recovering From Psychosis: A Wellness Approach," is designed to promote these outcomes. There are three principle course objectives: (a) identification of and differentiation among common daily symptoms, symptoms indicative of relapse, and relapse symptom triggers; (b) management of symptoms and symptom triggers; and (c) implementation of lifestyle changes needed to manage symptoms and symptoms triggers. Course content covers *DSM-IV* terminology, brain research and etiology, treatment and diagnostic issues, the role of anxiety, symptoms and their experiential correlates, lifestyle issues and medication, symptom management assessment, coping skills, and goal setting.

THE REHABILITATION PHASE

Rehabilitation focuses on implementation of a wellness plan that includes lifestyle changes needed to decrease symptoms and to increase coping with symptom triggers. The overall goal is to assist patients in achieving a self-determined satisfactory quality of life. Patients complete a course, "Symptom Management: A Wellness Expedition," which is accompanied by a workbook. The workbook can be completed individually, in one-to-one sessions, or in a formal group setting.

There is empirical support for the value of The Three R's Program in preventing relapse.[3] Compared to a randomized matched control group, for example, patients who participated in the 12-session course experienced significantly fewer inpatient days.

Supportive Family Training

Directed by family member/professional Sheila Shulman Le Gacy, the Family Support and Education Center for Transitional Living Services is a not-for-profit residential and rehabilitation agency in Syracuse, New

York.[4] The center offers a range of services for families of people with serious mental illness, including a family education and support program, Supportive Family Training (SFT). The program was selected by the New York State Office of Mental Health as a model for community-based family education and has served as a model for family education programs throughout the country. The course is being translated into Spanish to better serve the needs of the large Hispanic population in New York City.

The structured 12-week program covers the following topics: schizophrenia and major affective disorders, proper use of medication, signs of relapse and measures to avoid it, effective coping skills, management and self-care strategies, listening and communication techniques, problem solving and crisis care, community services and support networks, working effectively with mental health service providers, rehabilitation, and advocacy. At the beginning of each class, participants receive an outline of the information to be covered as well as related take-home material. At the completion of the course, graduates are encouraged to join their local NAMI affiliate.

The objective of SFT is not to provide family treatment, but rather to improve coping skills of family members, to highlight the primacy of self-care, to reduce their burden, and to enhance their quality of life. The program combines elements of support groups, adult education, peer counseling, bereavement work, and advocacy training. The SFT program is generally offered by a team consisting of a mental health professional and a family member. Participants may be parents, adult offspring, adult siblings, spouses, or concerned friends. A limited number of mental health professionals also enroll in the course, with the goal of providing opportunities for them to empathize with families and for families to learn about the professional perspective.

Le Gacy characterizes the SFT methodology as "working through the heart: a transpersonal approach to family support and education." She uses the term *transpersonal* to mean "beyond the self" or "larger than self," remarking that this transpersonal perspective allows for methods that extend family education deeply into the emotional and spiritual realm and that assist families in moving beyond their pain to attain meaning and connection in their lives. Affirming the value of SFT, one participant described the program as "immensely restorative," declaring: "Our hearts are less weary, our burdens lighter."

In an outcome study of SFT, almost all participants said they felt empowered by the course. A large majority reported improvements in their ability to deal with their relatives, to take care of themselves, and to understand their own emotional reactions. A 3-day Training Workshop prepares mental health professionals and family members to offer the SFT course in their local communities. Workshop topics include teaching methodology, recent research findings concerned with schizophrenia and major mood disorders, family coping skills and strategies, working with guilt and grief, and using disclosure effectively. Participants receive a 500-page teaching manual, which includes extensive handouts for each class. Enrollment is limited to 25 to 30 participants, the approximate size of the regular classes.

The MESA Model of Family Education

Over the course of their lives, family members have a spectrum of important and changing needs. Some needs are linked to their relative's phase and status of illness; others reflect their own concerns as family members with their own adaptational course. Thus, it is useful to think in terms of a continuum or network of family-focused services that can accommodate the needs of specific families over time. Developed and implemented in Virginia, the MESA model of family education incorporates many components of such a continuum.[5] The program is offered jointly by the Virginia affiliates of NAMI and Community Mental Health Center (CMHC) professionals throughout the state. The MESA program was accomplished through the collaborative efforts of family members and professionals, and with the support and sponsorship of both the NAMI state affiliate and the statewide association of CMHCs.

MESA is co-led by a family member and a mental health professional, which promotes the value of family-professional collaboration. Reflecting its acronym, the program emphasizes *mutual education, support*, and *advocacy*. This name acknowledges that families and professionals educate and support each other. In this process, an alliance is formed that creates a stronger voice for advocacy for people with mental illness. Although education is the primary focus, the group sharing and mutual support among family participants is equally important in relieving stress and in increasing feelings of confidence and competence.

As described in the *MESA Family Workshops Manual*, the program includes 14 (or more) sessions (each 1½ hours). The sessions are divided into three parts: (a) Information and Support, consisting of six sessions that cover mental illness, its impact on the family, symptoms of schizophrenia and mood disorders, impact of mental illness on sense of self, special concerns (substance abuse and suicidal risk), diagnosis and etiology, the impact of stress, and preventing relapse; (b) Skills Building, which consists of six sessions that target communication and problem solving and that offer specific guidelines; and (c) a Resource Series, which consists of a session that covers medication and research (presented by a psychiatrist), as well as optional sessions on community resources (presented by community representatives).

Three primary methods are used to conduct the MESA workshops: didactic presentations, group exercises, and group discussion. As specified in Table 15.1, a set of key concepts and guidelines are used throughout the series. Weekly homework assignments link the didactic material to real-life situations. A *MESA Participant's Workbook* is used for this purpose.

The MESA program includes "Train-the-Leaders Seminars," which are led by a family member-professional team, sponsored and coordinated by the state affiliate of NAMI. The 2-day training program is designed to prepare family members and mental health professionals to co-lead the workshops in their communities. Current information is provided on mental illness and its treatment and on the impact of mental illness on the personal lives of families and consumers. The training includes a review of the *MESA Family Workshops Co-leaders Manual,* which provides the curriculum for the MESA Family Workshops series. The statewide implementation of the MESA program fosters a "corporate culture" defined by a consistent philosophy, knowledge base, and approach to working with families, especially in community mental health centers, hospitals, and family support groups.

Participants report many benefits of the MESA program. One sibling wrote about her family's experience with mental illness, noting they "have felt helpless in the face of this intractable illness." After participating in the MESA program, she remarked that "all this has changed":

I understand mental illness, and no longer find it frightening. I have insight into how my sister feels, and what she is going through, and how hellish this is for her. This knowledge has opened a door for us that seemed closed. I have learned how to communicate with my sister, and she has responded to my efforts, and we have rekindled our friendship; on a different level than before her illness, but very rewarding nonetheless.[6]

Several other services have grown out of the alliance that develops as families and professionals work together in the MESA family education program. These collectively constitute an ideal for a Virginia continuum of services. In Virginia Beach, for example, the CMHC Office of Consumer and Family Affairs, directed by social worker Thomasine Cubine, offers a range of services and programs for family members, including educational literature, videotapes, audiotapes, and brochures on mental illness and community resources.

TABLE 15.1
MESA FAMILY WORKSHOPS: KEY CONCEPTS AND GUIDELINES

I. Mental illnesses, like other long-term illnesses, present themselves in different ways at different times in a person's life.
  A. The degree of intervention and support needs to vary depending on the stage of illness.
    1. During a stage when symptoms are most severe (acute episodes):
      a. families need to be more accessible and supportive;
      b. medication or hospitalization may be the most effective treatment.
    2. During recuperative/stable periods:
      a. families need to continue support,
      b. while gradually increasing expectations and levels of responsibility.
  B. The illness is not the person: Recognize that people who have a mental illness also have their own, unique personalities with strengths and contributions to make.
II. The stress of mental illness affects all the family members.
  A. Feelings of anger, hurt, resentment, and despair are typical responses for family members.
  B. Adjusting to a relative's mental illness is a painful process similar to grief and mourning.
  C. Blaming oneself or others is nonproductive.
  D. Support from others in a like situation helps relieve the stress imposed by mental illness.
  E. Outside activities and time for oneself are necessary in order to maintain health.
  F. Education about mental illness and resources helps families understand and cope.
  G. Educating others helps to combat the stigma of mental illness and to overcome the isolation that families experience.
  H. Families need to resume their own lives as they cope with and adapt to the illness.
  I. Joining with other families to advocate for the needs of people who have mental illness can be rewarding and productive.
III. Mental illnesses are biological illnesses that impair internal control over thought and mood processes.
  A. Order and structure in the environment help to provide external controls (for the person who has a mental illness).
  B. Expectations and life goals may need to be reevaluated.
  C. Maintenance of a calm mood (as much as possible) increases control over the situation.
  D. Clear and simple communications increase ability to understand and be understood.
  E. Reinforcement of reality can be reassuring to the person with mental illness when thoughts become distorted or delusional.

(continued)

TABLE 15.1 Continued

IV. Mental illnesses interrupt normal development of a sense of identity and self-esteem.
   A. Family members, the person with mental illness, and professionals need to work together to develop and support a rehabilitation plan.
   B. Families need to encourage the establishment of appropriate and attainable roles within the home and community.
   C. Families need to look for "health" and reward small gains.
V. People with mental illnesses tolerate stress poorly.
   A. An environment that is neither overstimulating nor understimulating helps reduce stress.
   B. Change, positive or negative, creates stress.
      1. Plan ahead, when possible, in order to minimize stress.
      2. Avoid making more than one change at a time.
   C. Identification of stress and individualized reactions to stress can help prevent relapse.
VI. Mental illnesses interfere with communication because thoughts and mood become disordered.
   A. Communication needs to be clear, specific, and focused.
   B. Verbal communication needs to be consistent with nonverbal communication.
   C. Communication of anger, hurt, or disappointment should be done in a clear, nonthreatening manner. (Suppression may foster resentment and the accumulated anger may resurface as hostility at a later point.)
   D. Emphasis in communication should be on acknowledging or praising positive actions or behavior.
VII. The complex nature of mental illnesses requires special guidelines for the whole family.
   A. The needs and rights of all family members must be considered.
   B. Overdoing for a person who has mental illness decreases his or her ability to do for himself or herself and increases the burden on the family.
   C. The member who has mental illness should not be allowed to dominate the whole family.
   D. The family needs to act as a unit. A consistent approach among family members and follow through in dealing with behavioral issues prevents manipulation.
   E. Hope and determination lead to solutions.

Note: From *MESA FAMILY WORKSHOPS: Mutual Education, Support, and Advocacy,* by T. Cubine and P. T. McCafferty, 1996, pp. 12–14. Reprinted with permission of the authors.

Services include a family support group offered by the local NAMI affiliate, a special support group for families whose relatives are incarcerated at the local correctional facility, a "buddy system" to encourage outreach and support to families of new patients coming into the CMHC, ombudsman services that provide assistance to families experiencing problems with the mental health system, special help for families seeking commitment of a relative to a mental hospital, and a community trust program to help families in planning for the future needs of their relative. An Advisory Council composed of consumers, family members, and professionals provides advice to the CMHC and forms work groups to address identified issues and to improve mental health services.

Occasional programs are designed to address specific family and community needs. These are cosponsored by the local NAMI affiliate and the CMHC. Recent projects have included workshops on mental disorders among children and adolescents and on new research in the treatment of mental disorders, a public forum on the new generation of antipsychotic medications, a NAMI Walk for Hope planned for fund raising, and participation in the Episcopal Mental Illness Network developed to support all those affected by serious mental illness. In addition, family members, consumers, and professionals jointly provide education to university and community groups using materials from the NAMI Campaign to End Discrimination; they also participate in various advocacy activities together.

The T.E.C. Network

Working at the Training and Education Center (T.E.C.) Network in Philadelphia, family member Marilyn Meisel and family therapist Edie Mannion have extensive experience in family education. A program of the Mental Health Association of Southeastern Pennsylvania, the T.E.C. Network offers an array of family education classes for groups of family members, as well as individual family consultation.[7] The classes are offered in the evenings; the daytime program consists of telephone and face-to-face family consultation. All of their family education classes are cofacilitated by a professional mental illness specialist and a trained family member (or "peer consultant"), which offers a model of family-professional collaboration and exposes class participants to both family and professional perspectives and areas of expertise. Their programs are limited to family members, who are likely to talk more openly and honestly than if their relatives were present.

One of their original educational programs is a 10-week Family Coping Skills Workshop, which has an optional extension that covers seven additional topics. The curriculum and philosophy for this course is contained in their teaching manual. Introductory material covers the workshop model, the role of the "peer consultant," role distinctions between teachers and therapists, developmental goals for participants, trends of participants, teaching skills, suggestions for developing a workshop, and recommendations for the first class. The introductory section also includes suggested readings, which are periodically updated. Portions of the program were used in the development of NAMI's Family-to-Family Education Program (formerly Journey of Hope).

The second section consists of the actual curriculum, handouts, and homework sheets for each class. The 10 basic chapters cover feelings of family members; the subjective experience of mental illness; creating a low-stress atmosphere; communication skills; problem definition skills; limit setting skills; skills for managing violent, disruptive, and self-destructive behavior; stages of accepting illness; planning for the future; and a wrap-up. The seven optional chapters address siblings, problem solving skills, common challenges, handling anger constructively, holidays, accessing the mental health system, and introduction to advocacy.

The final section includes regularly updated handouts on schizophrenia, mood disorders, schizoaffective disorder, and personality disorders (with a focus on borderline and schizotypal personality disorders). The manual is an excellent resource for practitioners who plan to offer an educational program for families. The training sheets contained in the manual include actual lectures, experiential exercises, role plays, and "process notes" that offer suggestions for handling challenging sections of each class.

Research findings from a large clinical trial indicated that workshop participants who had never participated in a family support or advocacy group developed increased understanding of mental illness and effective coping strategies (self-efficacy).[8] Although the group workshop was well liked by family members, there was evidence that individualized family consultation may be more beneficial. For instance, family members who received individualized consultation demonstrated greater self-efficacy whether or not they had prior experience in family support or advocacy groups.

As a result, Meisel and Mannion have modified the workshop model to assess educational needs at the start of the workshop, to include elements of individualized family consultation ("relatives group consultation"), and to offer illness-specific workshops.[9] They currently offer a 6-week family workshop on schizophrenia and schizoaffective disorder, a 6-week family workshop on mood disorders, and a 4-week family workshop on borderline personality disorder. They have also added a 4-week workshop for family members who have first learned of their relative's diagnosis within the last 2 years.

The T.E.C. Network Spouse Coping Skills Workshop

Upon noticing the high attrition rate for spouses who registered for the family workshop, Mannion and Meisel realized that the curriculum, which was primarily developed for parents, was not addressing the needs of spouses. Working with a Spouse Task Force, they developed a new curriculum. Although much of the content was changed from the original workshop, the key features of their model were maintained, including cofacilitation of the classes by a professional and a trained family member (in this case, a spouse "peer consultant"), as well as the exclusion of the partners with mental illness. Participants who complete the workshop are given the option of joining a monthly spouse support group that offers continuing emotional support and reinforcement of the material taught in the workshop.

The manual for the spouse workshop has the same format as the general manual, with identical introductory and final sections. Lesson plans, handouts, and homework sheets for the 12 classes are contained in the middle section. Some material from the general manual has been adapted to the needs and perspectives of spouses; other chapters are completely new. New topics include tips for living with a partner's mental illness, financial issues, helping children cope, and looking at the future of the marriage. Recent handouts have been developed to address the following: managing the bipolar cycle, coping with a partner who has depression, normal challenges of couples facing illness and disability, and building a support system. As with the general manual, the lesson plans contained in the spouse manual include actual lectures, experiential exercises, role plays, and "process notes" with suggestions for each class.

The specialized spouse workshop has significantly reduced the attrition rate of spouses (to about 5%). In addition, there is evidence that participation in the workshop results in increased understanding of mental illness and coping strategies, as well as decreased personal distress and negative attitudes toward partners with mental illness.[10] The following spouse affirms the value of the workshop:

My anger at my husband is now being redirected in avenues to help him and myself. My emotional reactions to his poor judgment or manic episodes compounded the problem. I'm trying. I really can endure, I can be strong, and I do have worth! I learned to empathize with what he is going through and to treat his illness as more of a "sickness." You taught me skills I can use to change both of our lives.

Her only complaint: "I just wish the course were longer." With the generous permission of Mannion and Meisel, Table 15.2 is a handout adapted from their manual for spouse workshops.

TABLE 15.2
HELPING CHILDREN COPE

---

1. Some basic questions children may be asking themselves (either consciously or unconsciously) when a parent shows symptoms of mental illness:
   - Why is Mom or Dad acting this way?
   - Is this my fault?
   - Will things stay like this?
   - Do Mom and Dad still love me?
   - What will happen to me if our family falls apart?

2. Helping children to understand the illness and develop healthy attitudes:
   - Some advantages to explaining the illness to children and directly or indirectly addressing the above questions:
     (a) Children often imagine things that are worse than reality.
     (b) Being honest with children helps them to trust you.
     (c) Understanding that there's an illness involved can help them to empathize with and respect their parent with mental illness.
     (d) Discussion may possibly reduce some of their anger and guilt about what is happening.
     (e) Discussion may reduce any anger and mistrust toward you if left to discover on their own the ways that their family life differs from their friends' during episodes of illness.
     (f) Discussion may reduce some of their vulnerability, sensitivity, confusion, and surprise when confronted with negative comments from others about their parent with mental illness.
     (g) Research indicates that information aids coping.
   - Tips for explaining the illness to children:
     (a) Start with yourself. Assess your attitudes and knowledge base about the illness.
        - The more you know, the better you'll be able to answer their questions matter of factly.
        - The stronger your attitude that the illness is somebody's fault, the greater the risk you can run of saying and doing things that can:
           (1) Put your children in a loyalty conflict.
              Example: "Mom says it's Dad's fault. Dad says it's Mom's fault. Whose side should I take?"
           (2) Teach children to blame and scapegoat when bad things happen.
              Example: "Mom says it's Grandma's fault that Dad can't handle anything."
     (b) Find out their way of explaining their parent's behavior.

TABLE 15.2 Continued

(c) Build on what they say:

- Acknowledge any truth in what they say.
- Respectfully correct anything that is based on wrong information or fantasy.

    Example: "Daddy isn't acting this way because of anything you or I have done."

(d) Use language and an explanation that is appropriate to each child's age and intelligence, using analogies and examples that are familiar to them.

    Example: (geared to a typical 5-year-old): "Do you remember when you had the chicken pox? You cried a lot, you didn't feel like doing anything, and you were grouchy toward all of us. It wasn't because you didn't love us or wanted to be that way, but because you didn't feel good. That's why Mom's crying a lot, not doing anything, and acting grouchy. She still loves you and me, but she can't show it right now."

    Example: (geared to a typical 10-year-old): "You know how parts of our bodies get sick sometimes, like when we get stomach aches or sore throats. Well, some people get sick in the part of their brains that controls feelings. That's what's wrong with Dad. He has a sickness in that part of his brain that controls feelings. That sickness has a name. It's called manic depression."

(e) If a child has witnessed violent or suicidal behavior, a situation requiring police intervention, or other traumatic incidents, don't underestimate how terrifying this experience can be. Helene Arnstein, in her book, *What to Tell Your Child about Birth, Death, Illness, Divorce, and Other Family Crises,* recommends the following explanation for any forcible removal of a parent from the home:

    Daddy didn't know just then what was best for him. He didn't know that the hospital is the safest and most comfortable place to be in while he was getting well. You know, there were times when you too had to do things you didn't want to, but which we knew were good for you. It was that way with Daddy, too. Other people needed to decide what was best for him.

(f) Let your children know there are books they may find helpful.

    Example: Books and videotapes for children and adolescents.[11]

    Example: Coloring book available through NAMI for children under 10.

(g) Children usually learn more from what their parents do than from what their parents say, so try as much as possible to practice using whatever information and attitudes you try to convey to them verbally.

(continued)

Table 15.2 Continued

Example: Role model being matter-of-fact with others about the illness.

Example: Role model protecting herself or himself from unacceptable behavior even though it is illness-based. (If the spouse can be firm and clear about the need to set limits on the partner, it may help children through any temporary distress and teach them that marriage does not mean sacrificing one's safety.)

3. Helping children with their feelings:

   - Predominant feelings may vary depending on a child's age and level of understanding.

     Example: Guilt or fear are often the predominant feelings for younger children whereas anger and embarrassment tend to be predominant for most adolescents.

   - Create an atmosphere that encourages children to talk about their feelings.

     (a) Talk about your own feelings so that they have a role model.

     (b) Take advantage of moments that lend themselves to a discussion of feelings.

         Example: Watching a TV show about a parent who develops a disability.

     (c) Be available to listen, but don't pressure a child to talk about feelings if he or she isn't willing.

   - Things to do when your children do try to express feelings:

     (a) Give your full attention. Make eye contact.

     (b) Check out what you are hearing in their words or interpreting from their behavior.

         Example: "So you're really angry at your father and me because of how much of my attention he takes?"

         Example: "You've been slamming doors all night. Are you angry about something? I'm here if you want to talk."

     (c) If the feelings shared by your children elicit strong feelings in you (e.g., anger, sadness, guilt), resist the temptation to jump in.

   - Getting judgmental or emotional can shut children up now and in the future.

   - It takes great self-discipline not to get judgmental if our children are having feelings that we think they shouldn't have.

     Example: "You should not be angry with me. You should be thankful. I'm the one keeping the family together."

     (d) You can sometimes spare children unnecessary disappointment by not telling them about planned events too far in advance.

TABLE 15.2 Continued

- Provide your children with skills for handling strong feelings:
  - (a) Explain that feelings are neither right nor wrong. It's okay and natural for them to have the feelings they're having.
  - (b) Emphasize that talking about feelings can be helpful, and that you'll always try to make special time when your children need to talk.
  - (c) Explain that feelings do not have to control what we do. Give examples.

    Example: "It's okay that you're angry at your father and me, but the way you're acting toward us is not okay."

    Example: "Being embarrassed about your mother's illness doesn't have to prevent you from explaining it to your friends."
  - (d) Humor can help to make the whole communication seem positive if it isn't used to discount or ignore your children's feelings.
4. Helping children learn effective verbal and behavioral responses:
   - Practical suggestions for responding to their parent with mental illness:
     - (a) Share any of the discoveries or skills you have acquired about what works and doesn't work in dealing with your partner.
     - (b) Make sure your children understand that even though their parent has mental illness, it's okay for them to protect themselves from any behavior that seems scary or dangerous.
     - (c) Give specific suggestions for how to protect themselves.
   - Make a rule that your children tell you whenever a situation involving your partner has scared them or made them uncomfortable.
   - Teach your children to tell their parent whenever he or she is scaring or upsetting them.
     - (d) Let your children know that showing their parent with mental illness they still love him or her is very important.
     - (e) Consistently discipline your children for acting disrespectfully toward either parent.
   - Practical suggestions for responding to others regarding their parent with mental illness:
     - (a) Involving children in keeping the illness a secret can be extremely burdensome to them.
     - (b) What *you* say and do with others regarding the illness will probably influence your children more than anything you tell them to do.
     - (c) Explain to your children that many people don't understand the illness:
       - It may scare them.
       - They may try to make fun of it.
       - They may have ideas that aren't true.
       - They may change the subject or say nothing.

(continued)

TABLE 15.2 Continued

(d) Teach your children how to explain the illness to others. The more your children understand, the easier it will be for them to explain it to others.

(e) Practice with them how they might respond:
Example: "That's the way God made my mommy."
Example: "I wouldn't make fun of your dad if he were sick."
Example: "If you understood what's wrong with my mother, I don't think you would say what you're saying."

Note: From *Teaching Manual for Spouse Coping Skills Workshop* by E. Mannion and M. Meisel, 1993, Chapter 10, pp. 13–21. Adapted with permission of the authors.

Project S.O.S.

Project S.O.S. (Stamp Out Stigma of Mental Illness) provides education about mental illness to students in elementary, middle, and high school.[12] Designed for educators, the three-level program is consistent with the mandate from the Ohio Department of Education to include mental illness as a content area in health curriculum.

The lesson plan for grades 4 to 6 centers on developing understanding and compassion for people who have mental illness. Objectives are to sensitize students to the pain caused by making fun of people with mental illness, to relate mental illness to other physical illness, and to inform students about the nature of mental illness. Students listen to a story about a student who reveals her brother's mental illness to her best friend, discuss the issues involved in the story, and write a friendly letter designed to explore some of the issues.

The lesson plan for grades 7 and 8 is designed to sensitize students to the negative impact of the stigma associated with mental illness and to inform students about the nature of mental illness and its treatment. Students listen to a story about a student who develops schizophrenia, discuss the relevant issues, and write a letter of complaint in response to a stigmatizing ad for a mountain bike.

Students in grades 9 through 12 learn to identify common fears and misconceptions about mental illness, discuss how stereotypes about mental illness are formed and affect our behavior, are given information about schizophrenia, and discuss the role that family, friends, community, and government can play in recovery. Materials include a personal account by someone who developed schizophrenia as a child.

Each lesson plan includes suggestions for further study, recommended reading and videotapes, a curriculum on mental illness, and possible speakers and tours. The response to the program has been very positive.

A seventh grade student commented, "Obviously, there are people who suffer with these problems and we need to understand them." A high school student wrote about a close friend who had been diagnosed with manic depression: "If my friend and I had been better educated on the signs of someone who is mentally ill, we could have gone for help before she became suicidal and extremely depressed."

BART's Place

At Northcoast Behavioral Healthcare System in Cleveland, Ohio, psychologist Janice Katz and other staff members have developed a program for children and teenagers whose parents have mental illness. BART's (Bring All Relatives Together) Place consists of a family room and a playroom that offer a safe atmosphere for healthy interactions between hospitalized parents and their children.[13] The need for such a program was compelling. Many of the hospitalized patients worried about their children and longed to see them; some of the parents were hospitalized for several months. Yet there was no opportunity for contact between these parents and their children. Prevented from visiting the ward until they were over age 16, children could often be seen waving to their parents from the parking lot.

At least 34% of psychiatric patients have children under age 19, yet there has been little attention to the parenting role of these patients or to the needs of their children. As Katz points out, children need reassurance that they did not cause their parent's illness, that the illness is not contagious, and that they are still loved by their parent. Likewise, mothers and fathers who are hospitalized for treatment of mental illness need reassurance that their children are safe during a potentially long separation and that their parenting role will be supported.

Goals of the program are to offer opportunities for constructive parent-child interactions; to provide support, education, and psychological tools for children; to create an environment that promotes positive family reintegration during or after a mental health crisis; to enhance parenting skills; and to furnish training for other professionals who are interested in offering similar programs. BART's Place provides the following opportunities for families:

- A place for supervised visits
- A place where children and families can learn about mental illness
- A place where patients and children can plan for discharge from the hospital

- Parenting classes for parents who are receiving inpatient or outpatient services
- Support groups for children and teenagers whose parents have mental illness
- A place to discuss family problems after discharge

The program is staffed by mental health professionals who are trained to work with children and families. Referrals can be made by hospital treatment teams as well as by patients, their family members, and outside agents.

Among the offspring who have been served are a 2-year-old girl who spent a week wandering around the house saying, "Daddy Okay? Daddy Okay?" after witnessing her father take an overdose; a 6-year-old child who witnessed the suicide attempt of his mother; a 12-year-old boy who called 911 after finding his father hanging from the rafters of the basement and cutting him down; and a 13-year-old by who led a nomadic existence with a homeless mother who was eventually incarcerated.

BART's Place has made a significant difference in the lives of these children and their families. Initially, a child therapist meets with each child to explain the purpose of the meeting, to describe BART's Place, to encourage the child to express his or her concerns, and to deliver a cuddly stuffed bear that proudly displays the name of the program. Other services are provided as needed for individual families. The program has developed a brochure, "Some Things to Keep in Mind When Talking to Children About Mental Illness," that assists staff in working with these families.

Based on patient and family satisfaction surveys as well as informal feedback, BART's Place has been enthusiastically received by all participating families. Families are grateful to have their needs addressed, to have parent-child relationships acknowledged and strengthened, and to have access to an educational, supportive, and safe environment. And, most poignantly, children no longer have to wave at their parents from the parking lot.

Notes

Chapter 1

1. Based on 1996 prevalence data from the Center for Mental Health Services, approximately 5.4 million adults (2.7 % of the population) have a "severe and persistent" mental illness (Kessler et al., 1996). At least 3 million children and adolescents (5 to 9%) have a serious emotional disturbance and "extreme functional impairment" (Friedman, Katz-Leavy, Manderscheid, & Sondheimer, 1996).
2. Lefley, 1989.
3. Marsh, 1992a, p. 10.
4. Marsh & Dickens, 1997, p. 23.
5. Marsh & Dickens, 1997, p. 28.
6. For discussions of the history of family-professional relationships, see Lefley, 1994a; Lefley & Wasow, 1994; Marsh, 1992a.
7. Lefley, 1994a.
8. Figures from Torrey, 1995.
9. For a penetrating examination of these problems, see Torrey, 1997.
10. Torrey, 1995, 1997.
11. For an excellent survey of family caregiving in mental illness, see Lefley, 1996.
12. Marsh, 1992a.
13. Keith, 1997, p. 9.
14. Lefley, 1994a.
15. Grunebaum & Friedman, 1988.
16. Marsh, 1992a, p. 16.
17. Marsh, Lefley, & Husted, 1996.
18. For disability, see Seligman & Darling, 1997; Turnbull & Turnbull, 1990. For chronic health problems, see McDaniel, Hepworth, & Doherty, 1992. For serious mental illness, see Marsh, 1992a.
19. For discussions of family coping and adaptation, see Hatfield & Lefley, 1987; Lefley & Wasow, 1994; Marsh, Lefley, & Husted, 1996.
20. For discussions of family effectiveness, see Beavers & Hampson, 1990; Dunst, Trivette, & Deal, 1994; Figley, 1989.
21. Dunst, Trivette, & Deal, 1994.
22. Hatfield & Lefley, 1987.
23. For a discussion of a competence paradigm, see Masterpasqua, 1989; for its application to family practice in mental illness, see Marsh, 1992a; for its application to family therapy, see Waters & Lawrence, 1993.
24. For discussions of family-professional collaboration, see Lefley & Johnson, 1990; Lefley & Wasow, 1994; Marsh, 1992a.
25. Spaniol, Zipple, Marsh, & Finley, 1998.
26. D. Johnson, 1987.
27. Marsh, 1992a.
28. Howells & Guirguis, 1985.
29. Marsh, 1994b, p. 108.
30. Marsh & Dickens, 1997, p. 29.
31. For a useful discussion of systemic principles and practice, see Anderson, Reiss, & Hogarty, 1986.
32. Lefley & Wasow, 1994; Marsh & Johnson, 1997; Mueser, 1996.
33. Lefley, 1996.

34. For further information, contact the central office of NAMI, 200 North Glebe Road, Suite 1015, Arlington, VA 22203.
35. For suggestions on family engagement, see Bernheim & Lehman, 1985; Glynn, Liberman, & Backer, 1997; Group for the Advancement of Psychiatry, 1993, Mueser & Glynn, 1995.
36. For discussions of family assessment, see Bernheim & Lehman, 1985; Glynn, Liberman, & Backer, 1997; Group for the Advancement of Psychiatry, 1993; Mueser & Glynn, 1995.
37. Bernheim, 1994a, 1994b.

Chapter 2

1. See, for example, the ethical code of the American Psychological Association (APA), 1992.
2. Glynn, Liberman, & Backer, 1997.
3. National Advisory Mental Health Council, 1993.
4. Basic Behavioral Science Research for Mental Health: A National Investment, 1995.
5. Kessler et al., 1996.
6. Schizophrenia: Treatment outcomes research, 1995; also see Lehman, Steinwachs, et al., 1998.
7. For example, see Goodwin & Jamison, 1990; Heston, 1991; Klein & Wender, 1994; Roth & Fonagy, 1996.
8. Substance Abuse and Mental Health Services Administration, 1994.
9. Wasylenki, 1992; also see Spaniol & Koehler, 1993.
10. Harding, Zubin, & Strauss, 1992.
11. Torrey, 1995.
12. Schiller & Bennett, 1996; Jamison, 1995; Styron, 1990; Spaniol, Gagne, & Koehler, 1997.
13. "John," 1997, pp. 7–8.
14. For example, see Andreasen, 1994; Bedell, Hunter, & Corrigan, 1997; Bentley & Walsh, 1996; Coursey, Alford, & Safarjan, 1997; Frances, Docherty, & Kahn, 1996; Gorman, 1995; Hirsch & Weinberger, 1995; Kahn, Carpenter, Docherty, & Frances, 1996; Lehman, Steinwachs, et al., 1998; Torrey, Bowler, Taylor, & Gottesman, 1994.
15. Amenson, 1998a, 1998b.
16. For example, see Glynn, Liberman, & Backer, 1997; D. Johnson, 1997.
17. Fink, 1988.
18. Moltz, 1993.
19. Yank, Bentley, & Hargrove, 1993.
20. Lefley, 1992, 1997.
21. Miklowitz & Goldstein, 1997.
22. Shimberg, 1991.
23. Papolos & Papolos, 1997.
24. Kitchener, 1984, 1986.
25. Lakin, 1988.
26. Marsh, 1992a.
27. Marsh, 1992a, pp. 57–58.
28. Thompson, 1990.
29. Lefley, 1996; Marsh, 1995.
30. Marsh, 1992a.
31. For example, see Carr, 1990; Lewis, 1989.
32. Marsh & Dickens, 1997, p. 109.

33. Marsh, Appleby, Dickens, Owens, & Young, 1994, p. 174.
34. Kitchener, 1984, 1986.
35. Begler, 1997.
36. For example, see H. Turnbull, 1989.
37. Perr, 1985; Smith, 1994a, 1994b; Watkins & Watkins, 1989.
38. R. Simon & Sadoff, 1992.
39. Berman & Cohen-Sandler, 1983; Smith, 1994a, 1994b.
40. Litman, 1989.
41. American Psychiatric Association, 1994.
42. Gutheil, Bursztajn, & Brodsky, 1984.
43. *Tarasoff v. Board of Regents of the University of California,* 1976.
44. Knapp & VandeCreek, 1990.
45. Melton, Petrila, Poythress, & Slobogin, 1987.
46. Wahl, 1995.
47. Torrey, 1997.
48. Marsh, 1997; Marsh & Johnson, 1997.
49. Petrila & Sadoff, 1992; Zipple, Langle, Tyrell, Spaniol, & Fisher, 1997.
50. For a sample release form designed for families, see Marsh, 1992b; Marsh, Lefley, & Husted, 1996.
51. Kaslow, 1993.
52. Kaslow, 1996.
53. Patterson & Lusterman, 1996.
54. Dixon & Lehman, 1995.
55. Bernheim, 1989, 1994a, 1994b.
56. Gottlieb, 1996.
57. American Psychiatric Association, 1994, p. 681.
58. For example, see Knapp, 1997.
59. Jamison, 1995.

Chapter 3

1. Backlar, 1994; Berger & Berger, 1991; Deveson, 1992; Dickens & Marsh, 1994; Moorman, 1992; Neugeboren, 1997; Sexton, 1994; C. Simon, 1997b; Swados, 1991; Wechsler, Schwartztol, & Wechsler, 1988; Wyden, 1998.
2. Marsh & Johnson, 1997, p. 229.
3. For an overview of family burden, see Lefley, 1996; for representative articles, see Biegel, Milligan, Putnarn, & Song, 1994; Carpentier, Lesage, Goulet, Lalonde, & Renaud, 1992; Clark, 1994; Gallagher & Mechanic, 1996; Hanson, 1993; Jones, Roth, & Jones, 1995; Maurin & Boyd, 1990; Reinhard, 1994; Sargent, 1992; Solomon & Draine, 1995; Song, Biegel, & Milligan, 1997; Winefield & Harvey, 1993.
4. Marsh, Lefley, Evans-Rhodes, et al., 1996, p. 4.
5. Greenberg, Greenley, & Benedict, 1994.
6. Marsh, D. T. (1988). [Mothers of children receiving mental health services]. Unpublished interviews and personal communications.
7. S. Atkinson, 1994; MacGregor, 1994; Solomon & Draine, 1996.
8. Marsh & Johnson, 1997, p. 230.
9. Flory & Friedrich, 1997.
10. Husted, 1994, p. 75.
11. Viorst, 1986, p. 264.
12. Marsh, 1992a, p. 74.
13. Marsh, 1992a, p. 79.
14. Marsh & Dickens, 1997, p. 26.

15. Terkelsen, 1987b, p. 141.
16. Torrey, 1995.
17. Torrey, 1995.
18. Lefley, 1996.
19. Lefley, 1996.
20. Husted, 1994, p. 75.
21. Marsh & Dickens, 1997, p. 14.
22. Flory & Friedrich, 1997.
23. Hanson, 1995; Hanson & Rapp, 1992; Skinner, Steinwachs, & Kasper, 1992; Solomon & Marcenko, 1992; Torrey, 1995.
24. Marsh & Dickens, 1997, p. 28.
25. Fink & Tasman, 1992.
26. National Institute of Mental Health, 1986.
27. Lefley, 1996.
28. Marsh & Dickens, 1997, p. 30.
29. Wasow, 1994.
30. Moltz, 1993.
31. F. Frese, 1994; quotes from pp. 80, 82, 83, 85.
32. Jamison, 1995; quotes from pp. 67, 89, 91.
33. Lefley, 1996; Solomon, 1996.
34. Marsh & Dickens, 1997, p. 132.
35. Gazarik & Acton, 1997.
36. Marsh & Dickens, 1997, p. 31.
37. For a discussion of the impact of disability on family functioning, see A. Turnbull & Turnbull, 1990.
38. Marsh & Dickens, 1997, p. 22.
39. Marsh & Dickens, 1997, p. 22.
40. Marsh & Dickens, 1997, p. 144.
41. Marsh & Dickens, 1997, p. 33.
42. Marsh & Dickens, 1997, p. 34.
43. Marsh, Lefley, Evans-Rhodes, et al., 1996; also see Doornbos, 1996; Hawley & DeHaan, 1996; F. Walsh, 1996.
44. Marsh, Lefley, Evans-Rhodes, et al., 1996, p. 10.
45. Marsh, Lefley, Evans-Rhodes, et al., 1996, p. 9.
46. Marsh, Lefley, Evans-Rhodes, et al., 1996, p. 7.
47. Marsh, Lefley, Evans-Rhodes, et al., 1996, p. 7.
48. Marsh & Dickens, 1997, p. 65.
49. Marsh & Dickens, 1997, p. 36.
50. Wasow, 1995.
51. Marsh & Dickens, 1997, p. 43.
52. Horwitz, Tessler, Fisher, & Gamache, 1992.
53. Ascher-Svanum & Sobel, 1989; Lefley, 1996; Scazufca & Kuipers, 1997.
54. Cook, 1988.
55. Lefley, 1996.
56. Carpentier et al., 1992.
57. Marsh & Dickens, 1997, p. 44.
58. McGoldrick, Giordano, & Pearce, 1996.
59. Figures from U. S. Bureau of the Census, *Statistical Abstract of the U.S., 1995.*
60. Kazdin, Stolar, & Marciano, 1995.
61. Marsh & Dickens, 1997, p. 98.
62. Plummer, 1996.
63. Finley, 1997.
64. Lefley, 1996.
65. Cook, Lefley, Pickett, & Cohler, 1994; Guarnaccia & Parra, 1996; Horwitz & Reinhard, 1995; Stueve, Vine, & Struening, 1997.

66. Pickett, Vraniak, Cook, & Cohler, 1993.
67. Finley, 1998.
68. Jordan, Lewellen, & Vandiver, 1995.
69. Lefley, 1994b.
70. Guarnaccia & Parra, 1996.
71. Finley, 1997.
72. For suggestions regarding cultural competence, see Cross, Bazron, Dennis, & Isaacs, 1989; also see Lefley, 1998.
73. Marsh & Johnson, 1997.
74. Marsh & Dickens, 1997, p. 100.
75. Marsh & Dickens, 1997, p. 102.

Chapter 4

1. Rolland, 1994; quote from Rolland, 1988, p. 454.
2. Sheehy, 1996.
3. Carter & McGoldrick, 1988.
4. Marsh et al., 1994, p. 173.
5. List, 1996, p. 37.
6. Marsh & Dickens, 1997, pp. 17–18.
7. Moltz, 1993.
8. Terkelsen, 1987b; quote from p. 128.
9. Marsh & Dickens, 1997, p. 81.
10. Marsh & Dickens, 1997, p. 49.
11. Marsh & Dickens, 1997, p. 72.
12. Marsh & Dickens, 1997, p. 69.
13. Marsh, 1992a, pp. 68–69.
14. Marsh, 1992a, p. 77.
15. Lefley, 1996.
16. Marsh, 1992a, p. 70.
17. Marsh & Dickens, 1997, pp. 17–18.
18. Pickett, Cook, & Cohler, 1994.

Chapter 5

1. Figley, 1989.
2. For example, Spaniol, 1987.
3. Figley, 1989.
4. Marsh, 1994b; Marsh, Lefley, & Husted, 1996.
5. Wikler, 1986.
6. Terkelsen, 1987b.
7. Reiss & Klein, 1987.
8. Taylor, 1983.
9. Antonovsky & Sourani, 1988.
10. Bateson, 1990.
11. Marsh & Dickens, 1997, p. 98.
12. Terkelsen, 1987b.
13. Chesla, 1989; Robinson, 1996.
14. Unpublished survey response; research reported in Marsh, Dickens, et al., 1997.
15. For example, Bandura, 1990; Lazarus & Folkman, 1984; Matheny, Aycock, Pugh, Curlette, & Cannella, 1986.
16. Marsh & Dickens, 1997, p. 97.

17. Marsh & Dickens, 1997, p. 97.
18. Vaillant, 1977, pp. 257–258.
19. Flynn, 1992.
20. Anonymous spouse (personal communication, October 15, 1997).
21. Marsh & Dickens, 1997, p. 81.
22. McCubbin & McCubbin, 1988.
23. Marsh & Dickens, 1997, p. 37.
24. Torrey, Erdman, Wolfe, & Flynn, 1990.
25. Marsh & Dickens, 1997, p. 99.
26. For example, Hatfield & Lefley, 1987; Kessler, Price, & Wortman, 1985.
27. Figley, 1989.
28. For example, Forman, 1993 (children and adolescents); Kessler et al., 1985; Matheny et al., 1986 (adults); Hatfield & Lefley, 1993 (people with mental illness); and Hatfield & Lefley, 1987; Zipple & Spaniol, 1987 (families of people with mental illness).
29. For example, see Meisel & Mannion, 1990; Mueser & Gingerich, 1994; Papolos & Papolos, 1997; Shimberg, 1991; Torrey, 1995; Woolis, 1992.
30. Spaniol & Zipple, 1997.
31. Phase theories of family adaptation to mental illness are discussed in Marsh, 1992a.
32. Terkelsen, 1987a.
33. Rando, 1984.
34. For example, see Marsh, 1992a.
35. Featherstone, 1980, p. 232.
36. Marsh & Dickens, 1997, p. 92.
37. Marsh, 1992a, p. 90.
38. Marsh & Dickens, 1997, p. 93.
39. Marsh, 1992a, p. 91.
40. Udwin, 1993.
41. Marsh & Dickens, 1997, p. 95.
42. Matsakis, 1992.
43. Marsh & Dickens, 1997, p. 96.
44. For example, Herman, 1997.
45. Marsh & Dickens, 1997, p. 65.
46. Marsh & Dickens, 1997, pp. xxiii–xxiv.
47. Flach, 1988, p. 29.
48. Wolin & Wolin, 1993.
49. Hudson, 1991, p. 209.
50. Marsh & Dickens, 1997, p. 1.

Chapter 6

1. For example, see Meisel & Mannion, 1990; Mueser & Gingerich, 1994; Papolos & Papolos, 1997; Shimberg, 1991; Torrey, 1995; Woolis, 1992.
2. Marsh & Dickens, 1997.
3. Shimberg, 1991, p. 169.
4. Ruocchio, 1997, p. 107.
5. Leete, 1997, p. 102.
6. Deegan, 1997, p. 77.
7. Copeland, 1994.
8. Jamison, 1995, p. 91.
9. Goldstein & Miklowitz, 1994; Miklowitz & Goldstein, 1997.
10. Cronkite, 1994, p. 214.

11. Styron, 1990, p. 84.
12. The Portable Medication Record (PMR) was developed by Victoria Conn and Nancy Edwards, and includes information about drug and food interactions provided by Mary Moller. For further information, contact MONTCO AMI, 100 S. Keswick Ave., Glenside, PA 19038. 215-896-0350
13. For a discussion of medication adherence, see Bentley, Rosenson, & Zito, 1990. One of the best sources of information about new medications is the NAMI newsletter, *The Advocate.*
14. For statistics regarding dual diagnosis, see Regier et al., 1990. For useful discussions of the topic, see Mueser & Gingerich, 1994; Ryglewicz & Pepper, 1996.
15. For discussions of long-term planning, see Mueser & Gingerich, 1994; Russell, Grant, Joseph, & Fee, 1995; Torrey, 1995; Woolis, 1992.
16. Husted, 1994; also see Torrey, 1995, 1997.
17. Many self-help materials are available from New Harbinger Publications, Inc., 5674 Shattuck Ave., Oakland, CA 94609. For trainers, educators, and group leaders, a resource is Whole Person Associates, Inc., 210 West Michigan, Duluth, MN 55802.
18. Resources are listed in Dickens & Marsh, 1994; Marsh & Dickens, 1997; Torrey, 1995. NAMI also has a list of books and other resources for purchase.

Chapter 7

1. Bernheim, 1989.
2. Wynne, McDaniel, & Weber, 1987; Wynne, Weber, & McDaniel, 1986.
3. C. S. Amenson (personal communication, September 14, 1997).
4. For discussions of the distinction between family consultation and family therapy, see Amenson, 1993; Bernheim, 1994a, 1994b; Glynn, Liberman, & Backer, 1997; Wynne et al., 1986. Some of their observations are reflected in Table 7.1.
5. Bernheim, 1994a, p. 148.
6. Bernheim, 1994a.
7. Amenson, 1993.
8. Bernheim, 1994a, 1994b.
9. J. R. Husted (personal communication, October 15, 1997).
10. Reported in Marsh & Johnson, 1997, p. 234.
11. Willick, 1997.
12. Amenson, 1993, 1998a, 1998b.
13. E. Mannion & M. Meisel (personal communication, October 23, 1997).
14. Solomon, Draine, Mannion, & Meisel, 1997.
15. Amenson, 1993.
16. Mueser & Gingerich, 1994; Woolis, 1992.

Chapter 8

1. Solomon, 1996.
2. Amenson, 1993; Dixon & Lehman, 1995; Mueser, 1996.
3. Unpublished data provided by A. B. Hatfield; reported in Marsh, 1995.
4. Abramowitz & Coursey, 1989; Ascher-Svanum, Lafuze, Barrickman, Van Dusen, & Fompa-Loy, 1997; Heller, Roccoforte, Hsieh, Cook, & Cook, 1997; Lefley, 1996; Mannion, Meisel, Solomon, & Draine, 1996.

5. Greenberg, Greenley, & Brown, 1997.
6. Dixon & Lehman, 1995.
7. Bernheim, 1994a, 1994b.
8. Amenson, 1998a, 1998b.
9. Mueser, 1996.
10. Lefley, 1996, p. 141.
11. Burland, 1992, p. 4.
12. Marsh & Dickens, 1997, p. 89.
13. Mueser, 1996.
14. Anderson, Reiss, & Hogarty, 1986.
15. See Marsh, 1992a, for a discussion of 10-week family education programs.
16. Family guides are available for schizophrenia (Mueser & Gingerich, 1994; Torrey, 1995); bipolar disorder (Berger & Berger, 1991); depression (Papolos & Papolos, 1997); and obsessive compulsive disorder (Foa & Wilson, 1991; Gravitz, 1998).
17. See Hatfield, 1990.
18. Marsh, Lefley, Evans-Rhodes, et al., 1996, p. 9.
19. Solomon, 1996.
20. Lefley, 1992.
21. Dixon & Lehman, 1995; also see Lehman, Steinwachs, et al., 1998.
22. Dixon & Lehman, 1995.
23. Falloon, Boyd, & McGill, 1984; Penn & Mueser, 1996.
24. Mueser & Glynn, 1995; also see Mueser, 1996.
25. Mueser & Gingerich, 1994.
26. McFarlane, 1994; McFarlane et al., 1995.
27. Miklowitz & Goldstein, 1997; quote from p. 5. Also see Goldstein & Miklowitz, 1994.
28. Spaniol, Zipple, Marsh, & Finley, 1998.
29. J. Atkinson & Coia, 1995; Bernheim & Lehman, 1985; Bisbee, 1991; Hatfield, 1990, 1994; Lefley & Wasow, 1994.

Chapter 9

1. Marsh & Dickens, 1997, p. 115.
2. For example, see VandenBos, 1996, for the special issue of *American Psychologist* concerned with psychotherapeutic outcomes.
3. *Consumer Reports,* 1995.
4. For discussions of differential therapeutics and therapeutic integration, see Clarkin, Frances, & Perry, 1992; Frances, Clarkin, & Perry, 1984.
5. Thompson, 1990.
6. For example, see Frances et al., 1984; Marsh, 1992a.
7. Marsh, 1992a, p. 204.
8. Howard, Moras, Brill, Martinovich, & Lutz, 1996.
9. Marsh & Dickens, 1997, p. 117.
10. For example, see Lefley & Wasow, 1994.
11. Reported in Marsh & Dickens, 1997.
12. Marsh & Dickens, 1997, p. 108.
13. Marsh & Dickens, 1997, p. 107.
14. For example, see Marsh, 1992a.
15. Marsh, Koeske, Schmidt, Martz, & Redpath, 1997.
16. Marsh & Dickens, 1997, p. 112.
17. Marsh, 1992a.
18. Marsh, 1994a, p. 122.

19. S. Atkinson, 1994; MacGregor, 1994.
20. Marsh, 1992a, p. 209.
21. Marsh & Dickens, 1997, p. 114.
22. See the discussion of negative treatment effects in Marsh, 1992a, 1994b.
23. See Lewis, 1989; also see Thompson, 1990, for a discussion of the principle of least intervention.
24. Marsh, 1992a, p. 212.
25. Marsh & Dickens, 1997, p. 109.
26. Marsh & Dickens, 1997, p. 109.
27. Ammons, 1996.

Chapter 10

1. Bernheim & Lehman, 1985.
2. Carlson, Sperry, & Lewis, 1997.
3. Le Gacy, in press.
4. See *Resident's guide to treatment of people with chronic mental illness*, 1993.
5. Woolis, 1992.
6. Bernheim & Lehman, 1985, p. 175.
7. McDaniel, Hepworth, & Doherty, 1993, p. 62.
8. Lefley, 1996.
9. Bernheim & Lehman, 1985.
10. Bernheim & Lehman, 1985.
11. Snyder, 1994.
12. For discussions of advocacy and system change, see Lefley, 1996; Torrey, 1995, 1997.
13. Hatfield, 1990.
14. Bernheim & Lehman, 1985, p. 187.
15. For discussion of some of the differences among family interventions, see Bernheim, 1994a, 1994b; Lefley, 1996; Marsh & Johnson, 1997; Solomon, 1996.
16. Pickett, Cook, & Laris, 1997.
17. Thompson, 1990.
18. Lewis, 1989.
19. Solomon, 1996.

Chapter 11

1. Wasow, 1995.
2. Marsh & Dickens, 1997, pp. 39–40.
3. Marsh, 1992a, p. 54.
4. Rando, 1986.
5. Deveson, 1992; Wyden, 1998.
6. Marsh, 1992a; quotes from p. 88.
7. Marsh, 1992a, pp. 120–121.
8. Hart, 1989, p. 266.
9. Marlatt, 1988, p. 7.
10. Bombeck, 1997, p. 45.
11. Marsh, 1992a.
12. Bernheim, Lewine, & Beale, 1982.
13. Marsh, 1992a, p. 115.
14. Marsh, 1992a, p. 61.
15. Marsh, 1992a, p. 79.

16. Marsh, 1992a, p. 87.
17. McElroy, 1987.
18. Marsh, 1992a, p. 215.
19. de Beauvoir, 1952, p. 473.
20. In Dally, 1982, p. 19.
21. For example, see Gilligan, 1993.
22. For a discussion of fatherhood and male gender roles, see Lamb, 1996.
23. Lefley, 1987b.
24. Rolland, 1994.
25. Marsh, 1992a, p. 69.
26. Marsh, 1992a, pp. 63–64.
27. Anonymous mother (personal communication, September 15, 1997).
28. Marsh, 1992a, p. 69.
29. Marsh, 1992a, p. 91.
30. Marsh, 1992a, p. 87.
31. Marsh, 1992a, pp. 151–152.
32. Real, 1997.
33. Marsh, 1992a, p. 103.
34. Featherstone, 1980; quote from p. 91.
35. Marsh, 1992a, p. 104; Mittleman, 1985, p. 302.
36. Marsh, 1992a; quotes from p. 122.
37. Marsh, 1992a, p. 185.
38. Greenberg, Greenley, McKee, Brown, & Griffin-Francell, 1993.
39. Marsh, 1992a; quotes from pp. 105, 107.
40. Chess, 1982, p. 96.
41. Marsh, 1992a, p. 19.
42. Marsh, 1992a, p. 166.
43. Marsh, 1994a, p. 108.
44. For a discussion of "mother blaming" in professional journals, see Caplan & Hall-McCorquodale, 1985.
45. Marsh, 1992a, p. 22.
46. Marsh, 1992a, p. 174.
47. Marsh, 1992a, p. 16.
48. Marsh, 1992a, p. 2.
49. Marsh, 1992a, p. 5.
50. Marsh, 1992a, p. 2.

Chapter 12

1. Demographic information from *DSM-IV*, American Psychiatric Association, 1994.
2. Lefley, 1996.
3. Spouses who commented in an early this chapter include Kathy Bayes and members of her support group, Penny Frese, Rita Packard, and several anonymous spouses. Quote from anonymous spouse (personal communication, October 31, 1997).
4. Wasow, 1995; also see Clausen & Yarrow, 1955; Gibbons, Horn, Powell, & Gibbons, 1984; Hooley, 1987.
5. Judge, 1994.
6. Mannion, 1996; The Well Spouse Foundation in San Diego estimates that 7 to 9 million spouses are living with partners who have serious mental illness (cited in Wasow, 1995).
7. Anonymous spouse (personal communication, November 10, 1997).

8. See Bernheim, Lewine, & Beale, 1982; Judge, 1994; Mannion, 1996; Wasow, 1995. Their work has contributed significantly to this chapter. For discussions of spousal burden, see Fadden, Bebbington, & Kuipers, 1987; Noh & Avison, 1988; Targum, Dibble, Davenport, & Gershon, 1981. Also see Strong, 1988, for a discussion of the spousal experience of chronic illness.
9. Naylor, 1977; quotes from pp. 102, 109, 204.
10. Graham, 1997; quote from p. 356.
11. Rice, 1994; also see Anonymous, 1994.
12. Mannion, 1998.
13. Bayes, 1997.
14. F. Frese & Frese, 1991.
15. Lefley 1987a.
16. Marsh, Lefley, Evans-Rhodes, et al., 1996, p. 10.
17. Judge, 1994.
18. Rando, 1984.
19. Judge, 1994.
20. Wasow, 1995, p. 72.
21. Rando, 1984.
22. Glick, Weiss, & Parkes, 1974.
23. P. Frese, 1996a, 1996b; quotes from pp. 53, 55.
24. Judge, 1994.
25. For discussions of spousal separation and divorce, see Judge, 1994; Mannion, 1996; Wasow, 1995.
26. Wasow, 1995; quote from p. 73.
27. Secunda, 1997.
28. Secunda, 1997.
29. Packard, 1992.
30. Anonymous spouse (personal communication, November 15, 1997).
31. Mannion, 1998.
32. Mannion, 1996, p. 17.
33. Packard, 1992.
34. Mannion, 1996, p. 18.
35. Packard, 1992.
36. Bayes, 1997; Mannion & Meisel, 1993.
37. Mannion, 1996, p. 17.
38. Bayes, 1997.
39. Quote from Mannion, 1998.
40. Quote from Mannion, 1998.
41. Mannion, 1996, p. 17.
42. Anonymous spouse (personal communication, October 31, 1997).
43. Mannion, 1996; quote from p. 16.
44. Judge, 1994; Mannion, 1996.
45. Anonymous spouse (personal communication, October 31, 1997).
46. For discussions of marital issues, see Judge, 1994; Mannion, 1996; Wasow, 1995.
47. Wasow, 1995.
48. Secunda, 1997.
49. Bayes, 1997.
50. Anonymous spouse (personal communication, October 31, 1997).
51. Hooley, 1987; Judge, 1994.
52. Mannion, 1996, p. 15.
53. Anonymous spouse (personal communication, October 31, 1997).
54. Bayes, 1997.
55. Mannion, 1996, p. 17.

56. Anonymous spouse (personal communication, October 22, 1997).
57. For discussion of social isolation, see Judge, 1994; Mannion, 1996; Wasow, 1995.
58. Anonymous spouse (personal communication, November 10, 1997).
59. Wasow, 1995, p. 69.
60. Wasow, 1995.
61. Anonymous spouse (personal communication, December 2, 1997).
62. See Judge, 1994, for a discussion of some of these spousal needs, as well as implications for intervention.
63. Anonymous spouse (personal communication, December 2, 1997).
64. Anonymous spouse (personal communication, October 31, 1997).
65. Anonymous spouse (personal communication, October 31, 1997).
66. Mannion (personal communication, December 4, 1997).
67. Mannion, Mueser, & Solomon, 1994.
68. Anonymous spouse (personal communication, October 31, 1997).
69. Anonymous spouse (personal communication, November 10, 1997).
70. Bayes, 1997.
71. Mannion (personal communication, December 4, 1997); also see Hulson, 1992.

Chapter 13

1. Our research was reported in Marsh & Dickens, 1997; Marsh, Dickens, et al., 1997.
2. Marsh & Dickens, 1997, p. 47.
3. Dickens & Marsh, 1994.
4. For representative studies, see Beardslee, Wright, Salt, & Drezner, 1997; Erlenmeyer-Kimling & Cornblatt, 1992; Maier, 1996.
5. For discussions of genetic risks, see Gottesman, 1991; Miklowitz & Goldstein, 1997.
6. For example, Radke-Yarrow, Nottelmann, Martinez, Fox, & Belmont, 1992; Thaker, Adami, Moran, Lahti, & Cassady, et al., 1993; Walker & Downey, 1990.
7. For example, Fendrich, Warner, & Weissman, 1990; Landerman, George, & Blazer, 1991; Tienari & Wynne, 1994.
8. Marsh & Dickens, 1997, p. 35.
9. Marsh & Dickens, 1997, p. 65.
10. Gallo, 1988.
11. See Powell & Gallagher, 1993, p. xiii, for a discussion of these issue in connection with sibling disability.
12. Marsh & Dickens, 1997, p. 45.
13. Marsh & Dickens, 1997, p. 41.
14. For general discussions of sibling relationships, see Bank & Kahn, 1997; Boer & Dunn, 1992; Klagsbrun, 1993.
15. Moorman, 1992; Neugeboren, 1997; C. Simon, 1997b; Swados, 1991.
16. Neugeboren, 1997; quotes from pp. 5, 165, 252.
17. C. Simon, 1997b; quote from p. 2.
18. Marsh & Dickens, 1997; Dickens & Marsh, 1994.
19. For sibling issue, see D. Weisburd, 1992. For family-oriented books see Carlisle, 1984; J. Johnson, 1988; Mueser & Gingerich, 1994; Secunda, 1997; Torrey, 1995; M. Walsh, 1985; Wasow, 1995; Woolis, 1992. For early articles see Hoover & Franz, 1972; Lidz, Fleck, Alanen, & Cornelison, 1963; Meissner, 1970; Pollack, Woerner, Goldberg, & Klein, 1969; Samuels & Chase, 1979; Stabenau, Turpin, Werner, & Pollin, 1965. For professional articles and

books, see Downey & Coyne, 1990; Gerace, Camilleri, & Ayres, 1993; Greenberg, Kim, & Greenley, 1997; Horwitz, Tessler, Fisher, & Gamache, 1992; Judge, 1994; Kendler, Karkowski, & Walsh, 1996; Landeen et al., 1992; Main, Gerace, & Camilleri, 1993; Marsh, 1992a; Riebschleger, 1991.

20. Riebschleger, 1991.
21. Goode, 1989, p. 63.
22. S. Weisburd, 1992, p. 13.
23. Wasow, 1995.
24. Neugeboren, 1997, p. 245.
25. Kelley, 1992, p. 28.
26. C. Simon, 1997b, p. 9.
27. Marsh & Dickens, 1997, p. 55.
28. Wasow, 1995.
29. For a discussion of the "replacement child syndrome" in biological death, see Poznanski, 1972.
30. For a discussion of similar issues in mental retardation, see Powell & Gallagher, 1993; in mental illness, see Leder, 1991.
31. Marsh & Dickens, 1997, p. 57.
32. Marsh & Dickens, 1997, p. 55.
33. Marsh & Dickens, 1997, p. 57.
34. Marsh & Dickens, 1997, p. 58.
35. Marsh & Dickens, 1997, p. 76.
36. Marsh & Dickens, 1997; quotes from pp. 77, 82.
37. Marsh & Dickens, 1997, p. 73.
38. Marsh & Dickens, 1997, p. 73.
39. Marsh & Dickens, 1997, p. 53.
40. Marsh & Dickens, 1997, p. 52.
41. Marsh & Dickens, 1997, p. 71.
42. Marsh & Dickens, 1997, pp. 73–74.
43. Marsh & Dickens, 1997, p. 73.
44. Marsh & Dickens, 1997, p. 59.
45. Marsh & Dickens, 1997, p. 57.
46. Marsh & Dickens, 1997, p. 81.
47. Marsh & Dickens, 1997, p. 82.
48. Marsh & Dickens, 1997, p. 80.
49. Marsh, 1992a, p. 127.
50. Marsh & Dickens, 1997, p. 62.
51. Marsh & Dickens, 1997, p. 86.
52. Marsh & Dickens, 1997, p. 83.
53. Marsh & Dickens, 1997, p. 84.
54. C. Simon, 1997a, p. C4.
55. Marsh & Dickens, 1997, p. 133.
56. Wasow, 1995.
57. Marsh & Dickens, 1997, p. 134.
58. Marsh & Dickens, 1997, p. 91.
59. Marsh & Dickens, 1997, p. 120.
60. Anonymous adult offspring (personal communication, November 10, 1997).
61. Kelley, 1992, p. 28.
62. Henderson, 1994; Swartz & Little, 1996.
63. Marsh & Dickens, 1997, Appendix C.
64. Secunda, 1997.
65. Marsh & Dickens, 1997, p. 107.
66. Rodman, 1986, p. 181.
67. Gravitz, 1998.

Chapter 14

1. Marsh & Dickens, 1997, p. 46.
2. For example, Downey & Coyne, 1990; Silverman, 1989.
3. Marsh & Dickens, 1997; quotes from p. 42.
4. For representative publications, see Anthony & Cohler, 1987; Beardslee, Bemporad, Keller, & Klerman, 1983; Gizynski, 1985; Goodman, 1987; Reid & Morrison, 1983; Weissman et al., 1984.
5. Atkins, 1992; DeChillo, Matorin, & Hallahan, 1987; Downey & Coyne, 1990; Guttman, 1989; B. Klein, 1990; LaRoche, 1989; Oates, 1997; Seifer et al., 1996; Silverman, 1989.
6. For example, Silverman, 1989.
7. For example, Guttman, 1989; B. Klein, 1990; Atkins, 1992.
8. Brown, 1989.
9. Holley & Holley, 1997; Karr, 1995; Lyden, 1997; Olson, 1994; Paterson, 1996; Sexton, 1994.
10. Olson, 1994, pp. 1, 6.
11. Lyden, 1997, pp. 18–19.
12. Dickens & Marsh, 1994; Marsh & Dickens, 1997. Also see Judge, 1994; Lefley & Wasow, 1994; Lucas & Seiden, 1997; Marsh, 1992a; Mueser & Gingerich, 1994; Secunda, 1997; Torrey, 1995; M. Walsh, 1985; Wasow, 1995; D. Weisburd, 1996; Woolis, 1992.
13. Marsh & Dickens, 1997.
14. For example, see Rutter, 1981.
15. Bruce, 1996, p. 15.
16. Marsh & Dickens, 1997, p. 40.
17. Bruce, 1996, p. 15.
18. Murty, 1996.
19. Marsh, 1992a, p. 66.
20. Marsh & Dickens, 1997, p. 24.
21. Larson, 1996, p. 23.
22. Anthony, 1975, p. 290; also see Guttman, 1989.
23. Marsh & Dickens, 1997, p. 32.
24. Bruce, 1996, p. 15.
25. Gavin, 1996, p. 19.
26. Oakes, 1996, pp. 42–43.
27. Marsh, 1992a, pp. 130–131.
28. Marsh & Dickens, 1997, p. 62.
29. Marsh & Dickens, 1997, p. 70.
30. Marsh & Dickens, 1997, p. 56.
31. Marsh & Dickens, 1997, p. 58.
32. Marsh & Dickens, 1997, p. 77.
33. Marsh & Dickens, 1997, p. 76.
34. Marsh & Dickens, 1997, p. 37.
35. Marsh & Dickens, 1997, p. 52.
36. Marsh & Dickens, 1997, p. 49.
37. Marsh & Dickens, 1997, p. 59.
38. For example, Sturges, 1977, 1978.
39. Marsh & Dickens, 1997, p. 54.
40. Marsh & Dickens, 1997, pp. 51–52.
41. Marsh, 1992a, p. 131.
42. Marsh & Dickens, 1997, p. 51.
43. Marsh & Dickens, 1997, p. 49.
44. Marsh & Dickens, 1997, p. 53.

45. Marsh & Dickens, 1997, p. 72.
46. Marsh & Dickens, 1997, p. 78.
47. Anthony, 1975, p. 290.
48. Bruce, 1996, p. 15.
49. List, 1996, p. 37.
50. Marsh & Dickens, 1997, p. 74.
51. Marsh & Dickens, 1997, p. 75.
52. Marsh & Dickens, 1997, p. 79.
53. Marsh & Dickens, 1997, p. 67.
54. Marsh & Dickens, 1997, p. 80.
55. Marsh & Dickens, 1997, pp. 81–82.
56. Marsh & Dickens, 1997, p. 83.
57. Marsh & Dickens, 1997, p. 15.
58. Marsh & Dickens, 1997, p. 81; for a discussion of relational problems among childhood caregivers, see Valleau, Bergner, & Horton, 1995.
59. Marsh & Dickens, 1997, p. 85.
60. Marsh & Dickens, 1997, p. 85.
61. Marsh & Dickens, 1997, p. 85.
62. Bruce, 1996, p. 13.
63. Marsh & Dickens, 1997, p. 60.
64. Marsh & Dickens, 1997, p. 80.
65. Dickens, 1996, p. 49.
66. Kinsella, 1996, p. 58.
67. Marsh & Dickens, 1997, p. 86.
68. Wasow, 1995, p. 14.
69. Marsh & Dickens, 1997, p. 19.
70. Wasow, 1995, p. 16.
71. Marsh & Dickens, 1997, p. 108.
72. Marsh & Dickens, 1997, p. 148.
73. Nicholson, 1996.
74. Spiese, 1996, p. 51.
75. Marsh & Dickens, 1997, p. 100.
76. Kinsella, Anderson, & Anderson, 1996.
77. Larson, 1996, p. 25.
78. Marsh & Dickens, 1997, Appendix C.
79. Secunda, 1997.
80. Ogren, 1996.
81. Marsh, 1992a, pp. 131–132.
82. Rodman, 1986, pp. 28, 187.
83. DeChillo et al., 1987.
84. LaRoche, 1989.
85. DeChillo et al., 1987.
86. Marsh & Dickens, 1997, p. 162.

Chapter 15

1. For example, contact Christopher S. Amenson, PhD, Director, Pacific Clinics Institute, 909 S. Fair Oaks Ave., Pasadena, CA 91105.
2. For information about the Three R's Program, contact Mary D. Moller, MSN, ARNP, CS, CEO, Psychiatric Rehabilitation Nurses, Inc., 12204 West Sunridge Drive, Nine Mile Falls, WA 99026.
3. Moller & Murphy, 1997.

4. For information about Supportive Family Training, contact Sheila Shulman Le Gacy, MA, Director, Family Support and Education Center, Transitional Living Services of Onondaga County, Inc., 239 W. Fayette St., Syracuse, NY 13202.

5. For information about the MESA model of family education, contact the Thomasine Cubine, LCSW, Director, Office of Consumer and Family Affairs, Comprehensive Mental Health Services, Pembroke Six, Suite 208, Virginia Beach, VA 23462.

6. Cubine, Bentley, Poe, & McCafferty, 1996.

7. For information about the T.E.C. Network Coping Skills Workshops (Meisel & Mannion, 1990) and the Spouse Coping Skills Workshops (Mannion & Meisel, 1993), contact Edie Mannion, MFT, and Marilyn Meisel, Directors, Training and Education Center Network, c/o Mental Health Association of Southeastern Pennsylvania, 1211 Chestnut Street (11th floor), Philadelphia, PA 19107.

8. Solomon, Draine, Mannion, & Meisel, 1996a, 1996b.

9. Mannion, Draine, Solomon, & Meisel, 1998.

10. Mannion, Mueser, & Solomon, 1994.

11. For a list of books and resources for young family members, see Dickens & Marsh, 1994; Marsh & Dickens, 1997.

12. For information about the S.O.S. Program, affiliated with NAMI of Ohio, contact Project S.O.S., P. O. Box 766, Berea, OH 44017.

13. For information about BART's Place, contact Janice G. Katz, MS, Northcoast Behavioral Healthcare System, North Campus, 1708 Southpoint Drive, Cleveland, OH 44109.

References

Abramowitz, I. A., & Coursey, R. D. (1989). Impact of an educational support group on family participants who take care of their schizophrenic relatives. *Journal of Consulting and Clinical Psychology, 57,* 232–236.

Amenson, C. S. (1993). *Education, consultation and treatment of families with a mentally ill member: A guide for effective professional intervention.* Pasadena, CA: Pacific Clinics Institute.

Amenson, C. S. (1998a). *Schizophrenia: A family education curriculum.* Pasadena, CA: Pacific Clinics Institute.

Amenson, C. S. (1998b). *Schizophrenia: Family education methods.* Pasadena, CA: Pacific Clinics Institute.

American Psychiatric Association. (1994). *Diagnostic and statistical manual of mental disorders* (4th ed.). Washington, DC: Author.

American Psychological Association. (1992). Ethical principles of psychologists and code of conduct. *American Psychologist, 47,* 1597–1611.

Ammons, D. (1996). It didn't need to happen! *The JOURNAL of the California Alliance for the Mentally Ill, 7*(3), 11–12.

Anderson, C. M., Reiss, D. J., & Hogarty, G. E. (1986). *Schizophrenia and the family.* New York: Guilford Press.

Andreasen, N. C. (1994). (Ed.). *Schizophrenia: From mind to molecule.* Washington, DC: American Psychiatric Press.

Anonymous. (1994). First person account: Life with a mentally ill spouse. *Schizophrenia Bulletin, 20,* 227–229.

Anthony, E. J. (1975). The influence of a manic-depressive environment on the developing child. In E. J. Anthony & T. Benedek (Eds.), *Depression and human existence* (pp. 279–315). Boston: Little, Brown.

Anthony, E. J., & Cohler, B. J. (Eds.). (1987). *The invulnerable child.* New York: Guilford Press.

Antonovsky, A., & Sourani, T. (1988). Family sense of coherence and family adaptation. *Journal of Marriage and the Family, 50,* 79–92.

Ascher-Svanum, H., Lafuze, J. E., Barrickman, P. J., Van Dusen, C., & Fompa-Loy, J. (1997). Educational needs of families of mentally ill adults. *Psychiatric Services, 48,* 1072–1074.

Ascher-Svanum, H., & Sobel, T. S. (1989). Caregivers of mentally ill adults: A woman's agenda. *Hospital and Community Psychiatry, 40,* 843–845.

Atkins, F. D. (1992). An uncertain future: Children of mentally ill parents. *Journal of Psychosocial Nursing, 30,* 13–16.

Atkinson, J. M., & Coia, D. A. (1995). *Families coping with schizophrenia: A practitioner's guide to family groups.* New York: Wiley.

Atkinson, S. D. (1994). Grieving and loss in parents with a schizophrenia child. *American Journal of Psychiatry, 151,* 1137–1139.

Backlar, P. (1994). *The family face of schizophrenia.* New York: Tarcher/Putnam.

Bandura, A. (1990). Conclusion: Reflections on nonability determinants of competence. In R. J. Sternberg & J. Kolligian (Eds.), *Competence considered* (pp. 315–362). New Haven, CT: Yale University Press.

Bank, S. P., & Kahn, M. D. (1997). *The sibling bond.* New York: Basic Books.

Bateson, M. (1990). *Composing a life.* New York: Atlantic Monthly.

Bayes, K. A. (1997, July). *Meeting the needs of spouses.* Presentation at the annual meeting of NAMI, Albuquerque, NM.

Beardslee, W. R., Bemporad, J., Keller, M. B., & Klerman, G. L. (1983). Children of parents with major affective disorder: A review. *American Journal of Psychiatry, 140*, 825–832.

Beardslee, W. R., Wright, E. J., Salt, P., & Drezner, K. (1997). Examination of children's responses to two preventive intervention strategies over time. *Journal of the American Academy of Child and Adolescent Psychiatry, 36*, 196–204.

Beavers, W. R., & Hampson, R. B. (1990). *Successful families.* New York: Norton.

Bedell, J. R., Hunter, R. H., & Corrigan, P. W. (1997). Current approaches to assessment and treatment of persons with serious mental illness. *Professional Psychology: Research and Practice, 28*, 217–228.

Begler, A. L. (1997). Legal issues in professional practice with families. In D. T. Marsh & R. D. Magee (Eds.), *Ethical and legal issues in professional practice with families* (pp. 27–49). New York: Wiley.

Bentley, K. J., Rosenson, M. K., & Zito, J. M. (1990). Promoting medication compliance: Strategies for working with families of mentally ill people. *Social Work, 35*, 274–277.

Bentley, K. J., & Walsh, J. M. (1996). *The social worker & psychotropic medication: Toward effective collaboration with mental health clients, families, and providers.* Pacific Grove, CA: Brooks/Cole.

Berger, D., & Berger, L. (1991). *We heard the angels of madness: One family's struggle with manic depression.* New York: Morrow.

Berman, A. L., & Cohen-Sandler, R. (1983). Suicide and malpractice: Expert testimony and the standard of care. *Professional Psychology: Research and Practice, 14*, 6–19.

Bernheim, K. F. (1989). Psychologists and families of the severely mentally ill: The role of family consultation. *American Psychologist, 44*, 561–564.

Bernheim, K. F. (1994a). Determining and implementing the family service plan. In H. Lefley & M. Wasow (Eds.), *Helping families cope with mental illness* (pp. 147–160). Newark: Harwood Academic.

Bernheim, K. F. (1994b). Skills and strategies for working with families. In D. T. Marsh (Ed.), *New directions in the psychological treatment of serious mental illness* (pp. 186–198). Westport, CT: Praeger.

Bernheim, K. F., & Lehman, A. F. (1985). *Working with families of the mentally ill.* New York: Norton.

Bernheim, K. F., Lewine, R. R. J., & Beale, C. T. (1982). *The caring family: Living with chronic mental illness.* Chicago: Contemporary Books.

Biegel, D. E., Milligan, S. E., Putnarn, P. L., & Song, L. (1994). Predictors of burden among lower socioeconomic status caregivers of persons with chronic mental illness. *Community Mental Health Journal, 30*, 473–494.

Bisbee, C. (1991). *Educating patients and families about mental illness: A practical guide.* Gaithersburg, MD: Aspen.

Boer, F., & Dunn, J. F. (Eds.). (1992). *Children's sibling relationships: Developmental and clinical issues.* Hillsdale, NJ: Erlbaum.

Bombeck, E. (1997). *Forever, Erma: Best-loved writing from America's favorite humorist.* Kansas City, MO: Andrews McMeel.

Brown, E. M. (1989). *My parent's keeper: Adult children of the emotionally disturbed.* Oakland, CA: New Harbinger.

Bruce, D. (1996). Thoughts about my mother. *The JOURNAL of the California Alliance for the Mentally Ill, 7*(3), 13–15.

Burland, J. (1992, June). On our own: A report on the final results of AMI-Vermont's first family education program. *Alliance for the Mentally Ill of Vermont, 25*, pp. 1, 4.

Caplan, P. J., & Hall-McCorquodale, I. (1985). Mother-blaming in major clinical journals. *American Journal of Orthopsychiatry, 55,* 345–353.

Carlisle, W. (1984). *Siblings of the mentally ill.* Saratoga, CA: R & E.

Carlson, J., Sperry, L., & Lewis, J. A. (1997). *Family therapy: Ensuring treatment efficacy.* Pacific Grove, CA: Brooks/Cole.

Carpentier, N., Lesage, A., Goulet, J., Lalonde, P., & Renaud, M. (1992). Burden of care for families not living with young schizophrenic relatives. *Hospital & Community Psychiatry, 43,* 38–43.

Carr, A. (1990). Failure in family therapy: A catalogue of engagement mistakes. *Journal of Family Therapy, 12,* 371–386.

Carter, B., & McGoldrick, M. (Eds.). (1988). *The changing family life cycle* (2nd ed.). New York: Gardner Press.

Center for Mental Health Services Managed Care Initiative: Adult Panel. (1997). *Core competencies for mental health providers.* Rockville, MD: Center for Mental Health Studies, SAMHSA.

Chesla, C. A. (1989). Parents' illness models of schizophrenia. *Archives of Psychiatric Nursing, 3,* 218–225.

Chess, S. (1982). The "blame the mother" ideology. *International Journal of Mental Health, 11,* 95–107.

Clark, R. E. (1994). Family costs associated with severe mental illness and substance use. *Hospital & Community Psychiatry, 45,* 808–813.

Clarkin, J. F., Frances, A., & Perry, S. (1992). Differential therapeutics: Macro and micro levels of treatment planning. In J. C. Norcross & M. R. Goldfried (Eds.), *Handbook of psychotherapy integration* (pp. 463–502). New York: Basic Books.

Clausen, J. A., & Yarrow, M. R. (Eds.). (1955). The impact of mental illness on the family [Special issue]. *Journal of Social Issues, 11*(4).

Consumer Reports. (1995, November). Mental health: Does therapy help? *Consumer Reports,* pp. 734–739.

Cook, J. A. (1988). Who "mothers" the chronically mentally ill? *Family Relations, 37,* 42–49.

Cook, J. A., Lefley, H. P., Pickett, S. A., & Cohler, B. J. (1994). Age and family burden among parents of offspring with severe mental illness. *American Journal of Orthopsychiatry, 64,* 435–447.

Copeland, M. E. (1994). *Living without depression and manic depression: A workbook for maintaining mood stability.* Oakland, CA: New Harbinger.

Coursey, R. D., Alford, J., & Safarjan, B. (1997). Significant advances in understanding and treating serious mental illness. *Professional Psychology: Research and Practice, 28,* 205–216.

Cronkite, K. (1994). *On the edge of darkness.* New York: Doubleday.

Cross, T. L., Bazron, B. J., Dennis, K. W., & Isaacs, M. R. (1989). *Towards a culturally competent system of care.* Washington, DC: National Technical Assistance Center for Children's Mental Health, Georgetown University.

Cubine, T., Bentley, K. J., Poe, J., & McCafferty, P. T. (1996, July). *The MESA model of family education: Virginia's experience in enhancing collaboration between families and professionals.* Presented at the annual meeting of the National Alliance for the Mentally Ill, Nashville, TN.

Dally, A. (1982). *Inventing motherhood: The consequences of an ideal.* New York: Schocken.

de Beauvoir, S. (1952). *The second sex.* New York: Bantam Books.

DeChillo, N., Matorin, S., & Hallahan, C. (1987). Children of psychiatric patients: Rarely seen or heard. *Health and Social Work, 12,* 296–302.

Deegan, P. E. (1997). Recovery as a journey of the heart. In L. Spaniol, C. Gagne, & M. Koehler (Eds.), *Psychological and social aspects of psychiatric disability* (pp. 74–83). Boston: Boston University Center for Psychiatric Rehabilitation.

Deveson, A. (1992). *Tell me I'm here: One family's experience of schizophrenia.* New York: Penguin Books.

Dickens, R. (1996). Looking-glass house. *The JOURNAL of the California Alliance for the Mentally Ill, 7*(3), 47–49.

Dickens, R. M., & Marsh, D. T. (Eds.). (1994). *Anguished voices: Personal accounts of siblings and children.* Boston: Boston University Center for Psychiatric Rehabilitation.

Dixon, L. B., & Lehman A. F. (1995). Family interventions for schizophrenia. *Schizophrenia Bulletin, 21,* 631–643.

Doornbos, M. M. (1996). The strengths of families coping with serious mental illness. *Archives of Psychiatric Nursing, 10,* 214–220.

Downey, G., & Coyne, J. C. (1990). Children of depressed parents: An integrative review. *Psychological Bulletin, 108,* 50–76.

Dunst, C. J., Trivette, C. M., & Deal, A. G. (Eds.). (1994). *Supporting and strengthening families. Vol. 1: Methods, strategies and practices.* Cambridge, MA: Brookline Books.

Erlenmeyer-Kimling, L., & Cornblatt, B. A. (1992). A summary of attentional findings in the New York High-Risk Project [Special issue: Genetics and gene expression in mental illness]. *Journal of Psychiatric Research, 26,* 405–426.

Fadden, G., Bebbington, P., & Kuipers, L. (1987). Caring and its burdens: A study of the spouses of depressed patients. *British Journal of Psychiatry, 151,* 660–667.

Falloon, I. R. H., Boyd, J. L., & McGill, C. W. (1984). *Family care of schizophrenia.* New York: Guilford Press.

Featherstone, H. (1980). *A difference in the family: Living with a disabled child.* New York: Penguin Books.

Fendrich, M., Warner, V., & Weissman, M. M. (1990). Family risk factors, parental depression, and psychopathology in offspring. *Developmental Psychology, 26,* 40–50.

Figley, C. R. (1989). *Helping traumatized families.* San Francisco: Jossey-Bass.

Fink, P. J. (1988). Response to the Presidential Address: Is "biopsychosocial" the psychiatric shibboleth? *American Journal of Psychiatry, 145,* 1061–1067.

Fink, P. J., & Tasman, A. (Eds.). (1992). *Stigma and mental illness.* Washington, DC: American Psychiatric Press.

Finley, L. (1997). The multiple effects of culture and ethnicity on psychiatric disability. In L. Spaniol, C. Gagne, & M. Koehler (Eds.), *Psychological and social aspects of psychiatric disability* (pp. 497–510). Boston: Boston University Center for Psychiatric Rehabilitation.

Finley, L. Y. (1998). The cultural context: Families coping with psychiatric disability. In L. Spaniol, A. M. Zipple, D. T. Marsh, & L. Finley (Eds.), *The role of the family in psychiatric rehabilitation.* Boston: Boston University Center for Psychiatric Rehabilitation.

Flach, F. (1988). *Resilience: Discovering a new strength at times of stress.* New York: Fawcett Columbine.

Flory, C. B., & Friedrich, R. M. (1997). Why do individuals with severe mental illness die before their time? *The CAMI Statement:Voice of the California Alliance for the Mentally Ill, 17*(3), pp. 1, 3.

Flynn, L. M. (1992). NAMI member survey offers advocacy tool. *NAMI Advocate, 3*(2), p. 12.

Foa, E. B., & Wilson, R. (1991). *Stop obsessing! How to overcome your obsessions and compulsions.* New York: Bantam Books.

Forman, S. G. (1993). *Coping skills interventions for children and adolescents.* San Francisco: Jossey-Bass.

Frances, A., Clarkin, J., & Perry, S. (1984). *Differential therapeutics in psychiatry: The art and science of treatment selection.* New York: Brunner/Mazel.

Frances, A., Docherty, J. P., & Kahn, D. A. (1996). Treatment of schizophrenia. *Journal of Clinical Psychiatry, 57*(Suppl. 12B), 5–58.

Frese, F. J. (1994). Psychology's role in a consumer-driven system. In D. T. Marsh (Ed.), *New directions in the psychological treatment of serious mental illness* (pp. 79–98). Westport, CT: Praeger.

Frese, F. J., & Frese, P. (1991). *Part 1: Schizophrenia: Surviving in a world of normals. Part 2: A love story: Living with someone with schizophrenia.* Beachwood, OH: Wellness Reproductions.

Frese, P. (1996a). Family life and mental illness: Making it work. *The JOURNAL of the California Alliance for the Mentally Ill, 7*(3), 52–54.

Frese, P. (1996b). When Daddy gets sick: Helping kids cope. *The JOURNAL of the California Alliance for the Mentally Ill, 7*(3), 54–55.

Friedman, R. M., Katz-Leavy, J. W., Manderscheid, R. W., & Sondheimer, D. L. (1996). Prevalence of serious emotional disturbance in children and adolescents. In R. W. Manderscheid & M. A. Sonnenschein (Eds.), *Mental health, United States, 1996* (pp. 71–89) (DHHS Publication No. SMA 96-3098). Washington, DC: U.S. Government Printing Office.

Gallagher, S. K., & Mechanic, D. (1996). Living with the mentally ill: Effects on the health and functioning of other household members. *Social Science and Medicine, 42,* 1691–1701.

Gallo, A. M. (1988). The special sibling relationship in chronic illness and disability: Parental communication with well siblings. *Holistic Nursing Practice, 2,* 28–37.

Gavin, T. (1996). The eternal dilemma continues. *The JOURNAL of the California Alliance for the Mentally Ill, 7*(3), 19–20.

Gazarik, R., & Acton, R. (1997, November 2). Journey into madness: Dead man's family blames system for failing mentally ill son. *Sunday Tribune-Review,* A1, 10.

Gerace, L. M., Camilleri, D., & Ayres, L. (1993). Sibling perspectives on schizophrenia and the family. *Schizophrenia Bulletin, 19,* 637–647.

Gibbons, J. S., Horn, S. H., Powell, J. M., & Gibbons, J. L. (1984). Schizophrenic patients and their families: A survey in a psychiatric service based on a DGH unit. *British Journal of Psychiatry, 44,* 70–77.

Gilligan, C. (1993). *In a different voice: Psychological theory and women's development.* Cambridge, MA: Harvard University Press.

Gizynski, M. N. (1985). The effects of maternal depression on children. *Clinical Social Work Journal, 13,* 103–116.

Glick, I. O., Weiss, R. S., & Parkes, C. M. (1974). *The first year of bereavement.* New York: Wiley.

Glynn, S. M., Liberman, R. P., & Backer, T. E. (1997). *Involving families in mental health services: Competencies for mental health workers.* Northridge, CA: Human Interaction Research Institute.

Goldstein, M. J., & Miklowitz, D. J. (1994). Family intervention for persons with bipolar disorder. In A. B. Hatfield (Ed.), *Family interventions in mental illness* (New Directions for Mental Health Services, No. 62, pp. 23–35). San Francisco: Jossey-Bass.

Goode, E. E. (1989, April 24). When mental illness hits home. *U.S. News & World Report,* pp. 55–57, 60, 62–65.

Goodman, S. H. (1987). Emory University project on children of disturbed parents. *Schizophrenia Bulletin, 13,* 411–423.

Goodwin, F. K., & Jamison, K. R. (1990). *Manic depressive illness.* New York: Oxford University Press.

Gorman, J. M. (1995). *The essential guide to psychiatric drugs.* New York: St. Martin's Press.

Gottesman, I. I. (1991). *Schizophrenia genesis: The origins of madness.* New York: Freeman.

Gottlieb, M. C. (1996). Some ethical implications of relational diagnoses. In F. W. Kaslow (Ed.), *Handbook of relational diagnosis and dysfunctional family patterns* (pp. 19–34). New York: Wiley.

Graham, K. (1997). *Personal history.* New York: Knopf.

Gravitz, H. L. (1998). *Obsessive compulsive disorder: New help for the family.* Santa Barbara, CA: Healing Visions Press.

Greenberg, J. S., Greenley, J. R., & Benedict, P. (1994). Contributions of persons with serious mental illness to their families. *Hospital & Community Psychiatry, 45,* 475–480.

Greenberg, J. S., Greenley, J. R., & Brown, R. (1997). Do mental health services reduce distress in families of people with serious mental illness. *Psychiatric Rehabilitation Journal, 21*(1), 40–50.

Greenberg, J. S., Greenley, J. R., McKee, D., Brown, R., & Griffin-Francell, C. (1993). Mothers caring for an adult child with schizophrenia: The effects of subjective burden on maternal health. *Family Relations, 42,* 205–211.

Greenberg, J. S., Kim, H. W., & Greenley, J. R. (1997). Factors associated with subjective burden in siblings of adults with severe mental illness. *American Journal of Orthopsychiatry, 67,* 231–241.

Group for the Advancement of Psychiatry. (1993). *Resident's guide to treatment of people with chronic mental illness* (Report No. 136). Washington, DC: American Psychiatric Press.

Grunebaum, H., & Friedman, H. (1988). Building collaborative relationships with families of the mentally ill. *Hospital and Community Psychiatry, 29,* 1183–1187.

Guarnaccia, P. J., & Parra, P. (1996). Ethnicity, social status, and families' experiences of caring for a mentally ill family member. *Community Mental Health Journal, 32,* 243–260.

Gutheil, T. G., Bursztajn, H., & Brodsky, A. (1984). Malpractice prevention through the sharing of uncertainty: Informed consent in the therapeutic alliance. *New England Journal of Medicine, 311,* 49–51.

Guttman, H. A. (1989). Children in families with emotionally disturbed parents. In L. Combrinck-Graham (Ed.), *Children in family contexts: Perspectives on treatment* (pp. 252–276). New York: Guilford Press.

Hanson, J. G. (1993). Families of people with a severe mental illness: Role conflict, ambiguity and family burden. *Journal of Sociology & Social Welfare, 20,* 105–118.

Hanson, J. G. (1995). Families' perceptions of psychiatric hospitalization of relatives with a severe mental illness. *Administration & Policy in Mental Health, 22,* 531–541.

Hanson, J. G., & Rapp, C. A. (1992). Families' perceptions of community mental health programs for their relatives with a severe mental illness. *Community Mental Health Journal, 28,* 181–197.

Harding, C. M., Zubin, J., & Strauss, J. S. (1992). Chronicity in schizophrenia: Revisited. *British Journal of Psychiatry, 161,* 27–37.

Hart, C. (1989). *Without reason: A family copes with two generations of autism.* New York: Harper & Row.

Hatfield, A. B. (1990). *Family education in mental illness.* New York: Guilford Press.

Hatfield, A. B. (Ed.). (1994). *Family interventions in mental illness* (New Directions for Mental Health Services, No. 62). San Francisco: Jossey-Bass.

Hatfield, A. B., & Lefley, H. P. (Eds.). (1987). *Families of the mentally ill: Coping and adaptation.* New York: Guilford Press.

Hatfield, A. B., & Lefley, H. P. (1993). *Surviving mental illness.* New York: Guilford Press.

Hawley, D. R., & DeHaan, L. (1996). Toward a definition of family resilience: Integrating life-span and family perspectives. *Family Process, 35,* 283–298.

Heller, T., Roccoforte, J. A., Hsieh, K., Cook, J. A., & Cook, J. A. (1997). Benefits of support groups for families of adults with severe mental illness. *American Journal of Orthopsychiatry, 67,* 187–198.

Henderson, P. (1994). Counseling children of parents with severe mental illness. *School Counselor, 42,* 147–154.

Herman, J. L. (1997). *Trauma and recovery.* New York: Basic Books.

Heston, L. L. (1991). *Mending minds.* New York: Freeman.

Hirsch, S. R., & Weinberger, D. R. (Eds.). (1995). *Schizophrenia.* Cambridge, MA: Blackwell Science.

Holley, T. E., & Holley, J. (1997). *My mother's keeper: A daughter's memoir of growing up in the shadow of schizophrenia.* New York: Morrow.

Hooley, J. M. (1987). The nature and origins of EE. In D. Hahlweg & M. J. Goldstein (Eds.), *Understanding major mental disorder: The contribution of family interaction research* (pp. 176–194). New York: Family Process Press.

Hoover, C. F., & Franz, J. D. (1972). Siblings in the families of schizophrenics. *Archives of General Psychiatry, 26,* 334–342.

Horwitz, A. V., & Reinhard, S. C. (1995). Ethnic differences in caregiving duties and burdens among parents and siblings of persons with severe mental illness. *Journal of Health & Social Behavior, 36,* 138–150.

Horwitz, A. V., Tessler, R. C., Fisher, G. A., & Gamache, G. M. (1992). The role of the adult siblings in providing social support to the severely mentally ill. *Journal of Marriage and the Family, 54,* 233–241.

Howard, K. I., Moras, K., Brill, P. L., Martinovich, Z., & Lutz, W. (1996). Evaluation of psychotherapy: Efficacy, effectiveness, and patient progress. *American Psychologist, 51,* 1059–1064.

Howells, J. G., & Guirguis, W. R. (1985). *The family and schizophrenia.* New York: International Universities Press.

Hudson, F. M. (1991). *The adult years: Mastering the art of self-renewal.* San Francisco: Jossey-Bass.

Hulson, B. (1992). Relationship problems and mental illness: Indications for couple therapy. *Sexual and Marital Therapy, 7,* 173–187.

Husted, J. R. (1994). The last asylum: The mentally ill offender in the criminal justice system. In D. T. Marsh (Ed.), *New directions in the psychological treatment of serious mental illness* (pp. 50–70). Westport, CT: Praeger.

Jamison, K. R. (1995). *An unquiet mind: A memoir of moods and madness.* New York: Knopf.

"John." (1997, Spring). Through my eyes. *Innovations: Stanley Center Newsletter for Providers, 2*(3), pp. 6–8.

Johnson, D. L. (1987). Professional-family collaboration. In A. B. Hatfield (Ed.), *Families of the mentally ill: Meeting the challenges* (pp. 73–79). San Francisco: Jossey-Bass.

Johnson, D. L. (1997). Overview of severe mental illness. *Clinical Psychology Review, 17,* 247–257.

Johnson, J. T. (1988). *Hidden victims: An eight-stage healing process for families and friends of the mentally ill.* New York: Doubleday.

Jones, S. L., Roth, D., & Jones, P. K. (1995). Effect of demographic and behavioral variables on burden of caregivers of chronically mentally ill persons. *Psychiatric Services, 46,* 141–145.

Jordan, C., Lewellen, A., & Vandiver, V. (1995). Psychoeducation for minority families: A social work perspective. *International Journal of Mental Health, 23,* 27–43.

Judge, K. (1994). Serving children, siblings, and spouses: Understanding the needs of other family members. In H. P. Lefley & M. Wasow (Eds.), *Helping families cope with mental illness* (pp. 161–194). Newark: Harwood Academic.

Kahn, D. A., Carpenter, D., Docherty, J. P., & Frances, A. (1996). Treatment of bipolar disorder. *Journal of Clinical Psychiatry, 57*(Suppl. 12A), 3–89.

Karr, M. (1995). *The liar's club: A memoir.* New York: Penguin Books.

Kaslow, F. W. (1993). Relational diagnosis: Past, present and future. *American Journal of Family Therapy, 21,* 195–204.

Kaslow, F. W. (Ed.). (1996). *Handbook of relational diagnosis and dysfunctional family patterns.* New York: Wiley.

Kazdin, A. E., Stolar, M. J., & Marciano, P. L. (1995). Risk factors for dropping out of treatment among white and black families. *Journal of Family Psychology, 9,* 402–417.

Keith, S. J. (1997). Working together. *The JOURNAL of the California Alliance for the Mentally Ill, 8*(3), 9–10.

Kelley, W. (1992). Unmet needs. *The JOURNAL of the California Alliance for the Mentally Ill, 3*(1), 28.

Kendler, K. S., Karkowski, S. L., & Walsh, D. (1996). The risk for psychiatric illness in siblings of schizophrenics: The impact of psychotic and non-psychotic affective illness and alcoholism in parents. *Acta Psychiatrica Scandinavica, 94,* 49–55.

Kessler, R. C., Berglund, P. A., Zhao, S., Leaf, P. J., Kouzis, A. C., Bruce, M. L., Friedman, R. M., Grosser, R. C., Kennedy, C., Narrow, W. E., Kuehnel, T. G., Laska, E. M., Manderscheid, R. W., Rosenheck, R. A., Santoni, T. W., & Schneier, M. (1996). The 12-month prevalence and correlates of serious mental illness (SMI). In R. W. Manderscheid & M. A. Sonnenschein (Eds.), *Mental health, United States, 1996* (pp. 59–70) (DHHS Publication No. SMA 96-3098). Washington, DC: U.S. Government Printing Office.

Kessler, R. C., Price, R. J., & Wortman, C. B. (1985). Social factors in psychopathology: Stress, social support, and coping processes. *Annual Review of Psychology, 36,* 531–572.

Kinsella, K. B. (1996). Helping children cope. *The JOURNAL of the California Alliance for the Mentally Ill, 7*(3), 58–59.

Kinsella, K. B., Anderson, R. A., & Anderson, W. T. (1996). Coping skills, strengths, and needs as perceived by adult offspring and sibling of people with mental illness: A retrospective study. *Psychiatric Rehabilitation Journal, 20*(2), 24–32.

Kitchener, K. S. (1984). Intuition, critical evaluation and ethical principles: The foundation for ethical decisions in counseling psychology. *Counseling Psychologist, 12,* 43–55.

Kitchener, K. S. (1986). Teaching applied ethics in counselor education: An integration of psychological processes and philosophical analysis. *Journal of Counseling and Development, 64,* 306–310.

Klagsbrun, F. (1993). *Mixed feelings: Love, hate, rivalry, and reconciliation among brothers and sisters.* New York: Bantam Books.

Klein, B. C. (1990). Survival dilemmas: Case study of an adult child of a schizophrenic parent. *Clinical Social Work Journal, 18,* 43–56.

Klein, D. F., & Wender, P. H. (1994). *Understanding depression.* New York: Oxford University Press.

Knapp, S. (1997). Professional liability and risk management in an era of managed care. In D. T. Marsh & R. D. Magee (Eds.), *Ethical and legal issues in professional practice with families* (pp. 271–288). New York: Wiley.

Knapp, S., & VandeCreek, L. (1990). Application of the duty to protect HIV positive patients. *Professional Psychology: Research and Practice, 21,* 161–166.

Lakin, M. (1988). *Ethical issues in the psychotherapies.* New York: Oxford University Press.

Lamb, M. E. (Ed.). (1996). *The role of the father in child development (3rd ed.)* New York: Wiley.

Landeen, J., Whelton, C., Dermer, S., Cardamone, J., Munroe-Blum, H., & Thornton, J. (1992). Needs of well siblings of persons with schizophrenia. *Hospital and Community Psychiatry, 43,* 266–269.

Landerman, R., George, L. K., & Blazer, D. G. (1991). Adult vulnerability for psychiatric disorders: Interactive effects of negative childhood experiences and recent stress. *Journal of Nervous & Mental Disease, 179,* 656–663.

LaRoche, C. (1989). Children of parents with major affective disorders: A review of the past 5 years. *Psychiatric Clinics of North America, 12,* 919–932.

Larson, A. (1996). Blue moon. *The JOURNAL of the California Alliance for the Mentally Ill, 7*(3), 23–25.

Lazarus, R. S., & Folkman, S. (1984). *Stress, appraisal, and coping.* New York: Springer.

Leder, J. M. (1991). *Brothers and sisters: How they shape our lives.* New York: St. Martin's Press.

Leete, E. (1997). How I perceive and manage my illness. In L. Spaniol, C. Gagne, & M. Koehler (Eds.), *Psychological and social aspects of psychiatric disability* (pp. 99–103). Boston: Boston University Center for Psychiatric Rehabilitation.

Lefley, H. P. (1987a). An adaptational framework: Its meaning for research and practice. In A. B. Hatfield & H. P. Lefley (Eds.), *Families of the mentally ill: Coping and adaptation* (pp. 307–329). New York: Guilford Press.

Lefley, H. P. (1987b). The family's response to mental illness in a relative. In A. B. Hatfield (Ed.), *Families of the mentally ill: Meeting the challenges* (pp. 3–21). San Francisco: Jossey-Bass.

Lefley, H. P. (1989). Family burden and family stigma in major mental illness. *American Psychologist, 44,* 556–560.

Lefley, H. P. (1992). Expressed emotion: Conceptual, clinical, and social policy issues. *Hospital and Community Psychiatry, 43,* 591–598.

Lefley, H. P. (1994a). An overview of family-professional relationships. In D. T. Marsh (Ed.), *New directions in the psychological treatment of serious mental illness* (pp. 166–185). Westport, CT: Praeger.

Lefley, H. P. (1994b). Service needs of culturally diverse patients and families. In H. P. Lefley & M. Wasow (Eds.), *Helping families cope with mental illness* (pp. 223–242). Newark: Harwood Academic.

Lefley, H. P. (1996). *Family caregiving in mental illness* (Family Caregiver Applications Series, Vol. 7). Thousand Oaks, CA: Sage.

Lefley, H. P. (1997). Prevention of schizophrenia: What does it mean? What's a family to do? *The JOURNAL of the California Alliance for the Mentally Ill, 8*(3), 24–26.

Lefley, H. P. (Ed.). (1998). *Families coping with mental illness: The cultural context.* San Francisco: Jossey-Bass.

Lefley, H. P., & Johnson, D. L. (Eds.). (1990). *Families as allies in treatment of the mentally ill.* Washington, DC: American Psychiatric Press.

Lefley, H. P., & Wasow, M. (Eds.). (1994). *Helping families cope with mental illness.* Newark: Harwood Academic.

Le Gacy, S. S. (in press.) Working through the heart: A transpersonal approach to family support and education. *Psychiatric Rehabilitation Journal.*

Lehman, A. F., Steinwachs, D. M., & the Co-Investigators of the PORT Project. (1998). At issue: Translating research into practice: The Schizophrenia Patient Outcomes Research Team (PORT) treatment recommendations. *Schizophrenia Bulletin, 24,* 1–10.

Lewis, W. (1989). How not to engage a family in family therapy. *Journal of Strategic and Systemic Therapies, 8,* 50–53.

Lidz, T., Fleck, S., Alanen, Y. O., & Cornelison, A. (1963). Schizophrenic patients and their siblings. *Psychiatry, 26,* 1–18.

List, A. B. (1996). On becoming authentic. *The JOURNAL of the California Alliance for the Mentally Ill, 7*(3), 37–38.

Litman, R. E. (1989). Long-term treatment of chronically suicidal patients. *Bulletin of the Menninger Clinic, 53,* 215–228.

Lucas, C., & Seiden, H. M. (1997). *Silent grief: Living in the wake of suicide.* New York: Jason Aronson.

Lyden, J. (1997). *Daughter of the Queen of Sheba.* Boston: Houghton Mifflin.

MacGregor, P. (1994). Grief: The unrecognized parental response to mental illness in a child. *Social Work, 39,* 160–166.

Maier, W. (1996). Onset and course of affective disorders in subjects at risk: A prospective family study. *Psychiatric Annals, 26,* 315–319.

Main, M. C., Gerace, L. M., & Camilleri, D. (1993). Information sharing concerning schizophrenia in a family member: Adult siblings' perspectives. *Archives of Psychiatric Nursing, 7,* 147–153.

Mannion, E. (1996). Resilience and burden in spouses of people with mental illness. *Psychiatric Rehabilitation Journal, 20*(2), 13–23.

Mannion, E. (1998). The ultimate acrobats. *The JOURNAL of the California Alliance for the Mentally Ill, 9*(2), 72–76.

Mannion, E., Draine, J., Solomon, P., & Meisel, M. (1998). Applying research on family education about mental illness to development of a relative's group consultation model. *Community Mental Health Journal, 33,* 555–574.

Mannion, E., & Meisel, M. (1993). *Teaching manual for spouse coping skills workshops.* Philadelphia, PA: Training and Educational Center (T.E.C.) Network, c/o Mental Health Association of Southeastern Pennsylvania.

Mannion, E., Meisel, M., Solomon, P., & Draine, J. (1996). A comparative analysis of families with mentally ill relatives: Support group members versus nonmembers. *Psychiatric Rehabilitation Journal, 20*(1), 43–50.

Mannion, E., Mueser, K., & Solomon, P. (1994). Designing psychoeducational services for spouses of persons with serious mental illness. *Community Mental Health Journal, 30,* 177–190.

Marlatt, J. (1988, January/February/March). The role of the family in rehabilitation. *Journal of Rehabilitation,* pp. 7–8, 77.

Marsh, D. T. (1992a). *Families and mental illness: New directions in professional practice.* New York: Praeger.

Marsh, D. T. (1992b). Working with families of people with serious mental illness. In L. VandeCreek, S. Knapp, & T. L. Jackson (Eds.), *Innovations in clinical practice: A source book* (Vol. 11, pp. 389–402). Sarasota, FL: Professional Resource Press.

Marsh, D. T. (1994a). The psychodynamic model and services for families: Issues and strategies. In H. P. Lefley & M. Wasow (Eds.), *Helping families cope with mental illness* (pp. 105–128). Newark: Harwood Academic Publishers.

Marsh, D. T. (1994b). Services for families: New modes, models, and intervention strategies. In H. P. Lefley & M. Wasow (Eds.), *Helping families cope with mental illness* (pp. 39–62). Newark: Harwood Academic Publishers.

Marsh, D. T. (1995). Families and serious mental illness: Ethical issues in professional practice. *Family Psychologist, 11*(1), 17–19.

Marsh, D. T. (1997). Serious mental illness: Ethical issues in working with families. In D. T. Marsh & R. D. Magee (Eds.), *Ethical and legal issues in professional practice with families* (pp. 216–237). New York: Wiley.

Marsh, D. T., Appleby, N. F., Dickens, R. M., Owens, M., & Young, N. O. (1994). Anguished voices: Impact of mental illness on siblings and children. In L. Spaniol et al. (Eds.), *An introduction to psychiatric rehabilitation* (pp. 162–175). Columbia, MD: International Association of Psychosocial Rehabilitation Services.

Marsh, D. T., & Dickens, R. M. (1997). *Troubled journey: Coming to terms with the mental illness of a sibling or parent.* New York: Tarcher/Putnam.

Marsh, D. T., Dickens, R. M., Koeske, R. D., Yackovich, N. M., Wilson, J. M., Leichliter, J. S., & McQuillis, V. (1997). Troubled journey: Siblings and children of people with mental illness. In L. Spaniol, C. Gagne, & M. Koehler (Eds.), *Psychological and social aspects of psychiatric disability* (pp. 254–269). Boston: Boston University Center for Psychiatric Rehabilitation.

Marsh, D. T., & Johnson, D. L. (1997). The family experience of mental illness: Implications for intervention. *Professional Psychology: Research & Practice, 28,* 229–237.

Marsh, D. T., Koeske, R. D., Schmidt, P. A., Martz, D. P., & Redpath, W. B. (1997). A person-driven system: Implications for theory, research, and practice. In L. Spaniol, C. Gagne, & M. Koehler (Eds.), *Psychological and social aspects of psychiatric disability* (pp. 358–369). Boston: Boston University Center for Psychiatric Rehabilitation.

Marsh, D. T., Lefley, H. P., Evans-Rhodes, D., Ansell, V. I., Doerzbacher, B. M., LaBarbera, L., & Paluzzi, J. E. (1996). The family experience of mental illness: Evidence for resilience. *Psychiatric Rehabilitation Journal, 20*(2), 3–12.

Marsh, D. T., Lefley, H. P., & Husted, J. R. (1996). Families of people with mental illness. In M. Harway (Ed.), *Treating the changing family: Handling normative and unusual events* (pp. 171–203). New York: Wiley.

Marsh, D. T., & Magee, R. D. (Eds.). (1997). *Ethical and legal issues in professional practice with families.* New York: Wiley.

Masterpasqua, F. (1989). A competence paradigm for psychological practice. *American Psychologist, 44,* 1366–1371.

Matheny, K. B., Aycock, D. W., Pugh, J. L., Curlette, W. L., & Cannella, K. A. (1986). Stress coping: A qualitative and quantitative synthesis with implications for treatment. *Counseling Psychologist, 14,* 499–549.

Matsakis, A. (1992). *I can't get over it: A handbook for trauma survivors.* Oakland, CA: New Harbinger.

Maurin, J. T., & Boyd, C. B. (1990). Burden of mental illness on the family: A critical review. *Archives of Psychiatric Nursing, 4,* 99–107.

McCubbin, H. I., & McCubbin, M. A. (1988). Typologies of resilient families: Emerging roles of social class and ethnicity. *Family Relations, 37,* 247–254.

McDaniel, S. H., Hepworth, J., & Doherty, W. J. (1992). *Medical family therapy: A biopsychosocial approach to families with health problems.* New York: Basic Books.

McDaniel, S. H., Hepworth, J., & Doherty, W. J. (1993, January/February). A new prescription for family health care. *Family Networker, 17*(2), pp. 18–29, 62–63.

McElroy, E. (Ed.). (1987). *Children and adolescents with mental illness: A parents guide.* Kensington, MD: Woodbine House.

McFarlane, W. R. (1994). Families, patients and clinicians as partners: Clinical strategies and research outcomes in single–and multiple-family psychoeducation. In H. P. Lefley & M. Wasow (Eds.), *Helping families cope with mental illness* (pp. 195–222). Newark: Harwood Academic.

McFarlane, W. R., Lukens, E., Link, B., Dushay, R., Deakins, S. A., Newmark, M., Dunne, E. J., Horen, B., & Toran, J. (1995). Multiple-family groups and psychoeducation in the treatment of schizophrenia. *Archives of General Psychiatry, 52,* 679–687.

McGoldrick, M., Giordano, J., & Pearce, J. K. (Eds.). (1996). *Ethnicity and family therapy* (2nd ed.). New York: Guilford Press.

Meisel, M., & Mannion, E. (1990). *Teaching manual for coping skills workshops* (rev. ed.). Philadelphia, PA: Training and Educational Center (T.E.C.) Network, c/o Mental Health Association of Southeastern Pennsylvania.

Meissner, W. W. (1970). Sibling relations in the schizophrenic family. *Family Process, 9,* 1–25.

Melton, G. B., Petrila, J. D., Poythress, N. G., & Slobogin, C. (1987). *Psychological evaluations for the courts.* New York: Guilford Press.

Miklowitz, D. J., & Goldstein, M. J. (1997). *Bipolar disorder: A family-focused treatment approach.* New York: Guilford Press.

Mittleman, G. (1985). First person account: The pain of parenthood of the mentally ill. *Schizophrenia Bulletin, 11,* 300–303.

Moller, M. D., & Murphy, M. F. (1997). The Three R's Rehabilitation Program: A prevention approach for the management of relapse symptoms associated with psychiatric diagnoses. *Psychiatric Rehabilitation Journal, 20*(3), 42–48.

Moltz, D. A. (1993). Bipolar disorder and the family: An integrative model. *Family Process, 32,* 409–423.

Moorman, M. (1992). *My sister's keeper: Learning to cope with a sibling's mental illness.* New York: Norton.

Mueser, K. T. (1996). Helping families manage severe mental illness. *Psychiatric Rehabilitation Skills, 1*(2), 21–42.

Mueser, K. T., & Gingerich, S. (1994). *Coping with schizophrenia: A guide for families.* Oakland, CA: New Harbinger.

Mueser, K. T., & Glynn, S. M. (1995). *Behavioral family therapy for psychiatric disorders.* Boston: Allyn & Bacon.

Murty, S. (1996). Can a support program for families make a difference? Two teenagers share their experiences. *The JOURNAL of the California Alliance for the Mentally Ill, 7*(3), 60–62.

National Advisory Mental Health Council. (1993). Health care reform for Americans with severe mental illnesses. *American Journal of Psychiatry, 150,* 1447–1465.

National Advisory Mental Health Council. (1995). Basic behavioral science research for mental health: A national investment. A report of the National Advisory Mental Health Council, Rockville, MD. *American Psychologist, 50,* 485–495.

National Institute of Mental Health. (1986). *Combating the stigma of mental illness* (DHHS Publication No. ADM 86-1470). Washington, DC: U.S. Government Printing Office.

Naylor, P. (1977). *Crazy love: An autobiographical account of marriage and madness.* New York: New American Library.

Neugeboren, J. (1997). *Imagining Robert: My brother, madness, and survival.* New York: Morrow.

Nicholson, J. (1996). Services for parents with mental illness and their families. *The JOURNAL of the California Alliance for the Mentally Ill, 7*(3), 66–68.

Noh, S., & Avison, W. R. (1988). Spouses of discharged psychiatric patients: Factors associated with their experience of burden. *Journal of Marriage and the Family, 50,* 377–389.

Oakes, B. (1996). The static bond: A daughter's experience with her mother's mental illness. *The JOURNAL of the California Alliance for the Mentally Ill, 7*(3), 42–43.

Oates, M. (1997). Patients as parents: The risk to children. *British Journal of Psychiatry, 170*(Suppl. 32), 22–27.

Ogren, D. J. (1996). Trauma and hope for healing. *The JOURNAL of the California Alliance for the Mentally Ill, 7*(3), 7–8.

Olson, L. S. (1994). *He was still my daddy.* Portland, OR: Ogden House.

Packard, R. A. (1992, June). *Living with mental illness: One wife's journey.* Presentation at the conference entitled, "Treating the seriously mentally ill: Educating professionals for the 21st century." Sponsored by the Medical College of Pennsylvania and the National Alliance for the Mentally Ill, Philadelphia.

Papolos, D. F., & Papolos, J. (1997). *Overcoming depression* (3rd ed.). New York: HarperCollins.

Paterson, J. (1996). *Sweet mystery: A book of remembering.* New York: Farrar, Straus and Giroux.

Patterson, T. E., & Lusterman, D-D. (1996). The relational reimbursement dilemma. In F. W. Kaslow (Ed.), *Handbook of relational diagnosis and dysfunctional family patterns* (pp. 46–58). New York: Wiley.

Penn, D. L., & Mueser, K. T. (1996). Research update on the psychosocial treatment of schizophrenia. *American Journal of Psychiatry, 153,* 607–617.

Perr, I. N. (1985). Psychiatric malpractice issue. In S. Rachlin (Ed.), *Legal encroachment on psychiatric practice* (pp. 47–59). San Francisco, CA: Jossey-Bass.

Petrila, J. P., & Sadoff, R. L. (1992). Confidentiality and the family as caregiver. *Hospital and Community Psychiatry, 43,* 136–139.

Pickett, S. A., Cook, J. A., & Cohler, B. J. (1994). Caregiving burden experienced by parents of offspring with severe mental illness: The impact of off-timedness. *Journal of Applied Social Sciences, 18,* 199–207.

Pickett, S. A., Cook, J. A., & Laris, A. (1997). *The journey of hope: Final evaluation report.* Chicago: The University of Illinois at Chicago, National Research and Training Center on Psychiatric Disability.

Pickett, S. A., Vraniak, D. A., Cook, J. A., & Cohler, B. J. (1993). Strength in adversity: Blacks bear burden better than whites. *Professional Psychology: Research and Practice, 24,* 460–467.

Plummer, D. L. (1996). Developing culturally responsive psychosocial rehabilitative programs for African Americans. *Psychiatric Rehabilitation Journal, 19*(4), 37–43.

Pollack, M., Woerner, M. G., Goldberg, P., & Klein, D. F. (1969). Siblings of schizophrenic and nonschizophrenic psychiatric patients. *Archives of General Psychiatry, 20,* 652–658.

Powell, T. H., & Gallagher, P. (1993). *Brothers & sisters: A special part of exceptional families* (2nd ed.). Baltimore: Paul H. Brookes.

Poznanski, E. O. (1972). The "replacement child": A saga of unresolved parental grief. *Journal of Pediatrics, 81,* 1190–1193.

Radke-Yarrow, M., Nottelmann, E., Martinez, P., Fox, M. B., & Belmont, B. (1992). Young children of affectively ill parents: A longitudinal study of psychosocial development. *Journal of the American Academy of Child & Adolescent Psychiatry, 31,* 68–77.

Rando, T. A. (1984). *Grief, dying, and death: Clinical interventions for caregivers.* Champaign, IL: Research Press.

Rando, T. A. (Ed.). (1986). *Parental loss of a child.* Champaign, IL: Research Press.

Real, T. (1997). *I don't want to talk about it: Overcoming the secret legacy of male depression.* New York: Scribner.

Regier, D. A., Farmer, M. E., Rae, D. S., Locke, B. Z., Keith, S. J., Judd, L. L., & Goodwin, F. K. (1990). Comorbidity of mental disorders with alcohol and other drug abuse: Results from the Epidemiologic Catchment Area (ECA) Study. *Journal of the American Medical Association, 264,* 2511–2518.

Reid, W. H., & Morrison, H. L. (1983). Risk factors in children of depressed parents. In H. L. Morrison (Ed.), *Children of depressed parents: Risk, identification, and intervention* (pp. 33–46). New York: Grune & Stratton.

Reinhard, S. C. (1994). Perspectives on the family's caregiving experience in mental illness. *Journal of Nursing Scholarship, 26,* 70–74.

Reiss, D., & Klein, D. (1987). Paradigm and pathogenesis: A family-centered approach to problems of etiology and treatment of psychiatric disorders. In T. Jacobs (Ed.), *Family interaction and psychopathology* (pp. 203–255). New York: Plenum Press.

Resident's guide to treatment of people with chronic mental illness. (1993). Group for the Advancement of Psychiatry, Report No. 136. Washington, DC: American Psychiatric Press.

Rice, J. (1994, September). *New roles for psychiatrists with members of patients families: Parents, spouses, and siblings.* Presentation at the Psychiatry Grand Round of Jefferson Medical College Department of Psychiatry, Philadelphia, PA.

Riebschleger, J. L. (1991). Families of chronically mentally ill people: Siblings speak to social workers. *Health and Social Work, 16,* 94–103.

Robinson, E. A. (1996). Causal attributions about mental illness: Relationship to family functioning. *American Journal of Orthopsychiatry, 66,* 282–295.

Rodman, F. R. (1986). *Keeping hope alive: On becoming a psychotherapist.* New York: Harper & Row.

Rolland, J. S. (1988). Chronic illness and the family life cycle. In B. Carter & M. McGoldrick (Eds.), *The changing family life cycle* (2nd ed., pp. 433–456). New York: Gardner Press.

Rolland, J. S. (1994). *Families, illness, and disability: An integrative treatment model.* New York: Basic Books.

Roth, A., & Fonagy, P. (1996). *What works for whom: A critical review of psychotherapy research.* New York: Guilford Press.

Ruocchio, P. J. (1997). The schizophrenic inside. In L. Spaniol, C. Gagne, & M. Koehler (Eds.), *Psychological and social aspects of psychiatric disability* (pp. 104–107). Boston: Boston University Center for Psychiatric Rehabilitation.

Russell, L. M., Grant, A. E., Joseph, S. M., & Fee, R. W. (1995). *Planning for the future: Providing a meaningful life for a child with a disability after your death* (rev. ed.). Evanston, IL: American.

Rutter, M. (1981). *Maternal deprivation reassessed* (2nd ed.). Harmondsworth, Middlesex: Penguin Books.

Ryglewicz, H., & Pepper, B. (1996). *Lives at risk: Understanding and treating young people with dual disorders.* New York: Free Press.

Samuels, L., & Chase, L. (1979). The well siblings of schizophrenics. *American Journal of Family Therapy, 7,* 24–35.

Sargent, R. J. (1992). Schizophrenia: The problem for the family. *Psychiatric Bulletin, 17,* 14–15.

Scazufca, M., & Kuipers, E. (1997). Impact on women who care for those with schizophrenia. *Psychiatric Bulletin, 21,* 469–471.

Schiller, L., & Bennett, A. (1996). *The quiet room.* New York: Warner Books.

Schizophrenia: Treatment outcomes research. (1995). [Special section]. *Schizophrenia Bulletin, 21,* 561–675.

Secunda, V. (1997). *When madness comes home: Help and hope for the children, siblings, and partners of the mentally ill.* New York: Hyperion.

Seifer, R., Sameroff, A. J., Dickstein, S., Keitner, G., Miller, I., Rasmussen, S., & Hayden, L. C. (1996). Parental pathology, multiple contextual risks, and one-year outcomes in children. *Journal of Clinical Child Psychology, 25,* 423–435.

Seligman, M., & Darling, R. B. (1997). *Ordinary families, special children: A systems approach to childhood disability* (2nd ed.). New York: Guilford Press.

Sexton, L. G. (1994). *Searching for mercy street: My journey back to my mother, Anne Sexton.* Boston: Little, Brown.

Sheehy, G. (1996). *New passages.* New York: Ballantine Books.

Shimberg, E. F. (1991). *Depression: What families should know.* New York: Ballantine Books.

Silverman, M. M. (1989). Children of psychiatrically ill parents: A prevention perspective. *Hospital and Community Psychiatry, 40,* 1257–1265.

Simon, C. (1997a, March 9). Haunted by my family's madness. *The Washington Post,* C1, 4.

Simon, C. (1997b). *Mad house: Growing up in the shadow of mentally ill siblings.* New York: Doubleday.

Simon, R. I., & Sadoff, R. L. (1992). *Psychiatric malpractice: Cases and comments for clinicians* (2nd ed.) Washington, DC: American Psychiatric Press.

Skinner, E. A., Steinwachs, D. M., & Kasper, J. D. (1992). Family perspectives on the service needs of people with serious and persistent mental illness. *Innovations & Research, 1*(3), 23–30.

Smith, S. R. (1994a). The legal liabilities of mental health institutions. *Administration and Policy and Mental Health, 21,* 379–394.

Smith, S. R. (1994b). Liability and mental health services. *American Journal of Orthopsychiatry, 64,* 235–251.

Snyder, C. (1994). *The psychology of hope: You can get there from here.* New York: Free Press.

Solomon, P. (1996). Moving from psychoeducation to family education for families of adults with serious mental illness. *Psychiatric Services, 47,* 1364–1370.

Solomon, P., & Draine, J. (1995). Subjective burden among family members of mentally ill adults: Relations to stress, coping and adaptation. *American Journal of Orthopsychiatry, 65,* 419–427.

Solomon, P., & Draine, J. (1996). Examination of grief among family members of individuals with serious and persistent mental illness. *Psychiatric Quarterly, 67,* 221–234.

Solomon, P., Draine, J., Mannion, E., & Meisel, M. (1996a). Impact of brief family psychoeducation on self-efficacy. *Schizophrenia Bulletin, 22,* 41–50.

Solomon, P., Draine, J., Mannion, E., & Meisel, M. (1996b). The impact of individualized consultation and group workshop family education interventions on ill relative outcomes. *Journal of Nervous and Mental Disease, 184,* 252–255.

Solomon, P., Draine, J., Mannion, E., & Meisel, M. (1997). Effectiveness of two models of brief family education: Retention of gains by family members of adults with serious mental illness. *American Journal of Orthopsychiatry, 67,* 177–186.

Solomon, P., & Marcenko, M. O. (1992). Families of adults with severe mental illness: Their satisfaction with inpatient and outpatient treatment. *Psychosocial Rehabilitation Journal, 16,* 121–134.

Song, L., Biegel, D. E., & Milligan, S. E. (1997). Predictors of depressive sympto-matology among lower social class caregivers of persons with chronic mental illness. *Community Mental Health Journal, 33,* 269–286.

Spaniol, L. (1987). Coping strategies of family caregivers. In A. B. Hatfield & H. P. Lefley (Eds.), *Families of the mentally ill: Coping and adaptation* (pp. 208–222). New York: Guilford Press.

Spaniol, L., Gagne, C., & Koehler, M. (Eds.). (1997). *Psychological and social as-pects of psychiatric disability.* Boston: Boston University Center for Psychiatric Rehabilitation.

Spaniol, L., & Koehler, M. (Eds.). (1993). *The experience of recovery.* Boston: Center for Psychiatric Rehabilitation.

Spaniol, L., & Zipple, A. M. (1997). The family recovery process. In L. Spaniol, C. Gagne, & M. Koehler (Eds.), *Psychological and social aspects of psychiatric disability* (pp. 281–284). Boston: Boston University Center for Psychiatric Rehabilitation.

Spaniol, L., Zipple, A. M., Marsh, D. T., & Finley, L. (1998). *The role of the family in psychiatric rehabilitation: A workbook.* Boston: Boston University Center for Psy-chiatric Rehabilitation.

Spiese, V. K. (1996). And what do we tell the children? *The JOURNAL of the Califor-nia Alliance for the Mentally Ill, 7*(3), 50–51.

Stabenau, J. R., Turpin, J., Werner, M., & Pollin, W. (1965). A comparative study of families of schizophrenics, delinquents, and normals. *Psychiatry, 28,* 45–49.

Strong, M. (1988). *Mainstay: For the well spouse of the chronically ill.* New York: Pen-guin Books.

Stueve, A., Vine, P., & Struening, E. L. (1997). Perceived burden among care-givers of adults with serious mental illness: Comparison of Black, Hispanic, and White families. *American Journal of Orthopsychiatry, 67,* 199–209.

Sturges, J. S. (1977). Talking with children about mental illness in the family. *Health and Social Work, 2,* 88–109.

Sturges, J. S. (1978). Children's reactions to mental illness in the family. *Social Casework, 59,* 530–536.

Styron, W. (1990). *Darkness visible: A memoir of madness.* New York: Random House.

Substance Abuse and Mental Health Services Administration. (1994). *Cost of ad-dictive and mental disorders and effectiveness of treatment* (DHHS Publication No. SMA 2095-94). Washington, DC: U.S. Government Printing Office.

Swados, E. (1991). *The four of us.* New York: Farrar, Straus & Giroux.

Swartz, R. M., & Little, C. A. (1996). Schools: A resource for offspring. *The JOUR-NAL of the California Alliance for the Mentally Ill, 7*(3), 63–65.

Tarasoff v. Board of Regents of the University of California, 529 P.2d 533, Cal. Reptr. 14 (1976).

Targum, S. D., Dibble, E. D., Davenport, Y. B., & Gershon, E. S. (1981). The Family Attitudes Questionnaire: Patients' and spouses' views of bipolar illness. *Archives of General Psychiatry, 38,* 562–568.

Taylor, S. E. (1983). Adjustment to threatening events: A theory of cognitive adaptation. *American Psychologist, 38,* 1161–1173.

Terkelsen, K. G. (1987a). The evolution of family responses to mental illness through time. In A. B. Hatfield & L. P. Lefley (Eds.), *Families of the mentally ill: Coping and adaption* (pp. 151–166). New York: Guilford Press.

Terkelsen, K. G. (1987b). The meaning of mental illness to the family. In A. B. Hatfield & H. P. Lefley (Eds.), *Families of the mentally ill: Coping and adaptation* (pp. 128–150). New York: Guilford Press.

Thaker, G. K., Adami, H., Moran, M., Lahti, A., & Cassady, S. (1993). Psychiatric illnesses in families of subjects with schizophrenia-spectrum personality disorders: High morbidity risks for unspecified functional psychoses and schizophrenia. *American Journal of Psychiatry, 150,* 66–71.

Thompson, A. (1990). *Guide to ethical practice in psychotherapy.* New York: Wiley.

Tienari, P. J., & Wynne, L. C. (1994). Adoption studies of schizophrenia. *Annals of Medicine, 26,* 233–237.

Torrey, E. F. (1995). *Surviving schizophrenia: A manual for families, consumers and providers* (3rd ed.). New York: HarperCollins.

Torrey, E. F. (1997). *Out of the shadows: Confronting America's mental illness crisis.* New York: Wiley.

Torrey, E. F., Bowler, A. R., Taylor, E. H., & Gottesman, I. I. (1994). *Schizophrenia and manic-depressive disorder.* New York: Basic Books.

Torrey, E. F., Erdman, K., Wolfe, S. M., & Flynn, L. M. (1990). *Caring for people with severe mental disorders: A rating of state programs.* Arlington, VA: National Alliance for the Mentally Ill.

Turnbull, A. P., & Turnbull, H. R. (1990). *Families, professionals, and exceptionality: A special partnership* (2nd ed.). Columbus, OH: Merrill.

Turnbull, H. R. (1989). *Disability and the family: A guide to decisions for adulthood.* Baltimore: Brookes.

Udwin, O. (1993). Annotation: Children's reactions to traumatic events. *Journal of Psychology & Psychiatry & Allied Disciplines, 34,* 115–127.

Vaillant, G. E. (1977). *Adaptation to life.* Boston: Little, Brown.

Valleau, M. P., Bergner, R. M., & Horton, C. B. (1995). Parentification and caretaker syndrome: An empirical investigation. *Family Therapy, 22,* 157–164.

VandenBos, G. R. (Ed.). (1996). Outcome assessment of psychotherapy [Special issue]. *American Psychologist, 51*(10).

Viorst, J. (1986). *Necessary losses.* New York: Simon & Schuster.

Wahl, O. F. (1995). *Media madness: Public images of mental illness.* New Brunswick, NJ: Rutgers University Press.

Walker, E. F., & Downey, G. (1990). The effects of familial risk factors on social-cognitive abilities in children. *Child Psychiatry and Human Development, 20,* 253–267.

Walsh, F. (1996). The concept of family resilience: Crisis and challenge. *Family Process, 35,* 261–281.

Walsh, M. (1985). *Schizophrenia: Straight talk for family and friends.* New York: Warner Books.

Wasylenki, D. A. (1992). Psychotherapy of schizophrenia revisited. *Hospital and Community Psychiatry, 43,* 123–127.

Wasow, M. (1994). A missing group in family research: Parents not in contact with their mentally ill children. *Hospital & Community Psychiatry, 45,* 720–721.

Wasow, M. (1995). *The skipping stone: Ripple effects of mental illness on the family.* Palo Alto, CA: Science & Behavior Books.

Waters, D. B., & Lawrence, E. C. (1993). *Competence, courage, and change: An approach to family therapy.* New York: Norton.

Watkins, S. A., & Watkins, J. C. (1989). Negligent endangerment: Malpractice in the clinical context. *Journal of Independent Social Work, 3,* 35–50.

Wechsler, J. A., Schwartztol, H. W., & Wechsler, N. F. (1988). *In a darkness* (2nd ed.). Miami: Pickering.

Weisburd, D. E. (Ed. & Pub.). (1992). Sibling issue. *The JOURNAL of the California Alliance for the Mentally Ill, 3*(1).

Weisburd, D. E. (Ed. & Pub.). (1996). Offspring issue. *The JOURNAL of the California Alliance for the Mentally Ill, 7*(3).

Weisburd, S. B. (1992). Adapting to the changed relationship: One sibling's perspective. *The JOURNAL of the California Alliance for the Mentally Ill, 3*(1), 13–15.

Weissman, M. M., Prusoff, B. A., Gammon, G. D., Merikangas, K. R., Leckman, J. F., & Kidd, K. K. (1984). Psychopathology in children (ages 6–18) of depressed and normal parents. *Journal of the American Academy of Child Psychiatry, 23,* 78–84.

Wikler, L. M. (1986). Family stress theory and research on families of children with mental retardation. In J. J. Gallagher & P. M. Vietze (Eds.), *Families of handicapped persons: Research, programs, and policy issues* (pp. 167–195). Baltimore: Brookes.

Willick, M. S. (1997, January). *What kind of psychotherapy is most effective in treating chronic schizophrenia?* Presentation at the meeting the Columbia Psychoanalytic Society, Panel on Psychosis, New York.

Winefield, H. R., & Harvey, E. J. (1993). Determinants of psychological distress in relatives of people with chronic schizophrenia. *Schizophrenia Bulletin, 19,* 619–625.

Wolin, S. J., & Wolin, S. (1993). *The resilient self: How survivors of troubled families rise above adversity.* New York: Villard.

Woolis, R. (1992). *When someone you love has a mental illness.* New York: Tarcher/Perigee.

Wyden, P. (1998). *Conquering schizophrenia: A father, his son, and a medical breakthrough.* New York: Knopf.

Wynne, L. C., McDaniel, S. H., & Weber, T. T. (1987). Professional politics and the concepts of family therapy, family consultation, and systems consultation. *Family Process, 26,* 153–166.

Wynne, L. C., Weber, T. T., & McDaniel, S. H. (1986). The road from family therapy to systems consultation. In L. C. Wynne, S. H. McDaniel, & T. T. Weber (Eds.), *Systems consultation: A new perspective for family therapy* (pp. 3–15). New York: Guilford Press.

Yank, G. R., Bentley, K. J., & Hargrove, D. S. (1993). The vulnerability-stress model of schizophrenia: Advances in psychosocial treatment. *American Journal of Orthopsychiatry, 63,* 55–69.

Zipple, A. M., Langle, S., Tyrell, W., Spaniol, L., & Fisher, H. (1997). Client confidentiality and the family's need to know: Strategies for resolving the conflict. In D. T. Marsh & R. D. Magee (Eds.), *Ethical and legal issues in professional practice with families* (pp. 238–253). New York: Wiley.

Zipple, A. M., & Spaniol, L. (1987). Current educational and supportive models of family intervention. In A. B. Hatfield & H. P. Lefley (Eds.), *Families of the mentally ill: Coping and adaptation* (pp. 261–277). New York: Guilford Press.

Index